GETTING
YOUR MESSAGE
ACROSS

GETTING YOUR MESSAGE ACROSS

A Practical Guide to Business Communication

Craig E. Aronoff

Georgia State University

Otis W. Baskin

University of Houston at Clear Lake City

Robert W. Hays

Southern Technical Institute

Harold E. Davis

Georgia State University

WEST PUBLISHING COMPANY

St. Paul   New York   Los Angeles   San Francisco

Copyright © 1981 by WEST PUBLISHING CO.
50 West Kellogg Boulevard
P.O. Box 3526
St. Paul, Minnesota 55165

Library of Congress Cataloging in Publication Data

Main entry under title:

Getting your message across.

    Bibliography: p.
    Includes index.
    1. Communication in management. 2. Commercial
correspondence. I. Aronoff, Craig E.
HF5718.G47   658.4'5   80-29111
ISBN 0-8299-0362-3

Preface

This book has grown out of the academic and business experience of the four authors. Collectively they are or have been communication consultants to more than thirty companies listed on the New York Stock Exchange and more than thirty-five universities. Each is a teacher with many years of work with students in the classroom.

We believe that we have produced a work that is theoretically sound. The theories expounded in the book have been tested by each of us in differing settings and circumstances.

We are convinced that we have produced a book that is practical. It addresses the kinds of problems and situations found daily in the world of business.

We shall be especially pleased if the readers find this book easy to read and understand. It was written with that in mind.

A book that is theoretically sound, practical and understandable should lay the basis for a sound educational experience. A short memorandum at the start of each chapter tells the student what can be expected from the chapter. The Principles for Practice that follow each chapter offer a summary. And the questions for further study at the end of each chapter should, if dealt with conscientiously, give each student a chance for experience and, we hope, for growth.

Any book on business communication must contain certain standard subject matter. The authors have tried to treat these subjects with the respect due them, presenting them in a readable fashion. Yet even in treating old subjects, new approaches are used. In Chapter 3, the researches of James H. Couey on clear writing are reported in book form for the first time. And the use of the Empathy-Content-Action model in writing letters also is new in book form. Beyond this, we believe that this work is the most comprehensive in the field to date because it integrates the full range of business communication activities. By that, we mean not only writing, editing, and rewriting, but speaking, listening, nonverbal communication, interpersonal communication, and group communication. It recognizes the expanding function of communication in business by including the various media now in use, both print and audio-visual.

Diane Exum of Georgia State University and the editorial and production staff of West Publishing Company are already aware of how much their help has been appreciated. We merely wish others to know, which is why we make it a matter of record here.

Craig E. Aronoff
Department of Management
Georgia State University

Otis W. Baskin
Department of Management
University of Houston at Clear Lake City

Robert W. Hays
Department of English
Southern Technical Institute

Harold E. Davis
Department of Journalism
Georgia State University

Contents

GETTING
YOUR MESSAGE
ACROSS

SECTION
I

An Overview of
Communication in Business

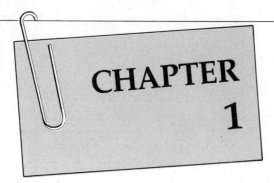

CHAPTER 1

To: The Reader
From: The Authors
Subject: Communicating in Business

After reading this chapter you will know that:

1. Communication skills are among the most important
   abilities that a person can bring to a career.

2. Communication is the most pervasive activity for
   managers.

3. Effective managing and selling depend upon effective
   communication.

4. Business communication includes not only good speech
   making, clear writing, and well-organized meetings, but
   also building relationships, nonverbal communication, and
   listening.

5. Effective business communication depends not only upon
   skills, but also upon attitudes and values.

Communicating in Business

"What we have here is a problem of communication," said the plant manager gravely. He did not smile; he was serious. He did not realize that on that same day he had labeled four distinctly different difficulties "problems of communication." Ever since he attended that advanced management seminar at the university, he had labeled every problem that had come up "a problem of communication." Some of the younger people on the plant staff jokingly suggested putting a new sign on the plant gate saying "You are now entering a problem of communication."

Of course, the plant manager was partly wrong. By attributing every problem to communication, managers reduce their opportunities to deal effectively with any one of them. But the plant manager was also partly right. Communication was a component of every problem he faced. Indeed, communication is an important aspect of virtually everything a manager does.

This book will facilitate your study of communication in business. We will help you to understand the process and nature of communication, to place it in its proper perspective in the business environment, and to develop or improve certain communication skills, attitudes, and values, so that you can perform more effectively and successfully in business organizations. We want you to be able to deal with communication problems when they occur, to prevent them to begin with, and to be able to distinguish between problems that have communication solutions and those that do not.

You may have heard the slogan of campus activists, "if you're not part of the solution, you're part of the problem." We hope to help you become part of the communication solution, instead of being part of the communication problem.

COMMUNICATION'S IMPORTANCE

In a world where it is difficult to find consensus on anything, the extent of agreement among business executives and educators about the importance of communication in business is amazing. In one survey of chief executive officers, all of those responding acknowledged that communication skills played a part in their climb up the executive ladder. Two-thirds said that communication skills played a major part. A survey of personnel directors found that communication ability is the most significant factor influencing promotions in business organizations. On the basis of this and other evidence, it is safe to conclude that communication abilities are among the most important a business person brings to a career. To some, communication is the sum total of executive job description. Chester Barnard, in his classic book *The Functions of the Executive,* maintained that the executive function is to develop and maintain a system of communication.

Communicating is the most pervasive activity for managers at all levels of business organizations. Research has shown that communication activities of all types occupy nearly ninety percent of a typical manager's day. Listening and reading to gain knowledge, insight, and understanding; raising questions; probing; proposing solutions; giving feedback; winning support; dealing with objections; and many other communication activities are the stuff of the managerial function. In the final analysis, the job of every executive or supervisor is communication. Management, it is said, is getting work done through others. Therefore, if managers are to get work done, they must communicate effectively with those through whom the work is to be done. As Peter Drucker, famed management consultant, says, "The manager has a specific tool: Information. He does not handle people; he motivates, guides, organizes people. . . . His only tool to do all this is the spoken or written word or the language of number."

Think for a moment about the organizational functions usually ascribed to management. Leadership, direction, and motivation, planning and decision-making, goal setting, implementation of change, coordination, evaluation, and control are traditionally considered the interrelated parts of the manager's job. And every single one of these functions is, in turn, a function of communication.

The importance of communication ranges far beyond the field of management. Selling, obviously, depends heavily on salespeople's ability not only to persuade, but also to assess the needs of the client. Even in the professions, such as the law, engineering, accounting, and medicine, communication is a critical skill. Because advancement in business or professional groups inevitably leads to managerial responsibilities, let us concentrate for a moment on the communication components of managerial functions.

COMMUNICATION AND MANAGERIAL FUNCTIONS

Since communication is the means by which human abilities and physical resources are productively combined to meet business goals, every aspect of management relates in some way to communication. Let us explore the relationship between communication and the various aspects of management.

Leadership: Leadership is a basic aspect of a manager's role. The relationship between leadership and communication is fairly obvious in that leadership involves interpersonal influence directed through communication to meet business goals. Consequently, the communication skill most frequently associated with leadership has traditionally been persuasion. Behavioral research has shown, however, that in addition to persuasive skills, leadership capabilities include such communicative abilities as developing relationships, encouraging participation, and maintaining openness with subordinates.

Direction and motivation: To provide direction and stimulate motivation, managers have become aware that they must attend not only to the needs of the organization but to individuals' needs as well. Complicating matters further, it has been found that human needs are not universal. Different people have different needs. The same person has different needs at different times. Whether a given reward fulfills an individual's needs depends on how the individual interprets the reward.

To discover individuals' needs, managers must improve their own abilities to perceive those needs and improve the opportunities for individuals to express their needs. As organizational pychologist Norman Maier has suggested, "The objective is to treat each person in accordance with his needs. . . . The person with the needs is in the best position to communicate them, but this requires an understanding listener."

Individual behavior is motivated by the subjective needs of the individual. Therefore, management's motivational task is to perceive individual needs and then to create the means by which individuals can fulfill both their own needs and those of the organization simultaneously. Motivation depends upon processes and skills, and communication lies at the heart of those processes and skills.

Planning and decision making: The communication process is the central nervous system of a business. Through it flows information that supplies the business's various parts with the technical and human data by which plans are made and upon which decisions are based.

In classical decision theory, economic man has perfect knowledge. He does not depend upon communication for the information upon which he bases decisions. But those of us who lack perfect knowledge must somehow acquire the limited information we need when we make plans and decisions.

Every step of the decision-making process, from awareness of the need for decision making through the implementation of decisions and plans, depends on communication effectiveness. Decision making cannot occur without communication; a major function of communication is to aid organizational planning and decision making.

Goal setting: A business without appropriate goals is like a ship without a rudder. But to have appropriate goals, the organization must maintain effective goal-setting procedures. Such procedures have these characteristics: individuals throughout the organization are involved in setting organizational and specific work goals; employees can relate personal goals to organizational goals; and employees perceive organizational climate as supportive and helpful. If employees are to take part in the goal-setting process, they must have ready access to organizational communication networks. They must receive information about the business and its environment and be able to make inputs. Managerial communication capabilities must include abilities to develop relationships, to encourage participation, and to maintain openness with subordinates.

Implementation of change: In a world in which the pace of change is speeding up, continued business success depends on the ability to respond effectively to change. Every manager in today's business environment is a change agent in that the manager helps change to come about.

Change agents depend on communication to understand both demands for change and capabilities to change. The flow of accurate information from outside and inside an organization is the basis upon which managers learn of problems requiring change. The capacity for change in a business directly results from its capacity for communication.

Coordination: Coordination has been defined as the conscious process of assembling and synchronizing differentiated activities in a business so that they function harmoniously in the attainment of business objectives. Again, the obvious prerequisite to assembling and synchronizing different activities is gathering, processing, and communicating information. Coordination, it has been said, is synonymous with management. Management has been equated with communication; thus, coordination is equated with communication.

Evaluation and control: Controlling is the activity that measures performance and guides actions toward a predetermined goal. The fundamental
basis of control is feedback—a process of observation, evaluation, and adjustment based on monitoring of information about past and present performance. Goal setting is the process of setting a business's course, and
evaluation and control is the process of maintaining that course.

The most common forms of control are financial control, production control, quality control, and inventory control. All of these, and any other
activity involving controls, operate through the communication of information about existing conditions, comparing that information with expected conditions, and making corrections based on the difference. Once again,
communication is that which makes all control possible.

CHANGING PRIORITIES IN BUSINESS COMMUNICATION

Until recent years, business communication usually meant the skills of
speaking and writing. Training in these skills stressed the development of
the ability to communicate information and instructions clearly and concisely with emphasis on form and style.

As you may have gathered by now, business communication includes
more than good speech making, clear writing, and conducting well-
organized meetings. The study of business communication now stresses
employee interaction and participation as well. With the increasing recognition that actions really do speak louder than words, nonverbal communication is emphasized along with verbal communication. Listening is considered just as important as—if not more important than—speaking.

Traditional communication training dealt with fact gathering and logical
presentations. But research has shown the equal importance of the attitu-
dinal and emotional aspects of communication. Many difficulties in business communication involve organizational practices and procedures and
the nature of management's relationships with employees. Consequently,
the effective communicator in business must realize that the structure of
relationships and expected roles in organizations make tremendous contributions to the meaning of work.

Finally, the communication media available for business communication
have expanded. Newsletters pumped off the mimeo machine are still popular, but many companies now publish four-color magazines. The bulletin
board is still a workhorse, but multimedia exhibits using slides and audio
tapes are increasingly popular. Closed-circuit television, videotapes, and
films are finding more and more uses in the business world. Business
communicators must be acquainted with all these media, their capabilities
and uses, to utilize the full range of communication potentials.

THE SKILLS OF BUSINESS COMMUNICATION

Exploring the relationship between management functions and communication and looking at changing priorities in business communication help to place communication in perspective. But what are the specific skills required?

Several studies of necessary business communication skills have been made by surveying graduates of business schools, educators, and supervisors in business. The following skills were identified:

- *writing:*   The ability to assimilate, organize, and present information in written form as memos, letters, and reports.

- *speaking:*   The ability to think through, organize, and present oral information concisely and coherently in both prepared and extemporaneous settings.

- *listening:*   The ability to receive, interpret, understand, and respond to both verbal and nonverbal messages from client or employees, both in terms of the information given and the feelings expressed.

- *questioning techniques:*   The ability to ask questions that precisely, clearly, and logically secure relevant and complete information.

- *interviewing:*   The ability to assess individual capabilities and establish rapport with potential employees or those already on the job.

- *motivation:*   The ability to motivate others in given job situations by being sensitive and responsive to their needs.

- *persuasion:*   The ability to persuade clients or employees, as individuals or groups, to accept policies, believe statements, or take specific actions.

- *relationship building:*   The ability to facilitate positive and productive relationships between co-workers and other people at all levels of the organization.

- *conflict resolution:*   The ability to handle conflict between individuals or groups within an organization by diagnosing the conflict and selecting strategies to achieve resolution of the conflict.

- *problem solving/decision making:*   The ability to analyze problems, to make decisions concerning specific strategies, to solve problems, and to evaluate the effectiveness of these solutions.

- *small group facilitation:*   The ability to develop and facilitate effective functioning of small groups within an organization, both in accomplishing the group's task and in building an atmosphere of cooperation within the group.

- *public relations:*   The ability to establish communication that invites credibility, trust, and confidence between a business and the public.

WHAT'S AHEAD IN THIS BOOK

We shall try to help you develop the understanding, the attitudes, and the abilities necessary for effective business communicators. This book is an aid, a tool that you can use in pursuit of your own communication goals. It will not make you a better communicator by itself. We can only assist you, because communicating is a changing, highly personal activity with roots deep in each individual's personality.

We believe that communication skills cannot be studied in isolation. In fact, most people are relatively good communicators in that they have been communicating since the day they were born.

Failure to understand the communication process coupled with inappropriate attitudes in communication situations contribute more to communication ineffectiveness than does any lack of skills. To improve your understanding of the process, our next chapter will deal with principles and concepts of communication. We have already begun to deal with attitudes toward communication and will continue to do so throughout this book.

Sections II and III of this book take a "how to" approach, dealing primarily with writing skills. Section II deals with writing letters, not love letters (though this section may offer some insights there as well), but letters designed to inform, to persuade, and to sell.

"Getting Your Message Across Through Memos and Reports," the third section of this book, is focused on presentation and gathering and preparing data for memos and reports.

Section IV deals with "Getting Your Message Across Face-to-Face." We begin this section with a chapter dealing with a subject that has been taught ever since Aristotle's time in ancient Greece. Aristotle called it "rhetorica," but we simply call it "speaking." We focus on presenting the reports you will have learned about in Section III. Our second chapter in this section deals with the most common communication activity, listening. Despite listening's paramount importance in the interpersonal communication process, it is an ability that we too often take for granted.

In the final three chapters of Section IV we explore nonverbal communication, interpersonal communication, and communication in groups.

Section V explores "Getting Your Message Across through Other Media." Here we look at everything from the company bulletin board to newsletters, magazines, closed-circuit television, video cassettes, and film in terms of their expanding applications within business organizations.

A Note of Caution   Few words are used more glibly and with less agreement as to meaning than the word "communication." Business management spends millions of dollars every year on "communication improvement" through training and media. And yet, communication problems in business persist. W. H. Whyte probably put it best: "The greatest enemy of communication is the illusion of it."

The importance of communication in business cannot be overestimated. But at the same time, communication is not a panacea, a philosopher's stone to solve all ills, nor the brass ring. There is no such thing as perfect communication. There is only a process requiring understanding, positive attitudes, constant attention, unending concentration, diligent effort, acceptance of responsibility, sensitivity, plus skills and abilities. With so much required, it is no wonder that communication often breaks down.

We offer you guidance, information, and the opportunity to gain insights through the use of this book. The final responsibility is yours.

To improve your communication through the use of this book, you should recognize four things:

1. Learning is not a passive process. It requires your active participation.

2. Knowledge is not behavior. You cannot become a more effective communicator simply by memorizing new terms and concepts.

3. To become a more effective communicator, you must recognize and come to grips with your own style of behavior and your own attitudes, values, and assumptions about people, relationships, and the world around you.

4. What you learn about communication here and now is only the beginning. Effective communication is a lifelong process.

PRINCIPLES
FOR
PRACTICE

1. By attributing every problem to communication, you reduce your opportunities to deal effectively with any of them.

2. Communication skills necessary for effective leadership include persuasion and abilities to develop relationships, encourage participation, and maintain openness.

3. To motivate employees, managers must improve their ability to perceive employees' needs and improve their opportunities to express these needs.

4. To take part in organizational decision making, employees must receive information about the organization and its environment and be able to make inputs.

5. The capacity for change in a business depends directly on its capacity for communication.

6. The process of control in a business depends on the organization's ability to gather information about ongoing processes.

7. Learning about communication, like communication itself, is an active, rather than a passive, process.

FOR FURTHER STUDY

1. How would you define communication?

2. Why do people so easily label difficulties "problems of communication"?

3. What kinds of attitudes might make communication more effective?

4. What factors have led to the changing priorities in business communication?

5. How does business communication differ from communication in other contexts?

6. What is the difference between active and passive learning?

7. Has the majority of your education so far stressed active or passive learning?

CHAPTER

2

To: The Reader
From: The Authors
Subject: Communication Theories and Models

After reading this chapter you will know that:

1. Theories are the foundation of the generalizations on
   which we base our everyday actions.

2. Scientific theories present relatively accurate
   conceptions of reality because they are developed through
   a process of rigorous testing.

3. Systems are hierarchical, interdependent, synergistic,
   and regulated.

4. Systems function through information gathering and
   feedback.

5. Systems are analyzed by describing them and exploring
   their goals, components, environments, condition, and
   potential for change.

6. Communication is the process of constructing meanings
   through the exchange of messages.

7. Meaning is not contained within the message; rather it is
   a function of interacting situational, personal, verbal,
   and nonverbal factors.

Theories of Communication

"Theory" has always been an imposing, even frightening, word. We usually react to the word with feelings of intimidation and rejection. We are intimidated by the names of theories that we have heard: the theory of relativity, the theory of evolution, the theory of celestial mechanics. Because we do not understand relativity, evolution, or celestial mechanics, we think that we cannot understand theories.

We frequently discount or dismiss that which frightens or confuses us. Confronted with scientific theory, many of us say, in effect, "Ah, that's just a theory," as if to say, "It's unproven; therefore, it's valueless."

Actually, theories are not valueless. They are not necessarily distant, complex formulations. All of us have theories about how the world works, how people relate to one another, what is right and what is wrong, and we all have theories about communication, although we might be hard pressed to put them into words. We have beliefs about the nature of meaning, how we perceive, and what is proper and effective communication behavior. To a large extent, your effectiveness as a communicator depends upon the correlation of your personal theories with reality. Since scientific theories are developed through rigorous testing, they are likely to be closer to reality than are our informal theories. By studying scientific theories, we can modify our personal theories toward greater accuracy. Consequently, we become more effective in terms of our behavior.

SOME "COMMON-SENSE" THEORIES OF COMMUNICATION

Because we are all experienced communicators (and often miscommunicators as well), we have developed theories of our own. If questioned, we usually defend such theories on grounds of "common sense" or popular acceptance (everyone does it or everyone knows that). Here are eight of those theories:

The "Decibel" Theory: According to the Decibel Theory, the best way to get your message across is to state it frequently and loudly. Parents who follow this theory rapidly escalate from mildly saying, "Please don't do that, Billy," to blasting, "Stop that, Billy!" Sometimes public speakers start softly and wind up screaming. Supervisors in business frequently employ similar techniques. Advocates of the Decibel Theory need reminding that "shouting only makes poor communication louder."

The "Sell" Theory: The Sell Theory assumes that the speaker is the only active agent in a communication situation. The listener is seen as passive and pliable. Thus, influence is believed to be a one-way process. One person "sells" information or ideas and the other person "buys." Communication based on the Sell Theory increases competition and raises barriers between individuals. Consequently, the chances of real meaning ever being found, much less shared, are reduced.

The "Minimal Information" Theory: The Minimal Information Theory assumes that receivers probably are not too interested in what is being communicated or anything else that is going on around them. (Supervisors adhering to this theory, for instance, assume that most employees are interested only in "wages and hours.") Following this theory, communicators tell individuals only "what they need to know"; consequently, the receiver has little to object to, little to ask questions about, little to use in forming possible negative judgments. But there is also little on which to build motivation, commitment, creativity, or to use in developing possible positive judgments. This theory appeals to those who feel that they do not have the time to communicate.

The "Mechanistic" Theory: The Mechanistic Theory holds that communication is a mechanical process. It maintains that words are like levers or buttons which produce certain predetermined results when pulled or pushed. Thus, when John wants to communicate an idea to Bob, he will select certain words to describe the idea from their reservoir of shared words. Since Bob has approximately the same pool of words, his mind translates John's words into the proper idea. Although this sounds simple and logical, its major problem is that it is not true. Two people seldom define the same word in exactly the same way, because meaning does not exist solely in words. People construct meaning through a process of which words are only a part.

The "If-I-Were-Him" Theory: The "If-I-Were-Him" Theory assumes that communication will be successful if the communicators can place themselves in the position of the receiver and then communicate appropriately. Actually, this is one of the better informal communication theories, growing as it does from the Golden Rule: "Do unto others as you would have them do unto you." George Bernard Shaw, however, found it necessary to rewrite the Golden Rule: "Don't do unto others as you would have them do unto you because their tastes may be different." Shaw's revision lends insight into the major problem with the "If-I-Were-Him" Theory. While it is often helpful to place oneself in the situation faced by the receiver (as we indicate in later chapters), like the Mechanistic Theory, this theory overlooks the fact that different people respond in different ways to the same situation.

The "If-They-Would-Only-Understand" Theory: The "If-They-Would-Only-Understand" Theory is another relatively enlightened idea. It rests on the notion that people respond favorably to messages that they understand. This theory is often represented by statements such as: "A worker will follow company orders and policies if he understands the reasons for them." What this theory overlooks is that honest people with good intentions who are confronted with the same information can understand each other and still disagree. In fact, people can agree to disagree. Adherents of this theory tend to explain their point over and over again, believing that understanding has not been achieved as long as disagreement exists.

The "Put-It-In-Writing" Theory: In some organizations the "Put-It-In-Writing Theory" results in the production of everything in octuplicate. This theory holds that meaning is unambiguous when words are on paper. In fact, meaning may be more ambiguous in written messages. There is no opportunity for immediate interaction, clarification, and feedback. Adherents of this theory would pass memos back and forth for three weeks before they would solve a problem that could be solved with a five-minute conversation.

The "Tool" Theory: The "Tool" Theory views communication as a hammer with which to nail disintegrating relationships back together or a hose to spray water on burning interpersonal conflicts. Followers of this theory are concerned with "communication techniques" to be used in case of "communication breakdown." They do not realize that many "breakdowns" are caused when communication is used as a tool to fix problems, rather than a process that must be constantly cultivated if problems are to be avoided.

THE SYSTEMS APPROACH

To make the "common-sense" approaches we have listed above more accurate and scientific, researchers have developed a variety of theories and models that attempt to further understanding of the communication process. The most broadly accepted theoretical framework for understanding communication behavior (indeed, all behavior) is known as systems theory, or the systems approach.

One thing that communication researchers now seem to agree upon is that communication is a *process*, not a thing, not a tool. It is not something that one person does to another. It is dynamic, not static. It has no discernible beginning or end. To say that communication is a process is also to say that it operates in the form of *systems;* therefore, to understand how communication operates, we must understand how systems work.

A system is a set of smaller systems grouped by sets of relationships. Thus, all systems have subsystems. A system exists in and interacts with its environment. Thus all systems have suprasystems (also called contexts, environments, and ecosystems). The entire universe can be organized in this way. An atom can be seen as a system. It consists of subsystems called neutrons, protons, and electrons, and exists in the suprasystem of a molecule. A two-person conversation can be seen as a system. Consider a system called Dick and Jane existing in the suprasystem of a cocktail party. The solar system consists of subsystems including the sun, planets, asteroids, comets, dust, and gases and is contained in a galactic suprasystem called the Milky Way. Any subsystem can be a part of several systems simultaneously, and any system can have several simultaneous suprasystems. Actually, whether something is a system, subsystem, or a suprasystem depends primarily on how you analyze a situation—what *level of analysis* you use.

A business organization is a good example of an operating system. Various departments are its subsystems. Its industry or its community are among its suprasystems.

To understand systems theory, we must understand four propositions that underlie it: hierarchy, interdependence, synergy, and regulation. The subsystem, system, suprasystem vantage point suggest the first proposition of systems theory, that *behavior is structured hierarchically*. Let us examine this proposition more closely.

Behavior connotes action, motion. Systems move. They are always evolving, changing, growing, decaying, Of course, some systems move more quickly or obviously than others. A language is a communication system made up of sounds and the relationships between sounds. Over generations and centuries it evolves, changes, and grows. Individuals using language are part of language systems. People as well as sounds are subsystems of language, while language exists in the suprasystem of society, a culture, or the human species. A table is a system. So is a building, a forest, or a dog. All contain elements that relate to each other and that act upon each other, even if we cannot see the action.

Structured connotes that these actions occur in relatively consistent and predictable ways. Rules govern behavior. Again, some systems are more rigidly structured than others. The right combination of oxygen, hydrogen, and heat will always produce water. But a smile and a friendly hello will not always get the same response. Nonetheless, to understand behavior, especially communication behavior, systems theory suggests that we first understand rules governing behavior. The rules themselves vary in terms of their explicitness and flexibility; they are often called norms, rules, values, expectations, boundaries, agendas, laws, policies, procedures, or the like.

Hierarchically suggests, as we have mentioned, the organization of behavior into successive subsystems, systems, and suprasystems. To understand a system of behavior fully, one must examine its subsystems and the suprasystems of which it is a part, as well as the behavior itself.

The second proposition of systems theory says that all elements of a system are *interdependent*. Interdependence is the opposite of independence. In this context, the word suggests that elements of a system cannot act alone. They cannot behave unilaterally. Thus, whatever affects any element of a system in some way, however minute, affects every element of a system. The actions of any system element must be seen as an outcome of the system rather than of the element itself, or of some isolated causal element or elements.

In practical terms, the principle of interdependency says a great deal about how we seek to understand, predict, and control behavior. When somebody does something that strikes us as out of the ordinary, we wonder why. We try to identify a particular thing or things that make the person behave in that peculiar way. If we are unable to do so, we give credit to the individual's internal state.

Both of these explanatory procedures assume simple linear cause-and-effect frameworks. They frequently restrict our understanding of behavior. Interdependency suggests that we must move beyond notions of cause and effect or credit and blame. We must recognize that the "responsibility" for behavior is not simply assigned. Rather, while it appears that an individual is "doing" the behavior, the behavior should be seen as the product of the interaction of the many systems to which the individual or the behavior belongs.

A simple example of these differing perspectives can be found in the way that some managers explain their employees' work behavior. Confronted with workers who are lax producers and are generally unmotivated, one manager may assume that each of these people and, in fact, workers as a group, are, by their nature, lazy. Another manager, however, realizing that workers in other situations are quite energetic and productive, may realize that elements of the particular situation in which these people are working create conditions that reinforce unproductive behavior.

The first manager may try to effect a change in behavior by using threats, rewards, firings, or tearing out hair. The second manager would probably look at the structure of the work environment, the interaction norms of the people in the environment, and other behavioral factors in an effort to change the system that resulted in unproductive behavior. While the first manager may achieve some temporary improvements, the second manager is more likely to achieve long-term success.

The principle of *synergy* is the third proposition of systems theory. Synergy is most simply defined as "the whole is greater than the sum of its parts." If a system were broken down into all of its components, and the behavior of each element were explained, the behavior of the system as a whole would not be explained. The relationships between the elements of a system, a very real and important aspect of systems, are lost when the system is broken up. The Eastern philosopher Jiddu Krishnamurti says the same thing: "One cannot take one problem separately and try to solve it by itself; each problem contains all the other problems. . . ."

Synergy suggests a perspective, the necessity of understanding the "big picture." Of course, it is difficult to examine a system whole. But at the very least, as one examines a system's parts, one should bear in mind that they are only parts and that the purposes of examination should be to understand how these parts behave in relation to the other parts.

The fourth systems proposition is *regulation*. The behavior of any system is a function not only of the interaction of its elements, but also of the interaction of the entire system with other systems. Thus, the behavior of any system is constrained or regulated. Behavior occurs within acceptable limits. If behavior exceeds those limits, compensatory behavior will occur.

The clearest example of regulation occurs in economic systems. Producers of goods and services must behave within limits if they are to survive as businesses. One limit is set by the necessity of profit. The other is set by the necessity of providing goods and services at levels of price and quality acceptable to customers. When a business fails to perform within these limits, regulatory behavior called "bankruptcy" occurs.

Everyday human behavior is similarly regulated. If you walk what has been appropriately called the "straight and narrow," you have no problems. But if you increasingly deviate from the norm, you meet compensatory regulatory activities of increasing severity. Friendly ribbing becomes criticism. Criticism becomes scorn, which becomes ostracism, which can become incarceration in prison or a mental hospital, exile, or even death. It is not that you must walk the straight and narrow, but you should have a good idea of acceptable ranges of behavior (whch vary from situation to situation) and venture near or beyond accepted limits at your own risk.

Regulation offers another means for understanding human behavior from a systems perspective. It suggests that we ask not only why something happens, but also why alternatives do not happen.

Systems Theory and
Understanding Communication

Systems theory is not a communication theory per se. It does apply, however, to all forms of behavior. Because communication is a form of behavior, and all behavior is at least potentially communicative, systems theory applies directly and appropriately to communications.

More important, transfer of information is what allows human systems (and the systems that humans invent) to work. Systems interact with their environments by gathering information about the environment and then interpreting that information. On the basis of that interpretation, appropriate responses are formulated. The appropriateness of the system's behavior can be ascertained by the *feedback* received from the environment.

The study of ways that systems use communication for direction and control is called *cybernetics*. The word is derived from the Greek word for the pilot of a ship who scans the sea for information and takes corrective action as necessary to keep the ship on course.

ANALYZING COMMUNICATION SYSTEMS

Professor Robert Hopper in his book *Human Message Systems* suggests six questions that you should ask in analyzing almost any system:

1. What system is being examined?
2. What are its goals?
3. What are its components?
4. What is its environment?
5. How well is the system working?
6. How could the system be changed to work better?

Let us say that we are interested in analyzing the communication behavior of supervisors in relation to their subordinates. What system is being examined? Are we observing a series of two-person relationships? Do we consider these people in terms of group communication? Or do we analyze organizational structure—rules, norms, attitudes, climate? What about the backgrounds of the supervisor and the workers? Do we restrict ourselves to semantics, the words used in the situation? How we define the system of communication in which we are interested will largely determine the nature, validity, and usefulness of our analysis.

In the case that we are considering, the system's goals refer to the purposes of communication between supervisor and subordinates. Some possible purposes of this system include informing, controlling, motivating, directing, enforcing rules, building relationships, seeking information and ideas, or introducing change. In analyzing the system, we want to know both the extent to which the system's goals are appropriate and the extent to which they are being accomplished.

As mentioned, all systems have subsystems. Once a system has been defined and its major functions described, the system's operation can be broken down into its component parts. Each part, in turn, should be described in terms of its own operation and its contributions to the system as a whole. In our example, each individual in the system could be described as a subsystem with particular attention paid to personality, attitudes, communication tactics, personal goals and relationships. Other subsystems that would require analysis are communication rules, norms, and roles present in the system.

All systems exist within suprasystems. Thus, the system's environment is important to its operation. A system's environment includes the things that are important to the system's goals and that cannot be changed from within the system. Relevant environmental considerations in our case may include organizational expectations, norms and rules imposed from outside the system, and the relationship between the supervisor and his boss.

To determine how well the system is working, you evaluate (using system questions 3 and 4) whether the system (question 1) is achieving its objectives (question 2).

The final question is, "How can the system be changed so that it works better?" Proceed with caution. System changes frequently have unintended and sometimes negative consequences. In the case of the supervisor and subordinates, needed changes could range from a mild suggestion that the supervisor provide more feedback to the workers, to putting everyone through intensive communication training, to restructuring relationships by altering rules, norms, and roles, to transferring or firing personnel. Of course, once a change is made, the system has been changed, and anlaysis must begin anew.

THE PROBLEM OF CONSTRUCTING MEANING

The heart of the communication process is meaning. We constantly attempt to understand the meanings inherent in people's words and actions. We forever try to get our meanings across to others. Communication is the process of constructing meanings through the exchange of messages.

Many people believe that meaning is contained in words themselves. A glance at a dictionary, however, will convince you that a single word has many meanings. Meaning cannot be said to reside "inside" a word; rather, factors outside of the word determine its meaning.

Meaning is an excellent example of systems theory in action. The late anthropologist Gregory Bateson discusses meaning in the following way:

> A phoneme (a basic sound fragment) exists as such only in combination with phonemes which make up a word. The word is the context of the phoneme. But the word only exists as such—only has meaning—in the larger context of the utterance, which again has meaning only in. . . .

Bateson points out hierarchy, interdependence, synergy, and regulation as they relate to meaning.

Many factors influence the meaning of any word, action, or thing. One factor is the message itself, but that is only one. Another is called meta-communication, literally communication about the communication. Meta-communication includes vocal inflection, timing, stress, pitch, vocal rhythm, or the use of space or touch, or perhaps a wink or a nod or any of a number of acts.

Other factors influencing meaning may include realtionships (trust, liking, status) between the source of a message and the receiver; the perception of the source's intention and motivation by the receiver; the pre-existing cognitive structure of the receiver (attitudes, values, beliefs, expectations, world-view, previous experience in similar situations); and the context in which communication occurs (situation, emotion, surroundings, goals, etc.).

Ultimately, communication theory aims at describing and understanding the process of constructing and transferring meaning. The intent of the theory presented has been to improve our capacities to understand others' meanings and to make our own understood.

Lewis Carroll, author of *Alice in Wonderland* and other fantasies, was interested in the process of meaning, as is evident from the following dialogue:

> "When I use a word," Humpty Dumpty said in a rather scornful tone,
> "it means just what I choose it to mean—neither more nor less."

"The question is," said Alice, "whether you can make words mean so many different things."

"The question is," said Humpty Dumpty, "which is to be master—that's all."

If you recall what ultimately happened to Humpty Dumpty, you can guess the answer to the question. Our study of communication theory shows that if we hope to be effective communicators, meaning must be master.

PRINCIPLES
FOR
PRACTICE

1. Your effectiveness as a communicator depends upon the correlation of your personal theories with reality.

2. Many "common-sense" theories of communication have limited usefulness.

3. Systems theory provides a framework for the understanding of all human behavior including communication.

4. Behavior is more accurately viewed as the output of a system than as a product of isolated causes.

5. The whole is greater than the sum of its parts.

6. The behavior of a system is regulated by its interaction with other systems.

7. Ask not simply why things happen; ask also why other things do not happen.

8. You can judge the appropriateness of your behavior by the feedback you receive.

9. You can help others to judge their behavior by the feedback that you give.

10. Understand that factors outside of a word determine its meaning.

11. The transfer of meaning is the ultimate goal of purposeful communication.

FOR FURTHER STUDY

1. Analyze various communication situations from the systems theory perspective. Use the six questions applicable to analyzing systems.

2. Which of the "common-sense" theories of communication apply to you?

3. How would the systems approach apply to letter writing? To memo and report writing? To speech making? To leading a group meeting? To preparing an in-house publication?

SECTION
II

Getting Your Message Across Through Letters

CHAPTER 3

To: The Reader
From: The Authors
Subject: The Principles of Effective Writing

After reading this chapter you will know that:

1. Sentences that on the average are short will help to make
    your writing clearer.

2. Short, simple words of Anglo—Saxon origin will also help
    to make your writing clear.

3. The use of personal examples and personal words will help
    to make your writing interesting.

4. In simplifying your writing, editing and rewriting can
    help.

Letter form →

1. *empathy*
2. *content*
3. *action*

The Principles
of Effective Writing

People who are geniuses do not need rules for effective writing. Shake-speare did not need rules, and neither did Thomas Wolfe nor Dylan Thomas nor Ernest Hemingway. But few people fall into their category. The rest of us need all the help we can get.

For a long time, scholars and stylists have been seeking rules to help people of talent, but not genius, to write interestingly and effectively. They started by asking a question: "Can a person who understands basic grammar and punctuation take specific steps to help make muddy writing clear and dull writing interesting?" From many sources the answer has come back "Yes." You can use three principles.

In this chapter, we shall look at them. They apply to writing letters, reports, and memoranda, all fundamental tools of business. Later in this book, in Chapters 4–11, you will see how these principles apply to these tools. At the end of this chapter are some exercises that will help you to begin mastering the techniques. You will find that they work beautifully in everyday bread-and-butter usage.

THE FIRST PRINCIPLE (THE COUEY PRINCIPLE)

Shortly after World War II, a young man working on the *Birmingham News* was selected to attend a seminar at Columbia University. His name was James H. Couey, Jr. The seminar was the American Press Institute, one of the most prestigious of the educational institutes for working journalists. For many years, journalists from all over the country went to Columbia, usually for two weeks, to sit around a huge table with their peers and with invited experts to discuss what they did for a living and to figure out ways to do it better. As a seminar member in 1948–1949, Couey pressed his colleagues to tell him what made some writing clear and easy to read and some writing hard to understand. No one at the seminar had any simple answers.

Couey made such an impression upon the seminar leaders at Columbia that he was invited to return as an expert discussion leader 20 times between 1951 and 1959. At first, he was not positive that he really was an expert, but he set out to become one. His insight was a simple one: sentence clarity is related to average sentence length.

The discussion groups that Couey led at Columbia (the Institute has since moved to Reston, Virginia) were rather large in those days, averaging 25 to 28 members each. J. Montgomery Curtis, a justly famous director of the Institute, described Couey's work this way in a letter to one of the authors of this book.

> The Seminar members would send three copies of their paper to Jim at least six weeks in advance. Jim then set to work reading the local news in each paper. He would thus determine the *average* (and there is no more important word than that in describing the Couey method) number of words per sentence. His next step was to have proofs pulled of a typical story for each paper. He would take these proofs to any meeting of small groups. His favorites were of a local of the CIO Steelworkers Union, a club of textile plant executives, a PTA, and so on. He preferred groups which met in the evening so there would be time to do the job. Jim would distribute the proofs of one story to all present at the meeting. He would give them a reasonable time to read the story—usually about seven to 10 minutes for a story of one-column length.

After the story had been read, the proofs would be taken up, and the participants would be asked a set of questions to see how much they had retained. After he had finished testing the stories in Birmingham, he would take the results to New York to show to the representatives of the papers in which they had appeared. At one seminar, there was a representative of a paper that specialized in stories about the textile industry. In that newspaper, Couey found one of the worst examples ever. Here it is, as preserved in the files of the American Press Institute:

> American London Shrinkers Corporation has spent a year and a half experimenting and compiling data on the shrinking and finishing of man-made fibers used in combination with woolen and worsted yarns and is now equipped to handle all types of blends, it is made known by Theodore Trilling, president.
>
> The trend toward blends in suiting and coating woolens and worsteds brought with it the need for a variety of alterations in the shrinking and sponging operation, Mr. Trilling adds, pointing out for example, that the Orlon content in a fabric turned yellow, the rayon and acetate content tended to moire and the 15 to 20 percent of nylon now often used to give added strength tended to shine.
>
> No new machinery is involved, just alterations in the processing, such as a change in the action or the weight of the apron or the leader, but it took a lot of trial and error observations, testing to make sure that further shrinkage would not take place, and tabulation of the data before the "we are now in a position" statement could be made, it was added.
>
> Special reports of the tests and their results have been passed along to the mills and sealing agents of these blends, and in some cases, they have served as a guide in the correction and improvement of these fabrics, Mr. Trilling states.
>
> He adds that his firm has been offering its 100 percent woolen and worsted finishing and shrinking service to the industry for the past 55 years and that with the alterations to handle blends now completed, an important step has been made.

We scarcely need any formal analysis to know that this piece of writing is not clear, but Couey wanted to make his point. He noted that the piece contains 271 words, but only five sentences. Thus each sentence is slightly longer than *54 words*. A sentence is a package for ideas, but readers struggle to get huge, blocky packages into their heads. When Couey asked people who had read the piece a series of questions about it, their answers showed little understanding.

> Who is making the statement? 26 percent knew.
> What firm is doing the work? 18 percent.
> How long have the experiments been underway? 30 percent.
> What kinds of materials are involved? 11 percent.
> What, briefly, is this story about? 9 percent.

The last question is most important. What is the story about? Only nine out of every 100 persons who read it could say. The story was a failure.

The young man representing the newspaper in which this piece appeared attempted to defend his publication. "We write strictly for experts in the textile business," he said, "and they would understand the piece." "Very well," said Couey. "We have a lot of textile people in Birmingham. I will take your story and test it with these people and send the results to you." He did and reconfirmed what he already knew, that the textile people could not understand the story either.

Couey was convinced that the trouble with the story was that the sentences were too long. So he mechanically edited the piece to reduce sentence length. He took care not to invest the edited work with literary excellence, as that would have thrown off the results of his test. Taken as literature, his "corrected" version is as bad as the original one. The second version has 265 words and 21 sentences, meaning that the sentences average a little more than 12 words. Here is the edited version:

> American London Shrinkers Corp. has come to the end of an 18-month search.
>
> One year and a half ago, that firm set out to find a safe way to shrink, sponge, and handle blended materials without damage. Much experimentation was required. Many volumes of data gathered. The trial and error method was given a thorough test.
>
> And now—success.
>
> Theodore Trilling, president of American London Shrinkers, has announced that the problem has been solved.
>
> Exactly what was the problem?
>
> The trend towards blends in suiting and coating woolens and worsteds created the necessity for developing some alterations in shrinking and sponging operations.
>
> Mr. Trilling mentioned the "change color" problem. He pointed out that the Orlon content in a fabric turned yellow. The rayon and acetate content tended to moire. The 15 to 20 percent of nylon, used to give strength, tended to shine. The "color changes" do not occur in the new process.
>
> No new machinery is needed, Trilling said. He made clear that only alterations in the processing are necessary. He referred to alterations such as a change in the action, the weight of the apron or the leader.
>
> The firm's president emphasized that many tests were required to make sure no further shrinkage would occur.
>
> Reports of the tests and results have been passed on to the mills and sealing agents of the new blends, Mr. Trilling said. In some cases, the new information has served as a guide in the correction and improvement of these fabrics, he said.
>
> This is an important step in the industry, according to Trilling.

When another test group was asked the same questions about this piece, the results were interesting. Readers in this group retained much more.

Who is making the statement? 68 percent knew.
What firm is doing the work? 55 percent.
How long have the experiments been underway? 71 percent.
What kinds of materials are involved? 29 percent.
What, briefly, is this story about? 64 percent.

On the most important question—What is this story about?—the number of persons understanding the story went up from 9 out of 100 to 64 out of 100 when the sentence length was dropped from about 54 words per sentence to about 12.

In preparing to conduct twenty discussion groups, Couey repeated experiments of this kind dozens of times. The results were always the same. Short sentence length meant greater understanding. It was pointed out to Couey that his "clear" writing usually had one idea per sentence; when you write a short sentence, it often contains only one idea. A one-idea sentence is clear and easy to digest. Whether or not clarity results from one-idea sentences could be debated. Couey demonstrated, however, that short sentences will do the job. Here is another example, not nearly so bad, from another newspaper. It is also preserved in the files of the American Press Institute. It has 288 words, 10 sentences, and an average of about 29 words per sentence.

A rock found last fall near Lake Pelican and inscribed with dates, an Indian symbol and a cross has been termed a hoax by Will G. Robinson, Pierre, secretary of the state historical society.

In a letter to Wright Tarbell, Watertown, who now has possession of the rock, Robinson said the fact that the inscriptions on the rock haven't weathered as bad as the rest of the rock's surface would indicate to him that the rock is a "plant."

Oblong in shape and measuring about 12 inches long, 10 inches wide and four inches thick, the rock bears the dates, 1511–1671. Above the dates is a cross-like inscription and below the dates appears a symbol representing a face with rays emanating from it, which Tarbell says is probably the old Indian symbol for a turtle.

The rock was found on the northwest side of Lake Pelican by Richard Torgerson, 707 B. Avenue, Northeast. Torgerson was crossing a sidehill to go fishing when he discovered the rock. Indian graves had been discovered in that general area several years previous.

Robinson, in his letter to Tarbell, cited the discovery of a rock near Big Stone Lake several years ago which bore the inscriptions "Plymouth" and "1620." Robinson said this rock had been discovered by a person who had no connection or interest in the rock and that no proof or evidence could be obtained relating the rock in any way with the Plymouth Colony.

The state historian added that newspaper accounts of the discovery of the rock near the Big Stone Lake may have prompted "some of the mischievous minded gentry to provoke a mystery" by inscribing the rock found by Torgerson and placing it where it would be discovered.

And here are the questions that Couey asked about the piece and the percentages of those who could answer them.

Where was the object mentioned found? 27 percent.
Who found it? 33 percent.
What was inscribed on it? 30 percent.
Who is the expert giving the opinion? 16 percent.
Who has possession of the object? 10 percent.
What, in general, is the story about? 40 percent.

An editing job reduced the story to 269 words, with 22 sentences and an average of about 12 words per sentence.

The mysterious rock found last fall near Lake Pelican is a hoax. That's the opinion of Will G. Robinson, Pierre, secretary of the state's historical society.

Robinson states his opinion in a letter to Wright Tarbell, Watertown, who now has the rock. Robinson studied the inscribed dates, an Indian symbol and a cross on the stone. He decided that those inscriptions haven't weathered as badly as the rest of the rock's surface. That fact indicates to him that the rock is a "plant."

The rock is oblong in shape. It measures about 12 inches long, 10 inches wide, and four inches thick. It bears the dates, 1511–1671. A symbol resembling a face with rays emanating from it is cut below the dates. Tarbell says the letter symbol is probably the old Indian symbol for a turtle.

Richard Torgerson found the rock. He was crossing a sidehill to go fishing when he saw the object. Torgerson lives at 707 B. Avenue, Northeast.

Indian graves had been discovered several years before in the area where the rock was found.

Robinson cited the discovery of another rock several years ago. That one was found near Big Stone Lake. It bore the inscriptions "Plymouth" and "1620." Robinson said no proof or evidence could be obtained relating the rock in any way with the Plymouth Colony.

He added that newspaper accounts of the Big Stone Lake find might have prompted "some of the mischievous minded gentry to provoke a mystery" by inscribing the rock and placing it where it would be discovered.

Torgerson discovered it.

The percentage of readers who could understand this story jumped sharply.

Where was the object mentioned found? 54 percent.
Who found it? 80 percent.
What was inscribed on it? 47 percent.
Who is the expert giving the opinion? 49 percent.
Who has possession of the object? 31 percent.
What, in general, is the story about? 83 percent.

As average sentence length dropped from about 29 words to about 12, general understanding more than doubled, rising from 40 percent to 83 percent.

No one would base a broad proposition on two pieces of evidence, or even on 10. But Couey repeated the experiment so many times, and always with similar results, that he formulated a rule now called the Couey Principle. It says: Use sentences that on the average are short. And when all his work is analyzed, it seems to show that 17 is about the breakpoint. When you use sentences that average 17 words or fewer, your readers generally can understand you. When you go over 17, you start losing your readers fast.

Again, Couey emphasized *average* sentence length. He will let you have a sentence 30 or 35 words long, provided you follow it with one that is five or six. Within limits like that, you can achieve variety, beauty, and aesthetic delight. Your work need not be choppy and monotonous.

Neither Couey nor his principal supporters ever pretended that short sentence length is everything. It is where you start. Says Montgomery Curtis: "There is a lot more to the art of writing than average words per sentence. But without that, you are lost." Scholars who criticize this approach say that counting the words in your sentences will reduce you to writing by formula. It need not do so. Once you train yourself to keep your sentences short *on the average,* variety will take care of itself and you need not count. You will have developed good habits, and they will carry you along on their own jetstream.

A personal word about Couey. This brilliant journalist was also an excellent teacher. He taught writing at Howard College (now Samford University) in Birmingham while he was working on the newspaper there, and his former students recall him as a man who looked for the philosophical underpinnings of what he was doing. After leaving Birmingham, he worked on a newspaper in Tampa, Florida, and in 1971 he became publisher of the *Honolulu Star-Bulletin*. That year, he and Mrs. Couey attended an international meeting in Helsinki, Finland. They were passing through the airport in Rome when Couey died suddenly. He was still in his forties. His research survives him, however, and many regard his idea as the cornerstone of clarity for writers.

THE SECOND PRINCIPLE

Long before Couey was born, scholars were debating as to which words in English are the most powerful and effective. Are they the Latin-based part of the language, much of which came in through French, or does effectiveness lie in words of Anglo-Saxon origin? Some 100 years ago, Dr. William Mathews, in his book, *Words: Their Use and Abuse,* pointed out that words of Anglo-Saxon origin are the dialect of the nursery, and their later use is tied to the feelings of those who use them by their early use. They "are full of secret suggestions and echoes," says Mathews, "which greatly multiply their power. . . . All passionate expression,—the outpouring of the soul when moved to its depths,—is, for the most part, in monosyllables."

However, more recently, a United States senator made a national reputation, and made himself a national resource, by using extremely long words cleverly. The late Senator Everett McKinley Dirksen of Illinois used long words and involved sentence constructions to be funny. He did not use the word "filibuster" to describe a long-winded speech when he could assure his hearers that "the measure will die of a semantic injection." Everyone laughed. He was being intentionally amusing by being preposterous. One day, when speaking on the Senate floor, Dirksen used the word "euphemism," and a senator who did not admire him asked him to explain. That was a mistake. Dirksen never broke his stride, but turned to his questioner and said: "If your father had been hanged as a horse thief, you wouldn't say it that way. You would say, 'He died at a public gathering when the platform gave way.'" Dirksen, being a gentleman, had the exchange removed from the *Congressional Record* so that the other senator would not be permanently embarrassed.

The point of this little story is this: So long as Dirksen was speaking for comic effect and for display, he loaded his language with words of Latin and even Greek origin. When he was hard pressed, he stopped using such words and spoke Anglo-Saxon. He did it instinctively. Look at the foregoing paragraph once more and see what he did and how he did it.

Few of us are as quick or clever as Senator Dirksen, but we can learn to take some steps. For example, the following words have two or more syllables. Each one can be replaced by a shorter word, usually a word of one syllable. The short word is the strong word, being for the most part Anglo-Saxon in origin. The longer words are for the most part of Latin origin, although words of Greek origin would fall into the same category. Look:

effectuate	encounter
endeavor	facilitate
initiate	occasion
proceed	procure

purchase

transmit

approximately

initial

presently

sufficient

assistance

discrepancy

objective

utilization

contribute

demonstrate

terminate

utilize

equivalent

optimum

subsequent

aggregate

compensation

modification

obligation

ascertain

construct

Now, let us replace each of the longer words with a shorter word that means the same thing. The long words on the list were chosen intentionally. Many people use them in their writing. Depending upon context, there can be more than one substitute word, but the ones given are common. This list could be longer, of course, but these will give you the idea.

effectuate: *do*

endeavor: *try*

initiate: *start*

proceed: *start, go*

purchase: *buy*

transmit: *send*

approximately: *about*

initial: *first*

presently: *soon*

sufficient: *enough*

assistance: *help*

discrepancy: *error*

objective: *goal, aim*

utilization: *use*

contribute: *give*

demonstrate: *show*

encounter: *meet*

facilitate: *help, aid*

occasion: *time*

procure: *get*

terminate: *stop*

utilize: *use*

equivalent: *equal*

optimum: *best*

subsequent: *after*

aggregate: *total*

compensation: *pay*

modification: *change*

obligation: *debt*

ascertain: *learn*

construct: *build*

Hereafter we shall not "ascertain" that the game "commences" at 7 P.M. We shall "learn" that it "starts" then. We shall not "demonstrate" a new product, but "show" it; we shall hereafter find "errors" rather than "discrepancies."

Look at this sentence: "In view of the fact that the instructor performed poorly, we feel he should be afforded another opportunity in the near future to demonstrate his ability." It is stronger to say: "Because the instructor did poorly, he should be given another chance soon." Some time ago, a young secretary was writing a letter for a state governor's signature. Before his election, the governor had been a rural newspaper publisher, and he knew about effective language. He looked at the letter the secretary had written and saw that it was loaded with long words. He smiled, gave the letter back, and said: "Boil the fat out of it." In the example above, we have boiled the fat out, and there was a lot of it.

What impulse makes people lapse into words of Latin or Greek origin the minute they start writing? They do not talk that way. Three or four centuries ago, most people who could read and write were members of the upper classes, or they had been trained to serve the state or the church. They were educated in Latin grammar schools where classical language and literature were emphasized. They naturally used words other than the basic Anglo-Saxon ones. Doing so put a social distance between them and the common people who spoke simply.

Today, we can all read and write, but many people still think it is a sign of status to use long words. Some scholars call this phenomenon "urbanization," or trying to be more "up town" than you are. Once, President and Mrs. Eisenhower visited an American city, and as they came down the ramp of their plane at the airport, President Eisenhower spoke a few words into the waiting microphones. "I thank you for being so kind to Mrs. Eisenhower and I," he said. He was urbanizing. He should have said, "to Mrs. Eisenhower and *me*," but he tried too hard and overshot the mark. Most people do not urbanize by making errors in the objective case, as President Eisenhower did. They do so by using long words. Some probably use fancy words because they think the organization they work for approves. We all know the effects of peer pressure, and if we believe that our organization likes certain pieces of jargon, or that it prefers language that is bloated, we use it. Besides, it is easier to do what everybody else is doing. Probably it makes us feel like a member of the team. The only problem is that it has little distinction. You sound just like everybody else—pompous. For reasons now forgotten, many of our police departments appear to attach caste status to words of Latin and Greek origin. Today, they do not "catch the men and women." They "apprehend the subjects." To them, mugging is "an unsolicited contact." When a victim of a mugging once wished aloud that she had had some Mace to squirt in the mugger's face, a policeman assured her that to have done so would have "caused the male subject severe optical damage." He meant the Mace would have hurt the criminal's eyes badly, which was the idea in the first place.

On the basis of what has been said so far, we have a new rule or principle. *Use words of Latin or Greek origin sparingly; instead, use simple words of Anglo-Saxon origin.* Please notice that the rule does not say to *avoid* words of Latin or Greek origin. That would be unwise. There is a time and a place for everything, and many Latin and Greek words are effective and easily understood. Many are beautiful and add variety to your writing. Some are technical words and must be used. Some are also everyday words: *item, alibi, vim, bonus, animal, veto, vacuum, recipe,* to name a few. The rule means that you should ordinarily avoid Latin or Greek words when you can find short words to take their places, words like those we looked at above. Obviously, you should never apply this principle mechanically. If a Latin- or Greek-based word has no exact synonym, then use the Latin- or Greek-based word. Also, do not use the same Anglo-Saxon word repeatedly in your writing. You will sound monotonous. You can achieve variety by using an occasional Latin- or Greek-based word that means the same thing. A common-sense application of the principle will mean that you will use shorter words overall, and that is the idea. If you do not know how to spot Latin and Greek words, then just use short words.

What we have just said raises an intellectual problem. We all know that college entrance examinations, intelligence tests, and other proficiency measurements are based partly upon vocabulary. If we are saying that you should ordinarily use short words when you write, are we also attacking the values of vocabulary? No. First, you will need a good vocabulary to understand the writings of people who have not read this book.

But that is not the best reason. George Orwell, in his book *1984,* created a world in which a new language had been developed, a language called Newspeak. Newspeak was language stripped to its essentials, and it robbed people of their power to think. The authorities invented the language for just that purpose. If stripping the language restricts the power to think, then is the other side of the coin also true? Does having a rich vocabulary help you to think better? Probably so. However, having a rich vocabulary does not mean that you should show it off when you write. And if you do so, do it to be intentionally funny or effective, as Senator Dirksen did, not to be unintentionally funny like a lot of unfortunate people.

THE THIRD PRINCIPLE

At the end of World War II, the Army asked a much-decorated American lieutenant to speak before civic clubs and other public gatherings upon his return to the United States from Europe. This young man, twenty-one years old and no public speaker, was frightened. He was sure he would rather face Germans than Rotarians.

He had a highly developed sense of duty, however, and he felt he had to try. In preparation, he started sketching out what he would talk about: "The superb quality of the American fighting man. The high ideals for which the war was fought." And so forth.

As he was preparing his notes, a senior officer assigned to help him, a man involved in the Army's public relations program, happened to come by and glance at what he had written. "Are you going to tell those people that?" he asked. The young man said he thought he was. And then the senior officer gave the young man the best advice he was to receive in his adult life, advice that meant money and advancement to him in later years:

> You have been commanding a military outfit which had a good many interesting characters in it. You know them all. Why not just think about these men, pick out five or six, and remember something interesting that each did? Tell about these people. Tell first about one, then make a little transition, tell about another, and so on. And finally, when you have told about the fifth or sixth, you will have spoken about seventeen minutes. That's as much as people are accustomed to hearing. Then, tell a funny one and sit down.

The lieutenant did it, and the result was remarkable. People were on the edges of their chairs. He was modest. He did not need to talk about himself, for the person who introduced him had already done that.

The point here is not that he made a successful speech. The point is that he learned *how* to make a successful speech. (It has often been said that it was not so important that the Wright brothers flew the first plane at Kitty Hawk. The point was that they knew how to build a plane that would fly. And so it was with this young man.) Today, he is in demand as a public speaker. Long ago, he stopped talking about World War II and started talking about interesting happenings and interesting people in his current line of work, in which he is happy and successful.

The senior military officer gave him advice that was based upon a sound principle. He had told him how to hold people's interest. Put simply, the principle is this: *Talk about people to hold other people's interest. Talk about things only when you must.* We are, as a rule, more interested in people than we are in things. Thus the principle is soundly based. When you talk about people, you will almost certainly hold interest. When you talk about things, attitudes, or high ideals, you may hold interest. When you talk extremely well, you almost certainly can. But it is harder, and the chances of failure are real.

Turn your mind back to the beginning of this chapter. You remember James Couey because he was an interesting man who did something interesting. You know what he did, and you will continue to know and to use it. You remember what Senator Dirksen did when he got into trouble. You recall that President Eisenhower urbanized a bit. You remember these *points* because you were told them in terms of people. You might not have recalled the points without the people. This device has been in use a long time. Everybody recalls Jonah and the whale, the prodigal son, and George Washington and the cherry tree.

A story is a stepped-up device for holding attention, and most ordinary business writing cannot be cast in that form. Occasionally, a letter or a memorandum can, and when it can, it works beautifully. For example, when a piece of writing tells what happened to people in a given situation, why not just tell what took place? That most certainly is a story. But even when a story is not being told, people can be referred to. Their names can be mentioned. You can relax and use *he, him, his, she, her, hers, we, our, ours, they, them, theirs.* And do not forget *I, me, mine,* or *you, your, yours.*

At this point, we must quickly say that there are firms, agencies, and institutions that do not allow such usage. They wish their correspondence to be formal, without personalization. What do you do then? You know perfectly well that any wise person taking a job will first find out what the boss wants and then try to deliver it. If your boss does not wish you to use personalized words—either in the form of stories or names or personal pronouns—then do not try to swim upstream. You could not anyway.

Do your best to use the third principle, but if your organization forbids or discourages it, you can still find plenty to do using the first two.

Examples   Following is a letter that uses all three of the principles. Jennifer Altmann owns an electric supply business. For seven years, she has made occasional sales to the owner of the largest automobile repair shop in the area. She has sold him some of the electrical motors, drills, hammers, and other equipment he needs. She would like to sell him more. Ms. Altmann has just gotten an order from him for an ABX-24 electric motor, a model noted for its dependability and its flexibility. This customer has not ordered this motor before, and Ms. Altmann wants him to know its virtues. She sends a truck to deliver the motor along with this letter:

```
Dear Mr. Ebersole,

   I am glad that you have ordered one of our ABX-24s.
These motors have a proven record of usefulness and
dependability. They can do a lot of different things.
   Four years ago, I sold an earlier model (ABX-21) to a
truck farmer who has used it to pump water from a deep
well to irrigate his crops. Two weeks ago, he came into
my office to buy ABX-24s for some new wells he has dug.
The ABX-21 has run for four years with no more
maintenance than normal lubrication.
   Some time ago, I sold seven larger models to the
operator of a lumber mill. They have served him
faithfully.
```

```
    I believe that you will find this engine to be
everything you wish for. You will probably find it to be
the most adaptable electric motor you have had.
    In a few days, I shall call upon you to discuss other
ways that we may serve you. We have other new lines of
electrical equipment which we believe could save you
money in your operation.

                           Sincerely,


                           Jennifer N. Altmann
                           President
```

The sentences are short. There are 178 words and 12 sentences. The average sentence length is less than 15 words. Couey would have found that quite acceptable. This letter does not mechanically avoid all Latin- and Greek-based words, but it is mostly Anglo-Saxon—short words. There are two little "people" examples in it—the irrigation farmer and the lumber operator. Mr. Ebersole will remember them, and he will also remember that they like the motor.

Had Ms. Altmann not known what she was doing, she might have sent the following:

```
Dear Mr. Ebersole,

    In reference to yours of November 23, please note the
delivery of motor ABX-24 which has been utilized by
business people in many diversified enterprises. I would
like to offer some suggestions as to how you can utilize
our service further, and for that purpose, I will be
calling upon you, making a definite appointment in
advance for the mutual convenience of all concerned.
Thank you for your order which we have been pleased
to fill on a rush basis.

                           Sincerely,


                           Jennifer N. Altmann
                           President
```

Unfortunately, more letters go out like this than like the first one. They give the impression of "thickness" and are heavy reading. The words and the sentences are too long, and the subject matter deals almost entirely with things, not people.

Edit or Rewrite

Two processes can improve what you have written or what somebody else has written. First, you can *edit* it. That is: you can take the piece of writing and go over it, changing it where it violates the principles. When you edit, you usually do not change the basic sentence structure. However, you may choose to do so. Starting over and changing the sentence structure is called *rewriting*. Both editing and rewriting are good and there is little to choose between the two. Sometimes you will use one, sometimes the other. Sometimes you will change one sentence only slightly; you may completely revise another.

   Always remember that for bread-and-butter writing of the kind that we are discussing, there is seldom only one way to write something. There are many correct ways. We should count ourselves happy if we can produce clear, interesting, and effective writing. The ability to do so has made many people happier, and some people richer.

PRINCIPLES
FOR
PRACTICE

1. Sentences that on the average are short are easier to understand.

2. When sentences average more than 17 words in length, your reader's ability to understand drops off fast.

3. A good average sentence length might fall between 11 and 14 words.

4. Short words of Anglo-Saxon origin produce clearer writing than long words of Latin or Greek origin.

5. However, words of Latin or Greek origin should not be avoided altogether, only used sparingly.

6. People are more interested in people than they are in things. Therefore, use personal names and words in your writing to increase the interest.

7. Editing and rewriting are devices you can use to improve quality of writing.

FOR FURTHER STUDY

1. Edit or rewrite the following. Count the number of words you saved by reworking the sentences.

a. On a monthly basis, he will visit a total of some 40 stores in the chain.

b. Are there newly developed ways and means of accomplishing the desired objective?

c. She was paid in the amount of $400.

d. In the event of inclement weather, the horse show will be rescheduled for another day.

e. I do not like to be forced into the role of serving as a lackey when my job description clearly states what jobs I am supposed to accomplish in this company.

f. In reference to your letter of June 27, I am pleased to state that the order will be processed immediately.

g. They did it in conjunction with their teachers.

h. The joint sponsorship of the two excellent companies should guarantee that the general public will respond and will attend the ceremonies.

i. Notwithstanding any agreement to the contrary, a company selling credit cards may not, as a condition to participating in a credit card plan, require that a purchaser procure any other services from the company selling the credit cards.

j. I would like to make the assertion that there are certain principles which have as their objective the maximization of verbal communication.

k. What recompense should a company offer to an employee who has been injured in a job-related accident?

l. An overwhelming preponderance of medical practitioners feel it necessary to purchase malpractice insurance policies.

m. He achieved a position of eminence within his profession.

n. What must we do after this undertaking is accomplished?

o. Proceed to expedite the order, as the customer asserts that she will be forced to terminate several accounts if the order does not arrive directly.

p. At the risk of losing what little credibility I have due to my short placement period, I suggest that we either provide the services delineated in our official publications or desist from performing in this field.

q. The hospitality desk will be situated adjacent to the registration desk, and you are urged to partake of the various kinds of hospitality that are being provided under multiple sponsorships.

r. Our production year was divided into two separate phases—production before Christmas and production after Christmas.

s. It was a rewarding experience for us to observe the interest and enthusiasm of the various participants in the charity benefit program.

t. I am myself struggling to deal with the concerns of bringing about broad changes in the detailed operations of this institution.

2. Write a letter to a friend who has helped you, explaining how you were helped and expressing thanks. Use the principles you learned in this chapter.

3. The following memorandum was written by a person working for a power company. It is not terrible, merely poor. You can improve it by editing or rewriting. Look carefully for words that are wasted and remove them.

Dear Mr. Thomas,

On Tuesday, July 18th, the Skills Training Center was pleased to welcome Ms. Bertha Lilly, a Research Associate with Technical Education Research Center in Wilmington, North Carolina. She was accompanied by two members from Power Generation Services. The purpose of the visit was for Ms. Lilly to become acquainted with the training techniques of the company and especially the Instrument Technician training that we are now developing.

After touring the facility and observing several classes being conducted, Ms. Lilly examined the Instrument Technician Program and discussed the research that she was presently doing. She was very complimentary of our training effort here and was very interested in the Instrument Technician Training Program materials that we had already developed. She asked for a copy of the questionnaire that we are planning to use. This writer offered to assist her in obtaining copies of the materials that she requested.

If there are any questions, please contact me.

Sincerely,

Theodore Ragsdale

4. The following letter is from a high school principal. It contains wasted words and phrases. Edit them out.

Dear Parents:

Recently, I had the occasion to attend and participate in the "Fifth Annual Southwestern Drug Conference." This conference was specifically concerned with the harmful effects marijuana use has on American youth.

The conference was highlighted by the presentation of
the voluminous amount of medical and scientific
research, which indicates beyond any doubt in my mind
that adolescents' regular use of marijuana is both
physically and mentally harmful.

I am so concerned over the harmful effects that
marijuana can have on young people that I am personally
involved in trying to share these recent scientific
findings with the community.

Enclosed you will find two articles from the *Abilene
Enterprise*. The facts presented in these articles were
based on very sophisticated scientific research.

I hope that you will take time to read it and if you
are interested in any more information, please contact
me or Mrs. Thornberry.

Sincerely,

Henry Raines
Principal

5. Following is a terrible example. It was produced in a federal agency in
Washington and sent to regional offices. Edit or rewrite this letter and
improve it.

Dear Regional Directors:

In order to facilitate automated generation of the new
SF-113A., Monthly Report of Federal Civilian Employment,
for the U.S. Civil Service Commission, the National
Office is planning to enhance our Payroll/Personnel
System to enable it to generate the total number of
employees occupying temporary positions.

In order to initialize the Employee Master File at the
Detroit Data Center, please provide us with the Social
Security Numbers and indicative name of all employees
within your office occupying temporary positions as of
November 4. Your reply should be received in this office
no later than December 23. Negative responses are
requested.

Sincerely,

6. This letter from the director of a seminar for business executives is typical

of much business correspondence. It can be improved. Rewrite or edit it.
Please use the principles learned in this chapter.

My colleages and I at Terrytown are delighted to learn
that you will be participating in our Executive Seminar
Program. As Seminar Director, I am looking forward to
meeting you and to the collaborative relationship which
is so intrinsic an aspect of this residential executive
education program.

The Executive Seminar Center, located in Terrytown,
offers an intensive educational experience in an
academic environment for select groups of career
executives. In a setting removed from the busy stream of
regular work, participating executives hear
presentations by and partake in dialogues with a
distinguished visiting faculty comprised of senior
scholars and policy—level government and corporate
officials. An important aspect of seminar participation
is the shared learning experience in which approximately
thirty—six executives partake. Representing a broad
cross—section and a wide spectrum of professional
backgrounds, these executives have unique opportunities
to informally share experiences and ideas with one
another and with the resident staff. The vigorous pace
is both intellectually stimulating and educationally
rewarding.

You will soon receive materials describing our
facilities, available services and other items of
personal interest. This package will include a copy of
the program agenda and preparatory readings which should
be reviewed prior to your arrival.

The Seminar has been conceptualized and designed as an
intensive learning experience for participating
managers. We hope you will derive optimal benefit from
participation in this residential program.

Telephone us if we may respond to any needs that arise
before your arrival here.

Sincerely,

Edward N. Langworthy
Director

7. This letter from the president of a student financial aid group to high

school seniors is better than average. Read it carefully. List the reasons why it rates fairly high marks.

Dear High School Senior,

    The current year is a big one for you. One of the most important things you will do this year is choose the college you will attend.

    It may seem that you have lot of time to make up your mind about college and a career. But may I offer a word of caution?

    1. Don't wait until you've decided on the one college you want before you decide what alternative you may have to take.

    2. Don't wait until the year is almost gone to find out that your parents can't afford the college you want.

    Believe me, I speak from experience. I've put three children through college. And, through the years, I've talked to a lot of American youngsters. I've urged them to look early to find ways of getting some of the $500 million in college funds that are available each year.

    The key? Do it early. Beat the crowd. Get your application for scholarships, grants, and aid to the right places as soon as you can.

    Right now. It is not too early to start looking for money for college. Now is the time.

            Sincerely,

            Alfred R. Sacks
            President

CHAPTER 4

To: The Reader
From: The Authors
Subject: Things You Must Know Writing a Letter

After reading this chapter you will know:

1. How the letter should look on the page.

2. The parts of the letter.

3. The advantages of *writing* the letter out.

4. The principles of dictation.

5. The importance of accuracy.

6. The effects of positive and negative language.

7. How to use precise words.

8. How to use the active voice.

9. The ''You'' Approach.

10. The Empathy-Content-Action model.

11. Good News Letters.

12. Bad News Letters.

Writing Letters—An Overview

HOW SHOULD THE LETTER LOOK?

How your letter looks will tell the reader more about you than you might expect. A smudged place or a struck-over letter or figure becomes the most important spot on the page. The eye goes to it at once. If there is a misspelled word, for some reason the eye leaps to find it. These kinds of slips can mark you as indifferent, careless, or ignorant.

Even those who are normally scrupulous about making their correspondence look good can send a bad letter if they are careless for a single instant. A good many years ago, a young American who was collecting autographs wrote to the Duke of Windsor, formerly King Edward VIII, to ask him for his. The Duke was then Governor of the Bahamas. He did not answer the letter personally, but one of his staff did. The letter said that the Duke "regreats his inability to comply with your request." Presumably, he "regretted" it. It is doubtful that he "regreated" it. The English language includes no such word. Although this happened about forty years ago, the American still remembers when a former King of England let one word get away from him.

Recently, the president of a public relations firm in a large city got a letter from a student at a nearby university. The student wanted information about the public relations business. In the inside address, he misspelled the name of the firm to which he was writing. The letter follows, edited only to protect the guilty:

```
    I am a mmember of the State University Student
Government and a Master Degree Candidate in Public
Relations and Administration. I am doing some research
for an in depth paper on Public Relations. I would
appreciate it very much if you could assist me by
sending me the answers to the following questions about
you agency:

1.  What basis is used for charging your customers? Or is
    it on a sistuational basis?

2.  Do you find P.R. a growing business in your state?

3.  Do you have a brochure giving you customers a gener-
    al idea of your services and costs?

    If you can answer these questions for me it would be of
great assistance to me and my disertation.

    Please forward any response to:  James Furness
                                     1642 Elmwood Street

ADD: 4. Are you a member of a P.R. organization such as
the PRSA?

Thank You for your cooperation.

                               Sincerely,


                               James Furness
                               Secreatary of Academic
                               Affairs
```

The public relations president answered the questions. Then he wrote:

> Were I a member of faculty of the university at which you are studying public relations on the graduate level, I should be alarmed at the poor quality of the letter that you sent to me.

The letter reflected discredit on the university, and it certainly made the student who signed it look stupid and slovenly.

We must not expect easy forgiveness for sloppy letters. People judge us quickly. Readers accept no excuses for misspelled words. You can buy good dictionaries today in both hardback and paper bindings. You can probably afford several, and you should keep one wherever you do any serious writing. Also you have less excuse for bad production now than ever before. Good-quality bond paper that can be erased easily is readily available. A white opaquing fluid is widely used to paint over typing errors, making them scarcely noticeable. The correction ribbons put out by many typewriter manufacturers can make mistakes invisible. Fast-correcting typewriters are being used in many offices.

The Paper

Most business letter sheets measure 8½ by 11 inches, although some people favor odd sizes to attract attention or serve some special need. Most business paper is white, although there is no reason not to use colored stock. Be sure to buy a good-quality bond paper.

How the letter looks is important. Margins of about one inch at each edge, including the bottom, will create a pleasing effect, although short letters should be placed on the page to create an impression of balance. The left-hand margin should be parallel to the left-hand side of the paper to avoid an out-of-kilter effect. There are many kinds and qualities of paper, and there are many kinds of typefaces (see chapter 14). Many electric typewriters use changeable type balls. You can choose almost any kind of type from a graceful script to a heavily authoritative face. Use the kind that fits your need. Always use a good quality of ribbon.

An electric typewriter is recommended, as it is faster than a manual and gives prettier results. Many companies use automatic typewriters when they need many copies of a letter. These automatics are expensive, but they produce perfect work rapidly. They stop at points where special information—a name and address, a figure, a date—should be typed in by a secretary, and letters are personalized.

Most business letters are single-spaced with a double space between paragraphs. Paragraphs usually are indented a uniform number of spaces; five is most common. It is proper, however, not to indent at all and to type everything flush left. Block pargraphing, as it is called, is preferred by some individuals and firms.

Here is an example of an indented paragraph:

```
Dear Sir,

     We shall expect you promptly at 8:30 a.m., as the
seminar will begin on time.

     I am enclosing a parking permit and you should be
able to park within a half-block of the door.

               Sincerely,
```

Block paragraphing would look like this:

```
Dear Sir,

We shall expect you promptly at 8:30 a.m., as the
seminar will begin on time.

I am enclosing a parking permit and you should be able
to park within a half-block of the door.

Sincerely,
```

The Parts of the Letter

Letters have several parts. They are listed and described below.

The letterhead and date: A company or institution usually has a letterhead preprinted. It carries the full name of the company or institution, its address, and perhaps the department in which the individual who is writing the letter works. Occasionally, it carries the individual's name and title. However, the date must be typed in at the top a few lines under the printed heading. The date can usually be placed toward the right margin, but should not extend beyond it. It can go flush left (even with the left margin) where block paragraphing is used.

If you have no preprinted letterhead, your full address and the date should appear at the top toward the right or flush left for block paragraphing. Single-space.

The inside address: Formal correspondence always carries an inside address, which is the name and the address of the person receiving the letter. It also carries the person's title, if there is one.

```
Mrs. Adrienne Horak
90 West 14th Street
New York, New York 10011
```

Single-space the inside address and place the ZIP code number one space after the state name. Unfortunately, there is no universal stylebook that tells us which words to capitalize, which to abbreviate, and which to spell out. (We shall have some suggestions in Handbook B, however.) Because styles vary, you could have written:

```
Mrs. Adrienne Horak
90 West 14th St.
New York, NY 10011
```

Whatever style you follow, be consistent. The Post Office Department is urging two-letter abbreviations for the states, the district, and the territories, such as NY in the example above. They are being used increasingly:

Alabama	AL	Montana	MT
Alaska	AK	Nebraska	NE
Arizona	AZ	Nevada	NV
Arkansas	AR	New Hampshire	NH
California	CA	New Jersey	NJ
Canal Zone	CZ	New Mexico	NM
Colorado	CO	New York	NY
Connecticut	CT	North Carolina	NC
Delaware	DE	North Dakota	ND
District of			
Columbia	DC	Ohio	OH
Florida	FL	Oklahoma	OK
Georgia	GA	Oregon	OR
Guam	GU	Pennsylvania	PA
Hawaii	HI	Puerto Rico	PR
Idaho	ID	Rhode Island	RI
Illinois	IL	South Carolina	SC
Indiana	IN	South Dakota	SD
Iowa	IA	Tennessee	TN
Kansas	KS	Texas	TX
Kentucky	KY	Utah	UT
Louisiana	LA	Vermont	VT
Maine	ME	Virginia	VA
Maryland	MD	Virgin Islands	VI
Massachusetts	MA	Washington	WA
Michigan	MI	West Virginia	WV
Minnesota	MN	Wisconsin	WI
Mississippi	MS	Wyoming	WY
Missouri	MO		

In the example above, we knew in advance that Mrs. Horak is married or widowed, and we addressed her appropriately as "Mrs." However, "Ms." is acceptable. It is a great time-saver, because you can use it without having to know whether a female is married or single. A good rule of thumb is to call each woman whatever she wishes to be called, if you know. Some prefer "Mrs." If you do not know, use "Ms."

The salutation: Most people are comfortable using the friendly salutation "Dear." Few of us would have a problem writing "Dear Mrs. Horak." It is true that we probably do not love her, but "Dear" is a conventional usage.

It is a social lubricant that makes correspondence easier. Several decades ago, "My dear Mrs. Horak" would have been all right, but that style is considered a bit formal now. If you know Mrs. Horak, you can probably say "Dear Adrienne."

If a form letter is set up on an automatic typewriter, the machine will stop for the inside address and the salutation to be put in by a secretary or typist. Yet even automatics are too slow where hundreds or thousands of copies must be sent. In such a case, the letter will be typed minus the inside address and salutation (although the salutation may say Dear _____), and then printed by the offset method. The printing is most often done on company stationery and is of such quality that it resembles an individually typed letter. A secretary will then type the inside address and salutation, using a typewriter that types as much like the printing as possible. If "window" mailing envelopes are used, it will be necessary to type the address only once.

The body of the letter: Again, there is no agreed-upon stylebook to tell us how to capitalize, abbreviate, or even to punctuate. Try to be consistent, however, and to follow the style of your company or institution, or the suggestions made later in this book. If your letter runs longer than one page, put enough copy on the second page (or third or subsequent pages if necessary) to make those pages look significant. Number the pages at the top. Plain white sheets, rather than letterhead, are used for all pages after the first.

The closing: You have many options here. You can say "Sincerely," "Sincerely yours," "With kind regards," "With best wishes," or fall back upon the old standby, "Yours truly," or "Truly yours"; or you can use "Respectfully" or "Cordially" as they seem proper. Almost any phrase that sounds natural and is suitable to the letter will do. If you are in doubt, "Sincerely" is recommended. It is simple and is recognized as appropriate in every case.

Most people put the closing two or three spaces below the last line of the letter and to the right, usually in line with the date at the top of the letter if they are on the same page. If block paragraphing is used, the closing can be typed flush left.

The signature: The signature is more than just the name of the person sending the letter. It usually includes the title as well. (In letters signed by more than one person, the person with the highest rank is listed first, with title. The others follow in descending order of rank. If all the signers are of equal rank, they are listed in alphabetical order, with titles). The name (or names), together with the address, which is always at the top of the page, will enable the receiver to address a reply accurately. Three spaces normally separate the "Yours truly" and the name. This allows space for signing. A typical closing and signature might run like this:

```
                    Yours truly,


                    Albert C. Shindall
                    Vice President for Production
```

If someone other than Albert C. Shindall has typed the letter, that person may show his or her initials following the writer's over against the left margin, as follows:

```
                    Yours truly,


                    Albert C. Shindall
                    Vice President for Production
    ACS/dlp
```

If Shindall has typed it himself, a relatively rare occurrence, he may wish to indicate the fact as follows:

```
    ACS/o
```

The "o" means "original." However, it is equally appropriate not to indicate anything if the letter is typed by the writer.

You also will show enclosures and carbons, unless you send blind carbons, which are not indicated.

```
    ACS/dlp

    Enclosure (or Encl.)

    cc: Mr. Robert Enloe
        Ms. Emmaline Franklin
```

If there should be more than one enclosure, write

```
    Enclosures, or
    Enclosures 2
```

Remember, the person who signs the letter, not the typist, is responsible for the contents. The responsibility is both moral and legal. So be cautious about authorizing others to sign your name.

For an example of an acceptable letter with all its parts marked, please see Exhibit 4-1.

EXHIBIT 4-1

DATE	June 28, 19—

INSIDE ADDRESS

Mr. Wade H. Simmons
187 Hampton Road, N.E.
Atlanta, Georgia 30305

SALUTATION Dear Wade,

BODY

The department of journalism is inviting some of its special friends to an exhibition of early American printing during the month of July. The imprints will be on display in the reading room of the department from 8:30 a.m. until 5:15 p.m. each weekday during the month.

This collection, which is on loan from the American Antiquarian Foundation, is made up mainly of newspapers. The oldest is Benjamin Harris's *Publick Occurrences, Both Foreign and Domestick* in 1690. The collection has representative newspapers from every period of our national life.

The display has not been seen in this part of the nation before. We hope that you will be our guest during the forthcoming month.

CLOSING   Sincerely,

SIGNATURE

Thurmond E. Davenport
Chairman
Department of Journalism

TED/dlp

WHETHER TO WRITE OR TO DICTATE

Now that we know how a proper letter looks, we must ask how to prepare its contents for the page. Theoretically, you may either write out the letter in longhand or rough it out on a typewriter and give it to a typist for final production; or you may dictate it. Letters roughed out before being typed are usually those on sensitive or complicated subjects. They require working over with great care. Dictation is used for much ordinary correspondence.

Some perfectionists rough out everything they do, and if they have learned the lessons of correspondence well, they probably produce the best letters. They not only write their letters out, but also perfect them through editing. Still, most companies and institutions expect their staffs to dictate correspondence and have provided for dictation. It is faster and saves the time of busy people.

Since most of us can speak fluently enough, you might suppose that dictation is easy. It is not. It often brings out the worst speech patterns. Give some people—even most people—a dictating machine or a secretary to take their words down, and they stop speaking simple English and start using long sentences loaded with words of Latin and Greek origin. Just why they do so probably goes back to that thing we called "urbanization." Just about everybody else seems to be doing it, which has made it a sort of bad standard. Take this sentence from a dictated letter: "Deepest regret is felt by all concerned that your suggestion cannot be utilized at this time." An easy way to say the same thing in words you might actually speak is, "We are sorry we cannot use your idea now." So be wary. Dictation often produces overblown results.

There are many kinds of dictating machines—portable ones; machines that look like a telephone and sit on your desk and record your dictation elsewhere; self-contained units that take up only a small space on one corner of your desk. All come with instructions from the manufacturer. Working the machine properly is up to you. It will not flash you a signal when you are using it badly. A secretary will, if you are dictating to one, and many people still do. But the machine is being used increasingly because it can take dictation at night and on the weekends, long after the secretary has gone home. What you have put into the machine will be ready for transcription at the opening hour of the next business day.

Before you start dictating, you must review the correspondence you intend to initiate or answer, and to *think*. You might make a few notes as an outline, and if you need pertinent files, you should have them at hand.

You may have access to word-processing equipment that greatly speeds up the typing and editing of letters. If so, see the section on word-processing in Chapter 8.

Accuracy

Technical accuracy will be discussed in a later chapter, but remember always that you will get low marks for mistakes. If you produce a beautiful letter that is 99 percent correct and 1 percent in error, you can be sure that the 1 percent will be noticed. It will discredit everything you did that was right. It may even land you in court. So have your data and materials at hand and use them. Our memories are often good, but they can play tricks, and we need to make as few mistakes as possible.

Give full instructions at the start. Do you want your message on a special letterhead? It will be too late to say so after the typing is done. Tell the typist how many carbons you need before the typing starts.

You will need to spell a great deal, whether you are using a dictating machine or speaking to a secretary. If, for example, you were writing or referring to a person named "Speight," you would have to spell it out— S-P-E-I-G-H-T. A typist trying to spell that name from its sound could make three or four wrong guesses. Even common names should be spelled. "Joe" sounds easy, but most people know somebody named "Jo." People are sensitive about names, so take care.

Most of us have taken information over the telephone that called for some spelling by the caller, and we know that many letters in the English language sound alike: *B, C, D, E,* and so on. To avoid confusion, it is helpful to say "B as in Boy," "C as in Cat," "V as in Victory," and so forth. Many an error has been avoided that way.

Numbers are tricky, too. If you dictate "one hundred and twenty-five," always follow by calling out the numbers individually—1-2-5. Where the numbers are six or seven digits long, this becomes all the more necessary.

A drawback of dictating as opposed to roughing out your copy lies in punctuating. If you dictate, you must dictate the punctuation, not trusting your typist to know what you need. Where there should be a period, say "Period"; a comma, "Comma." Many people find this difficult, but you must do it.

When you dictate to another person, you can correct mistakes easily or even change your mind on major points. You just speak to the person taking your words down. What about machine dictation? Corrections are possible. Some machines will make a little mark showing where corrections are needed, but the details of making changes vary from machine to machine. Be familiar with all the possibilities of the one you are using.

One Other Possibility

There is another way of producing good correspondence, and many people use it. They dictate a rough draft to a machine or a secretary, have it typed double-spaced, then get it back. They correct and edit between the lines. The corrected draft is then given to a secretary to be prepared in final form. This method probably is as good as doing your own rough draft, but it has the same disadvantage. The additional typing takes time. Excellent correspondence is regarded by some enlightened companies as such a plus factor that they cheerfully provide this service.

A Word of Caution

You will see your piece of correspondence once more after it is in final form—when you get it back to sign or to initial. You then have your last chance to make sure that everything is all right. Even the best typists make mistakes, and if you have dictated, incredible things can occur.

Among the world's most experienced dictationists are newspaper reporters, who are skilled at dictating news copy over the telephone on or near deadlines. Not long ago, a reporter on a large daily covered a religious meeting, and dictated his copy, including the words "Roman Catholic Church," to a person in the newsroom. The first edition came out with an account of the meeting at the "Women's Catholic Church." It is hard to know who was more upset, the reporter or the Archbishop. The young man who took the dictation was not concerned at all. He said it was the reporter's responsibility to speak clearly. The reporter caught the error after the first edition, corrected it, and somehow satisified the Archibishop.

However, your letters will not be having any second editions. If you do not check them, some slips and typographical errors will go out from your desk over your name. Next best to checking everything yourself is to have a careful and trusted secretary or aide do it. But the final responsibility—and the final blame or praise—is yours.

IMPORTANCE OF TRAINING

The frightening thing is how little it takes to damage a company's reputation. Recently, a man who has four children went on a short business trip. Going home, he passed a distinguished college, one that one of his children was considering attending. Since he had not been there in years, he pulled into the campus to take a look at it. A guard stopped him at the gate. "What do you want?" asked the guard. The man said he wanted to see the campus. "How long will it take?" "About ten minutes." "Well, you've got three minutes, mister."

The man did not go into the campus at all; he went on home, and his child went to college elsewhere. What was behind this episode? The college had had trouble with small fires in its dormitories. They were set by arsonists, who were never caught. The college put guards on its gates to let people know that security was being maintained. However, somebody forgot to train that guard. The damage he did to the college was difficult for its able president to repair. The man who was rudely treated happened to be a friend of the president, and he called him and told him what was happening. The guard was replaced with somebody who could do the job correctly.

A bad letter can be as damaging as this guard's behavior was, if not more so, since a letter can be read again and again. Increasingly, companies are training their people to write better letters, reports, and memoranda. Among the firms that seem to be doing a good job at it are the nation's utility companies, which are under public regulation and must take extraordinary pains. Colleges and universities that prepare students for business careers are providing good training in business writing. Opportunities to learn are multiplying and should be used.

Accountability

A few companies and institutions send out letters just to keep their names before their customers, but these letters account for only a small part of the total correspondence. Most letters are sent to do something practical: Sell or renew a subscription to a magazine. Sell an electric coffee pot. Offer a service. Make a contact for an insurance salesman. Soothe a dissatisfied customer. Adjust a claim for damaged goods.

Each letter has to compete for the attention of the person who receives it. It has to compete with other letters, ringing telephones, staff meetings, office emergencies, and so forth.

If all of that were not enough to sober us as letter writers, we must realize that we are accountable. It is easy to evaluate the effects of a letter. We were not shooting in the dark. If we mailed out a particular letter to accomplish a purpose, we know that someone will look to see whether the letter worked. If we sent out 50,000 letters to sell an electric coffee pot, we know that somebody will check to see whether the letter produced results. Did we receive a 4 to 5 percent response? We might get away with that. If we get as much as 10 percent, we have done well.

Tone

A business letter is no place to accentuate the negative, sound defensive, or work off personal guilts and hostilities. Many people do, especially when answering a critical letter from someone who has unleashed a blast. We shall shortly discuss how to answer negative letters, but first let us consider "tone."

When you get a letter, what do you want it to be like? You usually want it to be positive, optimistic, and helpful. People you send letters to want the same things, and you can make your own correspondence more acceptable by accentuating the positive and reducing the negative. One would be unwise to say that negative words should be avoided altogether, for there is a place for everything. But such words as the following usually set a negative tone:

unreasonable	unjust	cheated
totally unexpected	complaint	overcharged
rude	without fail	mistaken
falsely represented	incorrectly informed	displeased
misled	neglect	misconception

Take this letter:

> Dear Sir: We think your complaint about our bill is unreasonable, as we are ethically satisfied that we performed the service for which the bill was submitted. You must pay the bill by return mail, or we must unfortunately inform you that we will terminate doing business with you in the future.
>
> Sincerely,

This example is a slightly modified version of a real letter sent by a company in just such a situation. It is not a small company either, but one listed on the New York Stock Exchange. The tone is bad, and the letter is not likely to get the desired result. Since the customer questions the bill, and will have to have answers before paying, the best bet is to set up a situation where the bill can be discussed. It is in the company's interest that the discussion be pleasant. This letter might do the job:

> Dear Sir: It is often true that people have questions about the bills they receive. It is good for all of us, and for business in general, to have everyone satisfied when a business agreement is finally finished. We realize that you have questions, and we wonder if we could arrange a meeting to go over the matter together?
>
> Sincerely,

Perhaps the person who is slow to pay is right and the company is wrong. Maybe the company is right. Still, to collect anything, the company may have to compromise. At that point, it can (if it must) consider not doing any further business with this person. One thing is sure: the original letter would have made an enemy and quite possibly would not have collected any money either.

What was wrong with the first letter? It used a clutch of negative words which correctly mirrored a negative approach—*complaint, unreasonable, ethically, must pay, we must unfortunately inform you, terminate doing business.*

The second letter sets a better tone. It uses positive words to reflect a better attitude—*questions (rather than complaints), good, satisfied, agreement, we wonder if we could arrange, go over the matter together.*

You cannot build a good house out of bad materials, and you cannot build a good letter out of negative words. Negative words will cost you and should be used with the greatest care.

Precise Words

In addition to avoiding negative words wherever possible, you should seek to use words that say exactly what you mean. Occasionally, you will find a person who uses vague language to confuse or to mislead other people. Most of the time, however, that person's problem is that nobody has pointed out that imprecise words will not do the job that needs to be done. Look at this sentence:

My daughter fell down the stairs and broke a bone.

What bone? Her leg? Arm? Wrist? The reader is missing key information. This is better:

My daughter fell down the stairs and broke a leg.

Do not say: "She is an executive with the company." You will leave people guessing. Is she president; vice-president; treasurer? Give your readers the whole picture by using precise language.

The Active Voice

In addition to giving your readers specific facts that they can picture, do one other thing to lend muscle and action to your writing. *Use the active voice.* In the active voice, the subject of the sentence is the one doing the acting:

The company learned a great deal from the experience.

The subject is "company." The predicate, or verb, is "learned." As you see, the company "acted" by learning.

If you had written this sentence in the *passive* voice, the subject would not have been the actor:

Much was learned by the company from the experience.

The passive voice places the emphasis upon the person or thing receiving the action. Sometimes that is desirable, and there will be times when you will wish to use the passive voice. But most business correspondence benefits from strong and direct language. The active voice delivers those valuable qualities, and you should cultivate it as a friend to be used often.

Following are three examples. Notice that the active voice delivers a more direct statement.

Passive: A lot of good work can be done with an in-house publication.
Active: An in-house publication can do a lot of good work.
Passive: Richard Delaney had never been placed under real scrutiny by top management.
Active: Top management had never placed Richard Delaney under real scrutiny.
Passive: When a mistake has been made by you, say so at once.
Active: When you make a mistake, say so at once.

The "You" Approach

We now come to a principle that applies not only to letter writing but to human relations generally. It is called the "You" approach. It means that you put yourself in the other person's shoes insofar as you can. You try to *understand* the other person's point of view even though you might not agree with it.

Most people do not insist upon being *agreed with* to be reasonably satisfied. *Understanding* is often enough, or it is at least enough to help. When writing a letter, put yourself in the place of the person who will get it. You ask: Would I like to receive a letter like the one I am writing? That question can apply to all correspondence. It is especially apt for letters in which there is stress or bad feeling.

THE EMPATHY-CONTENT-ACTION MODEL

We should practice looking at things from the other person's viewpoint. We will now learn a model that will force us to do just that if we use it correctly. We could have saved the model and learned it later when we take up writing "bad news" letters. We shall mention it again then, but it is never too early to start practicing the "You" approach.

In 1976, two scholars, B. J. Winship and J. D. Kelley, published an article in *The Journal of Counseling Psychology* in which they gave the model. An adaptation of the work of earlier scholars, it is aimed principally at helping people handle stressful situations. A stressful situation is easily defined. It is one in which you do not like the outcome of a transaction, or you are in the middle of the transaction and you fear you will not like the outcome. How do you handle this?

Most people start out by stating their point of view vigorously. They emphasize all the reasons why their position should prevail, hoping to win over the other party. Winship and Kelley say that is not the best approach.

You do not stand a good chance of winning by emphasizing your own point of view at the start. Instead, you should start by showing that you understand the other person's position.

Let us get a mental picture of what the model to accomplish a good result looks like. Until after World War II, cars had gearshifts on the floorboard. The driver would shift from one gear to another after pushing in the clutch. A driver who used the clutch incorrectly could very well tear the teeth out of the gears. It usually took three gears to get up speed going forward— low gear, sometimes called first; second; and third gear, or high. The car started in low to build up speed, moved to second, and then into third, the running gear. You might get the car moving by starting in second or even in third, but it involved risk and you might have choked down. Consider the three steps in Exhibit 4-2 as gears. Take them one at a time. (Later, when you have had a lot of experience, you might do a little mixing, but it is not a good idea for beginners.)

EXHIBIT 4-2.
The Empathy-
Content-Action
Model

> Empathy—This means emphasizing where the other person is, or what the other person's proper interests are.
> Content— Emphasizing your own proper interests.
> Action— Saying what you wish the outcome of the situation to be. Frequently, you will compromise between your own position and the other person's to make both of you reasonably happy.

The model works as well in oral exchanges as it does in written ones. Let us take an oral example to demonstrate. Suppose that you are a fifteen-year-old girl who has been babysitting for a family down the street for three years. You like the job. You sit for the family two or three times a week; you always come upon call; you know the house; and you like the children. You have such a good arrangement that you do not sit for anybody else. There is only one problem. You started sitting for this family three years ago when the going rate was $1.50 an hour. Now the going rate is $1.75.

The family down the street does not seem to know this, and you have been too shy to tell them. But now you have decided to pluck up your courage and ask for a raise.

You enter the living room of the house about six in the evening and find the father of the household reading the newspaper.

> Mr. Addison, may I speak to you for a moment? I want to talk about my babysitting job with you. When I started babysitting for you three years ago, everybody in town was paying $1.50 an hour, but now everybody is paying $1.75, and I wonder if you could pay me that?

Is that a clumsy approach? Absolutely not. It is the way most people would do it. But if you use it, you may get the raise or you may not. Although it is not clumsy, there is a better way. In terms of our model—Empathy, Content, Action—you have started out on Content, which is second gear. You may get your car going or you may not.

How would we start in first gear? Empathy. That means showing that you understand the other person's proper interests. And what are Mr. Addison's interests? There are several: you always come when called; you like the children and they obviously like you; you know the house well; and you can handle emergencies reliably.

The following approach would be better, for it starts you in first gear and shows right away that you understand Mr. Addison's concerns. "Mr. Addison, I enjoy babysitting for you and your family because I really like the children, and they like me. I know the house well, and I am almost always available to come when you need me."

At this point, you have empathized enough, and what you have said is all true. You now switch into second gear, the Content part of the model, where you tell what is worrying you. That is the easy part, for you were upset enough to take on a man older than you are, a man you may be a little in awe of, an authority figure. After you have finished with Empathy, just say "but" or some other connecting word and shift into second gear. After you have said what is worrying you, use another connecting word, "therefore" or something like it, and tell what you hope the outcome can be: "I wonder if you could pay me the current rate?"

Anybody can handle gears two and three. First gear is hard, because you must think about the other person. In gears two and three, you are thinking mostly of yourself.

A word of caution must be said about first gear, Empathy. It must be based upon truth. If the young girl had said to Mr. Addison, "I think you are as handsome as my favorite movie star," it would have been a bad attempt at empathy, because the comment does not relate to the problem and is probably not true. Empathy is not flattery; it is understanding. And if it is false or strained, people will see through it and it will not serve your purposes.

The example of the babysitter actually happened. Many people working in business have used the same model to ask for raises in an acceptable way. Many of them have gotten what they asked for, or some part of it.

Another example based upon a real occurrence will show how empathy is the key. One evening recently, a man entertaining some business guests at a celebrated restaurant had an unpleasant experience. The next morning, he got the name of the manager of the restaurant, a Mr. Herbert Lindstrom. Still angry, he wrote Mr. Lindstrom the following:

```
Dear Mr. Lindstrom,

Last night, a female colleague and I took two business
guests to "Le Chancel" expecting to show them an
enjoyable evening. I am going to tell you what happened.

The waiter put us at a table where the tablecloth was
torn and they had tried to cover up the tear by putting
a candlestand on it. The service was slow, with a half-
hour wait between courses. We had ordered the roast beef
with potatoes for the main course. What we got was veal
with rice. The waiter didn't even apologize. We were so
furious that we didn't even stay for the dessert.

You are supposed to have a good restaurant, but this was
so lousy that I can assure that you won't be ruining
another evening for me and my friends. I am sending a
copy of this letter to the local newspapers so that they
can see that you don't run your business very well.

                 Sincerely,


            William A. Prufrock
```

Prufrock is rightly upset. He has paid to make a good impression on his friends, and he has been embarrassed. Yet his letter serves no purpose except to tell Lindstrom a thing or two. What will Lindstrom's reaction be when he gets the letter? He will feel bad about it, but he will probably not do anything to make this bad experience right for Prufrock. He will be afraid that if he even calls Prufrock on the telephone, he may get a receiver slammed down in his ear. So he throws the letter in the trash can.

Prufrock could have done better. First of all, this restaurant really has an excellent reputation, and such reputations are not built on the kind of service that Prufrock got. The fact that the reputation is generally good means that Lindstrom must be a conscientious manager who wants to serve his guests and that Prufrock's experience was unusual.

Prufrock himself is an executive with a large company and he knows how many thing can go wrong in managerial situations. His people have made mistakes, too. He should be able to empathize with Lindstrom easily. Suppose that he had decided to write a different kind of letter, one that might cause Lindstrom to pick up the telephone and invite him and a guest back to Le Chancel for a free evening, one in which everything would be done correctly. Would the following have done it?

```
Dear Mr. Lindstrom,

The good reputation of Le Chancel tells me that you are
a careful and conscientious manager, as such reputations
are not built by accident. I am a manager myself and I
know you cannot be in touch with everything that is
going on in your restaurant at all times. Therefore, I
believe you would wish me to tell you about a less-than-
ideal situation that happened there last night.
```

It would then be a simple matter to tell him what happened. After Prufrock has done so, how should he close?

```
I hope that you will not consider this to be a blanket
criticism, but as I know what pride you take in your
establishment, I believe that you would wish to know
these things.
```

The last paragraph, of course, is a rather modified Action section, or third gear. Since Prufrock is calling for no action, it is really just a pleasant sign-off. Since Prufrock did not write a letter like this, we do not know what kind of answer Lindstrom would have given. He might have asked Prufrock to return to Le Chancel as his guest; even if he did not, Prufrock would have been right to send such a letter. It is good business. It is good human relations. It establishes Prufrock in a position of ascendancy. It emphasizes the "You" approach, and for a letter of complaint, it uses negative words sparingly.

We can often measure the effects of letters written with the "You" approach, but few examples are more dramatic than one involving one of the nation's leading telephone companies and a customer we shall call Mrs. R. A. Baggs. The Baggs case is well known, a model of its kind.

The facts, only slightly changed to protect identities, are as follows: Mrs. Baggs is a widow who lives in a large American city. She has been a customer of her telephone company for thirty-seven years, and she has never been a problem before. Nine months ago, however, she bought a new puppy, a Scottish terrier she named Sapphire. Like most Scotties, Sapphire had a teething problem, and she has gnawed on a great many things in Mrs.

Baggs's home, including the telephone cord to the upstairs extension. Three times she has gnawed the cord in two, and three times the telephone company has replaced it without charge. In doing so, the company went somewhat beyond its promise to repair "reasonable wear and tear" free. Now that Sapphire has gnawed the cord a fourth time, a representative of the company has told Mrs. Baggs that the cord will be repaired but that she must pay for it.

Her reaction has been explosive. She claims she understood that she was entitled to unlimited repairs and, knowing that the telephone company, like all utilities, is under constant scrutiny, she says she intends to go public with her case. She plans to notify a member of the state regulatory commission who was elected on an anti-utility platform, the editors of the two daily newspapers, and a man we shall call P.J. Arnold. Arnold is a member of the news team of an aggressive television station, and he runs a feature called "Complaint Desk." Dissatisfied consumers call Arnold and he, after he investigates, often makes their cases a public issue. Seldom does a company or an institution get a break on Arnold's program. If his investigation turns up material favorable to a company, he usually does not air the case.

The chief executive officer of the telephone company is not only a good manager, but also a diplomat. His style of leadership has been so effective that his company has avoided the bitter criticism directed at some utilities. He also is a consummate writer, and he personally sketches out much of his sensitive correspondence.

His idea of dealing with Mrs. Baggs is simple. He will write her a letter cast in the form of the three-step model, a letter that is concerned, fair, and decent. If any of the persons Mrs. Baggs is threatening to notify actually call the telephone company, the company will produce the letter in its defense.

The executive asked for ideas from his staff. One junior officer, not taking the assignment seriously, suggested the following:

```
Dear Mrs. Baggs,

Regarding the chewing done by Sapphire on the cord to
your upstairs extension, may we suggest that any future
chewing done by said dog be done on the cord to your
electric dryer. After a few moments, the problem will be
solved once and for all.

                    Sincerely,
```

The executive was not amused, and he wrote the letter himself.

Dear Mrs. Baggs,

As a dog lover, I sympathize with the problems you are
having with Sapphire. I know how teething puppies are. I
know also that you live alone and that both Sapphire and
your telephone are not only comforts for you, but
protection as well.

Still, with all the sympathy that our company feels for
you and for Sapphire, you will remember that we have
replaced your upstairs telephone cord three times
without charge after Sapphire chewed it in two. Our
pledge to our customers is to repair "reasonable wear
and tear," and we stretched the rules to fix it the
third time without cost to you.

Now Sapphire has chewed the cord a fourth time. We are
anxious to fix it but we must make a charge. If we do
not, the cost will have to be passed along to our other
customers and we do not think this is fair.

We shall fix the telephone on the same day that you
notify us we may. And I would suggest that you consider
putting a wall telephone upstairs so that Sapphire
cannot reach the cord again, or that we encase the wire.

Thank you for your thirty-seven years as a good and
dependable customer.
                    Sincerely,

After getting this letter, Mrs. Baggs decided to go ahead and take her
case to P. J. Arnold. To everyone's astonishment, Arnold read the letter,
checked the facts with Mrs. Baggs, and decided that the telephone company not only was right but needed to be commended publicly. On his
news program, he praised the company for protecting other consumers
from passed-on costs, and that was the end of the Baggs case.

Look again at the letter above. Paragraph one is Empathy. It is real Empathy. Most people can empathize with dogs and with people who live
alone. Paragraphs two and three are Content. They tell where the telephone
company is. Paragraph four is Action, the proposed solution. And the final
paragraph is a complimentary sign-off.

Because of the good leadership in this company, Mrs. Baggs would never
have received a letter that was critical or insulting. Like wise students of
the human condition, the people running the company know that there
are two ways to make people dislike you: one is to make them feel guilty;
the other is to make them feel foolish. No prudent person or company goes
through life collecting enemies, except for unusually compelling reasons.
There is another reason to use the "You" approach and to avoid using

language in correspondence that challenges the pride or status, or insults the intelligence, of the recipient. That reason: When you make such challenges, your letter will leave the reader in an emotional tumult. The tumult must be dealt with before you can deal with the issues at hand. Why start a firestorm when it will take a lot of time—perhaps an hour or two—to put it out?

Using the three-step model is one way to avoid such firestorms. No model is perfect, and sometimes it will not work. But even when it does not work, it does no damage, provided you have used it with real empathy and suppressed any barbs or needles you may have wanted to throw. Use the model well and you will open the road to deal with real issues, not explosive detours into human emotions.

TWO KINDS OF LETTERS

The "You" approach requires you to think of the person who will receive your letter. When you do, you ask yourself how that person will respond. What you write will depend upon the response you expect. Of course, you may sometimes guess wrong, but you still must prepare a letter that you *think* will get the best response.

No categorization will cover every kind of letter that you will ever write, but the best practitioners of business writing are aware of two kinds that cover many. They are Good News Letters and Bad News Letters.

1. Good News Letters give the recipient favorable news, or news in which he or she has a good bit of favorable interest.

2. Bad News Letters tell the recipient something that is not welcome.

Good News Letters are easy to organize. You can be direct. Start off with your strongest statement first. Because the reader is already interested, no build-up is needed. Sometimes, you may choose to lead up to the subject more gradually for reasons of style or to create an effect, but the direct approach is often perfect for Good News Letters.

Bad News Letters are another matter. Your opening paragraph(s) should prepare the way for the reader to receive bad news or news on a stressful subject. An indirect approach may be best. The "You" approach often works nicely. However, Bad News Letters sometimes take a direct approach, depending upon circumstances. Use your judgment. Never take the direct approach in writing Bad News Letters simply because it is easier.

A lot of letters do not fit the Good News, Bad News categories, both of which foresee a reaction from the reader—one good, one bad. Many letters get only a neutral reaction, and the degree of neutrality varies. Where you are fairly sure that your letter will get a neutral reaction, make a conscious decision to use either a direct or an indirect approach. Your problem is likely to be getting and holding the reader's attention.

Keeping these points in mind, let us move on to the next chapter: Letters: Hard Sell and Soft.

PRINCIPLES
FOR
PRACTICE

1. The appearance of the letter on the page is extremely important.

2. Formal business letters are made up of several well-defined parts.

3. A letter can be sketched out in advance or it can be dictated.

4. Dictation is harder than it seems. The person dictating must spell many words, must take care with numbers, and must dictate punctuation.

5. Scrupulous accuracy in spelling and in factual details is crucial. A single error will damage a piece of writing.

6. Words with negative overtones give a bad impression in a piece of writing. Positive words create a good impression.

7. Choose your words precisely. Imprecise words sound weak and tentative.

8. Using the active voice will make your writing more direct and muscular.

9. To write letters that will be well received, put yourself in the receiver's place. The Empathy-Content-Action model will help you do this in many cases.

10. The Empathy-Content-Action model will help you deliver bad or unpleasant news in a more acceptable way.

11. In writing letters that contain good news, you usually emphasize the most important thing first.

FOR FURTHER STUDY

1. Each of the following sentences contains negative words and creates a negative effect. Rewrite each one to create a more positive effect, even when what you must say is harsh. Also, simplify the sentences according to the principles learned in the last chapter.

    a. Your complaint was received today, and we are certain that it is based upon a misconception.

    b. We do not believe that you are attempting to be unfair, but you must see that there is another way of looking at this situation.

    c. We are convinced that the matter was misrepresented to us, although we are not charging at this point that this was done deliberately.

    d. You have neglected to make payment as you promised, and we must tell you that continued failure in this regard will result in an immediate cancellation on our part.

    e. Your uncalled-for comments seek to cast doubt upon our motives in this matter.

    f. We cannot permit an attitude of mistrust to develop between us.

    g. You learned that I was dissatisfied, and I am writing you so that you will not hear misinformation on the subject from others. I had rather that you learned the distressing facts from me.

    h. You must be upset at the failure of the clothes dryer to function properly.

    i. We are doing this for you at some inconvenience to ourselves.

    j. We hope that you will not consider these comments improper on our part.

    k. Let us determine where the fault lies in this regrettable episode.

    l. Your letter was totally unexpected and concerns us greatly.

    m. We must face some disagreeable facts.

    n. The result is unacceptable, and alterations must be made at once.

    o. This matter demands your immediate attention..

2. Using your imagination to supply specific details, strengthen these sentences, each of which uses imprecise language.

    a. She painted her bedroom a nice color.

    b. I telephoned your company to place an order and spoke to one of your officers.

    c. We shall leave soon for a vacation at the seashore.

    d. An object bought at your store has generally worked well, but now I have problems with it.

    e. We do not have in stock the item in question, but we shall order it for you from our plant, which is located in a western state.

3. A teacher of a college class in public relations admired a magazine published by a national firm that manufactures automobiles. The magazine comes out four times a year. It has a circulation of more than one million. The teacher wished to have 25 copies of each issue of the magazine to give to students as an example of a model publication. Each student, of course, is a potential customer of the company that publishes the magazine. Here is the answer that the teacher received from the editor of the magazine. Why is it a poor reply? Why did it make the teacher angry, even though the editor was doing everything that was requested?

```
Dear Sir:

    I have received your recent letter telling us of your
interest in using our magazine in your course in
Effective Public Relations.

    We cannot honor every such request and those that we
do honor must be reviewed periodically.

    We are arranging to have 25 copies of each issue of
the magazine sent to you for one year. After that, if
you should still be interested, we will consider a
request for renewal.

                        Sincerely,
```

4. The following letter successfully raised funds for a volunteer fire department in a mountain area. List three or four reasons why this letter is a good one.

```
Dear Friends and Neighbors,

    Your Fire Department has had a good year. We want to
bring you up to date on some of our exciting
accomplishments. And we need help in meeting an
immediate challenge.

    First, the members of this department extend thanks to
all those who responded to our last fund-raising drive.
We collected $4,090.42. Along with the monies we made
through a barbecue and the members working odd jobs
after work and on weekends, we paid off the balance on
our pumper. We also were lucky to have a 300 g.p.m.
floating pump given to us this year.

    Our Class A pumper, along with our 1,200 gal. tanker,
changed our insurance classification from a Class 10 to
Class 9. That has saved on fire insurance premiums for
many of you.
```

```
    Even so, we know that many of you live on poor roads,
impassable to ordinary vehicles at certain times of the
year. We are happy to say that this problem has been
solved. The State Forestry Commission has bought us a 4-
wheel-drive fire truck. It is called a mini-pumper and
can navigate the roughest roads. It has a 300 gal. water
tank and a 500 g.p.m. pump that can draft water from any
available source.

    NOW THE CHALLENGE!

    We are a three-fire truck department with a two-truck
firehouse.

    This calls for an addition to our existing firehouse.
It will cost $5,000 with the members doing all the
finish work.

    Please help us. We are asking you to give whatever you
can. This will be our last fund-raising campaign for a
while.

    Good news. You can take your gift as a deduction on
your Federal income tax. Let us hear from you.

                            With sincere thanks,


                            Edna Lee Colby
                            Fire Chief
```

5. You have a job at an office supply company near the school that you attend. You can work part time there without mising any classes. The company has had a lot of turnover recently, probably because the supervisor of the part-time employees is unusually shy and withdrawn. It is hard to talk to the supervisor. You wish to keep the job because it is convenient, and because you can do a good job. But you must have an increase in your hourly rate. You decide to send the supervisor a letter based upon the Empathy-Content-Action model. Write the letter. Pay especial attention to the Empathy section. If you fail there, you may not get the raise.

6. You have just returned from your dream vacation—a summer in Europe. Before you left, you paid your bills, including one from the gas company. Upon returning, you find that you have five letters from the gas company, a collection series, saying that you made out the check to them improperly. They want their money. The tone of the fifth letter sounds as though the next knock on the door will be the sheriff. You are upset. You call the gas company and get the name of its president, A. P. Lee. You send a letter to Lee in the Empathy-Content-Action model that is designed to do these things:

    a. Tell what happened.

    b. Say that you are enclosing a check.

    c. Ask whether your credit rating has been harmed.

    Write the letter. Again, take care with the Empathy. It must be real.

7. You attend a business college in the evenings. During the day, you work part time in a grocery store that is part of a nationwide chain. You stamp prices on items in the stock room and put merchandise on the shelves. You like the grocery business and intend to make it a career, hoping to become an assistant store manager, then a manager, and finally a top official in the chain. Soon you will finish your business course. Then you will be ready to seek admission to the management training program run by the chain. Theirs is a six-month course. Many people apply, and the competition is keen. A letter of application is required. Write one, using the Empathy-Content-Action model. The Empathy section should reflect your understanding of what the company wants in its managers.

8. You are personnel manager for a company. Write a letter to all employees giving the following information. Each letter will be individually addressed on automatic equipment, and will be personally signed by you.

    a. On August 27, the south gate to the plant will be closed until September 16. The company regrets any inconvenience that will be caused.

    b. The company is having the south parking lot and the south roadways on plant property resurfaced.

    c. All other company parking lots and roadways will be open during this period.

    d. However, other company roadways and parking lots will be resurfaced next year at a time to be announced.

    e. Anybody who has been parking in the south lot and using that entrance should use another entrance and park on Myrtle Street in the All-Way lot.

    f. Those who need passes to park at All-Way can get them by applying to the personnel office in Room 122, Althauser Building, on August 2 or thereafter.

When you have finished the letter, mark its parts—Date, Inside Address, Salutation, Body, Closing, Signature.

9. Write a Good News Letter in which you accept an invitation to attend a testimonial dinner for your favorite high school teacher.

10. Write a Bad News Letter saying that you cannot attend the dinner. (In the opening paragraph, use the indirect approach. Express your appreciation of the teacher.)

11. You are the representative in Connecticut for a manufacturer of razors and razor blades. You have a new model that will shave smoother and longer. One version is made for men, another for women. Your mailing list has the names of the managers of 412 stores that have carried your line in the past. Write them a letter. It will be produced on a typewriter and then printed. You will sign each letter after it is individually addressed on a typewriter with a typeface that looks like the printing. Your purpose: To ask each store manager to order the model and give it a special display.

12. You are personnel manager of a plant in which the president is unpopular with the workers. He insists upon having a Fourth of July picnic and inviting all the workers and their families to come. He intends to make a speech, which he hopes will improve relations. The invitations will be by letter sent to the employees' homes. Write a letter for the president's signature. Take an indirect approach.

13. The following letter arrived in August at the home of a woman whose college-age daughter had done summer work for a temporary employment agency. The daughter had worked on 14 jobs, lasting from two to 11 days. The daughter was preparing to return to college. Her mother was pleased at this letter from the agency:

```
Dear Mother, meet me at the Trailblazer Inn. . . . . .

   As the pace of summer slows and your sons and
daughters return to school, consider how you can best
use your time. We know you are familiar with our
service. We worked with at least one member of your
family this summer. With many of our employees returning
to school, we are faced with a serious shortage of
people. We need your help!

   Regardless of how rusty your skills may be, we have
jobs in all office and nonskilled classifications.
Homemaking skills are too often taken for granted and
many times can be used in business.

   Jennie Crowell, our Office Supervisor, and I will be
at the Trailblazer on Tuesday, August 21, from 9 to noon
to discuss an opportunity for you. The room number will
be posted in the lobby. Please schedule a few minutes
that morning to stop by and enjoy coffee with us. We'll
outline for you how rewarding it is to work as a
Temporary and still have the time to do the things you
want to do. If you have any questions before our get-
together, please call me or Jennie.

Sincerely,


Wendy Salzburger, Personnel Director
P. S. Bring a friend or neighbor. There will also be a
door prize!
```

Please answer these questions:

a. This letter does not include the name of the recipient in the Salutation. There is no Inside Address. The address on the envelope merely said Mrs. Allers, with the street address and city. No first name was given. Do these omissions weaken this letter?

b. Did the author of the letter follow the principles of effective writing learned in Chapter 3? How?

CHAPTER 5

```
To:          The Reader
From:        The Authors
Subject:     How to Write Letters that Sell
```

After reading this chapter, you will know:

1. A flexible guideline for writing sales letters.

2. The value and uses of enclosures.

3. The uses and sources of mailing lists.

4. How to write letters of congratulation.

5. How to write letters of thanks.

6. How to write letters of condolence.

7. The value of allowing time to write good letters.

Letters:
Hard Sell and Soft

One success story known to every student of merchandising in America is that of Sears, Roebuck and Co. Late in the last century, when most Americans still lived on farms and in villages, Sears and Roebuck decided to exploit this vast, untapped market by setting up a mail-order service for products of all kinds. Catalogues were sent to huge numbers of people, most of them living on rural routes. Thousands of families responded, marking their order cards by kerosene lamp and sending them in to the Sears office. In time, the goods they ordered came by mail, and Sears and Roebuck began to make merchandising history.

In the decades following, most Americans moved to town. (So did Sears and Roebuck, for the most part, although mail order remained an important part of its business.) Most retail buying in America today is done over the counter. But the mail still plays a big part in sales, regardless of whether a letter initiates a sale by landing an order, invites a potential customer to come into a store and buy, or to send for a catalogue, brochure, or for more information, or prepares the way for a salesperson to call.

HARD-SELL LETTERS

In this chapter, we shall look at sales letters—hard and soft. The hard-sell letters try to induce a customer to buy. The soft-sell letters seek to create a feeling of customer goodwill that will help business in the future.

Most hard-sell letters are mass produced. They can be made to look personal, but most recipients of these letters know they are not and do not expect them to be. (See the section on word processing in Chapter 8.) Still, they must be attractive and well written. The average American gets much unsolicited mail, and your letter must stand out if it is to win the reader's attention.

A Flexible Guideline

In our last chapter we looked at the Empathy-Content-Action model for handling correspondence in which there was stress or potential stress. We said that it is fairly inflexible. It is like three gears on an automobile—low, second, and high.

The model for organizing a sales letter is very flexible. You can start anywhere in the model, because the parts indicate only the four main ideas that ordinarily would be included in a sales letter. They do not constitute "gears." If you were making a sale in person, you would do these things:

1. Get the attention of the person to whom you are speaking.
2. Talk about your product and why it is special and good.
3. Get the order, or put events in motion that will lead to an order.

The Four P's

A model of a sales letter contains the same elements, which for simplicity's sake we call "the four P's":

1. *The Probe (or the part that gets attention).*
2. *The Product (or the part that describes what we are selling).*
3. *The Proof (or the section that indicates that the product is good).* Unfortunately, many sales letters omit, or do not emphasize, this important part.
4. *The Point (the purpose of writing the letter in the first place).*

This model naturally unfolds the sales process. You remember what was said earlier about getting the right tone, using positive rather than negative words, emphasizing the "You" approach. Before you write, figure out where your interests and the interests of the persons receiving the letter overlap and stress these points.

A sales letter has one vital requirement. You must know your product—everything about it. What will it do better than other products like it? How does it compare in price, convenience of use, ease of repair, as a time-saver?

You must know every positive feature and stress it. It is impossible to sell something that you do not know inside and out.

Here is a letter in which the author, weighing all the advantages of the product, used all four parts of the model. An insurance company in the Midwest sent it to parents of American high school students. The parts of the model are labeled so that you may analyze the way the letter was put together. The inside address was typed, as was the salutation, but the body of the letter was printed to look like an original. The signature was obviously printed.

EXHIBIT 5-1.

Dear Mr. and Mrs. Arundel,

PROBE

We know that family budgets are often strained and that many things must be omitted for good financial reasons. Because of that, we have set up a Young People's Insurance Plan that can easily be paid for, and that we believe suits your family needs and the needs of your child.

PRODUCT

Young people insured under our plan get excellent protection at low rates until they are 25 years old, and at good rates thereafter. For the first year, the cost is only $12.00, and from the second year until the 25th birthday, it is only $19.50. At age 25, it goes to $67.50 a year and will never be increased. These rates are for a $5,000 policy. This insurance is also available in a $10,000 policy, and you should double the amounts for it. By age 25, the child usually has taken over the premium payments. You or your child may cancel the coverage at any time, but we cannot, so long as the payments are made. This is true even though the child's health may take a turn for the worse.

PROOF

This policy has been sold by us for the past seven years, and we boast about 645,000 satisfied customers in more than half the American states. It is the most successful new policy that we have introduced in the last 18 years.

POINT

Enclosed is an addressed, stamped postcard for you to return to us. Please fill in the blanks on the back so that we may send you the simple forms needed for your child to have this excellent and inexpensive protection.

Sincerely,

EPHRAIM D. CASLON,
President

The person who wrote this letter focused it sharply. A major worry of middle-class American families, the most likely clients, is how to pay the bills. Knowing this, the writer overlapped that interest in the first sentence. The letter proved to be effective.

The writer also knew exactly what the Point was, what the reader was supposed to do. The writer made it easy for the reader by enclosing an addressed, stamped card that would take little effort to fill out and return.

Starting with "Point"

Another insurance company recently succeeded with a Good News letter designed to prepare the way for a salesperson to call. This letter did not need all four parts of the model. It did not start with Probe, but started with Point (unless you wish to say that the two were combined in this case).

```
Dear Mr. Feorino,

   May we offer you without charge or obligation a
pocket-sized engagement booklet to help you keep track
of your appointments? We shall be happy to stamp your
initials in gold upon the cover. If you would like to
have this useful item as a gift of Endymion Insurance
Company, please return the enclosed stamped card to us
and we shall see that you receive it with our
compliments.

                    Sincerely,


                    John A. Higgins
                    President
```

Mr. Feorino ordered the booklet and got it, delivered in person by a salesperson from the company, who immediately began to cultivate a new customer. Again, all the letter writer wanted Mr. Feorino to do was a simple thing—return the card.

Starting with "Proof"

An ingenious alumni director of a major American university recently sent out a letter that started with the Proof section, the part that shows the product is good. Endorsements, or statements of satisfied users, are frequently a successful sales method. They constitute Proof.

Dear Member,

This time last year, more than 240 of your fellow alumni
accepted our invitation to join us for an eight-day trip
to Greece. Judging from the letters we received from
them after the trip was over, they have been talking
about it ever since.

This trip was so successful that we are arranging it
again this year to fall over the Thanksgiving Holidays.
As last year, there will be accommodations at the Royal
Olympic in downtown Athens, tour of the city, the
Acropolis, and the museums. There will be options for a
short cruise to nearby islands, for visits to Delphi,
Argolis, and Cape Sounion.

Travel will be by two chartered jets.

Details, including the remarkably low cost, are
contained in the enclosed brochure. Please detach the
coupon and mail it back to us now so that we may reserve
a place for you.

Enclosures   Analysis of this letter shows that it started with Proof, which
was followed by Product, and then by Point. The Proof part was so well
done that, in effect, it also served as Probe.

This alumni director did something more than put together a good sales
letter, however. She made good use of the enclosure, a six-panel foldout in
four colors, giving all details of the trip, including one she deliberately did
not include in the letter—the price. Cost is a factor to most readers. These
readers will be sure to read the enclosed brochure promptly and carefully
because of the intentional omission in the letter. In so doing, they will get
a second sales pitch, in color and with pictures.

Although many successful sales letters have no enclosures, a great many
do. One way to use them effectively is to direct the readers to the enclosure
for full details.

For example, a good many American magazines now sell things other
than subscriptions—books, maps, personal and decorative items, novelties.
One of the nation's most successful magazines sent out the following letter
one October:

Dear Subscriber,

   The Christmas season will shortly be upon us with all
its rushing and bustling about. For many years, we have
helped to ease your shopping burden by making guest
subscriptions available, and by offering other
carefully-selected items which you can buy by mail.

```
As a valued reader, you are already familiar with the
quality of our magazine. Execute the enclosed gift
subscription card, and everyone on your list will
receive beautifully printed announcements, sent in your
name shortly before Christmas.

Also, browse through the enclosed catalogue to see
what options we have selected for you this year. An
order blank is at the rear. All purchases will be
delivered to you well before Christmas, if postmarked by
December 1.
```

Once more, the letter did not tell everything, but led the reader to enclosures to learn details.

Department stores are great believers in enclosures. They find many occasions for sales—Back-To-School sales, Harvest sales, Thanksgiving sales, After Christmas sales, and so forth. Their customers receive sale announcements containing large numbers of enclosures, sometimes ten or twelve, promoting special items. Customers also get letters promoting lines or changed lines. The body of the letter often gives no more than a suggestion of the information in the enclosures.

Mailing Lists If you keep a good tone by using positive rather than negative words, emphasize the "You" approach, use good grammar, good taste, and the active voice, and remember in a general way the four parts of the model, you can produce sales letters that will deliver results. They can deliver, however, only if they go to the right people. An old saying holds that there are two ways of getting rid of something: throw it away or give it to somebody who does not want it. The implication is that one method is as effective as the other. Because department stores, as mentioned above, do most of their mailing to former customers, they know they are dealing with interested people.

Here is an example of what can happen when you do not use an appropriate mailing list. In a large American city, a community center attempted to promote a fund-raising dance in a huge gymnasium by sending out a general letter to the community. The center served an area of more than 10,000 people, but these people had no common interests other than their place of residence. A good letter was prepared and sent out bulk mail. It failed to produce the desired results because the mailing went to large numbers of people who did not dance, who were past the age of thinking much about dancing, who were not interested in the old-fashioned kind of dancing being planned, or who just did not care to get involved in a community event. People who do a great deal of direct mail selling would say that the sponsors of the dance had used an "impure" mailing list. That means that many people who got the letter were not prospects for the service or the product being promoted. Sending a letter to them was the same as throwing it away.

Where would the dance sponsors have found a proper mailing list with a high degree of purity? A dance studio or dance clubs in the community would be good places to start. You would start with their membership lists even if you had to list them as co-sponsors of the event to get them. The heart of your list, then, would be the membership rosters of organizations already dealing with the kinds of people likely to respond to your letter. You would add to their lists by asking friends and acquaintances for the names of persons who might be interested in such a dance.

Consider the letter that Ephraim Caslon wrote to the parents of American high school students. Where do you suppose he got his mailing list? He approached the publishers of two magazines published mainly for teen-agers, one for boys and one for girls, and he bought their subscription lists. These magazines had the names of the parents of the children as well as those of the subscribers themselves. And, of course, they had the correct addresses. The best lists have the *full names* of your prospects and always have their *correct addresses*.

What about the letter that Mr. Feorino got from John A. Higgins? Mr. Higgins, or his secretary, got the name out of the newspaper. Mr. Feorino's engagement had been announced, always an item of interest to those who sell insurance. He would probably want an appointments booklet to keep track of all the new things happening in his life.

The alumni director had her list already prepared—her membership rolls. So did the magazine that sought to make Christmas easier for its subscribers by selling to them through the mail. An organization's own business records usually constitute the purest list you can find anywhere. Among the impure lists are directories and public lists of all kinds (voter records, records of automobile sales, etc.).

Exhibit 5-1 lists some sources of mailing lists:

EXHIBIT 5-1.
Sources of Mailing Lists

1. The records of your own company, organization, or institution, showing who has done business with you before.
2. Membership lists of organizations, churches, special interest groups whose concerns overlap with yours.
3. Newspapers and magazines, which give information about people whose lifestyles are changing through marriage, promotion, transfer, etc. Classified advertisements also can tell something.
4. Bought mailing lists. Many public relations firms will assemble a mailing list for you for a fee. Bought subscription lists of special interest publications.

EXHIBIT 5-1.
(continued)

> 5. Names suggested by friends and acquaintances.
> 6. Lists (of what may prove to be a low degree of purity) from public records. You can purify them, but doing so will take effort.

Remember this, too: Mailing lists never stay the same. You must update, prune, and add to them if they are to keep their value.

SOFT-SELL LETTERS

The letters thus far have all been of the hard-sell kind. They asked their recipients to do something specific and to do it right away. Not all sales letters are of this type, however. Some seek merely to create good feeling that can be translated into a fruitful business transaction later.

Letters of Congratulation

There are several kinds of "soft" letters. They usually fall in the Good News category. One of the common ones is the letter of congratulation. The owner of a sporting goods shop in an American city assigned a secretary to read the newspapers carefully to identify outstanding high school and elementary school athletes of both sexes. The daily newspapers did cover school sports, but the secretary soon found that community and suburban weekly newspapers gave fuller coverage. The president of the firm asked the secretary to prepare short letters of congratulation to two young athletes each working day, which meant sending more than 500 letters a year. Care was taken to send the letters to athletes in all sections of town, and not to send too many to one section in a short period of time. After a time, the secretary began to include young men and women who had distinguished themselves in the Boy Scouts and Girl Scouts, since they, too, might be expected to have an interest in sports and outdoor life.

What elements should be included in a letter of congratulation? Such letters should be personal and should be signed by the president of the firm or someone else with an impressive title. They should be short and direct. They should be sincere. Sincerity means that each letter must be personal and individual. You cannot use the same language on everybody and get the effect you want. People are quick to spot insincerity, and they just might compare letters. Would this do for the sporting goods owner?

Dear Jack,

Your splendid run in last Friday evening's game against
the Falcons has given a lot of pleasure to your
classmates and to many of us in the community. It is a
pleasure to hear of something that was so flawlessly
done.

I read of your accomplishment in the newspaper and I
hope that I may have the opportunity to congratulate you
in person. When you are next in McDaniell's Sporting
Goods Company, will you come by my office and let me
shake your hand?

                    Sincerely,

                    William A. McDaniell
                    President

This theme has many variations. This one would also serve:

Dear Jack,

All accounts say that you covered your team with glory
last Friday evening in the game against the Falcons.
Good performance is always noticed and is its own best
advertisement.

I am proud of you, and I also like to talk football.

Put your head into my office the next time you are in
McDaniell's Sporting Goods Company and let's see who
knows the most ball scores.

                    Sincerely,

                    William A. McDaniell
                    President

Neither of those examples sounds like a form letter, and neither is. There
are at least fifteen other ways to vary the letter, and each variation invites
the young person to come by the store and meet the owner. Mr. McDaniell
knows his strengths, and he knows that he can charm his callers, once they
get there, and make them want to come back. He also gives them a small,
inexpensive gift. These letters draw young people with many years ahead
of them into the sporting goods shop. They have a pleasant experience
there and talk about the store to their friends. Thus, the effects of the letters
are multiplied several times over.

We can learn much from Mr. McDaniell's letters, which succeed, but we may learn almost as much from a letter that fails. The president of a college decided to build community support by having an aide write a letter every day for him to send to someone in the community who had achieved distinction. The newspapers were searched for names, and then the letters went out. Some, such as this one, were not very good:

```
Dear Mr. Holcombe,

    Congratulations on your election as president of the
Northside Civic Association. We are proud of everyone
who is willing to assume a role of civic leadership in
this great city of ours.

    We at Albion Mechanical College salute you, and invite
you to let us know how we can serve you better.

                    Sincerely,


                    John A. Harcourt
                    President
```

The letter was acceptable down through the end of the first paragraph, although it sounds cut and dried, like a form letter to anybody who was recognized for civic accomplishment. It *was* a form letter. But the second paragraph is silly. Would Harcourt really give Holcombe any time to tell how to serve him better? If not, he had better not pretend that he would. Holcombe took Harcourt up on his offer. He wrote back to say that in addition to serving as president of the Northside Civic Association, he was also heading the local United Fund drive and asked Harcourt to supply students from Albion to do door-to-door solicitation.

Harcourt had made a blanket offer, and he had to make it good. Never again did he use such expressions as:

"Please let us know what we can do for you."

"We are ready and anxious to be of service to you."

"We invite you to let us know how we can serve you better."

Today, he merely uses a complimentary sign-off: "We at Albion Mechanical College salute you, and wish you and the Northside Civic Association every success."

The real difference between the letter-writing operations of William McDaniell and John Harcourt, however, is not at once apparent. McDaniell thinks the letters are important and shows it; to Harcourt they are just routine. In both instances the detailed work is done by assistants; what makes the real difference is the attitude of the sender. McDaniell shows that he cares and the spirit is catching. Harcourt does not do much more than sign the letters. He cannot understand why they produce so few results. Although he has switched the letter-writing chore around several times among different assistants, the letters still fail to produce the desired results. For a brief time, the job passed into the hands of a super-eager young man, who broke one of the cardinal rules of writing congratulatory letters. That rule says, "Don't overdo it." Harcourt had attended his Rotary Club meeting, and he told the letter-writer that Thomas Exley, a fellow Rotarian, had made some good points in a talk to the club that day, and asked that a letter to Exley be prepared. Here is the result:

```
Dear Tom:

Your speech today at the Rotary Club was excellent. You
are getting to be the William Jennings Bryan of the
speaking circuit. You really struck a great chord of
music today. Congratulations.
```

Exley's speaking style has about as much kinship to that of William Jennings Bryan as lawn grass does to an orchid. He is a speaker of modest accomplishment. What Harcourt meant was that Exley had made a point or two worth thinking about, not that he had struck any chords of music or added luster to the history of oratory. The letter lacked sincerity. It was overdone. The following letter, which was much better, is the one that finally was sent:

```
Dear Tom:

Real thought went into the remarks that you made today
at the Rotary Club and they have given me some new
insights.

If you should have a copy of your comments, I would like
to have them so that I may share your point of view
with others on my staff.
```

Letters of Thanks

The letter above has brevity, sincerity, and reasonableness to recommend it. Letters of thanks—another way of building general good will—should have the same qualities. Care should be taken that the letter does not extend thanks beyond what the service rendered was worth. If it does, it loses credibility. Suppose you have been visiting the office of a friend, one whose line of business differs from yours, and you have been cordially introduced to another visitor. You have managed to open a business contact with this other visitor. You might write your friend as follows:

Dear Jeanine,

It was good of you to introduce me to Fred Thelmus when
I was visiting you the other day. It appears that he and
I may be able to do business together.

I hope that I can please him as well as you apparently
are doing.

Thanks for this contact. I hope that I may return the
favor.

                    Sincerely,

                    John Rappaport
                    Vice-President for Sales

This letter is warm, friendly, and sufficient, but not lavish. It may cause
Jeanine to look for other favors to throw your way. At least, it has created
a climate of goodwill and has indicated a spirit of reciprocity. Jeanine will
feel good about getting such a letter.

People can properly be thanked for an endless number of things. Any
act, service, or piece of business that has helped you will do. You should
not express thanks for favors not received. Some people tend to do this.
The following two letters do not, however. Both are reasonable, and both
have a good tone.

Assume that you have just received an unusually large order from an old
customer.

Dear John,

You and I have been friends and have been doing business
together for a good many years now, but I need to say
occasionally how much I appreciate you and what you and
I are able to do together. I think it is profitable to
both of us, and I know it is a pleasure to me.

I am moved to write this little note by your recent
order which I received today. We shall fill it exactly
to your specifications.

Thank you for your continuing confidence in us, and
thank you for your personal friendship.

                    Sincerely,

Or suppose that you had a first-time customer last week.

Dear Mrs. Bowe,

Thank you for permitting Lanton Electric Company to
serve your needs with a new washing machine this week.
We value all our customers, and constantly seek to make
new friends who will permit us to serve their appliance
needs.

Please visit us again, and accept our appreciation for
your confidence in us and in our merchandise.

                    Sincerely,

Letters of Condolence

Letters of congratulation and letters of thanks normally do not seek to do
much more than create good will. Letters of condolence never do. People
are never more sensitive than when there has been a death in the family.
They remember every kindness extended to them. Except for a few intimate
friends who will be asked to help after someone has died, all that the rest
of us can do is to take notice of the loss. Dignity and good taste are needed.
Accuracy is also required. Check the facts. Spell all names correctly.

A letter of condolence is one form of correspondence that can be hand-
written. It is more personal if it is handwritten, and it shows that the person
who signed it really wrote it. Letters of condolence are usually quite short.

There are two kinds of letters of condolence. In one type you knew the
deceased person; in the other, you did not. If you knew the one who died,
it would be helpful to recall some pleasant circumstance in which he or she
is remembered. Suppose the wife of a friend you know in a civic club has
died. You did not know her well, but you saw her a number of times at club
dinners and social events.

Dear Bill,

   I learned only this morning of Joan's sudden death,
and my thoughts went immediately to you and to her and
to the family of which I have often heard you speak.

   Mary and I have often noticed Joan at our club events
and have commented about the gentle impression she
always gave. She seemed to give such pleasure to those
around her.

   Our thoughts are with you and your family, and our
hope is that you can find comfort at this time of loss.

This letter has many variations. You can find a variation to fit your personality and style. For example, the second paragraph can have as many versions as there are people and experiences. The experience referred to must be authentic. If it sounds authentic, it need not be long.

In letters concerning the death of someone you did not know, you must omit any personal reflections unless you know from a second-hand source something that you can mention appropriately. Say, for example, that the elderly father of a friend has died, and you know that he had an especially fulfilling life.

```
Dear Ed,

The death of your father is a sad event for your family
and your friends, and I know that this is a hard time
for you especially.

A number of persons have told me that he had a life that
was filled with much success and happiness.

I hope that you can now be comforted by the recollection
of a beautiful life well lived.
```

A good condolence letter has one other feature: it is adaptable. If you sketch out four or five good ones, you can use them, with modifications, again and again. After all, you seldom need to write the same person twice. Just find language that is brief, dignified, and that sounds like you at your best, and you can be a real comfort to your friends at a sensitive time.

TAKE TIME TO DO IT RIGHT

Effective letters cannot be dashed off in a minute. An employer who instructs a secretary or an assistant to write two letters of congratulation each day should recognize that such a request, if taken seriously, must be given a priority. Everything that has a priority requires time, an uninterrupted block of time, not a few minutes sandwiched in between answering the telephone, transcribing, typing, filing, and receiving callers. Letters are seldom excellent if they are written on stolen time. An expert may occasionally be able to turn out a good one quickly, but great letters are usually like other works of art: they must be done at the artist's pace. And to work at his or her own best pace, the artist needs the right amount of unbroken time.

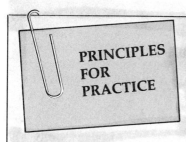

PRINCIPLES FOR PRACTICE

1. A flexible guideline called the Four P's can help you plan and organize sales letters.

2. Enclosures can help in the sales process.

3. Mailing lists are good only if they are up to date and if they get letters to people who are likely to want your product.

4. Letters of congratulation are useful in building goodwill.

5. Letters of thanks indirectly help the sales process by strengthening personal relationships.

6. Letters of condolence deal with the most sensitive of all subjects—death. People remember the good ones they receive and feel kindly toward those who sent them.

7. It takes time to write good letters.

FOR FURTHER STUDY

1. The following letter from the Director of Admissions of a university was received by a young woman early in her last year of high school. Find the four *P*'s. Is this a reasonably good sales letter? Why?

```
Dear Student,

    As a participant in the Spring Search of the College
Board, you will be inundated with information from
colleges and universities. We suggest that you examine
the information carefully. The selection of a university
is among the most important decisions you will make. We
invite you to consider Ellsworth Ingram University.

    A suburban campus of 1,700 students, Ellsworth Ingram
is a private, coeducational, four-year university
offering specialization in 45 areas. Classes are small
(averaging twenty students) and are taught by
outstanding faculty. Seventy percent hold doctorates.
```

Our alumni occupy places of leadership throughout our
state and region.

We feel that Ellsworth Ingram University might be the
place for you. You and your parents are invited to visit
throughout the year. The Admissions Office is open
Monday through Friday from 8:30 a.m. until 5 p.m. and
Saturday from 9 to noon. For further information, please
fill out the postage-paid reply card and return it.

We look forward to hearing from you.

Sincerely,

Sue Ellen Bosworth
Director of Admissions

2. One of the four *P*'s is missing in the following letter, which came from
your insurance agent. Is it a good sales letter? Would it be better if the
missing *P* were present? Using your imagination, supply the *P* in a short
paragraph you write to be inserted.

Dear Mr. Hidalgo,

We've all seen how sharply the costs of medical care
have gone up. American Hospital Association surveys show
that a relatively minor illness or accident can cost
hundreds of dollars. A serious problem can wreck the
best-planned budget.

That's why I'm pleased that we are now able to let you
examine an excellent Hospital Plan. Our company will
provide you and your family this insurance plan with
valuable benefits at economical rates.

The protection it offers can mean less financial
strain and more peace of mind for you and your family.

No matter what other coverage you have, this
supplemental policy gives you $90 a day in cash benefits
to help with unexpected costs. Why not review it in your
own home at no obligation?

All you need do is return the application form. Your
policy showing complete benefit information and
effective date will be sent. You send no money now. You
have 10 days to decide whether or not you want to keep
it.

```
     You can have your monthly premium automatically
charged to your bank account. It costs you nothing to
look into. You owe it to yourself, and to your family,
to consider this protection.

                         Sincerely,


                         Renee Kinard, CLU
                         Agent
```

3. Until March, you and John Poindexter were Vice-President–Production and Vice-President–Sales for a large manufacturer of carpentry tools—hammers, saws, nails, etc. Both of you resigned from that firm, Erbo and Company, Inc., and you have opened your own manufacturing company. You call it TexPro and Tennessee Company. You have a plant with 112,000 square feet of space, and you own 62 acres upon which to expand. You will produce lines that supplement those produced by Erbo and Company. Write a letter to the sales outlets that you have been dealing with over the years. You have a good mailing list. The purpose of the letter is:
  a. To announce formation of your company.
  b. To invite people to visit you at the Home Builders' Show in Milwaukee in June.
  c. To tell about your new plant located in Parrott, Tennessee.
  d. To enclose a catalogue of your merchandise.
  e. To enclose an order blank.
  Mark the four *P*'s in your letter.

4. You are Ellen Queler, processor of gourmet foods, many of which are bought for gifts. Write a letter to the retail outlets that sell your merchandise. Here is what you want the letter to do:
  a. Announce a fruitcake made by a new recipe.
  b. Announce a new plum pudding.
  c. Announce a new catalogue, a copy of which you enclose. The catalogue is expensive. You do not wish any to be wasted. You are limiting the number of free catalogues that each distributor may order on the basis of earlier sales to that distributor. You wish to favor those who have made the best effort to sell Ellen Queler's products.
  d. Distributors who wish to buy extra copies of the catalogue for their own mailings can have them for 27 cents each.
  e. Enclose an order blank for both the free and purchased catalogues.

5. Your company makes WIPECLEAN, the finest lens polisher in the world. As you know, you should never polish the lens of your glasses with a dry handkerchief or cloth, because you can scratch the lens. One drop of WIPECLEAN on the lens permits safe polishing. WIPECLEAN has a silicone base. WIPECLEAN is sold in drugstores, and your mailing list has the names of more than 2,000 outlets that handle your product. Because of problems in the marketing department, sales are down. Write a letter to your outlets to "resell" them on the product. Here are some points:

  a. WIPECLEAN does not evaporate and has a shelf life of 10 years.
  b. It will also polish photographic lenses.
  c. It is especially good for plastic lenses, which scratch more easily than glass ones.
  d. One small drop of WIPECLEAN will polish a lens.

6. You work for a pen manufacturing company. You make a desk set that retails for $29.79. The base of the set is simulated black marble, and the pen stands in a holder with a gold washer around the socket. For an additional $10.50, you will imprint the name of a person or a company in gold on the base. The Christmas season is coming, and these sets will make excellent business gifts. Write a letter to your outlets offering the new imprinting service and guaranteeing delivery within one month after orders are received at the plant.

7. You are president of the International Office Managers' Consortium and Association, a group that represents office managers in the United States and Canada. You and Elbert Hines, chairperson of the Department of Decision Mathematics at Ellsworth Ingram University, are sponsoring a two-day seminar entitled "Understanding the Office of the Future." The seminar will be held at the University on November 7–8. You are handling general arrangements. Hines and the Department of Decision Mathematics will provide space for the seminar at the University and will staff the program. The program will deal with computers and modern technology and how they will affect the office of the future. The seminar will make no profit. There is a $35 registration fee for meals and coffee breaks. Each person who attends is responsible for paying hotel and travel expenses. Write a letter to the members of the Consortium and Association inviting them to come. You will make two enclosures: the names, addresses, telephone numbers, and rates of three nearby hotels where registrants may stay; a registration form for the seminar. You need not write the enclosures, but you should refer to them in or on your letter.

8. You are chairperson of the board of directors of the Whispering Oaks Civic Association. The association is a quarter of a century old. It represents residents who live in the Whispering Oaks section of your city. It is nonprofit, concerned only with betterment of the neighborhood. A major concern has been traffic. A seven-year-old child was killed last week by a hit-and-run motorist. Write a letter to your membership making these points:

  a. Members of the association should write, call, or otherwise communicate with the mayor and members of the city council. This is urgent. Ask them to take action at once.
  b. An attachment to your letter gives names, addresses, and telephone numbers of these officials.
  c. The civic association four months ago submitted a traffic plan to the city, but no action has been taken.
  d. The plan called for traffic lights at key intersections to slow down traffic and for the installation of several four-way stops.

9. You are senior vice-president and trust officer of the First National Bank of Jackson City. You want to encourage "living trusts" for people who qualify for them. A person needs a minimum of $200,000 in cash or securities to qualify. You have identified about 300 people who qualify. You write each a personal letter, individually typed on an automatic typewriter and signed by you. Your points:
  a. First National's investment staff is experienced and has an excellent record.
  b. Economic conditions and uncertainties make "living trusts" a valuable option.
  c. "Trust" is a confusing word. "Living trust" means professional management of your investments by the bank on a full-time basis.
  d. A "living trust" can be set up to produce maximum income, maximum growth, or a combination of the two.
  e. Return the form in the enclosed stamped envelope and a senior trust officer will call to explain further the benefits of this arrangement.

10. The sixteen-year-old son of an important business associate will become an Eagle Scout next Tuesday. Write the young man a letter of congratulation. He is an honor student in high school, and he plays guitar in a band. Work carefully on the tone of the letter. Say enough, but not too much. (You may be sure that the young man will show your letter to his father.)

11. You sell vacuum cleaners to retail outlets. For several years, Ted Estes has been a good customer. Ted has been eased out of his highly desirable store at Wampo City, however, and transferred to a less desirable one in Tellico Heights. You know that Ted was transferred because he could not control his temper and he offended many people. You will continue to sell to Ted in Tellico Heights. You cannot exactly write him a letter of congratulation, but write the closest thing to it that you can. Acccentuate the positive.

12. You are director of a tutorial program in a large public school system. You have worked with many 11th- and 12th-graders who volunteered to tutor students in lower grades who need special help. It is the end of the year. Write a letter of thanks to your young tutors.

13. You own a small dry goods store at 123 Cain Street. Last night, Police Officer J. D. Riley, who patrols the area, saw a would-be burglar trying to break in one of the rear windows of your store. Officer Riley stopped his patrol car, and when the would-be thief ran, Riley pursued him on foot. The would-be thief shot twice at Riley before finally getting away. Riley was not hurt. He is a married man with two small children, ages 4 and 2. Write a letter to Riley and indicate carbons to Police Chief R. N. Hofstadter and to Mayor Rhonda Suarez.

14. A business acquaintance, Theodore Ratcliffe of Guy Walter and Company, lent you his cabin on Lake Trainer for a weekend. You have just returned to work on Monday morning. Ratcliffe has occasionally bought building supplies from you for Guy Walter and Company. Write a letter thanking him for the use of the cabin. You hope that Mr. Ratcliffe's loan of his cabin, and the good feeling it indicates, will open the way to an expanded business relationship.

15. You are loan officer of the Waldrop City National Bank. Three years ago your bank approved a loan of $4,700 to Mrs. Gail Riggs to help her pay for her daughter's college education. Mrs. Riggs made the last payment on her note last week. Write her a letter thanking her for her business, congratulating her on her excellent credit rating, and expressing a desire to do future business with her.

16. You own a catering service. Your bookkeeper reminds you that five years ago, Ms. Melinda Kunz asked you to cater a special party at the Ransom House Inn. She is director of special services at the Inn. In the last five years, she has asked you to cater 27 events. On this fifth anniversary of her first order, write a letter to Ms. Kunz thanking her for her business and invite future business.

17. Edward Wylly, vice-president of Rim Iron Works and one of your good customers, has died suddenly. Write two letters of condolence. One goes to his wife of 36 years. They have recently returned from a trip to Europe. The other goes to Sampson Reidler, president of Rim Iron Works.

18. Mrs. Annette Friedlander, mother of Cy Friedlander, one of your most important customers, has been killed in an automobile wreck. She was 63 and a widow. Cy was devoted to her. Write him an appropriate letter of condolence.

CHAPTER 6

To: The Reader
From: The Authors
Subject: Some Other Kinds of Business Letters

After reading this chapter, you will have guidelines for writing:

1. Order letters and acknowledgments

2. Inquiries and acknowledgments

3. Claim letters

4. Adjustment letters

5. Credit letters

6. Collection letters

7. Form letters

Other Kinds
of Business Letters

Up to this point, we have emphasized clarity and simplicity in business writing. We have discussed achieving a good tone. We have learned to use negative words and phrases sparingly, to use precise words, and to favor the active voice. We have studied the "You" approach. Keep these considerations in mind as we look at several common forms of business correspondence.

ORDER LETTERS AND ACKNOWLEDGMENTS

Businesses are happy to get order letters. They are the "stuff" upon which profits depend. Whether you are the sender or the receiver of an order letter, it needs several elements to be effective.

1. The writer must state *exactly* what is wanted. The receiver cannot guess, and delays and expensive mistakes will occur if exact information is not given. Here is a checklist.
   a. The number of items wanted and the unit, where there is one (7 boxes; 364 lbs.; 99 doz.; 44 gr.).
   b. The price per item or per unit ($34.67 per lamp; $19.23 per 1,000 cards; $17.46 per box).
   c. A description of the item (claw hammers, staplers, rubber cement, bond paper).

d. The catalogue number, if there is one.

e. The model number, if there is one.

f. Special information, such as color and weight.

2. The writer must specify how the items are to be delivered: U.S. mail, United Parcel Service, Federal Express, truck, railway.

3. The writer often must say how payment is to be made: C.O.D., regular 30-day account, open account. If the writer already has an account with the company, this information may be omitted.

The key to a good order letter, indeed, to all good business correspondence, is clarity. To assure that complete information is sent, most companies preprint purchase order forms on which customers fill in the blanks or check appropriate boxes. Use of these forms minimizes errors and omissions. However, order letters are still common and are likely to remain so. The following letter to the Ulal Bag Company has the elements needed:

```
Dear Sales Manager,

    Please send us sixteen boxes of size 12 burlap bags at
$52.00 a box. These should be your boxes holding 50 bags
each. The size 12 bags are catalogue number 172.

    We want normal burlap color with no imprint.

    Payment will be made upon the terms of our 30-day
account.

    We need delivery by November 21. We ask that you
deliver prepaid through an authorized trucking line.

                    Sincerely,
```

So long as the order letter gives the required information, it need not be long. Two or three short paragraphs will often do the job. Likewise, there is no reason why the *acknowledgment* of an order letter should be long. It often can be a form letter in which you fill in the blanks:

```
Dear Customer,

    Your order, dated _____, has been received. We
are happy to have your business.

    We shall ship your order by      (kind of conveyance)
on      (date)     , and we hope that
you will find everything to be satisfactory.

                    Sincerely,
```

Sometimes it is not necessary to acknowledge a routine order in which there are no problems. Quick delivery of the merchandise will be enough. However, acknowledgments build good will. They, like order letters, are in the Good News category, and they show that you have the customer's welfare in mind. It is always good policy to send them to new customers.

Some order letters present problems, however. If a customer's order is not clear, you must ask for more information. Let us say that you got this letter:

```
Dear Sales Manager,

    Please ship 50 boxes of Sizemore erasers by October
3d. We need them by October 10th.

    Ship prepaid any method you choose, and bill us on our
account.
                        Sincerely,
```

The problem here is that Sizemores come in three sizes. The letter neither specifies size nor mentions the price per box, which might have given us a clue to the size. It is necessary to write a letter like this:

```
Dear Customer,

    Thank you for your order of 50 boxes of Sizemore
erasers, which came today. By checking the enclosed
stamped card, indicate whether you wish size 12, size
14, or size 16 Sizemores. The price of each per box is
shown on the card.

    We shall fill your order promptly upon getting this
information.

                        Sincerely,
```

Occasionally, you must decline to fill an order. You do not stock the item requested, you have run out of the item, or the line has been discontinued. Acknowledgment letters for orders of this kind fall into the Bad News category and should be worded tactfully. You still hope to get future business from the customer.

```
Dear Customer,

    We have received your order for 4 dozen RalTest self-
sealing one-quart jars. We regret that the one-quart
sizes are no longer made because of the switch to the
metric system.
```

```
We make the jars now in liter and half-liter sizes.

    Attached is a schedule of sizes and prices, and we
hope that we may have the pleasure of getting a re-order
from you.

                              Sincerely,
```

Sometimes, an acknowledgment letter must disappoint a customer al-together. In such cases, tact is important. Remember the "You" approach.

```
Dear Customer,

    We are glad to have your order for three size-19
aluminum garbage cans.

    Because these items are bulky and shipping costs are
high, we regret that we cannot fill orders that total
less than $200.

    Please give us an opportunity to serve you again. We
are glad that you thought of us.

                              Sincerely,
```

INQUIRIES AND ACKNOWLEDGMENTS

Letters of inquiry fall into two categories:

1. Those that may lead to business, and, it is hoped, to profit for the recipient.

2. Those that request information or some item or service that will not lead directly to a business transaction. However, an appropriate response to such letters may produce good will.

Businesses are always eager to answer the first kind. If the inquiry is about prices, about lines of merchandise, or about services offered, the business probably has a form letter ready to give the information. The business certainly will have a printed or mimeographed schedule of prices, or items or services for sale, which can be included in a short letter of acknowledgment.

```
Dear Mrs. Ritter,

    We at Eldridge Bakery can easily supply 12 freshly
baked cakes for your reception.
```

```
    We are sending a schedule which shows the variety of
cakes and other baked goods that we offer. The prices
cited for each item are competitive and, in many cases,
are lower than the local rate.

    Send us your order and we shall do our best to give
you cakes that will taste as good as they look.

                    Sincerely,
```

Suppose that you are dean of admissions at a college and get an inquiry like the following:

```
Dear Admissions Office,

    I am a high school senior and am considering where I
shall go to college next fall.

    Will you please send me your catalogue and any other
information about your college that you think I need?

                    Sincerely,


                    Tara Triegle
```

The Admissions Office has a form letter and some printed materials ready:

```
Dear Ms. Triegle,

    We are happy to have you consider our college. We are
enclosing the catalogue, which contains information
about curriculum, fees, and requirements, and the
Student Handbook, which contains information about
social opportunities and housing on our campus.

    Thank you for writing, and let us hear from you again.

                    Sincerely,
```

The letter of inquiry was simple and to the point. It was clear. The acknowledgment said what was being done about the inquiry and expressed thanks.

Both of the acknowledgments given above are standard Good News letters. They go directly to the point, and they may produce business for your company or institution. But suppose you got an inquiry in which there is no immediate profit for you, but from which you might derive good will. You are director of public relations for an electric power company, and sometimes you supply door prizes and small gifts to be distributed at luncheons and meetings. Each of these gifts has the logo of your company imprinted. You receive this letter:

```
Dear Mr. Tate,

   The West Norcross P.T.A. will hold its annual
Parent—Teacher dinner on May 30, and we should again
like to inquire whether you can contribute 120 ballpoint
pens as individual gifts for each teacher and parent,
and also contribute four electric lamps as door prizes
to be given away in a drawing.

   We also would like to have any other small items that
you could give us, also for distribution through a
drawing.

   We shall give full credit to your company for its
generosity.

                              Sincerely,


                    J. A. Tubman
```

Mr. Tate is happy to give the 120 ballpoint pens. They are inexpensive and are an easily justifiable public relations expense. He balks, however, at giving four lamps, because they cost almost $150 each and he has only seven left. (The logo is worked tastefully into the glass shade of the lamps.) Mr. Tate wishes to give only part of what is requested, and he must be tactful.

```
Dear Mr. Tubman,

   Quincy Electric Company will be happy to furnish 120
ballpoint pens with our compliments for distribution at
the annual Parent—Teacher dinner of the West Norcross
P.T.A. We are happy to be asked to have a part once more
this year.

   Rising prices have affected our ability to make our
electric lamp available, however. The lamps are
expensive and we have virtually been forced to stop
giving them for door prizes.

   I am happy to say that I will be glad to make
available six boxed packages of playing cards. Each card
is tastefully imprinted on the back with our company
logo, and it is our hope that they will serve as a
pleasant reminder of Quincy Electric.
```

```
      Please let me know when you would like to pick these
   items up, as it will be my pleasure to welcome you to
   our headquarters.

                        Sincerely,
```

Pleasing Mr. Tubman cost Mr. Tate's company a small sum of money, since there is a cost to supply the items. However, a great many inquiry letters do not ask for *things,* but for *information* that cannot be supplied with prepared schedules. Assembling information and preparing it in written form involves a cost too because it takes the time of one or more employees. When writing a letter asking for information such as this, consider three approaches:

1. Make your request as simple as you can without obscuring your purpose.

2. Promise confidentiality where appropriate. Many people are willing to give information if they are assured that they will not be quoted by name.

3. Where practical, offer to do something for the person, firm, or institution giving the information. Usually this is done by offering to supply a copy of the findings of which the information will become part. This is especially important if those supplying the information go to a great deal of trouble on your behalf.

A university president recently received the following request for information from a national foundation:

```
Dear Mr. President,

You are familiar with the work of the ERNOE Foundation
in supporting higher education throughout America. In
line with national goals well established by Congress,
the courts, and the President of the United States, the
ERNOE Foundation is making selected grants to
institutions to help them open their doors wider to
women and to minority groups.

To make these grants wisely, we must have information
about the status of these groups in higher education at
the present time. We are aware that you receive many
requests for information, but if you execute the
enclosed questionnaire, or have it executed by a
knowledgeable person on your staff, you would be helping
us to serve the profession of which you are a part. And,
of course, you are eligible to make a grant application
to us.
```

```
We promise confidentiality. The information will be
used, but no institution will be referred to by name
unless permission is given by that institution.

The results should be significant. When this nationwide
survey is completed, those institutions taking part in
it will be supplied a copy of the findings.

                    Sincerely,


                    J. A. Halpern, Ph.D.
```

It is quite likely that the university president will supply the information. It would be good to have a copy of the findings; it may be desirable to apply for a grant; and the last thing the university wants is a reputation for being uncooperative. So the following acknowledgment might be written to the secretary of the foundation:

```
Dear Dr. Halpern,

  We shall be glad to supply the information requested
in your letter of September 24, and we are glad to have
your assurance that confidentiality will be observed.

  You can appreciate the fact that a great deal of work
is involved in getting this information together. I am
asking Assistant Vice-President Marguerite Ellison to
undertake this as a project, and I shall review her
findings before sending them to you. Her work will
require four weeks.

  We appreciate your inquiry.

                    Sincerely,
```

Note that the acknowledgment gives explicit information. It leaves no loose ends hanging, but tells what will be done, who will do it, and when.

Suppose, however, that it was necessary to say no. You then have a Bad News letter, and tact must be used. Consider using the Empathy-Content-Action model, which we learned in Chapter 4.

```
Dear Dr. Halpern,

  I am impressed with the value of the survey that you
are making on behalf of your foundation, and I know that
the findings will be significant nationally.

  However, at the moment I am having a difficult staff
situation, as the assistant vice-president who would
```

```
assemble and computerize the information is involved in
a lengthy project that takes her full time.

    I regret that we cannot take part at present, but we
know that others can and we wish for you a happy outcome
from this venture.

                    Sincerely,
```

This letter uses the model to deliver a nice "no." It also minimizes the damage that the "no" does. When you really must say "no," you usually can find a way to use the model truthfully and diplomatically.

CLAIM LETTERS

Your business will be getting and perhaps sending claim letters. When something has gone wrong—an item your company has bought from another firm is defective, an order has not been filled, goods you ordered were damaged in transit—a letter is usually written about it. This is called a claim letter. If there is urgency about the matter, you might make a telephone call reporting what has happened, but such a call should always be followed by a letter. A letter is permanent and can be read again next year or three years from now, long after the substance of a telephone conversation has become hazy.

In writing a claim letter, *be sure to be precise.* Do not say: "The machine that we bought from your firm recently is unsatisfactory." You have not told the recipient of your letter enough. Instead, say: "The ALC electric motor, Model 1323-B, that we bought from you on April 17 is unsatisfactory. You may check the details of this purchase on Invoice 1876." You have now given the selling company enough information to find the needed documents. Do not say: "Upon finding the machine was not working, we immediately notified one of the officials in your service department." Instead, say: "Upon finding that the Model 1323-B was not working, we immediately notified Joseph Dale, assistant manager of your service department." Imprecise language is weak and tentative. Facts and specifics are strong and command attention.

When you write a claim letter, do three things:

1. Get all your facts together. Be prepared to say exactly what is wrong; describe precisely what the cost in time, money, and inconvenience has been to you, if this should be pertinent.

2. Ask yourself: "What do I want to accomplish with this letter?" A precise understanding of the kinds of redress you want will help you get a good focus.

3. Resolve not to let your letter sound antagonistic.

Of these, the latter is the hardest. When things go wrong, when your plans and needs are frustrated, indignation and anger may boil up, and it would be easy to start lashing out at those you think responsible. At that point, remember the "You" approach. Put yourself in the other person's place. In any business, in any undertaking, a certain number of things inevitably go wrong. Most successful companies are interested in seeing that they are put right again. Such companies are successful in great part because they get repeat business—customers come back again and again— which means that mistakes are corrected. So start with the assumption that the other person will wish to make the situation right. If that is not the case, consider what your priorities are and take appropriate action.

Here is an actual case. You work for a family-owned business in a large city. The business owns its building, which is heated by a gas furnace in the basement. Once a year for seventeen years, Edwards Brothers Plumbing and Heating Company has serviced the furnace. Two weeks ago, they came on special call. The furnace was not performing properly. They repaired it and left. A few days later a bill arrived and it was paid promptly. Two days after the bill was paid, the furnace broke again in what you are sure was the same place it was broken before. You call Edwards and they come again and fix it. This time it really is fixed. But then you get another bill, which you do not believe you owe. You have paid once to have the furnace repaired, and you should not have to pay twice. Here is the letter that was sent:

```
Dear Mr. Edwards,

    For the past seventeen years, my company has had the
satisfaction of doing business with you, and we know
that you take pride in your work. We have never had the
slightest problem with your service.

    Now, however, we do have one. Our furnace broke on
November 17 and your representatives came and fixed the
automatic shut-off valve, which you had installed new
the year before. Your bookkeeper then sent us a bill for
the service, which we paid.

    Two days after we sent you our check, the automatic
shut-off valve broke again, and your representatives
came and fixed it a second time. We are pleased with the
job, as the valve apparently is fixed. However, we have
now received a second bill.
```

```
I am not sure that you wish to bill us twice. Will you
please check your records and give me a telephone call?

                    Sincerely,
```

You will notice that this letter is patterned upon the Empathy-Content-Action model. Paragraph one is Empathy, two and three are Content, and four is Action. It is a good use of the model, and it produced the desired result. The second bill was canceled.

Not all claim letters will be cast in the form of this model, but if you do not use this form, you should take care to consider the other person's point of view in some other way, and to assume at the outset that good intentions exist. You can change your approach later if you must.

ADJUSTMENT LETTERS

Very often, when customers are making a claim against your company, you must write a letter telling them what you intend to do about it. That is called an adjustment letter. It is a sensitive letter because, as noted before, successful firms build upon repeat customers. You want to do everything within reason to keep the people who do business with you happy.

There is one rule that applies to all business correspondence, and it applies doubly to adjustment letters, in which, by definition, you are dealing with people who are upset. *Never promise more than you will deliver.* In world affairs, revolutions have been set off by statesmen who promised results they could not produce; many a business has been ruined by the same thing. You do not even have to make a specific promise to get into trouble. An implied one can be just as damaging; so weigh your words with care.

Adjustment letters vary widely because the party at fault varies. In fact, the fault can fall into four categories:

1. Your company is at fault.
2. The buyer is at fault.
3. Another person or firm is at fault.
4. You have not yet learned who is at fault, but you are investigating.

These are the variables in adjustment letters. There are also certain *constants*. The first one is, by now, a familiar friend:

1. Emphasize the "You" approach. Unless the other person is killing your profit by being a difficult customer, you want his or her future business.

2. Avoid negative words as much as you can while stating the facts.

3. Say what you intend to do.

4. Invite further business.

Which of these parts is more important? (In some letters, parts can be combined.) They are all important. However, people resent situations less when the facts are kindly explained to them—not condescendingly, but kindly and fully. Reduce resentment by full disclosure delivered in your best tone.

Take an example where *your company is at fault* (Exhibit 6-1).

EXHIBIT 6-1.

Dear Mrs. Bernstein,

We intend to see that your new AUTOMAX washing machine, which you bought from us eight weeks ago, gives you the service you have a right to expect.

Our service representative has been to your home, checked the machine, and found that a slightly imperfect cycle-regulator was installed in the factory. This is fully covered in your warranty and it will be made good at no expense to you.

Very shortly, we shall telephone you to fix a time when our representative may come to your home to replace the part. On the same trip, we shall have your entire machine checked and serviced.

Thank you for your confidence in us. We value your business, and are enclosing a notice of our sale on electrical appliances, which runs for one week beginning on the 15th of this month.

Sincerely,

Paragraph one takes the "You" approach. Paragraph two says what the facts are, using positive words insofar as possible: *slightly imperfect, fully covered, made good.* Paragraph three says what you will do, and paragraph four invites further business—in this case, at a specific time. You should not expect that the parts will always unfold in just this order, but each should be represented in all adjustment letters except the most exceptional, even when used in combination with another part.

Where the *buyer is at fault,* you will wish to use the recommended parts of the letter, but you must be especially conscious of tone if you wish to keep the buyer's business. Suppose that the buyer (a firm) has bought an electric motor from you, has failed to have the machine serviced properly as required by the warranty, and now complains that the machine is giving problems. (See Exhibit 6-2.)

EXHIBIT 6-2.

Dear Mr. Cisneros,

  The concern about the trouble you are having with the ALC electric motor, Model 1323-B, which you bought from us April 17, is understandable. You need reliable performance from this equipment for your business to function properly.

  The sales agreement guaranteed the performance of the machine provided it was checked and serviced every four months during the first year you had it.

  Although two such inspection periods have passed, the equipment has not been checked and serviced by any of the firms which we certified as authorized to do it. The machine will work properly only if its upkeep is maintained.

  We value you as a customer and want you to have the best service, so we shall, with your agreement, send one of our representatives to your city to put the machine in good working order. We shall bill you at actual cost, as we value your satisfaction in this instance more than we value our own profit.

  Will you let us know whether this arrangement is satisfactory, and let us know how else we may serve you?

                Sincerely,

Let us say that *a third party was at fault*—a railroad, for example, which delivered the motor in damaged condition. (See Exhibit 6-3.)

EXHIBIT 6-3.

Dear Mr. Cisneros,

  We understand your need to have your ALC electric motor, Model 1323-B, running properly at the earliest moment. We received your order for it on April 17.

  Our careful investigation shows that the railroad damaged the motor in transit. This does not happen

EXHIBIT 6-3.
(continued)

often, and happily we know how to repair the motor so that it will be as good as new.

We stand ready to repair the motor at cost to us, and the matter will have our top priority. After the repair, we shall join with you in certifying damages against the railroad so that you may make a claim against them. In case you wish to begin preparing the claim papers immediately, we are enclosing the standard forms used in making railroad claims.

We value you as a customer and wish to help you in every way in this distressing situation. If you have other ideas as to how we should handle this emergency, please call us immediately. Or perhaps you will be good enough to call us anyway, so that we may know how you wish to proceed.

Sincerely,

In case *you do not know which party is at fault,* a letter like the following one in Exhibit 6-4 would help to "contain" the situation while you find out.

EXHIBIT 6-4.

Dear Mr. Cisneros,

We understand your concern at the imperfect condition in which your ALC electric motor, Model 1323-B, arrived. We received your order on April 17 and shipped it promptly the next day by rail express.

We have conducted a preliminary investigation, but because of the temporary absence of the superintendent of our warehouse, we cannot yet say whether the fault is ours, or whether the fault lies with the railroad. We shall continue to look into the matter until we find out.

In the meantime, we are sending a service representative to your plant to make the motor as good as new. If later investigation shows we are at fault, we shall absorb the full expense of setting things right. If it shows that the railroad is at fault, we shall join you in pressing a claim.

We are anxious that you be satisfied, and we hope that we may continue to serve you well.

Sincerely,

CREDIT LETTERS

Much business is done on credit. The decision whether to grant a line of credit to a firm, institution, or individual is usually made by a professional staff (in large firms) or by the topmost officers of the organization (in smaller firms). The decision is not a mechanical one arrived at after putting certain elements into a formula. An element of judgment is required.

If a decision is made to grant credit in a given instance, the job of writing a letter saying so is fairly easy if care is taken to include certain points (see Exhibit 6-5):

EXHIBIT 6-5.

Dear Mrs. Ullman,

We at DIETRICK's are happy that you applied to us for credit and are pleased to tell you that we are extending credit privileges to you immediately. Enclosed you will find two charge cards and an announcement of our forthcoming sale, which begins the tenth of this month.

Your line of credit with us is $1,200. If your account should go over this sum, we shall ask you to withhold further charges until it has been reduced or to make a special arrangement.

You will be billed during the last week of each month, and full payment is expected within thirty days. For balances left unpaid more than thirty days, a finance charge of 1½ percent per month will be added.

Otherwise, no conditions are attached. We hope that you will enjoy using it as much as we expect to enjoy serving you.

Sincerely,

1. The terms of payment must be stated. Is full payment expected within thirty days, and will an interest charge be made on the unpaid balance thereafter? The conditions must be spelled out so that the customer knows what they are.

2. What is the customer's credit limit? Can an individual charge up to $1,500, or $2,000? Can a firm charge up to $10,000? State the credit limit clearly.

3. If the account is of a special kind, or if there are other conditions connected with it, declare them plainly.

4. If credit is being granted, express your pleasure.

5. Invite business.

6. Do laws require you to explain details of the credit policy? If so, do you have a printed explanation to enclose?

Mrs. Ullman can scarcely fail to be pleased. But suppose you had to tell her "no." Your credit officers have checked her credit rating with her bank and with a professional credit-checking organization and you think she is a questionable risk. She already owes other people a good bit of money. However, it is possible that she may still do some cash business with you, and, of course, her credit rating can improve in six months or a year. You do not wish to lose her as a cash customer or as a potential credit customer. You also do not want her to tell her friends how unreasonable you are. Be very tactful (see Exhibit 6-6):

EXHIBIT 6-6.

Dear Mrs. Ullman,

   We are pleased that you have applied to DIETRICK's for a line of credit. We greatly value the business that you give us and the confidence you have in us.

   We believe that, for the present, however, you might be more comfortable dealing with us on a cash basis. We shall be happy to reconsider opening a charge account for you later if you would care to reapply.

   We are currently scheduling a series of large sales, the first of which will open on the Monday after Easter. Please don't fail to visit us in order to see the variety of bargains that will be offered in every department in the store.

                    Sincerely,

This letter, of course, is making the best of a sticky situation. Yet you were considerate in that you invited her to reapply for future credit. That will make her feel better. She probably will not do so unless her financial situation really has improved.

COLLECTION LETTERS

The first thing to know about collection letters is that you have a perfect right to write them. Many people are embarrassed about money, and they become uncomfortable when they must remind or tell others that it is time (or past time) to pay money that is owed. Yet collections must be made. Businesses must show a profit or go out of existence, taking jobs and trade down the drain with them. Nonprofit organizations must have income or they will close.

If a person or firm has bought the goods or services of another person or firm, then there is an obligation to pay for them provided the goods and services were satisfactory. The loss of the money due on only one account kills the profit that a firm made on many. Therefore, you do not wish to lose payment. You must be *persistent* in your collection efforts, even if it takes months of writing letters at fifteen- to thirty-day intervals. (Toward the end of the collection process, you narrow the interval.)

Keep these points in mind:

1. Do not be antagonistic or sarcastic in your collection letters. Bad feeling will result, and such attitudes can be self-defeating. Be as positive and as considerate as circumstances will permit, especially at the beginning.

2. Start with the premise that most people are honest and will pay; avoid an "injured" tone.

3. Seek to collect what is owed as promptly as possible. Failure to do so could, in extreme cases, mean that your company or institution must run on borrowed money until debts are collected.

4. Keep the customer's goodwill if possible. Satisfactory future business can come from customers who have been slow to pay.

5. And, to repeat the point made earlier, *persist*. Start trying to collect when the bill becomes due and do not stop until the final recourse has been exhausted. (There might be an occasional exception. If the amount owed is small and the customer is a big one, you must consider where your best interests lie.)

Let us now look at the stages of the collection process. We begin with the early stage.

1. *Normal billing.*   Firms or individuals having accounts normally get a bill at or near the end of each month. This bill, which gives the sum owed and says what the charge is for, is the first stage in the process. It is not at all stressful. People expect to get bills for goods or services that they have honestly bought. Bills often are delivered at the same time that goods and services are delivered or performed. This also is a normal part of the process, involving little stress.

2. *Second notice, or reminder.*   Second notices are not threatening either. Although most people are conscientious about paying, bills sometimes are misplaced or overlooked. Sometimes a customer, with or without a twinge of guilt, discovers that finances make it necessary to delay payment for a month. When you send a second notice, you still assume that the customer intends to pay. You just send another bill, usually identical to the first except that you may pen a note on the bottom saying "Past due" or "Overdue"; or you may use a rubber stamp or sticker that says "Second Notice," "Please send us your check," or something similar. Third notices are not uncommon. They still fall within the early stages of the process. These bills and notices are not heavily personalized and this is deliberate. It makes them less threatening.

3. *Special consideration letter.*   At this point, we leave the early stage of the process. The customer has not answered the original bill or the second (or third) notice. We are now into the middle phase, where there is stress. The following "special consideration letter" went from a physician to one of his patients. The patient is a conscientious person who had turned his bills over to his insurance company for payment, and who thought they were being handled. They were not. The patient had not paid out in medical expenses the $150 minimum that his insurance company requires each year before it will start picking up bills; so the doctor had not been paid. The patient had ignored the second and third notices, thinking he had paid.

```
Dear Mr. Wilson,

   I know that economic times are not good, and I wonder
if you are having a problem about which I do not know.

   My office has sent you three bills for professional
services and we have not heard from you. I am always
happy to work with patients on their accounts and to
give consideration to circumstances.

   You can understand, however, that the expenses of my
own office continue to go on and that I must inquire
about money that is owed.

   We are enclosing another bill, and I hope that I may
hear from you soon.

                    Sincerely,
```

The bill was paid immediately. Mr. Wilson was a little embarrassed but the matter was cleared up satisfactorily. Remember: in this stage, be considerate, but do not give up your claim.

4. *Persuasion letters.* Usually you write only one letter like the example above. If such a letter is going to work, it will usually work with one usage. If it fails, you must apply stress. You can send several "persuasion" letters at intervals of about fifteen days. At this point, you can no longer assume that the customer has failed to pay through oversight or misunderstanding. You definitely have a problem with this customer.

What persuasion "appeals" can you make? All appeals should be directed to the *customer's* self-interest, not yours. Your company may really need the money that is owed, but if the customer has been unmoved by three or four communications that were routine or considerately written, he or she is unlikely to be concerned about your company's needs.

What can we assume about the customer's needs? How shall we address them? We can assume that the customer is a normal human being who wishes to keep his or her self-respect and to avoid the serious inconvenience that would result from loss of credit.

You cannot legally threaten the customer with loss of reputation. To publicize a customer's problems and poor record of debt-paying is unthinkable today. So use the other approaches. The self-respect theme would normally run through almost anything you write in this instance. Also, you still wish to retain good will if possible, and for that reason you will be as considerate as you can, while deliberately increasing stress. To retain good will, you can use certain "cushions": expression of thanks for past payments (if true) and for past business; promotion of sale or product; continued use of the techniques discussed in sales letters. Here is a letter from a department store to a customer who failed to answer four communications:

```
Dear Mrs. Wylie:

  On September 7, RAHNER's will begin a two-week Fall
Festival Sale and there will be bargains in all of the
store's departments. We hope that you will visit us and
inspect the many opportunities for money-saving
purchases.

  We notice, however, that you owe us $189.60 on your
30-day account, and that $101.62 of this sum has been
due for more than 90 days.

  We value you as a customer and we wish your credit
always to be good.
```

```
Enclosed is a bill. Please let us have your payment
right away, or let us hear from you.

                    Sincerely,
```

The first paragraph is a "cushion," notice of a forthcoming sale.

This letter raises the idea of credit loss but does not threaten it. There are many ways to phrase this idea:

"Your good credit rating has been built slowly and we know its value to you."

"A good credit rating in today's society is a valuable asset."

"It is a matter of serious inconvenience when a good credit rating becomes impaired." (This is slightly stronger.)

"You will wish to be able to continue charging merchandise up to your credit limit merely by presenting your charge card."

"You will wish to be fair with yourself about the matter of maintaining good credit."

"The responsibility for keeping in good repair the great convenience of ready credit is in large part yours."

Where the customer is a company rather than an individual, you might raise the specter of possible economic loss.

```
Dear Mrs. Enserl,

   We know that NELLY's is one of our newer accounts and
that NELLY's is a new store. We are happy to extend
credit to you.

   Your account is now more than 80 days in arrears, and
I am enclosing a new bill for the amount.

   You will wish to pay it at once. NELLY's will want to
have the latest line of cloth goods to offer its
customers this fall, and we wish to be able to fill your
orders promptly and fully.

                    Sincerely,
```

Persuasion letters are the heart of the middle phase of the collection process. They can be repeated as often as desired—until it is finally clear they are being ignored. They appeal directly to the delinquent's self-interest, and they usually suggest that the customer can avoid the loss of something that is valuable. These appeals can be stated in as many ways as you have the imagination to devise.

If you fail to collect at this point, you must accept the fact that the normal billing process of the early phase has not worked, and neither have the appeals of the middle phase. It is now time for the final phase. You must play your ultimate cards.

5. *"We are close to the end" letters.*   These letters usually are signed by high company officials. They suggest that the delinquent account has come to the attention of the highest persons in the company and that the matter is moving toward a rapid end. Such letters may renew appeals to the customer's self-interest and may contain such sentences as:

"The costs of legal action run high, and they would devolve upon you if this matter should be brought to court."

"It would be a serious matter for us to turn this matter over to our attorneys."

"Our company has an arrangement with a collection agency to help us in cases where those who owe us money will not take their obligations seriously."

Notice, however, what these sentences have *not* done. They have not set a definite date on which you will take the actions you have mentioned. They merely suggest what might happen and imply that the end cannot be far away.

Even at this point, with stress building rapidly, the high company official signing the letter will wish to appear reasonable and conciliatory. Toward the end of the letter, such language as the following might be appropriate:

"We are aware of business conditions today, and we stand ready to work with you toward reasonable methods of discharging this debt."

Or,

"We keep the door open to work with our customers so long as we see signs of sound intentions on their part. May we hear from you?"

6. *Final action letters.*   You have failed thus far. You no longer have satisfactory contact with the customer. You decide what action you will take and you write a letter notifying the customer of the forthcoming action and the date you intend to take it. You also may use telephone or personal calls. Telegrams also carry a special authority. Here is a typical letter:

```
Dear Mrs. Enserl,

   NELLY's has now owed us $1,723.79 on account for more
than eight months without making payment. You have heard
from us twenty times about this unpaid sum.

   Within ten days, you will be contacted by our lawyers
and you will shortly be served with papers preparatory
to a suit.
```

```
    Unless the bill is paid within ten days, you may
 confidently expect these things to occur.

                    Sincerely,
```

One caution: do not threaten a suit unless you mean it. Many firms prefer to use collection agencies which collect money on percentage. When you reach the "final action" stage, always do what you say you are going to do unless the final threat causes the delinquent to pay or to make some satisfactory arrangement.

FORM LETTERS

Form letters are not highly regarded by most people. When those receiving them say, "That's a form letter," they do not mean it as a compliment. But even those who criticize such letters in an off-handed way sometimes read and respond to them. A well-done form letter is an excellent business tool.

It has several advantages for the sender:

1. It is much cheaper than an individually prepared letter.

2. It saves time.

3. It frees you from having to write the same letter over and over.

4. It reduces boredom in offices where large numbers of letters must be sent.

Form letters deal with situations that come up again and again. For example, many sales letters are form letters. The early letters in a collection series can be form letters, as can answers to inquiries, credit letters, acknowledgments, adjustment letters, and many others. There are three basic kinds of form letters, each of which will be discussed in turn:

Whole letters, written to deal with situations that recur.

Fill-in-the-blank letters, where special information must be included.

Form paragraphs.

Looking first at *whole letters*, we see that they are just what the name implies. They are usually printed in large numbers and are not personalized. Many of them have been typed and then printed by offset. They may look individually typed, but they are not. The signature is usually printed also.

Here is an example of a sales form letter from a mail-order house. It refers the reader to two enclosures—a brochure showing items for sale, and an order blank. It is a perfectly satisfactory form letter with enclosures, and it should produce results. This letter, with minor changes, has been used by this mail-order house every third year for the past nine Christmas seasons. It has been unusually effective.

```
Dear Christmas Shopper,

    What is the worst thing about shopping at this time of
year? Tired feet? Worry about unbought presents? Finding
time for endless looking when the pressures of the
season already have you over-committed?

    The enclosed brochure lists 507 quality items which
you can order from us by mail. Each item is fully
described and is pictured. The cost is often lower than
the manufacturer's suggested retail price. Both figures
are given for your information.

    Our order form will make your shopping task easy.
Return yours to us as soon as you have finished studying
the brochure.

    REMEMBER: We must receive your order by December 1 to
insure delivery to you by December 23.

                Sincerely,


                Elaine M. Travis
                Sales Director
```

Not all *whole letters* are printed. Some are recorded on tape and are produced on automatic typewriters. These, however, are much more expensive than the printed kind.

Fill-in-the-blank letters differ from whole letters in that certain information must be added to them. A typical one might say:

```
Dear _____,

    We thank you for your order of _____(date)_____ . We
shall be sending _____ items _____ to you by Railway
Express. You may expect delivery by _____(date)_____ .

    Your bill totals _____(amount and itemization, if
necessary)_____ . We shall look forward to receiving your
check and we invite your future business.

                Sincerely,
```

These letters are sometimes printed to look typewritten; then the blanks can be filled in with an identical typeface. Probably the letter just cited could not have been produced that way, because the blanks to be filled in vary widely from letter to letter. It most likely will be produced on automatic typewriters. If so, the letter will type automatically, stopping at the proper points for the needed information. A good operator can keep several machines going at once.

The letter in Exhibit 6-7 from a bank did not need much information typed in—just the date, inside address, and salutation. The rest was printed in an identical typeface. Notice that this is not an especially good letter. The bank included all the information that was needed, but it broke the principles of effective writing discussed in Chapter 3. The sentences are long, and so are some of the words.

EXHIBIT 6-7.

January 21, 19—

Mr. Edward N. Burrell
141 Oak Street
Sacramento, CA 95813

Dear Mr. Burrell,

  Previously, we have called your attention to the matter of your checks being returned for the reason of insufficient funds. Since then we discover that it has been necessary for us to return other checks for this same reason. We feel that we cannot continue to carry indefinitely accounts that we must return checks for, because as you know return items necessitate special handling and the cost to us as well as to yourself is prohibitive.

  We hope that you will cooperate with us in taking the necessary steps to correct this situation, as it is serious and could necessitate the termination of our business status.

                    Sincerely,

                    Brandon T. Lipschutz
                    Vice President

Form letters are prepared for *situations* that arise regularly. *Form paragraphs* are prepared for *recurring points*. Members of the United States Congress get thousands of letters a year that require them to state their positions on issues. A great many Congress members now prepare individual paragraphs to cover the points they wish to make. They may have several versions of the same idea prepared in different ways with different shadings. These paragraphs are numbered and put in a computer. When, for example, a letter from a constituent arrives expressing an opinion on energy and federal aid to education, an assistant to the member of Congress can call the computer and order paragraphs 92, 31, 45, 79, and 22. After supplying the date, inside address, and salutation, the assistant can let the computer do the rest.

There is one risk. A careless or unskilled assistant can order up an answer that does not deal with the letter the constituent sent or one that deals with it badly. Recently, one constituent wrote his Congressman expressing concern on two points: the slowness of Congress in adopting a federal energy policy (he urged the Congressman to speed things up), and worry that the U.S. Department of Education is interfering too much in the operation of the nation's school system. Here is the answer he received:

```
Dear Mr. Tutwiler,

    Thank you for your comments on the nation's energy
problems.

    Our reliance on undependable foreign sources of energy
supply poses a great threat to our country's future
security and it is imperative that we take prompt and
effective action to combat this problem. Clearly, that
was the President's intent in urging Congress to act
upon an ambitious program for increased domestic energy
production. While I'm sure all would agree that this is
a worthy goal, I can understand some of your concerns.

    On June 26, I was one of only 25 members of the House
to vote against legislation which granted broad
authority to the President to stimulate the development
of a synthetic fuels industry by providing subsidies for
private industry to build synfuel plants. It also
established standby authority to involve the federal
government in the actual production of synthetic fuels
if private industry failed to meet certain production
goals. I opposed the bill because of its cost, estimated
by the Congressional Budget Office at $18 billion over a
five-year period, and its provisions for direct
government involvement in energy production.

    A central element of the overall energy program is the
decontrol of oil prices. I do support price decontrol
and am a member of the House task force seeking to win
Congressional approval of this measure. Higher oil
prices will promote some reduction in demand and will
produce some increase in domestic oil supplies. In
addition, these higher prices will make alternative
energy sources more economically competitive.

                    Sincerely,
```

This response does not directly address the points raised by the inquirer. It talks generally about energy, but does not explain why Congress was slow to adopt a coherent program. It does not mention the U.S. Department of Education, which was a major subject of the inquirer's letter. The member of Congress came off looking less than good because of this letter, which was produced inexpertly from form paragraphs on a computer.

However, form paragraphs can deliver good work. Even small offices can keep a loose-leaf binder with one or two hundred sheets in it, each sheet including a form paragraph that discusses a frequently recurring point. A good executive or assistant who can find the right paragraph and order numbers 11, 16, 93, and 14 (or some other appropriate combination) will produce correspondence that is both intelligent and pertinent.

PRINCIPLES FOR PRACTICE

1. Order letters and their acknowledgments are the "stuff" of which business profits are made.

2. Some inquiry letters will lead to a profit and some will not. It is important to take pains with both kinds.

3. A good claim letter must be precise. It should never sound antagonistic.

4. The key to writing a good adjustment letter is finding out whose fault it is that something went wrong. Once that is determined, you can proceed rather easily.

5. Credit letters must set forth all the stipulations that are attached to the use of the credit. And when you must say "no" to a credit application, you must use tact.

6. The collection process involves a carefully graduated series of letters in six ascending steps. The key to writing collection letters is to persist in a proper way as long as necessary or feasible.

7. Form letters and form paragraphs save time, money, and brain-power. When well done, they can be effective.

FOR FURTHER STUDY

1. You, John Tyler, are president of a trucking company in Washington, Iowa. Every Christmas you give your customers a calendar for the forthcoming year with your company name imprinted upon it. It is inexpensive and effective year-round advertising. Write a letter to the Reliable Calendar Company ordering 2,000 calendars to be delivered to you by November 15. Your order is dated March 15. You want the following imprint:

John Tyler Trucking Company
944 Bason Street
Washington, Iowa 52353
Telephone: (Area Code 319) 653-4926

You want wall calendars measuring 14 by 20 inches, Style X-3. List price is 97 cents per unit. Prepaid delivery via United Parcel Service is requested.

2. Reliable Calendar Company has received the order. However, the company wishes to ship the calendars in mid-August for the following reasons:
  a. If an imprinting error is made, there must be time to correct the error.
  b. Late fall shipments are unreliable, because a heavy influx of parcels overloads all methods of transportation, including United Parcel Service.

Write a letter acknowledging the order, and asking that Mr. Tyler return an enclosed card giving his approval to the mid-August shipping date.

3. You are vice-president for inventory for a large firm that sells building supplies. You have ordered 2,000 sheets of aluminum siding from a regular supplier. You specified Catalogue No. 1423, but you were sent No. 1427a, which is a smaller size. You also paid $247.50 in trucking costs before you realized the error. Write a claim letter to your supplier requesting these things:
  a. That the 1427a siding be picked up at your warehouse.
  b. That the 1423 siding be delivered.
  c. That the supplier refund to you the $247.50 trucking costs.
  d. That the 1423 siding be delivered within five days, as a major customer needs it.

Indicate that your letter confirms an earlier telephone conversation.

4. You run a novelty sales business. A bank has ordered 200 small leather pouches with the bank's logo imprinted in gold on them. The bags will be given as favors at a banquet. You order them from a company in Texas and the bags are delivered directly to the bank. Because the imprinting is unprofessional, the bags are unacceptable. The bags cost you $7.72 each, and you sell them to the bank for $10.49. Write a letter to the company in Texas explaining that the bags are being returned to them. This adjustment letter is easier to write than most, because you have not yet paid the Texas bill. You ask the Texas company to send the bank a check for $28.64 to refund the money the bank paid Federal Express for delivering the bags.

5. Write a letter to the bank explaining what happened about the bags. (The imprint should have been stamped on three times. An inexperienced operator did it twice.) Offer to supply the bags on a rush basis from another company. You can have the bags in time for the banquet. Explain that you have requested that the bank be refunded the Federal Express expenses. Offer to pay these costs if the Texas company does not.

6. As owner of The Style Salon, a shop specializing in fashionable women's wear, you personally review all applications for credit and you sign all credit letters. You have received a credit application from Ms. Bonnie Clyde, and investigation shows that she is a good credit risk. Write Ms. Clyde a letter approving credit for her. Be sure to include all the elements suggested by the text.

7. Ms. Ruthanne Drexler also has applied to The Style Salon for credit. You have checked her rating and find that she is slow to pay, and that one department store in town has written off her charges as a bad debt. You still wish, however, to keep Ms. Drexler as a cash customer. Write a letter to her that is as considerate as possible, but that says "no" to the credit application while inviting cash business.

8. Banks sometimes have problems with customers who overdraw their accounts. Where the bank knows the customer, it will sometimes pay checks drawn upon such accounts, expecting to recover the sum from the customer. Assume that you are a bank officer. A small firm that has had an account with your bank for nine years is now in financial difficulty. The firm's account is $402 overdrawn. Remembering the six steps of the collection process, write one letter for each step to the president of the firm, Mr. Eric Dillham, seeking to collect. Go all the way to the last step, your sixth communication, and in that step close the account and inform Mr. Dillham that you are turning the matter over to a collection agency.

9. Following is a letter used by a bank in its collection process. It is a form letter. It could be much better. It falls into the second- or third-notice category of the collection process. Criticize this letter; then write one that is better:

```
Gentlemen of

  Emerson Garment Company
  $233.00
  Cust. #7339356

  Enclosed is a photocopy of this past due invoice. If you
```

```
need more information before it can be paid, please tell us.
If not, please send us your check in the return envelope.

                         Sincerely,


                         R. P. Smalley
                         Credit Manager


Enclosure
```

10. The very large company for which you work has its headquarters on the West Coast. It has been announced that in two years the headquarters will move to Richmond, Virginia. You have been sent ahead to Richmond to open a small advance office and to look after the company's interests there. You get a lot of letters of inquiry asking about the company, employment opportunities, and the company's products. You also get a good many requests for contributions to charitable organizations. After consulting your West Coast superiors, you decide to make no contributions for some time, possibly two years. You wish to assess the local situation carefully before you start giving money. Write a *form letter* explaining this and giving good reasons why. The letter should be general enough to refuse all requests without unduly ruffling feathers.

11. In relation to the question above, write a *form paragraph* expressing your company's pleasure in coming to Richmond. You will use this paragraph to lead off all your letters responding to inquiries.

12. The following form letter, used by a small factoring company (three employees) in the South, acknowledges orders. The blanks are usually filled in neatly with pen and ink and the signature at the bottom is real. This is an acceptable use of a form letter by a small company. Using it as a guide, prepare a form letter that your own small company might use to order materials and goods.

```
Dear Customer:

This will confirm your order of _____(date)_____ .

Enclosed you will find a photo-copy of your order giving
you all the details. Please check it carefully for
discrepancies; then sign in the lower right-hand corner
and return it to us at your earliest convenience. Should
you find any discrepancies, simply correct them right on
the face of the order before signing and returning it to
us.
```

You can expect shipment of your order to be made
_____(date)_____ by ___(conveyance)___ . In the meantime,
if there is any further way we can help you, please let
us know.

Thank you very much; we appreciate your business.

               Sincerely,

               Rena M. Gottschalk
               President

13. Analyze the following form letter. It could be softer in tone and still be effective. Rewrite this letter. Consider using the Empathy-Content-Action model.

Dear Customer:

  Your net billing for the calendar year of 19— was
under $3,000.

  As we have advised you in several letters and
mailings, and at various trade shows, rising costs and
distribution expenses have made it prohibitive for us to
service an account whose total net billing for the
calendar year was not at least $3,000.

  We deeply regret the necessity of instituting a policy
of minimum billing; however, to offer good service and
quality products we are unable to keep accounts on our
books who did not meet the requirements as established.

  In these difficult times, I feel sure you will
understand the necessity of this decision.

               Yours very truly,

SECTION
III

Getting Your Message Across Through Reports and Memos

CHAPTER 7

To: The Reader
From: The Authors
Subject: The Strategy of Writing

After reading this chapter, you will have learned:

1. The extent and importance of writing memos and reports on many jobs.

2. That the general principles of effective writing apply to memos and reports as well as to letters.

3. The use of strategy in planning to write.

4. Criteria for a good memo or report.

5. An approach to analysis of a reader and a situation.

6. The value of planning.

Strategies for Writing Memos and Reports

This chapter will help you sense even more the importance of learning to write well. It will also show you the need for planning your strategy. The rest of this section, Chapters 8 through 11, will help you improve your skill in writing memos and reports, *using the principles you learned for letter writing*. Please study these chapters carefully. Many of the suggestions included in them will apply to you.

PAPERWORK

"A river," said "Cap" Stone, production foreman.

"Troublesome," said Ern Moore, salesman.

"Costly," said Bill Freely, expeditor.

"Keeps me in business," said Jill Jenks, office manager.

"Still necessary," all four chorused.

These comments and names are fictional, but they could all be answers to a real question: "What do you think about paperwork in your organization?"

Paperwork indeed is like a river in flow, sometimes in flood. It goes on and on. Paperwork is troublesome and costly. And written reporting does keep Jill Jenks and all the operators, collators, and mail people busy.

Written reporting increases the cost of almost any product or service. In some industries, such as insurance and banking, paperwork accounts for most of the operating overhead. Even in industries like steel rolling and auto assembly, where "production" is the key word, some paperwork is necessary. You can scarcely imagine carrying on any business activity in a complex society without some letters, memos, and reports.

How much does all this paperwork cost? Current estimates suggest that a routine business letter costs more than a casual lunch. This estimated cost of a letter covers only writing or dictating, typing, mailing, and providing supplies—just the cost of getting your thoughts on a piece of paper and getting the piece of paper to a reader. The cost does not include the time spent researching the files to answer an inquiry, checking the account to mail a collection letter, studying the claim before sending an adjustment letter, and the like. Moreover, the basic cost does not pay for any reader's time.

The cost of writing memos and reports probably far exceeds the per-page cost of writing a letter. Writing a memo or report usually takes more time per page than writing a one-topic business letter does. Also, some business letters can be form letters with a lower per-letter cost. Again, the cost of a memo or report goes far beyond the simple cost of getting words on a page. In fact, preparing even a single page in a technical report or proposal could easily cost several person-days.

The obvious costs of paperwork are not the major costs. Paper, supplies, and postage usually account for only a minor part of the total cost of a letter, memo, or report. The time spent in researching and thinking usually costs most in a reporting project. But other major costs come from writing or dictating, typing, editing, retyping, reproducing, and sending the paperwork. Then come the costs of time spent reading.

Behind every letter, memo, or report lurks a greater, even more dangerous, cost: the cost of an error. A mistake in a proposal can result in a bid so high that it costs the bidder a contract, or a mistake can turn a planned profit into a terrible loss. A mistake in a simple memo explaining a new system of overtime can cause chaos in a plant; a faulty research report can commit a company to produce a money-losing product. Thus the costs of bad paperwork may far exceed the other costs of producing a memo or report.

Why do we need to discuss the extent and cost of producing memos and reports? The preceding discussion should lead you to these conclusions:

1. Paperwork, although costly, is necessary—at least some of it. Large organizations cannot run without memos and reports. Government regulations, geographical separation, complexity of work, and many other factors make written messages indispensable. Even small companies or agencies need some paperwork.

2. Almost any responsible job in business, industry, or government will require you to write memos and reports.

3. People will judge you at least partly by the memos and reports you write.

4. Therefore, the question you should ask yourself is not "Should I write memos and reports?" Instead, you should ask yourself: "How can I write better memos and reports?" "When must I write a memo or a report?" "How can I write more efficiently, spending less time and getting better results?"

Now you have learned three key ideas: first, report writing costs time and money on the job. Second, in many courses in school and almost every organization you are required to write reports. Thus, if you are a student, better reports should lead to better grades. Or if you are a typical employee rising in the ranks, you can expect to write many memos and reports in your lifetime. Third, improving your skill in writing memos and reports is a worthy goal.

REPORTS AND MEMOS—THE NERVOUS SYSTEM OF ORGANIZATIONS

Suppose that you are sitting at your desk with a yellow legal pad that is blank. You have just completed a study of your small company's data-processing needs. Jerry Hines, president, founder, and majority owner, had assigned you this project. You have worked hard for more than three weeks, talking with your own company's data-processing users and talking with people from other small companies. You have talked to the folks in finance. You even talked to the manufacturing people at a special meeting.

Now the time for talk has passed. Mr. Hines expects your report in final form Friday. Today is Tuesday, and you must write your report in time to get it edited, typed, and checked.

The talking steps were pleasant. You find the ideas stimulating, the responsibility challenging.

But now you must *WRITE* that report. And if you are like most people, you dislike writing.

We shall deal with actual writing a little later. Let us first put report and memos in perspective.

Reports and memos are the nervous system of organizations, regardless of type. Service companies, manufacturers, distributors, government agencies, and even nonprofit organizations differ widely in their specific goals.

For example, foundations try to give away money. Private companies usually try to make a profit. Government agencies try to concentrate on a mission and prevent a budget cut. But one characteristic all organizations share is a need for written records.

Written reporting is vital for several reasons:

1. People are often widely separated. A report written in Chicago may go to an accountant in St. Louis and then to field offices in Atlanta, Denver, and San Francisco.

2. Events in an organization's history may span a long time. A report protects an organization against the fallibility of human memory. For example, results of tests of a proposed engine for an automobile may not appear in an automobile until four years after the testing ended.

3. Legal restrictions, government regulations, court decisions, and contracts often call for written documentation of facts and decisions.

4. Complex decisions must dovetail with other complex decisions. The sheer complexity of many products defies mere oral discussion. Even if the designers of a main frame computer and related software tried to rely only on each other's discussion, manufacturing people and eventually the customers would still demand production specs, parts lists, service and installation manuals, training manuals, and reference manuals.

5. Employees do not stay on their jobs forever. They die, retire, transfer, and are fired or demoted. If the organization depended solely on their oral commitments or their own knowledge, departure of even lower-ranking employees would cause chaos.

6. No organization today can depend on the irreplaceable person. Instead of entrusting its destiny to an employee's memory, the organization protects itself with the contents of its filing cabinets.

Thus reporting systems serve the organization as the nerve networks serve the human body. The nerves carry instructions to the body's parts. The nerves carry pain and other sensations to the body's control management (the brain). Just so, the reports carry orders out to subsidiaries, divisions, and even individuals, and they carry responses back to the control management.

Every organization that includes more than a very few people depends on the written report to carry on its work. Recommendations, reports of investigations, studies, surveys—all sorts of findings from lower-ranking employees—move up the "chain of command." Instructions, decisions, orders—the product of higher management—go back down the channels. Very often, the only tangible output from conferences, investigations, or other activities is some sort of written document.

But the very complexity of organizations and their goals demands reports that make the report writer's job difficult. You can grasp this problem by imagining that you are any of the following employees of an electric utility company:

- Bert Halloran is an electrical engineer working in power distribution. He holds a master's degree in electrical engineering.
- Cathie Poll is a biologist working in environmental protection. She monitors the water quality in the company's hydraulution lakes. She has a Ph.D. in microbiology.
- Steve Jordan is a quality assurance inspector in nuclear power generation. He writes quality surveillance reports on the vendors' products bought by his company. He retired from the Navy's nuclear sub force and has many years' experience plus training in service schools.
- Lucius Pressly is an accountant by job and training. He serves as an internal auditor checking company expenditures.
- Callie Stewart sells the company's product. She calls on architects and prospective building owners to offer her expertise in designing lighting systems, power circuits, etc.
- Joseph Kelly is a line installation crew chief. His crew puts up poles or lays underground cables. He came up through the ranks. Although he has had no formal training, he has two decades of experience behind him.

Now, if you were any of these people (fictitious names, but real jobs), you would speak somewhat the same language they all speak. But you might find yourself referring to reports or instructions from someone whose technical background differed from your own. And your reports might go to some readers whose backgrounds differed from yours.

Reports vary in purpose, length, and formality, and they can flow to and fro in almost all major activities: research, development, planning, design, operations, buying, selling, and collecting. Reports vary in length from a filled-in form or a brief one- or two-paragraph memo, to documents of hundreds of pages. Reports vary in formality from hand-written, informal notes to printed, heavily illustrated documents. Some typical reports include:

- research and test reports
- literature reviewing and state-of-the-art reports
- proposals and requests for proposals
- investigation reports, inspection reports, and trip reports
- minutes of meetings and conferences

- recommendations for decisions
- audits
- progress reports based on time intervals
- annual reports
- vendor visitation and inspection reports
- recommendations
- instructions
- installation, service, and training manuals
- descriptions

Regardless of their type, almost all reports meet one or more of these purposes: to inform the reader(s); to get some type of action; or to serve as a written record.

You may dread writing a report. But being asked to write a report can be flattering. When someone asks you to write a report, you are being asked to render management an important service. Your readers need your report because they either (1) know less about the subject than you do, or (2) do not have the time to gather the information your report provides. In either case, your reader trusts you and respects what you offer in writing; otherwise, your report would be an idle exercise.

You must recognize that writing a report is a uniquely human activity. When you are writing a report, you are rendering a service that the most sophisticated computer cannot match.

Given the importance of reports and memos, the following chapters will help you to make them

- more useful to you and your employer
- more accurate and more nearly correct
- clearer, more readable, and more understandable
- more concise
- less costly

The important steps in planning are (1) developing your strategy, (2) analyzing your reader and the situation calling for a memo or report, and (3) thinking of the end-results of a memo or report. These steps should increase your chances of solving problems with better reports; improving your organization's operations; and, quite frankly, attracting favorable attention to yourself.

Planing a memo or report (handwritten annotation in left margin)

Developing Your Strategy

The strategy of writing is usually more important than the actual word-by-word process of writing. Most of us have had some training in the mechanics of writing. Long-suffering English teachers tried to teach you to use language *correctly*. That is, you learned to obey the rules of grammar, spelling, and sentence structure (syntax). Such training is valuable. After all, as you rise toward the higher levels of your organization, your readers will notice your language habits, just as they will your other habits.

Despite the importance of language habits, your first thoughts should be concerned with the "big picture." You must first consider the entire process of generating your memo or report so that you can develop an overall strategy. Exhibit 7-1 shows you the general steps involved in preparing a formal report. Although the process may vary somewhat for differing reports, you should be acquainted with the entire process and keep it in mind from the very beginning.

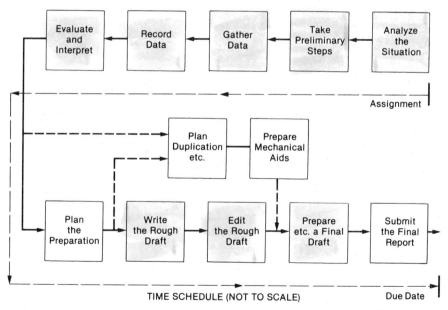

EXHIBIT 7-1.
Steps in Preparing a Formal Report

The Price of Writing Without a Strategy

The rest of this chapter will discuss the importance of strategy, that is, of your overall approach. Here are some actual situations that show the folly of ignoring sound strategy or of paying attention only to the mechanics of writing. (Pretend that you are each of these writers. The people have fictitious names, but the situations have occurred many times.)

Situation 1 Murphy is a staff expert on computer graphics for his plant. Highest management sent Murphy to a manufacturer's seminar. Although the seminar was free, Murphy's company paid his expenses and relieved him of his duties for three days. Murphy knew how important computer graphics could be to his plant; so when he returned, he spent many hours on his report. It included every detail—an hourly schedule of each day in the seminar, even the times he went to lunch! He revised the draft until it was in flawless English. He asked his wife, who had always gotten good grades in English, to check his report.

However, Murphy's boss, Sarah H., did not like the report. She wanted to know, quickly and clearly, "What did you learn from this seminar?" or more importantly, "What did you learn that we should apply? Should we buy that manufacturer's equipment? Should we send other people to the seminar?"

Question: If you were Sarah, how would you tell Murphy to change his report?

Situation 2 Jonathan L. faces a real problem. His group is falling behind schedule despite all his efforts. He sees only three ways to get back on schedule: (1) hire two more machine operators, (2) bring some people in on overtime, or (3) subcontract part of his group's work to an outside vendor. He recommends taking all three steps.

Paul, his immediate supervisor, nearly explodes when he reads Jonathan's memo: "Jonathan, where have you been? You knew we were in an austerity program. You knew the V.P. was on a cost-cutting crusade. Yet you asked for three steps, any of which will increase expenses!"

Question: What would you have suggested to Jonathan, assuming that he felt he had to take all three steps?

Situation 3 Martie suspects that some employees are taking company tools home. Sets of drill bits seem to vanish. Before he left on vacation, Julian, her supervisor, told her, "I want to find out why inventory changes so much in tool crib. Harry [the big boss] is raising the devil, and he told me to find out. While I'm on vacation, look into this, and get me a report."

Martie thinks she has solved the mystery. She writes a report outlining her suspicions, presenting the facts on inventory. She has it typed to be ready for Julian's return next week.

Then she thinks: "I'd better get this report to Harry, so he can take action now." So she sends the report to Harry. Julian returns from vacation to find that:

• Harry is demanding a plan to stop the theft, but Julian has not seen Martie's memo when Harry confronts him.

• The secretary who typed the memo gossiped about Martie's secret findings. Rumors are flying.

Question: If you were Julian, what would you tell Martie?

Situation 4   Tim heads your company's Data-Processing Committee. After its last meeting, Tim summarized the discussion that took place: "So we have decided that we do not have enough computer power. One, we have only a low-level compiler. Two, we have only 36K storage. We need on-line 18K. Three, we need much faster RAM time. Four, we need more real-time terminal modes to replace our batch modes."

And Tim writes just these words to ask top management for a quarter of a million dollars for new equipment. His request is a masterpiece of assembling unfamiliar data. He has graphs and charts to show random access times, flow charts to show inputs, and so forth.

In the management dining room about three days later you overheard the comptroller talking to the manager of finance: "Tim is trying another 'snow-job.' He thinks if he can intimidate us with that computer jargon we'll sign a blank check."

Tim is shocked to learn that top management has turned down his request for a larger computer system. He complains bitterly to you, "This outfit is 'horse-and-buggy.' We act as though the computer had just been invented. I give up. What can I do?"

Question: What can you say to Tim?

THE IMPORTANCE OF STRATEGY

These four situations had two factors in common:

All the writers were serious, dedicated people. All tried to do a good writing job. All had carefully checked their reports or memos, and all had produced writing that was mechanically perfect. An English teacher would probably have given each of them an "A" for correctness.

But:

All these writers neglected the strategy of writing. All seemed to think that writing is intended only to produce words. All seemed to think that a memo or report is an end unto itself, that an assignment to write is an assignment only to produce a memo or a report.

Thus all these writers failed to study the strategy of writing in a real-world situation. *Strategy* means *the overall, general approach*. Strategy differs from *tactics, the specific ways of carrying out the overall approach.* You are already familiar with strategy in many fields. You might speak of military strategy as the general plan of winning a war, such as whether to fight on land or sea. The tactics of warfare involve moving individuals or small groups. In business the overall strategy may be to increase profits through new product research; business tactics may involve particular sales campaigns. But in any activity, those who succceed plan their strategy before they choose tactics.

When you write, you should plan your strategy—the desired end-results for a given set of conditions and for a particular reader (sometimes for more than one reader). Only then can you select your tactics—the way you put your report or memo together, the words you choose, the charts or other visual aids you use. If you start writing (carrying out tactics) before you plan strategy, you will almost certainly waste time. You will miss your target and fail to meet your deadline. In fact, if you bury yourself in detail before you plan your approach, you may even write a needless memo or report. Strategy might have led you to make a phone call instead of writing.

You will learn shortly how to plan your strategy. But first, you need to study the desired end-result.

"This memo is all wrong, Farnsdale...Didn't you see my latest memo on how to write a memo?"

GRIN & BEAR IT by George Lichty © Field Enterprises, Inc., 1980
Courtesy of Field Newspaper Syndicate

Criteria for a Good Memo or Report

Obviously, part of your strategy is to produce a "good" memo or report. The memo below offers guidelines for good memos and report. Indeed, had the "Bureau of Memos" chief in the cartoon given Farnsdale the following memo, their problems might have been avoided.

```
      To:  The Reader
    From:  The Authors
 Subject:  Criteria for good memos and reports
```

Good memos and reports meet the following criteria:

- usefulness: A good report meets a need, yours or your reader's. You have seen that memos and reports are costly. You must make sure that your on-the-job writing really has a purpose. You must determine what that purpose is.

- accuracy: Many decisions depend on reports. If yours presents wrong ideas or recommends unwise steps, a wrong decision may be made. Your readers have a right to expect that they can depend on what you tell them.

- readability, understandability, and clarity: These characteristics are related. All of them affect your reader's ability to absorb your ideas. Your writing must be readable; thus your reader should understand your words and sentences. Moreover, the pattern of your writing—beyond your words, phrases, and sentences—should be easy to understand. Finally, the idea you are trying to convey must be clear from what you have written.

- conciseness: Concise writing carries your ideas with a minimum of wordage. Because your words use up a reader's time, you must make them work for you. If you write long, rambling, padded sentences, you risk (1) wasting your reader's time and (2) confusing your reader(s) by burying key ideas.

- suitability to your reader's needs: Your memo or report must supply what your reader either wants to know (if the reader has asked for your report) or *should* want to know.

- timeliness: Ideally, your memo or report will reach your reader just when he or she can give it attention and act on your recommendation.

- appropriateness: You must employ proper "mechanics"—spelling, capitalization, abbreviation, and use of numbers.

- formality: A brief note to a fellow worker differs from an important report to top management. You follow

```
habits of dress and dress according to circumstances.
In deciding how formal writing should be, follow the
same principle.
```
- efficiency: The most important costs in report writing come in preparing for the report (gathering and interpreting the facts). However, the in-between costs can be high. Your writing should be as low-cost to produce as possible.

These criteria should serve as guides for every memo and report.

ANALYZE YOUR READER AND THE SITUATION

As you have seen, correctness of grammar, spelling, and punctuation is important. But you should not emphasize the mechanics of writing at the expense of the purpose of good writing, which is to communicate ideas. For several reasons, a good report is more than just a correct piece of writing. Your memo or report always faces competition for the attention of your reader. Furthermore, your reader almost surely knows less about your subject than you know, and an idea may lose some meaning when it is transmitted from one mind to another. Although you will not convey every thought exactly the way you intend, you must try to transfer ideas as effectively as possible.

Let us see how to analyze your reader, your reader's situation, and the way these two factors can affect your writing. (As Chapter 12 shows you, you would follow this same approach in analyzing an audience for a presentation.) First, you need to know the ways in which your readers differ.

Readers differ in:

- general knowledge developed through training, education, and experience
- specific knowledge of the particular topic on which you are writing and level of decision making (what they *can* do about your recommendations, for instance)
- relationship to and regard for you: (1) how much faith they have in what you say and (2) whether they have found your previous written work to be reliable
- preferences—their likes and dislikes or biases
- attitude toward your topic—their interests and concerns

You do not write in a vacuum. Your readers are not isolated. Other factors—what you might call readers' "situations"—affect the way you write any memo or report. Readership situations include:

● other factors competing for the readers' attention—distractions, pressures, reports from other people

● the seriousness of your subject—the issues involved, the problems, even the "booby traps"

● the risk/reward ratio—what your readers will gain or lose from paying attention to your writing

● the "ground rules"—your organization's policies; regulations affecting your subject; any guidelines (such as requests for proposals or bid specifications); any other decisions or rules; and any laws or government regulations affecting your proposals

● the schedule—when and where your memo or report will be done and any delivery time needed for your memo or report to reach your reader

● the "track record" of your other communications—how receptive your readers have been to your earlier memos or reports

You must also analyze the end-result for your report. A report is a management tool, intended to meet a need or solve a problem. Borrowing a term from finance, you might consider the final use for a report the "bottom line." Ask yourself: "Where will my report go? Who will use it?" Many of your reports will focus on a single idea. For example, your progress reports will answer the bottom-line question from your boss: "How is your work going?"

You must focus on the end-result use of your report before you start writing, or even before you start gathering information. Otherwise, you will not know which facts to use and which to discard. You will not know what visual aids and attachments to get or to start planning.

All these factors can affect:

● what you write (what details you include and what questions you answer)

● the style of your writing (the formality, tone, and organization)

● the priority and urgency of your work (how much time you spend, and whether the writing is "quick and dirty" or polished)

● the assumptions you can make (what your reader knows, wants to know, or needs to know)

These factors and the whole matter of strategy should not frighten you. Analyzing the reader and the situation is simple; it requires only a few minutes. But reader/situation analysis can be the most worthwhile few minutes you spend.

You can see how to analyze the reader and the situation and how to plan your writing by studying the following problems:

Problem 1:   Study has shown that you need to upgrade your computer. This costly step will need top management approval.

Your decision: You translate the technical data and terms into ideas top management will understand—faster "turnaround" of print-outs, faster reports, better control; more jobs the upgraded computer can handle; and lower per-job costs for computing.

Problem 2:   Sam White, your boss, tells you that he must be in Washington *tomorrow morning* to give the Nuclear Regulatory Commission a review of what happened at your reactor generator plant. You have already gathered the facts but thought you had at least a week to assemble them. He wants notes on which to base his discussion.

Your decision: You drop every other job on which you are working. You ask for a secretary for the rest of the day. You outline (in five minutes) what you will write. You then dictate the notes hurriedly. As soon as the typist completes a page, you edit it. You remember that your notes will be only notes, not a finished report. When the typist completes the last page of the edited first draft, you ask that a second draft be typed. Then you check the second draft carefully. You then have a final draft typed, check it, and have it duplicated. You also prepare the attachments (tables of data). When you take the final draft to Sam, you warn that you wrote it under pressure, and you promise a full report for next week.

Problem 3:   You have represented your company at a hearing before a government agency. You committed your company to certain construction work. (Higher management had approved this commitment in advance.) Your written report must do two tasks: (1) advise top management of the decisions and commitments you made and (2) tell your operating, engineering, and construction people of the details of these commitments.

Your decision: You write two reports. The first report summarizes decisions and commitments and goes only to top management. It refers to the second report, which contains full details, in case top management wants a copy. The second report, with the first report as an introduction, goes to the heads of the operating, engineering, and construction branches.

Problem 4: You must write your monthly progress report on the Shim-Stamping Section, which you supervise. You know that your organization's progress reporting system works like an inverted filter. That is, people on each level abstract the main ideas from the reports coming upward, summarize the ideas, and then group the items.

Your decision: You make the reading easy for the reader. You (1) start your report with an overview, a summary, of progress for the month, (2) cover the major items, and (3) close with a forecast for the coming period. You move the details (production records, safety record, and hours worked) to attachments. You pattern these attachments on the format Jake Besler, your boss, uses in his own report.

SUMMING UP

An ounce of strategy . . . is worth a pound of cure. This adaptation of the old cliché holds true. Every one of the situations above actually happened. In some cases the writer did not follow the strategy suggested—with sad results!

PRINCIPLES FOR PRACTICE

1. Paperwork is part of the cost of almost every product or service.

2. People will judge you by your memos and reports.

3. The strategy of writing is usually more important than the actual word-by-word process of writing.

4. A good report is useful, accurate, readable, and concise.

5. A good report is suited to your reader's needs in terms of information, language, timing, and formality.

6. Planning for writing takes little time; writing without planning invites disaster.

These situations differ widely, but they all teach one lesson: You must develop a strategy before you start writing. To write without a strategy is to invite disaster.

Developing a strategy requires little time. You could have done it in a few minutes for some of the situations above.

FOR FURTHER STUDY

1. If you spend fifteen minutes in writing a one-page memo, how much would writing it cost? (What salary do you assume you would make?) Do not forget the indirect cost—your fringe benefits, the pro-rated cost of equipment and office space, and other indirect costs.

2. How long would you probably need to write or dictate a one-page, single-spaced memo or letter? Do not forget the time you spend in revising and checking what you have written.

3. Why do larger organizations usually require more paperwork per employee than smaller organizations require? (Note that the question refers to "more paperwork *per* employee," not just to "more paperwork.")

4. Some simple societies have little need of writing. What are the major factors that cause our complex society to create so many memos and reports?

5. Why not transact nearly all business orally?

6. How much does a piece of paper cost? How much do you suppose your college or university's paperwork increases the cost of your schooling?

7. Think about the people in some organization you know well, for example, your school or a place where you have worked. How many of them seem to handle paperwork as a major part of their jobs?

8. Sam Fork, Office Manager, thinks your organization needs a policy on how to write reports. He has invited you to write the first section. What would you include?

9. How would a proposal to offer a company's product differ from a service manual for that product?

10. You are proposing a company's services for a maintenance program in a Middle Eastern country. Can you merely revise a proposal submitted previously in the United States? Why?

11. These people will get your next report: Jere Wonder, Production Supervisor; Sarah Queen, Public Relations; and R. T. Small, Accounting Manager. Your real story depends on technical data that only Jere Wonder understands. What will you do to translate the unfamiliar data for your other readers?

CHAPTER 8

To: The Reader
From: The Authors
Subject: Planning Memos and Reports

After reading this chapter, you will know:

1. The general principles of planning to write a memo or
    report.

2. The method of organizing ideas in a logical and
    psychological order.

3. The techniques of focusing a memo or report on the
    ''bottom—line'' question.

4. Ways to plan word processing.

5. Ways to use visual aids to reinforce your writing.

6. Methods of gathering information for your memo or report.

Planning Memos and Reports

"Outline before you write." You probably heard this advice in every one of your English classes. But, like Sandra Hatchett, you may have considered that advice bookish nonsense. Sandra still thinks that "making an outline takes too much time, all that arranging and numbering." But she wonders why writing even a short memo is so hard. Her secretary wonders why dictation sessions are so painful and why Sandra marks up letters already typed and retyped. Sandra's readers find reading one of her memos very hard work. They must struggle through thickets of trivial ideas to find the main point.

Here is the moral, for Sandra, for you, and for everyone else: *Plan before you write.* Always make some sort of outline. For writing or dictating even the briefest letter, make a mental outline. For writing a longer memo or report, jot down on a scratch pad the ideas you will use, and then arrange them in the order you want.

Outlining can save your time in dictating or writing. It is like having a set of working prints in building a home. Moreover, your outline will help you determine what kinds of information you will need to write your memo or report.

Yes, a few people do seem able to write with no evident plan. But most of us, certainly Sandra and probably you, should plan. A plan offers you the best assurance of a logical order in your finished writing.

LOGICAL AND PSYCHOLOGICAL ORDER

You may ask, "If an outline is supposed to assure logical order, what is 'logical order'?"

Actually, writing in *logical order* in a memo or report means grouping like items in the same paragraphs or same sections. Someone has defined logical order as having all the bananas in one basket, the apples in another, and the oranges in a third. For example, a safety inspection report might discuss hazardous personnel practices in one section, plant engineering defects in a second section, and minor housekeeping problems in a third section. You can usually make sense of logical order by reviewing your outline before you write.

But grouping related items is not enough to ensure a sound *psychological order.* Writing in psychological order means presenting your ideas in the order in which a reader can best receive them.

Suppose you have just come back from a trip to a work site. Your boss, Dick Willton, asks: "How was your trip?" But that question is just social noise. Dick is really wondering, "What did you find that I need to know?" This question is Dick's "bottom line," that is, his major interest. Recall how the previous chapter urged you to focus on the bottom line, the end-result, even before you started getting your facts? Good psychological order demands that you answer the bottom-line question as early as possible. Then you can present your facts to justify that bottom-line answer. This approach is similar in philosophy to the inverted pyramid style that will be discussed in Chapter 17.

Some people believe in the gradual build-up. They urge you to start with details and then, eventually, lead to the conclusion. This approach is called *"inductive order."* (See Exhibit 8-1.)

EXHIBIT 8-1

```
        TO:  Peter R. Stable, President
      FROM:  James P. Roach
   SUBJECT:  Cost Reductions

   We have considered all available data and sampled
opinions from various responsible personnel over the
past few weeks. We now believe that by exercising
conservative measures and taking appropriate steps, we
can cut our utility costs. We can also save money by
more carefully controlling scrap, rework, and
rejections. Further, we must seek ways to make our jobs
more efficient. Cost reduction is feasible and therefore
should be a major factor in our long-range planning.
```

The inductive approach is a logical one in which similar topics may be grouped in the same paragraph or same section. It moves from fact to fact to conclusion, much as one actually thinks when analyzing facts. But inductive order is not usually the best psychological approach in conveying ideas to a busy reader. You waste Dick's time if you drag him through your own thought processes, withholding the main idea until you have presented everything else.

Writing in an inductive order would be like answering Dick's question "What did you find out?" by saying, "Well, Dick, I left the office at 10:00 because I had a plane at noon, and I caught the 'limo' to the airport, and wouldn't you know, the limo got caught in a traffic jam. Well, I missed my plane, and . . . and . . . and. . . ." Then after about ten minutes of detail you would say, "By the way, the plant I visited has run far over its planned costs."

Your inductive order makes Dick plough through all those details until he learns your key idea.

Instead, you would probably start out with the bottom-line idea that interests Dick most: "The plant is far over costs, and we should stop the line immediately. Here's why. . . ."

Such an approach is called the *deductive order*. Deductive order, with the main idea coming early in a report, offers you and your reader several advantages:

1. You start by stating what you intend to prove. By stating the main idea early, you tell your reader what to expect.

2. You give your reader a choice of how far to read. Dick may want to know only the main idea. He may be in such a hurry that he wants to wait until later to read the proof. Or he may have such confidence in you that he needs no proof.

3. By putting the main idea early, you make sure that Dick will get at least the main idea. There you save Dick's time.

4. Dick may really understand only the bottom-line idea in a highly technical report. He may not understand the details.

5. You can get across the main idea first and then put in as much detail as you need.

6. By setting forth the main idea soon, you make sure you do not lose *your own* thoughts in details.

The memo written in inductive order in Exhibit 8-1 appears in deductive order in Exhibit 8-2.

Deductive

EXHIBIT 8-2

TO: Peter R. Stable, President
FROM: James P. Roach
SUBJECT: Cost Reductions

Cost reduction is feasible and therefore should be a
major factor in our long-range planning. Cost reductions
can most likely be achieved through conservation
(utility costs); control of scrap, rework, and
rejections; and improved job efficiency.

You may be wondering right now, "Should I always put the key idea early? If my report faces resistance, should I not lead up to it to keep my reader from rejecting it as soon as he or she reads the first paragraph?" Shortly, you will see how to handle the exceptions.

Now note that if Dick reads past the first few sentences of such a deductive trip report, he will know what you learned that the company can use. The deductive order clearly gives Dick one more advantage. Suppose that Janet, Dick's boss, meets Dick at lunch and asks about the trip. Dick can confidently tell her the main idea(s) he learned. He may not recall (or may not have read) the details, such as the names of the people you took to lunch. Janet would not expect Dick to recall such details. But he will know "the bottom line". Dick would not want to admit, "I can't recall; that trip report was so cluttered with detail I never got to the conclusion."

BOTTOM-LINE QUESTIONS

To make sure you give the bottom-line answer early, you need to know the bottom-line question. Actually, as the previous chapter emphasized, you should have asked yourself the bottom-line question before you started gathering your facts. Here are the key questions for typical reports:

- *a trip report:* "What did you learn that we can use?"
- *a progress report, status report,* or *stage report:* "How—in a sentence or two—is this project doing?"
- *a feasibility study:* "Should we do it?"
- *a monitoring report* or *inspection report:* "What, in a few sentences, did you learn, and what should we do as a result?"

- *a set of instructions:* "What is the worker supposed to do, and what are the desired end-results?"
- *a request for funds:* "What will these funds allow us to do, or to do better?"
- *a proposal:* "In an overview, what can we do for the reader?"

Some Exceptions to the Rule

The deductive order you have just studied almost always works, because it is psychologically sound. But, as always, there are exceptions to the rule. These situations require variations on the general principle of deductive order:

1. *You have to write in a format set by policy or by the reader's directions.* Perhaps your organization's standard format calls for the summary at the end. If so, you must follow that format until you attain a high enough rank to change it. The same situation prevails if you know, or suspect, that your reader prefers an upside-down format.

2. *You may write a report that faces serious objections.* Normally, you begin by summing up your ideas or recommendations. However, you may decide that a better strategy would be to acknowledge the reader's likely objections before you summarize your own ideas. For instance, you may request new equipment or more personnel during an austerity program. A sound psychological approach might call for a "buffer" paragraph to start the memo. This buffer paragraph could (1) admit the opposing view and perhaps even validate the view and then (2) summarize your proposal.

Note how this example overcomes the reader's resistance:

> Guidelines for the austerity program set up this quarter are clear, and my group has already started its cost-reduction program. However, this report will show why we must have a third-shift inspector to meet the quality-assurance program. This report will also show how our cost-reduction effort will more than offset the added cost of the third-shift inspector.

If you do not admit the opposition, you will be accused of not having "done your homework." Someone will surely raise the opposition anyway. And admitting the opposition takes away some of its force.

3. *You may need to state at least some background information or define the problem before you summarize your solution to the problem.* In such a case, state the problem as concisely as possible.

PLANNING THE COMPLETE PRODUCTION OF A
MEMO OR REPORT

Planning a memo or report calls for more than just making an outline. You must treat a writing job as a production outline. You may organize your writing well, you may write clearly, and you may edit carefully. But you have not completed your writing task until you have the final report ready. After all, your report cannot become a useful management tool until it reaches your readers.

Along the route to a completed report you may face many obstacles:

- getting draft(s) typed
- getting appended materials or attachments ready
- (perhaps) reproducing, collating, and binding the copies
- getting the report or memo to the target reader(s)

Sandra concentrates on writing. She disregards the work done by support people who must help her get her report ready. Listen to the coffee-break talk:

SANDRA'S TYPIST: . . . nice person, but everything she does ends up as a hurry-up job. She's always bursting in to ask me to rush a job instead of rushing the rush job she asked me to rush yesterday. She pushes me so fast to meet deadlines that I make too many mistakes.

SANDRA'S BOSS: Sandra thinks well. But she gets behind schedule, and then she lacks time to check her important memos or reports. She even leaves mistakes in arithmetic in reports.

THE SUPERVISOR OF DUPLICATION: Sandra forgets that we can reproduce typed pages easily, but some things we can't do easily. She calls for half-tone illustrations and multicolor runs. Often her bar graphs and pie graphs could be made with cross-hatched lines and therefore run easily instead of needing many-color runs.

THE MAIL ROOM CLERK: Sandra doesn't realize that mail delivery takes time. Also, she forgets that packaging takes time and that we close the postage meter at 4 o'clock every day.

THE ILLUSTRATOR: Sandra likes to use graphs in some of her reports for the "big wheels" upstairs. And I like to do good graphical work. But Sandra thinks I can knock out a decent bar chart as fast as she can sketch it. So she waits until the last minute to bring me the sketches. Then she expects the camera-ready chart in thirty minutes. I know she has thought about what she wants to show. Why can't she talk with me early? Then I'll draw her charts, and we'll only need to put on the page number.

Sandra's main problem is that she acts as though producing a report involves only writing. She does not work into her plans the nonwriting tasks someone must do.

PLANNING FOR WORD PROCESSING

If your workplace offers word-processing equipment, you can save time in editing; mass-produce typed letters, with minor changes in each letter; or produce final copy ready to reproduce. But to get best results from word processing, you must plan the work.

"Word processing" refers to a system for rapid typing of documents. This system of treating editing or typing like any other production problem cuts the cost of typing, editing, and final production of memos, letters, and reports. The per/unit cost for such documents should decrease with word processing. Any given word-processing system may call not only for high-speed equipment but also for centralizing of some secretarial work, realigning of certain duties, and learning of new skills.

Most word processors try to speed up one of two operations. One system displays the editing of drafts on a screen or other display. The other system commands a typewriter by memory storage. With the latter system the typist can hand-type an inside address and salutation, and the memory control will complete the typing. A few word-processing systems have both major capabilities. Other word-processing systems rely on simpler equipment, such as telephones to a central recorder or recordings sent to a typing pool.

Planning is most important in the key steps of word procesing: (1) typing the first draft, (2) recording the typing of the first draft, (3) revising the first draft, and (4) producing a final draft. In word processing, steps (1) and (2) usually occur at the same time, with memory devices "fed" by a typewriter.

Proper planning can increase efficiency most in steps (3) and (4). Once in memory (and depending on the equipment), the draft can be either (a) edited, with changes stored in memory, or (b) used as a master, form letter, with typed-out letters varied. In step (4) the system produces material far faster than a human typist can type (300 to 400 words per minute for an electric typewriter, hundreds of lines per minute for a computer printer).

Too many people think that automatic equipment assures good results. But like any other powerful tool, word processing poorly planned can multiply mistakes. Poor planning can result in wasted motion, idle equipment, the same mistake on dozens of letters instead of only one letter, steps taken out of sequence, or a costly system focused on producing only a few letters.

USING TABLES AND VISUAL AIDS

Tables, graphs, and charts share one characteristic: they are all visual aids, that is, supplements to phrases and sentences. Therefore, we shall define visual aids in memos and reports as communication devices other than words. For additional discussion of visual aids, especially see Handbook C.

You probably will not prepare your own visual aids. You will depend upon typists, illustrators, or drafting people. But you should learn how to plan with illustrators and reproduction people the preparation and inclusion of visual aids in reports. You should also learn how to select proper visual aids and how to assess the quality of visual aids.

Depending on the situation, the reader, and other factors, you may use any of the following types of visual aids:

- tables and data sheets
- engineering drawings, working prints, or maps
- technical illustrations, shaded drawings, sketches, isometrics, exploded views, and presentation drawings
- graphs and charts
- photographs and reproductions of photographs
- samples and models

As you write or dictate, you should consider whether a visual aid can carry your message better than sentences. If so, what types of visual aid could you use? What type would be best? Your decision could depend on these criteria:

- readers' needs, backgrounds, and uses for reports
- ideas to be presented
- relative importance of reports
- access to illustrators and reproduction people
- budgets (in time and money) allowed for reports
- usable or adaptable materials "on the shelf"
- schedules, especially deadlines, for reports
- final drafts—sizes, reproduction methods, and quality
- your own talents for planning visual aids

Visual aids differ widely, from simple to complex. However, you can observe some general principles and "rules of thumb" for visual aids:

- Visual aids deserve as much attention as other parts of reports. You should plan visual aids before you edit your first draft, or preferably sooner.

- Visual aids should show exactly what they are intended to show—no more and no less. Visual aids usually cost more than the same number of pages of typed text. And visual aids should meet your readers' needs.

- You should (1) obey copyright laws and (2) give credit for ideas from someone else. (Thus, ideas in this set of notes were suggested by various engineering societies and the American National Standards Institute.)

- You must consider reproduction and binding. For example, reproduction of photographs (half-tone) and color visual aids (color separation or multi-run) is costly. Binding usually requires an extra margin allowance.

- Visual aids should come as close as possible after the first text reference. An exception would be multi-page visuals. Usually, these should be attachments at the end of the report.

- Visual aids should add substance to the report. They should never be used for mere "window dressing."

- All visual aids should carry clear titles. If a report has several visual aids, you should number them.

- If readers must turn reports to read visual aids, they should turn reports 90 degrees clockwise (see Exhibit 8–3).

For additional information on visual aids, see Handbook C.

EXHIBIT 8–3
Rotation of Visual
Aids

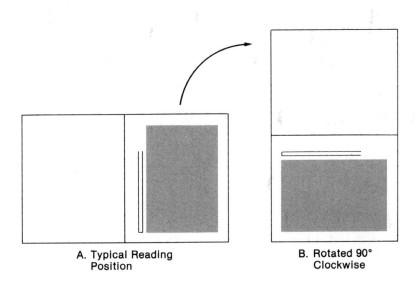

A. Typical Reading
Position

B. Rotated 90°
Clockwise

GATHERING INFORMATION

Now that you understand the importance of planning, you are ready to write. Right? Wrong! Now comes the time when you must gather and organize the information that will go into your report.

You have, of course, already determined the bottom-line question. Indeed, it is very likely that you already have much of the information that you will need once you have produced your outline. But it is important, at this point, for us to consider where information comes from, how you get it, and how you use it.

The information you will use in memos and reports comes from four main sources:

1. Observation.
2. Interviewing.
3. The library.
4. Surveying.

Observation

To some extent observation plays a role in all information-gathering efforts. It may involve simply looking or gathering impressions with no effort to validate or standardize data. Or it may involve "systematic observation" using standardized procedures, trained observers, or other control devices. *How* you might go about observing can be broken down into at least five types: (1) natural direct observation, (2) contrived observation, (3) mechanical observation, (4) indirect observation, and (5) records observation.

1. Natural direct observation means that the observer makes direct observations in a natural setting. Observers make no attempt to manipulate the circumstances; they simply record what they see or hear (or smell or taste).

2. Contrived observation is almost a kind of experiment in which a situation is established for the purpose of seeing what happens. This occurs, for instance, when airline executives fly unannounced on their company's flights to evaluate service given to regular customers.

3. Mechanical observation uses some kind of device (video cameras, stopwatches, turnstiles, audiometers) to make and record observations.

4. Indirect observation is a kind of Sherlock Holmes approach that seeks clues by which conclusions can be drawn about circumstances that cannot be observed directly. Physical evidence is most useful in this regard.

5. Records observation uses data already compiled. Production records, sales records, personnel records, computerized inventory data, or virtually any information that is systematically generated and stored can be useful in this respect.

Interviewing

It is often important to find out what someone thinks or knows when you are preparing your report or memo. Ranging from a few informal questions to highly structured, multiple sessions, interviewing can provide valuable data and insights.

Interviews should be planned in advance. You should know what information you need and develop a strategy for getting it. "Fishing expeditions" are usually a waste of everyone's time.

If you want similar kinds of information from several people, you will perform structured interviews. In these situations your questions must be prepared in advance and asked consistently.

You may develop a form for recording answers to certain structured interview questions. Shorthand and tape recorders are valuable tools when interviews are not structured.

The Library

Information needed to solve managerial problems is often found in books, pamphlets, articles, brochures, or other material located in public, university, or corporate libraries. You are probably not the first person ever to confront the situation you are dealing with; so it is likely that published materials can provide some information or insight.

The hard part, of course, is finding the information you need. A good reference librarian may be your best resource. But you should become familiar with basic, standard sources of information. Some of these include:

1. Atlases such as those published by *National Geographic;* almanacs such as *The World Almanac;* and yearbooks of various professions, trades, and countries.

2. Biographical directories such as *Who's Who in America; Who's Who in Commerce and Industry;* and *Poor's Register of Corporations, Directors, and Executives.*

3. Dictionaries such as *American College Dictionary, Webster's Collegiate Dictionary,* and *Webster's New International Dictionary.*

4. Encyclopedias such as *Americana, Britannica, Collier's,* and *Encyclopedia of the Social Sciences.*

5. Government publications such as the *Catalog of United States Census Publications* and the *Statistical Abstract of the United States,* which are published by the United States Government Printing Office in Washington, D.C.

6. Trade directories such as *Trade Directories of the World,* Ayer's, Kelly's, and Thomas's directories.

The standard source for locating books is the card catalog, which is cross-referenced in three categories: author, subject, and title. Periodical indexes are the best sources for locating articles. A few of the indexes important to business people are *Accountants' Index, Business Periodicals Index, Readers' Guide to Periodical Literature,* and the *Wall Street Journal Index.*

Surveying

Surveys are used quite frequently to gather information on a sample basis from large groups of people. They may be conducted by telephone, face to face, or most commonly, questionnaires. In any case, surveys involve series of questions.

In designing surveys you should make sure that your questions:

- are easy to understand
- elicit information specifically relevant to your needs
- are as simple as possible
- lend themselves to easy tabulation of results
- are valid and reliable

Entire books have been written on surveying techniques. Before attempting surveys, avail yourself of one.

SUMMING UP

Plan, outline, gather information: once you have completed these three steps, you are ready to write. Moreover, you will find your writing much easier. Writing, as the old saying goes, is 90 percent perspiration and 10 percent inspiration. Once you have planned, outlined, and gathered information, much of the sweat is behind you.

PRINCIPLES
FOR
PRACTICE

1. Plan before you write.

2. Outlines are necessary for organized and efficient presentation of information.

3. Good memos and reports follow both logical and psychological order.

4. Memos and reports start by answering the bottom-line question.

5. Good memos and reports require that the entire production process be planned.

6. Use visual aids when they convey messages better than words can.

7. Determine what information you will need and how you will get it before you start writing.

FOR FURTHER STUDY

1. Suppose you wanted to show enrollment in your school each fall for the past ten years. What types of graphs could you use? What type would you use?

2. You want to report on how you budget your time. You could, of course, use words. How else could you show your time allocations?

3. What problems would you face in using a pictogram to show employment in a large company?

4. You want to describe automobile ownership at ten-year intervals from 1900 until 1980. What types of visual aids might show your data? What problems would you face in trying to show your data by a bar graph?

5. Match the types of data in the left-hand column against the probable best way to convey the data to a reader. If two ways would work well, list both.

Type of Data	*Way to Show the Data*
_____ people's feelings about streets in your city	A. pie graph
_____ total sales and net income on those sales for ten years	B. bar graph

Type of Data	*Way to Show the Data*
____ prices of various books you have had to buy	C. segmented bar graph
____ your weekly schedule	D. line graph
____ locations of homes on lots in a subdivision	E. table
____ how an automobile gearshift works	F. pictogram
____ advantages of buying a certain make of car	G. cartogram
	H. histogram
____ regulations for conduct at your school	I. drawing
____ the pleasures of your favorite sport	J. sketch
____ the national budget this year	K. photograph
	L. area chart

6. Prepare an outline for the following topic: "Buying a home is an important decision that should be made carefully." When you finish your outline, write a draft. Do not edit the draft. Stop writing at the end of one hour.

7. What are the bottom-line questions for these reports?

- feasibility studies
- proposals
- job instructions
- job descriptions
- accident reports
- construction specifications
- recommendations for promotions

8. How would you arrange these topics in a plan for solving a problem?

- Option 1
- Option 2
- Option 3
- Statement of Problem
- Recommendation (of chosen option)
- Attachments
- Summary (brief)
- Detailed conclusions and recommendations

9. In any report recommending a course of action, what typical questions should you answer about the proposed course of action? (Hint: When is the action supposed to occur?)

10. Suppose you had to write a trip report to cover your vacation. Arrange these topics in a deductive order:

- problems faced
- difficulties overcome
- duration of trip
- purpose of trip
- routes taken
- method of transportation
- success (or failure) of trip
- places visited
- places stayed
- other topics (insert topics as appropriate)

CHAPTER 9

To: The Reader
From: The Authors
Subject: Writing Your Report

After reading this chapter, you will know:

1. The proper form for memos.

2. How to use headings and enumerations in reports.

3. The proper format for longer reports.

4. Ways to facilitate your writing.

Writing Your Report

After you have gathered all the necessary information, the next task is to put it in understandable form. Recall from Chapter 3 the three principles that can make all writing more understandable: keeping sentences short on the average; using simple words; and humanizing the content.

SHORT AND LONG REPORTS

Most reports are short. Although individual organizations may require differing formats, two forms are universally used: the letter report form and the memorandum report form.

The letter report form, starting with the date, letter address, and salutation and ending with a complimentary close and signature, is most frequently used when the short report is to be submitted to someone outside of your organization. The memorandum report form is used to communicate between people in the same organization. Usually, the memorandum report starts out with a heading similar to the following:

```
        TO:
      FROM:
      DATE:
   SUBJECT:
```

Complex problems usually require long reports including detailed information. To make the report easy to read, to emphasize important points, and to help their readers follow their thoughts from one point to the next, good report writers use headings and enumeration.

Headings and Enumeration

Headings are used by a report writer to help writing flow out of one idea and into another. They usually reflect the outline previously developed by the writer. In essence, they make the report easier to read. Just think how boring it would be to have to read an entire chapter of a textbook without some divisions in it with headings to help you make the transition from one idea to the next. Although the use of headings helps the reader to make the desired transition of thought, they should not replace the transitional sentence itself. The report should make sense even if the headings are not used. One technique is to repeat the words of the heading in the first sentence following it, such as was done in this paragraph.

Headings should be descriptive but as short as possible. They should also be used in a prescribed hierarchy: the relative importance of each is determined by the form and the position given it. Headings comprised of all capital letters are generally superior to those that include lower-case letters, and headings that are centered on a page are generally superior to those that are placed at the margin. Here is a brief memo on the use of headings:

```
     TO:  The Reader
   FROM:  The Authors
SUBJECT:  Headings

Here is a demonstration and explanation of the use of
headings in long reports.

              TITLE OF REPORT

Since all parts of the report are subparts of the
whole report, the title of the whole report should be
superior to all other headings. One way to do this is to
type it in all caps and spread it.

          FIRST-ORDER CENTERED HEADING

Your first-order heading, unnumbered, centered, and
typewritten in full capital letters, introduces a major
division of the report. If the heading is longer than
four inches, an inverted format should be used with
single spacing between the lines.
```

Second-Order Centered Heading

Second-order headings are centered, typewritten with only the first letter of each word capitalized, and undercored. Solid underscoring is preferred for typewriting ease and easy reading. The same four-inch rule applies for a second-order heading.

Third-Order Side Heading

The third-order heading, typewritten flush with the left margin and on a line by itself, introduces a subdivision of the part of the report that began under the second-order heading. Only major words are capitalized, and there is no end punctuation.

Fourth-Order heading. Fourth-order headings provide for a subdivision that is subordinate to the third-order side heading. Only the first word is capitalized; the heading is followed by a period; and the paragraph always continues on the same line.

When organizing the report, there are three important points to remember in using the headings:

1. Not all reports need to carry the same number of levels of subdivisions. Some reports may require all four and others may require only one or two.

2. There must always be at least two headings at any given level, because dividing a section must logically produce at least two subsections.

3. There must be at least one paragraph of writing under each heading. For ease of reading, never use two headings in succession without text between them.

Another way a report writer emphasizes certain ideas and at the same time writes about them concisely is to enumerate items, that is, to put them in a numbered list. By single-spacing, indenting the items, and making wider margins, the reader's attention can be drawn to the list as something of importance. An example of an enumerated list appears in the final paragraph of the preceding memo.

Format of Long Reports

The format of long research reports differs from that of memos. Long reports contain three categories of material: preliminaries, the body, and reference materials.

1. The preliminaries include:

    Cover
    Title page
    Letter of transmittal
    Contents
    Summary (or Abstract)

2. The body includes:

    Introduction
    Findings (development of subject matter appropriately divided into sections)
    Solution

3. The reference materials include:

    Bibliography
    Appendix

The Preliminaries

Cover: Covers come in all sizes, shapes, colors, and binders. If the contents of the report call for a cover that will attract attention, choose a design that does so; otherwise select a simple design. There are many kinds of binders on the market; be careful to select one that will hold the report securely. Many of the clamp-type and plastic molded–type binders are not adequate. Above all else, do not use a cover that has obviously been used already for some other paper or report.

Title page: These kinds of information are included on the title page: the title of the report; the name of the person, professional title, and organization; and the data on which the report is to be based.

Letter of transmittal: The letter of transmittal is written to the person to whom you will officially submit the report. You may appropriately start out by saying, "Here is the report. . . ." The letter might also include a brief statement of the problem and primary conclusions and recommendations. In addition, you will normally indicate that working on the report was an interesting opportunity, ask to discuss it further, and possibly offer to conduct future projects.

Contents: A contents page contains all the first-, second-, third-, and fourth-order headings, along with the page number on which each appears. An increasingly common heading for this page is "Contents" and not "Table of Contents." If the report contains several tables, graphs, or figures, a list of them should be provided on separate pages following the contents page. These pages are quite frequently headed "List of Tables" or "List of Figures."

Summary: The summary (or Abstract) tells the reader a capsule version of the report. Thus the reader learns (1) what to expect (2) whether to read the report.

The Body The report proper begins with the first page of the introduction, which follows the preliminaries listed above. For most reports, the body may be divided into an introductory section, findings section, and solution section.

Introduction: The introductory section of the report should contain

1. A paragraph or two giving background information.

2. A clear and sharply focused objective statement, together with an analysis and specification of any constraints.

3. Research methodology. Information in this section discusses the exact data collected to solve the problem, plus the sources of such data.

Findings: This section is the heart of the entire report. It includes tables and figures when appropriate and a nonevaluative analysis of the data. Organization of factual evidence in this section is extremely important because your solution, which follows, will be accepted or rejected on the basis of facts presented here. There is no room for editorial or subjective comments.

Solution: The solution to the problem needs to grow directly out of the findings. This solution may be stated with conclusions. If so, the conclusions must be based on data analyzed in the previous section. If the researcher has subjective suggestions, they are stated in the form of recommendations.

The Reference Materials Many reports include a bibliography, an appendix, and then a fly leaf as the last page.

Bibliography: The bibliography follows the body as a separate section of the report. It may list *all* references consulted for the project, or it may list only the references cited in the report.

Appendix: Questionnaires, correspondence, quotations from respondents, supporting legal decisions or laws, raw data, and tables that contain data of lesser importance than those presented in the body of the report are examples of items that might be included in the appendix. Many beginning writers want to know, "How do I decide what goes in the body of the report and what goes in the appendix?" Anything that is going to help the reader to agree with your solution should go in the body, because many readers will not read the appendix. If there are several items to be placed in the appendix, they might be subdivided and labeled A, B, C, D, etc.

COMPOSING YOUR DRAFT

Let us suppose that you now have a good outline for your report. You have gathered all of your information and carefully planned production of the report. How do you really write or dictate the report?

This whole subject of writing is perplexing. No one can really tell you how to bring words to the surface of your mind. Writing may come fairly easily to you or it may be very difficult.

Writing good reports, however, is not all art. For the most part, it is a craft to be learned and mastered. Some basic approaches to writing can be learned. If you have planned your writing project, you have already taken a major step. With a logical/psychological outline, your words will flesh out your framework. You may not find the actual writing easy. But you should be able to put words together acceptably. These rules will help you.

1. *Get the ideas on paper quickly.* Keep your thoughts moving as you change ideas into words. Write (or dictate) fast. Try not to stop writing to search for precisely the word or phrase you want. Leave a space blank if you lack a needed word, fact, number, date, or reference. If you stop writing to look for a specific number or word, your train of thought may well be derailed. And once it has jumped the track, it can be awfully hard to get moving again.

Once the words start flowing, you should keep writing as long as your thoughts move. Try to complete the full report or at least a section of it before you stop. If you must stop in midsection for a couple of days, you will have to review your writing before starting again.

2. *Write from your outline.* Look at your outline as a sketch, one to which you will add the fine lines. Or treat your outline as a skeleton to which you will add the flesh of sentences. If you think you will need to move several sentences to another place, keep writing. Just note in the margin (or with a sentence to the typist) that you will want to move the section to another place later.

3. *Write most paragraphs in the deductive order.* Start paragraphs with topic sentences. Using this style, your sentences in a paragraph will move from the broad and general to the detailed and narrow. A schematic of your typical paragraph would look like this:

> General, broad (most abstract idea) at the start
> Details to bear out the general idea, such as
> figures, examples, quotes, references,
> citations, logical arguments, and
> other "proofs"

You can consider the topic sentence in such a paragraph an umbrella. Your first (or at latest your second) sentence is like an umbrella, covering everything else in the paragraph. Or you can treat the paragraph as a lawyer's opening remarks to the court: "We will prove that the defendant is not guilty," and then present supporting ideas.

In this example of a deductive paragraph, note how the printing narrows, just as the ideas narrow as the sentences move from general to specific. The questions in parentheses could be the questions you asked yourself as you wrote:

> Housekeeping in this area is very poor. (How so?) The
> area has no general program of trash pick-up. (What
> else?) The bins overflow by the end of each
> week. Scraps of metal litter the aisles,
> and at the time of the inspector's
> tour, a cigarette was burning
> in one wastebasket.

Using this deductive approach, you in effect ask yourself about each idea in your outline: "What is the broadest statement I can make about this subtopic?" You phrase this umbrella sentence so that you can tell your reader the key idea.

Once you have written the umbrella sentence, you will use the rest of your paragraph to explain that sentence, prove it, and give examples. The other sentences in the paragraph flesh out the key idea. To flesh out the paragraph, you can ask yourself such questions as these:

"What will this sentence mean to my reader?"

"What would I say if my reader doubted the truth of this sentence?"

"What are the subideas of this main idea?"

"How can I 'prove' what I have just written?"

"What details would convince my reader that my umbrella sentence is sensible or true?"

4. *Keep writing and editing separate.* Do not stop writing to puzzle over the wording of a sentence. Especially, do not stop your thinking to search for the one best way to state an idea or the one precise word to use. As the next chapter will show you, editing is important. But to spend much time in editing what you are trying to write would distract you from your own thoughts.

Ideally, you should allow yourself a "cool-off" period between writing and editing. Then you can stand back from what you are writing and view it more objectively, as another person (such as your reader) would read it.

But what if you do not have enough time to edit carefully? What if your first draft will be your only draft? Suppose your boss is almost leaning over your shoulder, wanting your report to answer a question for higher management? In short, what if you must produce a "quick and dirty" version? Well, follow the same principle: write quickly, trying to complete the entire draft. At least your boss will have a complete document, together with your warning that you had to write hastily. Then, if your boss allows time, you can edit the draft.

5. *Plan your first-draft writing to make editing simple.*   If you dictate, tell the secretary to double-space. If you type or write long-hand, double-space your draft. The extra space will allow room for editing and be a help to the typist who prepares a second draft.

SUMMING UP

The ultimate objective of your writing is to communicate the information you have gathered and any conclusions you have drawn as effectively and efficiently as possible.

Readability is the ease with which a reader can obtain a message. The keys to readability have already been shared with you. They are:

- logical and psychological order of presentation
- paragraphs that are reasonably short and arranged in deductive order
- sentences that are short on the average
- words that are short
- writing that is humanized
- verbs that are active
- variety in word choice and sentence structure

These key suggestions will not ensure that what you write will be great literature. But they most assuredly will help you produce solid writing.

Of course, your job is not over when the first draft is written. Matters touched on in this chapter will be dealt with more extensively in the next chapter when we discuss revising and editing your draft.

PRINCIPLES FOR PRACTICE

1. Use headings to aid in transitions within longer reports.
2. Good writing is not necessarily an art.
3. Get your ideas on paper quickly.
4. Use your outline as a skeleton to which your words add flesh.
5. Write most paragraphs in the deductive order.
6. Keep writing and editing separate.
7. Plan your first draft to make editing simple.
8. Readability is the ultimate objective of your business writing.

FOR FURTHER STUDY

1. Write an "umbrella" (topic) sentence about each of these topics:
   a. a hammer
   b. tardiness in arriving at work
   c. the ideal supervisor
   d. good work habits

2. Which of these statements would you write as a topic sentence in a deductive paragraph?
   a. One step must be to control password access.
   b. This program will aim at better computer use.
   c. Our records show that we need better use of our computer.
   d. One step would be to save batch processing until off-peak hours.
   e. Our demand for computer time exceeds service availability during midmorning and late afternoon hours.

f. The program discussed in this section will increase the efficiency of our computer use.

3. Now reorganize the sentences listed under the previous question. Put a "1" to the left of the first umbrella sentence, a "2" to the left of the sentence that should come next, and so forth.

4. Copy the sentences in the order in which you have arranged them. You should sense that the ideas are in logical order, but the writing does not flow smoothly; that is, the ideas lack "transition." Add or delete words or phrases to smooth the writing.

5. Simone Jackson says, "I bet you can get nine-tenths of what you need to know by reading only the first sentence in each paragraph of my environmental impact statement." If Simone is right, what style does she use? Do you think a reader would like to read Simone's statement? What dangers could arise from such a reading practice?

6. You have just written this sentence: "Cost reduction must be a major factor in our long-range planning." One fact to support this umbrella idea would be a quotation from the vice-president. What other types of "proof" might support the topic idea?

7. You have prepared this outline for a memo:

Changes Needed in Traffic Flow

Summary
    problem—traffic jams
    solution—staggered working hours

Problems of Congested Traffic
    accidents
    delays
    wasted energy from idling engines
    obstruction of emergency vehicles

Solutions Considered
    better timing of traffic lights; but already OK
    police to keep traffic moving; not enough police
    widening streets; Department of Transportation no funds
    staggering office hours

Advantages of Staggering Office Hours
    spread out flow
    actually some net time

Problems and Solutions
    disagreements over hours; conferences among executives

conflicts with taking kids to school; no solution
inconveniences to motorists; but total time saved

Now write an umbrella sentence for each major heading and each sub-heading. Beneath each umbrella sentence list some typical types of proof. Beside each typical proof cite a visual aid that might show that proof. Invent proof items.

8. Read a major article in one of these magazines: *Business Week, Forbes, Fortune, Nation's Business.* Copy the umbrella sentence in each paragraph in outline form. Calculate the average paragraph length in number of sentences. Show your outline to a friend for brief study. Then ask your friend questions to test his or her understanding of the article and memory of the key ideas.

9. Read the main story on the front page of a daily newspaper. Underline the umbrella sentences. Then calculate the average paragraph length in sentences. Make the same calculation for a textbook. What differences do you find in typical length of paragraphs between a newspaper and a textbook? How would you account for this difference?

CHAPTER 10

To: The Reader
From: The Authors
Subject: Revising and Editing Your Draft

After reading this chapter you will know:

1. The major factors that will help you produce a good memo
    or report.

2. Ways to make sure your memo or report is accurate and
    adequate.

3. Methods of improving organization and arrangement,
    technical correctness, completeness, conciseness,
    readability, clarity, and usefulness.

4. By examples, how to revise and edit phrases, clauses,
    whole sentences, and an entire memo.

Revising and Editing Your Draft

You will do some of your best writing after you have completed a first draft of your memo or report. You may define *revising* and *editing* by many terms: *improving, debugging,* or *smoothing.* Regardless of what term you prefer, this chapter will show you how to improve a rough draft of a memo or report after you have written it (or at least a section of it).

First, we will look at the general principles of revising and editing. Then we will deal with specific ways to improve your writing by editing.

GENERAL PRINCIPLES OF EDITING

Rule 1:   Whenever possible, allow "cool-off" time between completing a draft and starting to edit.   This principle is sound, even if you find it hard to apply under job deadlines.

Rule 2:   Welcome help from a skilled editor.   No matter how well you write, you can always improve. The other person editing your work may offer the same comments your reader would offer or ask questions about your writing that will save you from making a mistake.

Rule 3:   Learn when to "leave well enough alone."   A change does not always improve a memo or report. Minor changes that you make in your own writing may result in no major improvement. Minor changes in someone else's writing may lead the other writer to accuse you of "nit-picking." Sometimes a draft suffers so many changes as it moves from one person to another that it ends up in what is virtually its original form. Also, a little editing usually greatly improves a rough draft. But as you spend more time in editing, you may reach the point of diminishing returns. You will never find the one perfect way to write a memo or report, no matter how much time you spend in editing. You must always judge editing by cost-effectiveness, your schedule, and the importance of the document.

Rule 4: Revise or edit with the reader and situation in mind. This is the same attitude you take when you write. For instance, ask yourself, "Will the reader understand this phrasing?" "Could I cut some of this wording?" "Does this idea need an example to explain it?"

Rule 5: If you have time, read a whole section or even the whole memo or report before you start revising or editing.

Rule 6: Focus on the major matters of accuracy and adequacy:

- organization—logical/psychological order for the target reader(s) and for the situation
- technical correctness (of fact and word usage)
- completeness
- conciseness
- usefulness
- readability
- clarity

As you revise to improve the major matters, you can check as many of these minor matters as your time permits:

- mechanics (grammar, spelling, punctuation, abbreviation, use of symbols, capitalization)—so long as these matters do not affect a major matter, such as technical accuracy
- word choice

Please note: These "minor matters" are minor only in being easy to correct. A mistake in even a minor matter can cause a major error. For more extensive discussion of these matters, see Handbook B.

Checking Organization

If you (or whoever wrote what you revise or edit) planned the writing carefully, there should be no need to rearrange ideas or paragraphs. However, if a rough draft does contain mistakes in order of ideas, editing should correct these mistakes.

As you check the order, you are, of course, trying to put yourself in your reader's place. The crucial question is this: "Does this writing present my ideas in an order that will help the reader's understanding and acceptance?"

You can usually correct errors in arrangement by a note to the typist, such as "insert this paragraph at * on next page"; or you can draw a circle around a misplaced sentence and show with an arrow the proper place for that sentence.

One warning, however. Moving a sentence to some other place can ruin the transition, the smooth flow between sentences, or confuse a reader who wants to follow a cross reference. For example, if you move a sentence starting with "However" to another part of the paragraph or page, that first word could puzzle a reader. Or you might move a sentence that reads: "The graph on the next page will show. . . ." If you move that sentence back several pages, you will confuse your reader.

Checking Technical Accuracy

Your reader has a right to expect accuracy in your memo or report. Your report may become the basis for a decision. If your statements are untrue, your calculations wrong, or your ideas not valid, your reader may reach a wrong conclusion. An incorrect report can not only result in bad decisions but also become a matter of serious conflict. Some reports result in lawsuits, criminal prosecution, injuries, or deaths. Just imagine, for example, the results of a mistake in a report on testing of food products or inspection of a rocket.

When you write (or later revise or edit), you should hone your senses, sharpen your alertness to detect likely sources of error. Errors can creep in at any stage of report writing. Danger zones are found:

- *in gathering data*
  built-in instrument error (such as a faulty meter in a science lab)
  procedural error (such as bias in sampling)
  errors of adjusting or reading instruments
  researcher bias
- *in using data from other people*
  garbled transmission
  errors in copying
  lies
- *in recording data*

- *in interpreting facts*
  selective perception
  inappropriate frame of reference
  many other types
- *in calculating*
- *in expressing ideas*
  word selection
  poor writing
  many others

Checking technical accuracy in your own writing differs from checking it in someone else's. In revising your own writing your biggest problem is that of repeating the same mistake you made in writing. Allowing yourself a "cool-off" period offers you your best chance of catching your own mistakes. Your problem in editing another person's writing may be that you do not have all of the data or you do not fully understand the subject of the report. You can help solve this problem by checking results of your editing with the writer.

Despite these two problems, you must still edit for technical accuracy. Within the limits imposed by your time, the importance of the subject, and your knowledge of the subject, check for:

1. *Freedom from carelessness.*   Mistakes can slip in from errors in typing, copying quoted material, recording or copying data, and many other situations. The best rule to follow is: "Be suspicious. Stay alert to spot any word, reference, or figure that does not look right."

2. *Internal consistency.*   Ask yourself such questions as: "Does the report contradict itself?" "Does the report promise anything that it fails to deliver?" "Do the figures add, and do other mathematical steps check?" "Are cross references within the report accurate?"

3. *Freedom from incongruity.*   An incongruity is a statement or calculation that, in the light of everything else you know, seems wrong or at least doubtful. You should ask yourself, "Does this report violate any commonly held ideas?" "Does this report violate law, regulation, custom, or policy?"

In checking for technical accuracy, be sure to: (1) Check all calculations, or have someone else check the figures. (2) Approximate the answer to every calculation for which you have the background data. If your guess differs greatly from an answer, check the calculation again (if you wrote the original draft) or ask the other writer.

How can you handle a statement or figure that seems wrong but really is not? Such an apparent mistake could "throw" a reader who was reading carefully. A good rule is: "Put in a note to explain any incongruity." For example, you could note at the bottom of a table: "Because of rounding off, some columns do not add to 100.00." Or you could note, "Under the revision of 1980, the specification read *seven* days." If a mistake appear in quoted material, you can put a note in brackets inside the quotation.

As you revise and edit for accuracy, you may also need to check value judgments. In effect, you ask yourself, "How valid are the conclusions?" In test reports, reports of investigations, or recommendations, a writer may answer the questions "So what?" "What do the facts really mean?" "What should be done?" The answers to these questions are not fact but opinions or value judgments. Value judgments always go beyond the facts on which they depend.

The value judgment or recommendation may well be the most critical part of a report. For example, the value judgment in a test report on a new product is far more than a mere array of facts; after all, the gathering of facts is often a fairly low-level job (done sometimes by automatic recorders). The crucial task is the use and interpretation of fact; value judgments must come from people with much expertise. You and any other writer really earn your paychecks when you move from answering such questions as "What happened" to the bottom-line question, "So what should we do?"

In editing reports, you cannot always correct all mistakes of judgment. Only time will reveal the inaccuracy of some statements. However, you can check some judgments by asking such questions as:

"How conclusive are the facts?"
"How far beyond the data do the conclusions go?"
"What other conclusions would the facts allow?"
"What commonly held ideas do the conclusions contradict?"
"What risks and rewards do the conclusions create?"
"What further data would be needed?"
"How will the reader accept these conclusions?"

Two of the most common errors in reasoning are (1) hasty generalization and (2) confusion between or uncertainty about cause and effect. Hasty generalization results from drawing a broad conclusion from insufficient facts. Sampling only a few pieces of lumber from a truckload shipment might lead to a report that the entire shipment is acceptable. The first few sales in a campaign might not represent the real trend. Uncertainty about cause and effect is the mistake of thinking that umbrellas cause rain. For example, suppose that after you decide to pay salespeople by direct commissions, sales quickly rise. Are you sure that the new way of paying sales people prompted them to work harder? Or did a new product line entice more customers? Or did your credit policy change? And will the change last?

Perhaps the best approach to avoiding these two errors is a mixture of common sense and healthy suspicion. Could the supplier have deliberately stacked the best lumber in plain view on the truck? Could any other major change have increased sales?

Editing for Completeness

The goal of editing for completeness is kin to the goal of editing for technical accuracy. Here there is no single rule of thumb. The amount of detail you include depends on so many factors: your reader, your reader's interest in the topic, the time available to prepare or read the report, his or her appraisal of your competence, the seriousness of the topic, the need to preserve data for future use, the amount of proof needed, and the challenges to conclusions.

As a general principle, include the amount of detail your reader expects and the subject deserves. You must walk the thin line between (1) not giving enough detail to support the judgments and to convince the reader that the report is a mature effort and (2) loading a report with so much detail that the reader is bored or the main ideas are buried.

You or the person who wrote the draft should already have solved this problem. If not, you must solve it when you revise the draft. You can consider this approach: give a general summary followed by details. You can make the opening section (or for a short report the first paragraph or two) brief. Many details may be included later in an attachment. Thus, a reader may elect to read only the first part of the report but not the details in the attachment. Incidentally, this principle offers you one more good reason for writing in the deductive style discussed in Chapter 8. By going from general to particular, you can summarize but still offer detail.

Of course, certain details may be essential. Some reports require certain certificates or standard phrases. You must make certain that the final report includes all required phrases, statements, certificates, or sections.

Reports may need details: (1) to "prove" the opening statements and support the conclusions and (2) to meet certain specifications. For example, a report may be one of a series; answer an inquiry; fulfill specific instructions or orders; or be controlled by government regulations.

Making sure that your report is complete does not mean you are saddled with excess wordage. While trying to supply all of the facts and ideas needed, you should edit writing to tighten it, to make it more concise. The next section will show you how to cut out the padding—the fat, flabby expressions—and thus increase the efficiency of your writing.

Editing for Conciseness and Simplicity

For three reasons you should revise your writing to make it more concise: First, conciseness saves production and reading time. Paperwork costs money, not just in the cost of paper (paper is *the lowest of costs*), but in the cost of preparing and reading reports. When your reader reads needless words, he or she is wasting time. Second, cutting out the padding makes your writing clearer. Pruned of dead words, your ideas stand out. Third, clean-cut, sharp writing *seems* easier to read; therefore it *is* easier to read. So cut out the useless words, the words that neither carry ideas nor make reading smoother.

However, edit carefully. Someone has said, "Be long on ideas, short on words." But be careful not to leave out vital words. You want to prune words, not ideas or facts, when you edit. Your editing should raise the efficiency of your writing. Engineers define *efficiency* as *the ratio of output to input*. You could define *efficiency of writing* as the ratio of ideas and facts conveyed to the wordage used to convey those ideas.

Another precaution: avoid "telegraphic English" except when you write telegrams. You gain very little by leaving out *a, an,* and *the;* the omission of these words can make reading seem like riding a wagon over a rough road.

The sections on writing letters in this book suggest many ways for you to make your writing more concise. You should refer especially to Chapter 3.

You can cut out excess words in several ways:

1. *Omit unnecessary words or phrases.* You seldom need the phrases "which is" and "who are." Note how you can cut these phrases:

This tool,—which is—used in measuring distance, is called "a chain."
John Jones,—who is—supervisor of production control, . . .

This sentence is about five words overweight:

It is necessary for you to specify clearly what you need.

The sentence really means:

You must clearly specify your needs.

2. *Cut any padding that hides the real subject or the verb.* Note how the useless words add weight to this sentence:

There were—three ways of measurement (were) available.

3. *Pick the shortest, simplest words that convey your ideas and tone correctly.*

You may often have to use some complicated technical words. Technical words, mainly from Latin (you remember our comparison of Latin- and Anglo-Saxon–derived words in Chapter 3), have precise meanings for which you cannot find simple one- or two-syllable word replacements. The word *depreciation* is an example. Of course, you might have to define *depreciation* for a reader, but your definition would call for many words, not just one simple word. Your topic dictates some of your word choices.

Editing to Improve Clarity

How can you make your ideas clear and focused on your message? You have already learned from the section on conciseness and simplicity how to use simple words and to cut out useless words and phrases. But clear sentence structure requires more than cutting word length and sentence length. Clear structure also depends upon the way you put phrases together.

Some teachers urge their students to attempt unusual sentence structures. Variety does have a place, because phrasing all of your ideas in the same pattern would bore your reader. But if you write in the practical world of business, industry, and government, you should usually employ the safe, direct English sentence. Leave stylistic cuteness to those who do not have to write in a busy, competitive setting. Instead, follow these principles:

1. *Try to keep the subject close to the verb.* The meaning of a sentence derives from the subject-verb connection, and that connection should be close. Notice the clumsy pattern of this sentence:

He, so far as we can tell from a quick check, has not balanced the accounts.

Instead of this clumsy structure, you could write:

A quick check shows that he has not. . . .

2. *Try to avoid splitting the verb.* Splitting the verb weakens the most important element in the sentence. This sentence is awkward:

He has, as far as we can tell from a quick check, not balanced the accounts.

If you need to keep the minor idea of "so far as we can tell from a quick check," put the pieces of the verb together:

So far as we can tell from a quick check, he has not. . . .

3. *Make verbs do the work in your sentences.*   And phrase your sentences so that the real subjects connect to the real verbs. For example, this sentence hides the real subject and real verb:

> There has been a noticeable improvement in our meeting of quotas.

Without the fat and the real subject/verb carrying the thought, this really means:

> Our meeting of quotas has clearly improved.

4. *Use the active voice whenever possible.*   (For further discussion of active voice, see Chapter 3.)

5. *Make each sentence emphasize its important ideas.*   Far too many sentences in reports focus on the trivial. For example, this sentence,

> Following is a report that represents our study of downtime on the package labels.

is a grammatically correct sentence. But this sentence emphasizes "Following . . . is." Surely, you would want to emphasize that the report presents (or "covers") the study, not that the report is following. Revised, the sentence would read:

> The following (or "This") report presents our study. . . .

In brief, if you are tempted to write an inverted sentence, ask yourself: "Why make my reader wait to get the meaning?"

6. *Pay special attention to the verb idea in each sentence.*   Make sure you build your sentence around the real verb. Because the verb carries the force of the sentence, you should revise any sentence in which the verb lacks clear, compelling force. Note how the following sentence from an actual report lacks verb-power:

> Savings in excess of two hundred thousand dollars per year can be obtained should all five job classifications be eliminated or combined per this report.

You might revise this sentence to read

> As shown in this report, eliminating or combining all five job classifications *would save* more than two hundred thousand dollars per year.

To focus on the real verb, cut out useless, distracting verbs. The italicized verb in a sentence like this serves no real purpose:

> We *have looked* at this situation and have developed two theoretical operational modes.

Instead, write

> For this situation we have developed . . . etc.

Here is another sentence (from an actual report) which you could prune to emphasize the real verb:

> This secondary agreement becomes part of the primary contract and has the effect of preventing a contractor from issuing a low bid in year one with the hope of making it up in subsequent periods.

If you focused on the real verb idea, you could trim the deadwood:

> By becoming part of the primary contract, this secondary agreement *prevents* a contractor from low bidding the first year in hope of raising rates later.

7. *Avoid jumbled constructions.*   Note that the phrase "glancing sideways" does not refer to any thing in this sentence:

> Glancing sideways, the belt was seen to slip off the pulley.

Revising to Improve Readability

Readability depends on many factors. Besides clarity and conciseness, readability depends upon transition and emphasis. Let us first review transition.

Just as you should avoid telegraphic English, you should avoid bumpy, jumpy writing. A string of clipped sentences will impress your reader as immature writing. How then can you write shorter sentences but not write rough sentences?

1. *Use transitional words or phrases for easier, smoother writing.*   Such words or phrases tie ideas together with threads of thought. Note how the italicized words connect ideas in this paragraph:

> Any *investment decision* involves the true *cost* of the investment. A *decision* to buy a new machine tool, for example, may *cost* $50,000. But the true *cost* may

far exceed the first *cost*. True *costs* may include interest on the *investment*, rising price of replacement, depreciation, obsolescence, and many other nonobvious *expenses*.

You can build good transition several ways:

- Repeat key words, so long as your writing is not monotonous.

- Use reflection words, which look backward to a previous item. Such words include *this, such, for example,* and *these.*

- Offer specific examples of general ideas.

- Use parallel structure effectively. For example, you could parallel main ideas: "The true cost includes taxes and depreciation; it does not include production improvement or satisfaction. (For more on parallel structure, see Handbook B.)

- Use numbers in a list of items, or words that show reference (*first, next, finally*).

2. *Do not stuff too many ideas into one sentence—or even into one paragraph.* If you do, you will lose your emphasis and your reader. A reader needs to group ideas into thought packages. If you fill a sentence with too many ideas, your reader cannot retain the main idea. For example, suppose you wanted to tell a reader how to check the oil level in an engine. If you crowded all of the steps into a single paragraph, you would blur your reader's thinking. To make your main ideas stand out, you can:

- Separate main ideas within a paragraph by putting each in a sentence starting with transitional words, such as *First, Second,* etc.

- Separate main ideas within a paragraph or even in a single sentence by separating them with "paren" numbers such as (1), (2), etc.

- Place key ideas below the paragraph and set them off by "bullets," as in this list, or numbers if the sequence of items is important.

3. *Keep your sentences and paragraphs short enough to form sense packages.* The term *sense package* means *a thought that the reader can retain easily.* The readability of your writing depends partly on conciseness and clarity, subjects already discussed. As you recall, readability also decreases as sentences get longer. The term *sentence* here does not mean the same as *sentence* meant in your early English courses in school. Readability improves as you break ideas into simpler units. Therefore, any device that divides ideas into sense packages can improve readability. For example, any statement ending with a strong mark of punctuation will suggest to your reader: "Here is a sense package I can handle."

Common marks of strong punctuation include

- period

- semicolon
- colon
- dash (double hyphen in typing)
- parentheses or brackets
- new paragraphs
- items set off by numbers in parentheses
- indention for lists
- items in a list set off by "bullets"

4. *Avoid twisted or complex sentence structure.* The more complex the structure, the harder the sentence will be to read. A general principle is this: do not force more than one main idea into a sentence. True, such a rule restricts the use of compound and compound-complex sentences. But you will do better saving such sentences for the times you really need them. Your reader will usually find simple sentences (one main idea) and complex sentences (one main idea and one or more minor ideas) easier to read than compound sentences (two or more main ideas). And certainly you should not bury your main idea in a pile of minor ideas, as in this sentence:

> When anyone who has a grievance contacts the shop steward, he should set forth his complaint very truthfully, whatever the seriousness of the complaint may be against someone who is in management.

The minor ideas bury the key idea, which is "he should set forth his complaint very truthfully."
Try revising this sentence:

> Anyone with a grievance against a member of management—whatever the seriousness of the complaint—should set forth the complaint truthfully to the shop steward.

or

> Anyone with a grievance (whatever its seriousness) against a member of management. . . .

5. *Stick to the normal subject-verb-predicate order.* Generally, avoid the twisted, periodic, or inverted sentence order. Most English sentences state ideas in the normal order of thought: a subject doing something to something or a subject doing something. This sentence pattern is so common that you can sense it even if you do not understand the words. Thus, in the sentence "The etaoin shrdlu the gizzmoes," the subject is clearly "etaoin," the verb is "shrdlu," and the direct object is "gizzmoes." Because this order reflects the way people think, it offers a normal pattern.

A periodic sentence delays the subject of the sentence until the end:

> To supervisors the most vital question arising every day is "What next?"

An inverted sentence places the verb ahead of the subject:

> Included in this part are the hammer, the anvil, and the barrel.

This sentence has two weaknesses. First, it places the subject after the verb, a reversal of thought order. Second, it may tempt the user to make the verb singular even though the real subject is plural. You would create a subject/verb disagreement by writing

> Included in this part *is* the hammer, the anvil, and the barrel.

6. *Whenever possible, express ideas with action verbs rather than linking verbs.* Because transitive verbs express action, they make more forceful sentences. To understand this principle, you need to know that English has three types of verbs:

- transitive verbs show action
  examples: *turn, adjust, close, drive, break*
- linking verbs show equivalency, "equal to"
  examples: *is, are, seems*
- intransitive verbs show a change in condition or location
  example: *become*

Some verbs show action in one meaning (transitive meaning) but change in another meaning (intransitive meaning). For example, "Sarah is *growing* the culture for the test" uses "growing" in the transitive meaning. But "Sarah is *growing* more competent" uses "growing" in the intransitive sense.

Of course, you cannot avoid linking verbs. Linking verbs *are* important parts of English (as you see from reading this sentence). But linking verbs cannot make sentences active and powerful. Look how this sentence, "June will be in attendance at the meeting," wastes the chance to express a thought more forcefully: "June will attend the meeting." The revised version not only states the real idea more forcefully, but also saves three words.

7. *Keep the point of view consistent.* "Point of view" means your choice—for subjects and verbs—of

- *number:* Is it singular or plural?
- *person:* Is it first person (*I, we, me, us,* etc.); second person (*you, your,* etc.); or third person (*he, she, it, they,* the name of a machine, the name of some material, etc.)?
- voice: Is it active (subject acting) or passive (subject being acted upon)?
- mood: Is it declarative (making statements); imperative (giving commands or instructions); interrogative (asking questions); or subjunctive (expressing a doubt)?

Choose your viewpoint according to the subject, the reader, and the circumstances. Because the circumstances usually stay constant throughout your memo or report, your point of view should remain constant. Note how the point of view changes awkwardly in this short paragraph:

> If this choice is not made (passive) soon by you, you (second-person active) will have to select a new line. The company (third-person) will not have enough funds for an entirely new program, so we (first-person plural) must find minor changes. It is my (first-person singular) opinion that. . . . Therefore, do (imperative) not scrap any of the existing grinders. The chosen vendor (third-person singular) has told us (first-person plural) that they (third-person plural). . . .

Changing from a varying to a single point of view produces much clearer and smoother writing:

> If you do not choose soon, you will have to select a new line. We will not have enough funds for an entirely new program, so we must find minor changes. . . . Therefore, you must not scrap any of the existing grinders. The chosen vendor has told us that. . . .

Sometimes you have to change point of view. When you do, warn your reader. For example, you might just have written some general principles in third person. Now you want to state certain rules in second-person imperative. Signal this change by such devices as (1) a heading, such as "Steps in Leveling the Transit," or (2) at least a transitional sentence, such as "In setting up a transit, the instrument operator should take these steps: . . ."

By now you should have grasped this truth: readability is both a logical and a psychological problem. That is, a reader finds material easier to read when you relate ideas logically and offer your ideas in easily grasped sense packages. The reader looks for the end of a sense package, unconsciously thinking: "Aha! I've got this idea before going to the next." The reader reads the way a person crosses a stream, stepping from one sure footing to the next.

IMPROVING USEFULNESS

Any memo or report you write must meet this test: Can the reader *use* the memo or report in solving problems, making decisions, keeping records, etc.? For your memo or report to serve your reader, it must (1) reach the reader at the right time and (2) be accurate, concise, clear, complete, and readable. Getting the report to the reader at the right time requires early planning. Previous sections in this chapter have shown you how to make the report clearer and faster and easier to read.

Now let us study a few other ways in which you can make your next memo or report more useful:

1. *Use specific terms; make your ideas carry as much force as possible.*   Note how easily you can understand the sentences in this paragraph:

> If you cannot turn the lid, you may have to change the temperature of the container so that container and lid are at different temperatures. Applying liquids near one end of the container will cause a difference in temperature between lid and container. This difference will cause one surface to expand and the other to contract, thus. . . .

But you still do not grasp the real facts. Changing a few of the general terms to specifics makes the ideas much clearer:

> If you cannot screw off the lid, you may have to loosen it by warming it. Applying cold water to the neck of the container and warmer water to the lid will create a temperature difference between lid and container. The warm lid will expand, and the cooler container will contract, thus. . . .

2. *Do not weasel.*   You should avoid weakening your own ideas by such paddings as

> The objective of this report is to review the stability test.

Either you reviewed the stability test or you did not review it. Almost surely you did review the test; if you did, your sentence should say:

> This report reviews the stability test.

If you did not review the test—and thus, your work did not meet your objectives—your sentence should read:

> This report was planned to review the stability test. However, ...

3. *Do not waste your reader's time and interest.*   Stating obvious and unneeded details distracts a reader and makes a report less useful. Of course,
the target readership determines the detail needed. But the first six words
in this sentence contain only one idea, an idea that the italicized words
could tell alone:

> Data from the *test results show* no relationship between screen size and extra-
> neous material.

This sentence states an unneeded idea:

> He then *proceeded* to explain the process.

Instead, you can merely write

> He then explained the process.

Sentences starting with the words *by, through, there,* and *if* can often waste
words:

> By filling each canister half full, spillage was prevented.
> Through the use of swash plates, fluid sloshing was decreased.
> There was a requirement for us to inspect each unit.
> If the nozzle is immersed in the fluid, it will stop air entrainment.

Revising these sentences will help you (1) avoid awkward sentence structure, (2) focus your thoughts on the real subject/verb ideas, and (3) most
important, make your writing more useful:

> Filling each canister half full prevented spillage.
> Swash plates decreased fluid sloshing.
> We had to inspect each unit.
> Immersing the nozzle in the fluid stopped the air entrainment.

Exhibit 10-1 shows how you could revise and edit a memo to improve
major factors:
Following these suggestions in writing, revising, and editing your draft
will assure you of a report that serves its intended purpose and reflects
favorably on you. All that remains is to see to it that your report gets where
it is supposed to go, in the proper form, at the proper time.

PRINCIPLES FOR PRACTICE

1. Revising and editing should focus on major matters of accuracy and adequacy including organization, correctness, completeness, conciseness, usefulness, readability, and clarity.

2. Ask yourself, "Does this writing present my ideas in the order that will help the reader's understanding and acceptance?"

3. Errors can creep in at any stage of report writing. Beware!

4. Include the amount of detail your reader expects and the subject deserves.

5. Conciseness saves time and money while making writing clearer and easier to read.

6. Clarity demands much of your verbs. Make them work, keep them active, do not split them, and keep their subject close.

7. Transitional words make for smoother writing and easier reading.

8. Your writing will be more useful if you use specific, forceful terms.

FOR FURTHER STUDY

1. Why should writers start any long report with a "Summary"?

2. How does a letter to someone outside your organization differ in length, formality, and arrangement of ideas from an internal memo?

3. How do revising and editing differ from checking and proofreading?

4. Why is technical accuracy so important in memos and reports? How can errors creep in—and remain in—memos and reports?

5. To make writing more concise, what words or phrases could you sometimes substitute for these phrases?

as a matter of fact _____

because of the fact that _____

in spite of the fact that _____

will give assistance in _____

EXHIBIT 10-1

ILLUSTRATION 10-1

EXAMPLE OF A MEMO WHICH NEEDS REVISION

December 16, 1980

To: John Haskins

From: S. L. Dunn

Subject: Trip Report for Monitoring of Training in Plant No. 2

On Thursday, December 15, I traveled to Plant No. 2. Because I would have had to rent a car even if I had flown commercial flight I drove. I arrived at the plant at 8:30 a.m.

Belongs in expense report, not in this memo.

I was met at the security section by L.R. Roomer, Training Specialist at Plant No. 2 and also coordinator of the outside vendor training. R. V. Able, the vendor's representative, did not meet me. He could not leave the skill trades training area since trainees were then being lectured on safety methods and techniques.

Contains Trivial Details

From 9:00 until lunch I monitored the vendor's class. The shop training area had enough tools; however, this area needs at least one more motor grinder, since it now has only one bench-top grinder.

I lunched with Ms. Roomer from 11:45 until the training session resumed at 12:30.

During the afternoon I interviewed four trainees. All four expressed their satisfaction with the training. They showed samples of their typical work pieces (drilling in 24ST sheet, after first sharpening drill bits). The samples revealed adequate workmanship.

Thursday night I stayed in the Rambling Inn, near the plant.

The next morning I interviewed four people who had completed the training and have been assigned to their work stations, plus their supervisor. Again all four and also their supervisor expressed satisfaction.

After lunch, I left the plant and drove back to the office.

These ideas belong near the start of the memo to answer key questions.

In summary, this training program supplied by Knox Skills Development appears to meet the terms of our contract. The only item was the need for another bench grinder. Otherwise the program is satisfactory. The vendor's representative, (name) assured me that another grinder would be obtained.

If you need more information, please contact me. I should check into this program again next February.

/s/

ILLUSTRATION 10-1 (cont.)

EXAMPLE OF A REVISED MEMO

December 16, 1980

To: John Haskins

From: S. L. Dunn

Subject: Trip Report for Monitoring of Training in Plant No. 2

     The training program supplied by Knox Skills Development meets
our contract in all respects but one. There is a need for another
bench grinder. Mr. R. V. Able of Knox Skills assures us that the
grinder will be ordered.

     These conclusions are based on discussions on December 15 and 16
with L. R. Roomer, Plant No. 2 training specialist and coordinator
of outside vendor training, R. V. Able, four trainees, and four
employees who have completed their training, and their supervisor. I
also monitored a class that Able was teaching.

     All parties expressed satisfaction with the training. The
trainees showed their progress by doing typical work pieces (drilling
in 25ST sheet, after first sharpening drill bits). Their work showed
adequate skill.

     Able taught the class competently. The training area was
adequately equipped with the exception of the bench grinder.

     This program should be checked again in February. If you need
more information, please call me.

     /s/

is not in a position to _____
at a time when _____
will provide with _____
in the meantime _____
until such a time as _____
few in number _____

6. Change the verb form or the sentence structure to improve these sentences: The inspectors are resistant to new methods.

_____

Inattention to specs must be brought to a stop.

_____

He, so far as is known to us, has not resigned.

_____

Rejection will, as a prediction on this date, be in excess of last year's.

_____

7. Underline the vague, padding, or "weasel" words or phrases:
This proposal will affect our next year's projections. Our per-unit costs will no doubt change. Therefore, it is the purpose of the chart to influence management's attitude regarding altered processes.

8. By inserting transitional words in the blanks and by changing sentence wording, make the following paragraph read more smoothly. (You may want to change capitalization to show a new sentence or to combine sentences):
"Chip" is a natural film used in paper making _____
Chip is used in making certain plastics. _____
Chip comes from wood pulp. Chip is the strongest component. Two major components are used—chip and rag—in paper making.

9. In the blank below each sentence, state a key step you would take (if someone else had not already taken that step) to make sure each report would be useful:
A request for approval of purchase of a new duplication machine

_____

A proposal for increasing employment each month for the next year

_____

A set of instructions for welding trainees

_____

A description of new office layout

_____

10. Suppose your company sent you to inspect a construction site. Draw a line through any topic listed below that might be useless for your report.

Then reorganize the topics by printing a number in each blank, with "1"
to represent the first topic, "2" the next, etc.

_____ materials shortages
_____ place you had lunch
_____ how you got in the main gate
_____ actual versus scheduled completion
_____ problems with materials vendors
_____ revised completion date
_____ work not within specifications
_____ summary of progress
_____ recommendations
_____ site superintendent visited
_____ day/date of visit
_____ location of site
_____ day/date of previous visit
_____ day/date of next visit

11. Underline the main idea in each sentence twice. Underline once any
useful idea that should be subordinated. Delete useless ideas or words.
"We are attaching a list of qualified bidders that will assist you in issuing
requests for proposals."
"We received your list of qualified bidders, and we will screen this list
carefully."
"Each employee should read the instructions, study them carefully, and
then follow them closely."
"On Monday, December 18, 19__, the boiler make-up pump failed."
"Please attend this meeting and bring a copy of any grievances recently
filed."
"Please answer at your earliest convenience, but no later than day after
tomorrow."
"The damaged crates, which have been returned, are not in the 'hold'
section of Central Receiving."
"This container is square in shape and has a weight of 181 pounds."

12. Check the following uses of data for any problems of factual accuracy.

HOURS SPENT IN INSPECTION

Day	Hours
Monday	6
Tuesday	5
Wednesday	4
Thursday	3
Friday	2
Total	21

"This square borrow pit, measuring 20′ × 20′ × 10′, requires excavation of 40,000 cubic feet of clay."

"Prills freely falling from the sprinkler will drop at a rate of 32 feet per second."

"The two-inch line will carry 1,000 gallons per minute, while the one-inch line carries only 480 gallons per minute. Thus the two-inch line carries approximately twice as much as the one-inch line at the same pressure."

13. Edit the following material to correct all major matters.

"Calculations of the lumber needed were made by an estimator. He has attached his full calculations to show all data. Of primary importance is the crucial matter, as is explained in the calculations, of shoring. Using the formula for board footage, it is shown that

$$\text{board footage} = \frac{110 \times 2 \times 6 \times 8}{12} = 980 \text{ board feet}$$

This is not in agreement with the estimate as originally made. Although at first seemingly inconsequential, this error is actually consequential, in that it is symbolic and representative of careless estimating. As a matter of fact, the estimator was in receipt of our verbal protest of two weeks ago. There is no excuse for such inconsistent treatment of calculations which are not in concurrence with the original estimates made at first."

CHAPTER 11

To: The Reader
From: The Authors
Subject: Checking and Sending a Memo or Report

After reading this chapter you will know how to:

1. Check memos and reports before signing or sending them.

2. Watch for the most likely sources of errors.

3. Teach others, such as secretaries, to check memos and
   reports carefully.

4. Plan the method and timing for sending memos and reports
   to your reader.

Checking and Sending
a Memo or Report

Suppose that you now have that memo or report in final draft. It is ready to go. You want to get it off your desk and on its way.

Wait!

Before you actually send it, you should take two steps: (1) proofread, or have someone else proofread, the typing or printing and (2) plan the distribution. Of course, even before you begin writing, you should have thought about sending the letter or report. Now you must send the document so that it will get to the right reader or readers at the right time.

Before signing a document, ask yourself: "What would happen if top management carefully read this document? What would happen if some hostile reader read this document?" Keep high standards for yourself and for anyone working for you. You can always relax standards when "quick and dirty" work is required. Insist that secretaries check their typing before they give it to you for signing, but let them know that you check anything you sign.

Even when you cannot check every detail, you should randomly inspect at least some work. For example, if you are sending a large report to many readers, you cannot check every page of every copy. Check at least a few copies; let your helpers know you care about and will be alert to check for quality.

In checking writing, as in editing, you should be playing two roles: hostile attorney and reader's representative. Always remember that even if you delegate the right to sign your name, your signature attaches the responsibility to you.

CHECKING (PROOFREADING)

When you or someone else edited the memo or report, you tried to improve technical accuracy, readability, clarity, conciseness, mechanics, and other features of the writing. When you check a final draft, you need not concern yourself with revising or editing. At the stage of "proofing" (proofreading) you are mainly trying to make sure the final typing or printing matches the last edited draft and is mechanically correct.

Here are some practical hints for proofing a vital memo or report. For routine or informal reports you may use your judgment in applying these tips.

1. *Try to have someone other than yourself or your typist check the final copy, reproduction, or stencil.* If you write a memo or report and someone else types it, both of you are too close to it. You will probably repeat earlier mistakes. Someone else might find those mistakes.

2. *If you or your typist must check your work, try to allow a "cool-off" period.* Waiting a day or two after you have written the report or the typist has typed it will increase your alertness to mistakes.

3. *If you do not have time for a "cool off," slow down your reading.* You can probably read fast, perhaps 500 to 1,000 words per minute. But reading rapidly will lead to poor proofing. As you skim-read, you miss mistakes. You can slow down your reading by either (1) reading the material backwards, from end to beginning, (2) reading the material aloud, or (3) reading by pointing your finger at each word. Any of these methods will slow you to perhaps 100 words per minute and will focus your attention on each word or number. Of course, you still need to read the material in regular fashion, beginning to end.

Learn to use standard proofing symbols, and train secretaries and typists to use them. Here are some proofreading symbols (Exhibit 11-1). They are modifications of printers' symbols as adapted for business use. Use of these symbols will save time and ensure more accuracy.

4. *Watch likely places for slip-ups.*
- long tables
- notes at the bottom of tables
- headings—number sequences, capitalization, spelling
- sentences running from one page to another
- spelling of proper names, especially trademarks, readers' names, and company names

EXHIBIT 11-1

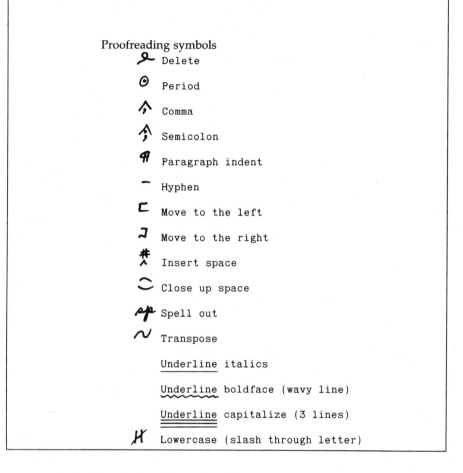

Proofreading symbols

✗	Delete
⊙	Period
⋀	Comma
⋀	Semicolon
¶	Paragraph indent
–	Hyphen
⊏	Move to the left
⊐	Move to the right
#	Insert space
⌒	Close up space
sp	Spell out
∼	Transpose
<u>Underline</u> italics	
<u>Underline</u> boldface (wavy line)	
<u>Underline</u> capitalize (3 lines)	
ℋ	Lowercase (slash through letter)

- words hyphenated at the ends of lines
- abbreviations and symbols
- syllables in long words
- doubled punctuation marks (quotation marks, dashes, commas, or brackets)
- tables of contents for long reports
- decimal points in monetary sums or other numbers
- internal digits in large numbers

5. *To the degree that time and the importance of the memo or report permit, verify calculations.*   At least guess or approximate answers to calculations, especially percentages. Check all totals in columns of figures. Verifying calculations is a good job to assign to a trainee, but you should still check them yourself.

6. *Check format for consistency.* Margins, indentions, and capitalization and underlining of headings should be consistent. Page numbers, heading numbers, and illustration numbers should be in proper order, and no gaps should remain.

7. *Check especially the spelling of trademarks and all other proper names for correct spelling and usage. Correct means as the owner prefers.* Remember that the normal rules of spelling do not apply to proper names. Misspelling a proper name can cause at least embarrassment, at worst (in the use of a trademark) a legal problem.

8. *Check spelling of all other words,* especially the troublesome words listed in Handbook B.

9. *Check all combined references to day/date.* For example, check Friday, October 13, to be sure Friday is October 13 and that this date is correct.

FINAL PREPARATION OF A MEMO OR REPORT

Before you send the memo or report, you must make certain that (1) you have enough copies and (2) it contains all the required parts. The widespread use of office duplicators has made preparation of one copy of a single-page memo easy. Preparation of many copies, however, requires that you tell the person preparing them how many you need, what type of paper you need, and whether you want the copies bound or stapled. Remember that rerunning is costly; better to have a few extra copies than risk a rerun.

Make sure your memo or report includes everything you planned. Verify the inclusion of all cross-referenced or other promised materials. Make sure that blanks are filled in and that promised attachments or appendices referred to are appended to the memo or report. Any phrases such as "the next page will show," "Appendix A gives . . . ," or "The graph on page 7 . . ." are warnings to keep you alert for any omitted materials.

Binding of reports may create problems. Your first planning steps should have included the binding method. But checking a large, bound report is costly. If you have many copies of a long report, have someone "fan" each copy, flipping rapidly as though shuffling a deck of cards. Such fanning may reveal a missing section, a badly printed page, or a section or page turned backwards.

SENDING OUT A MEMO OR REPORT

Again, you should have planned much earlier how to distribute your memo or report. If you did not, plan now before you deliver or mail the document. Here are some tips for sending memos and reports to your readers:

1. *Record the names or titles of everyone who will receive a copy of the document.* The memo or report can show these, either at the top right of the first page or at the end of the last page of a letter of transmittal.

2. *Build in a contingency time to allow for delivery of any document mailed.*

3. *For very important documents that are mailed, such as a proposal or tax report, ask for a "return receipt requested."* Remember: your copy may prove you wrote the report, but it does not prove that anyone got it.

4. *If receipt is essential, build in a "fail-safe" plan.* You can call the target reader to find out if the document got there.

5. *Time the receipt of the document carefully.* For instance, if you send a report to your boss and also to his or her boss, make sure your immediate boss gets a copy first.

6. *Keep a copy of any vital writing.*

7. *For proposals to be delivered by a certain time, arrange for delivery early.* For example, Joe Ransom's company is bidding on a big job, with the bid due in Des Moines by 4:00 p.m. on August 31. The person making the delivery goes to Des Moines on August 30, although the bid is not to be turned in until perhaps 3:30 p.m. the next day. Joe does not want to risk anyone opening his bid in time to reveal its details. Joe figures that preparing the bid cost $20,000. To protect the investment, he does not mind spending an extra day's pay and the cost of a motel room for the delivery person. Joe might deliver the bid himself.

8. *For important documents never risk not having enough postage.* If late arrival of a document would cost you a penalty, consider registered or certified mail.

9. *In planning your distribution, ask yourself: "What could go wrong?"* Remember Murphy's Law: "If anything can go wrong, it will."

10. *"Maintained" documents can create problems.* A maintained document is one that the writer promises to keep up to date. Typical maintained documents are service manuals for technical devices subject to change; policies and procedures manuals; and directives. Do not promise to maintain any document unless you really can do so. If you plan to keep the document up to date by sending the reader new pages, make sure that (1) the reader can replace the pages (replacement is hard with certain types of binders); and (2) you keep a master copy that shows both old and new pages.

PRINCIPLES FOR PRACTICE

1. When your final draft is finished, check it one more time.

2. Have someone who neither wrote nor typed your memo or report proofread it.

3. If no one else is available, let the report "cool off"; then read it slowly as you look for mistakes.

4. With all the time and money you have spent on preparing your memo or report, do not skimp on the cost of delivery.

FOR FURTHER STUDY

1. How many words do you find misspelled in these sentences? (Do not concern yourself about the meanings of the sentences.)

> The coorporation decided that the practises of previous steps had benefitted employes. As soon as the employe received the committment, he or she could at his or her convenience compair the allottment formally choosen with that of the present.

2. Today is Friday. Sue Schnell, a traveling salesperson, must send an important contact report to Sid Perry, regional manager (immediate boss), and to the regional manager, Marjorie Fraser (two steps up the line). Sue is in Toledo, Sid is in Chicago, and Marjorie is in San Diego. What should Sue do to send the reports properly?

3. You cannot use the U.S. Postal Service to send certain materials. The Postal Service puts weight and size limits on parcels, and it is not the cheapest way to send certain materials. Find out some basic facts about the Postal Service and other carriers. What materials can you send by carriers other than the Postal Service? What materials must you send by the Postal

Service? What are some advantages and disadvantages of the various ways of sending materials?

4. Why is misspelling a trademark bad? Why is misspelling or misusing your own company's trademark most serious?

5. Where could you find standards for abbreviations or symbols in your field?

6. Some people question the wisdom and even the morality of sending blind carbon copies. What do you think?

7. Suppose you wrote a report for your boss to sign. You sent the report to several people. A receiver called to point out a typographical error. Who is responsible—your boss, you, or the typist?

SECTION
IV

Getting Your Message
Across Face to Face

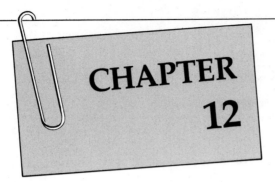

CHAPTER 12

To: The Reader
From: The Authors
Subject: Presenting Your Report and Other Speeches

After reading this chapter you will know that:

1. Words and language help us cope with daily life and partly determine how we perceive the world.

2. Public speaking is a form of expanded conversation accessible to normally intelligent people who have the desire to share ideas with others and who are willing to master a few skills.

3. Public-speaking situations are characterized by high structure, unbroken discourse, limited interaction, and the opportunity for preparation.

4. In public speaking you need: research, analysis, and organizational skills to put the speech together; language and transactional skills to deliver it.

5. In approaching the speech-making situation, you analyze your audience, explore the situation, and determine your speech's topic and purpose.

6. The three steps in speech preparation are research, organization, and construction.

7. Successful speech making depends both on content and delivery.

8. Effective delivery depends on establishing a good relationship with your audience, having necessary verbal skills, and using visual aids.

9. Accomplished public speakers are audience-centered rather than self-centered.

Presenting Your Report and Other Speeches

We live in a sea of words. Each of us is exposed to thousands—conceivably even millions—of words a day. Our words, our language, distinguish us from the other animals of the earth. Yet one thoughtful observer, Lewis Thomas, has said that we build our language and live within it as bees build and live within their hives.

Some dispute the importance of words. Children say, "Sticks and stones may break my bones but words will never harm me." They usually say this, however, when they have felt the lash of words or been cut by them. Samuel Butler claimed that "Words are but wind." Some communication scholars say that as a culture, we overemphasize oral communication at the expense of visual, tactile, kinesic, or even olfactory modes.

Nonetheless, it is hard to dispute the importance of words, language, and speech either from the individual viewpoint or from the broader perspective of history.

The impact of words and language on us and on history is shown by the work of anthropologists Edward Sapir and Benjamin Whorf. After studying differing cultures, they concluded that language determines how we perceive the world. And as to words' impact on historical events, the Old Testament puts the issue perfectly: "Many have fallen by the edge of the sword, but not so many as have fallen by the tongue."

Words help us cope with everyday problems of living. Bergen Evans used to say: "Words are one of our chief means of adjusting to all the situations of life. The better control we have over words, the more successful our adjustment is likely to be."

In most situations, even skillful speakers have little control over the words bombarding them. Even their own utterances are influenced by many variables when communicating interpersonally or in small groups. (We shall take up communication in interpersonal and small group situations in Chapters 15 and 16.)

This chapter, however, is devoted to the public presentation, or speech making, a situation in which the speaker can exercise a measure of control over the words spoken.

SPEECH MAKING

Speech is natural, yet people take to speech making like an eight-year-old takes to castor oil. For many people, standing before an audience is only slightly more desirable than standing before a wall facing six loaded rifles. In a survey of 3,000 Americans reported in David Wallechinsky's and Irving Wallace's *The Book of Lists,* more people said they were afraid of making a speech more than they were of any other thing. While 19 percent feared death and 32 percent feared heights, 41 percent feared speech making. Risking understatement, let us say that most people feel inadequate when called upon to say a few words.

This anxiety is partially a function of how we envision public speaking. We compare ourselves to a silver-tongued, full-throated orator whose word, voice, and gesture move people to tears one moment, laughter the next, then transform the audience from peace-loving Everymen to bloodthirsty warriors.

There was a time—before television, movies, or radio; before microphones or public address systems; indeed before literacy was widespread—when learning was passed on through oral tradition. Oratory was the primary means of education, information, persuasion, and entertainment. Vestiges of those days remain in college lecture halls, the "rubber chicken circuit" of after-dinner speeches, and in the pulpit. But the best evidence that oration's day is past is probably found in the United States Senate. The Senate, once known as the world's greatest debating society, is heir to the tradition of Daniel Webster and John C. Calhoun. Yet very few senators in the past decade can be described as great orators.

When you compare yourself to other public speakers, think of the majority of your college professors—the monotonous ones who bury their heads in their notes and come out when the bell rings. You can face an audience as well as they can!

We do not belittle the great responsibility that comes with public speaking. Jenkin L. Jones says: "A speech is a solemn responsibility. The man who makes a bad thirty-minute speech to two hundred people wastes only a half hour of his own time. But he wastes one hundred hours of the audience's time—more than four days—which should be a hanging offense."

Acceptable public speaking is not a fine art, but rather a form of enlarged conversation accessible to normally intelligent people. However, they must have the desire to share ideas and thoughts with groups of others, and they must master a few skills.

Speech making is a rich and complicated process, but its simplicity is understood less than its complexity. Perhaps for this reason, Charles Brown and Charles Van Riper wrote, "Speech . . . is our supreme tool, but like the ape who employs a flute to scratch himself, we have not yet learned all the uses of this greatest of human inventions."

Characteristics of the Public Presentation

Although we likened public speaking to conversation enlarged, there are factors that set speech making apart. These include: the structure of the communication situation; unbroken disclosure; limited interaction; and the opportunity to prepare before the speech. Looking at these differences will help us to understand public speaking.

Structure: Conversations are loosely structured. Participants may have varying norms, may constantly shift roles, may have any of a number of motivations or purposes, and need not have a set agenda.

Speech-making situations, however, are highly structured. Interaction norms are fully established. There is no question about who speaks to whom, or in what sequence. Roles are well understood, with all parties— introducer, speaker, and members of the audience—knowing how they are to behave. Motivations may differ, but they are pretty much limited to entertaining, informing, persuading, or getting an audience to take an action. Finally, a speech takes place within a specific time framework. It begins at a particular time or at a designated place in the agenda. It lasts for a given period, sandwiched between introductions and words of appreciation.

In short, there is little flexibility in the structure. This is both a bane and a boon to the speaker. Structure helps, because it gives the speech-maker guidelines for the presentation and situation. But it makes things harder because the audience has standards and expectations by which to judge the speech.

Continuous discourse: If you were in the middle of a conversation and someone launched into a speech lasting twenty to thirty minutes you would be
surprised. Why? Because we do not hold forth for long periods in daily
interaction. Thus, public speaking represents an unusual opportunity to
explore ideas more fully, to convey information more thoroughly, to draw
out logical rationales to support positions in argument, or to convince your
audience to take particular actions.

Limited interaction: In public speaking, most of the overt communication
is one way—from speaker to audience. This allows continuous discourse.
It is a mistake, however, to believe that *all* communication flows one way.
Interaction is limited, but there is interaction. Even as the speaker is speaking, the audience is giving feedback by laughing, yawning, nodding, sleep-
ing, staring into space, and in extreme situations, booing and tossing
tomatoes. The speaker must be sensitive to the audience's responses, adapt-
ing style, pacing delivery, and even changing speech content according to
the feedback received.

Prior preparation: Mark Twain quipped, "It usually takes more than three
weeks to prepare a good impromptu speech." We shall discuss speech preparation later, but let us say now that the opportunity to prepare in advance
is a major difference between conversation and public speaking. Preparation
is the main factor giving the speaker control. Conversationalists have little
or no time to consider their audiences, research their subjects, organize
their presentations, or edit their remarks. But the speech-maker can do all
of these things. When speakers fail to prepare, they lose the richest advantage available to them.

Speech-Making Skills

George Bernard Shaw claimed that he learned to speak in public the way
he learned to skate: "By doggedly making a fool of myself until I got used
to it." In fact, the best and maybe the only way to learn speech making is
to do it. The skills you need are much the same as those you have used in
conversations all your life. The problem is to get used to using them in a
different context.

You will need skills in research, analysis, and organization to put the
speech together. You will need language and transactional skills to deliver
it. All of these skills will be discussed later. Here we shall look at some
things common to all communication situations and apply them to public
speaking.

The first of these is sensitivity to others and to self. Henry Clay Smith says sensitivity is "the ability to predict what an individual will feel, say and do about you, himself and others." When speakers can predict responses, they can construct and deliver messages that better meet audience needs and expectations.

The basis of sensitivity is the desire to perceive others. It is the need to learn about their needs, attitudes, history, values, and expectations. Sensitivity also involves the highest use of our perceptual faculties, to gather and evaluate information about others. It helps us to understand our own biases, attitudes, and values as they relate to our perceptions of others. According to John W. Keltner, "To be senstive to others, one must be able to empathize with them; that is, we must be able to perceive another person's feeling, thoughts, and behavior as if they were our own." Of course, we can never completely know another person, much less an entire audience. But this is an ideal, and it points to the importance of gathering information about the audience both before and during the presentation.

Another skill relevant to all communication situations is the ability to cope with oneself. We have mentioned the need to understand one's own biases, attitudes, and values. But we also must learn to deal with what we understand about ourselves. The skill of self-coping is important in public presentations, where every statement carries messages about the speaker. Effective speaking tells an awesome amount about the person making the speech. Furthermore, self-disclosure is an important element in public speaking because it helps to establish credibility. It identifies the speaker with the audience.

In addition to coping with self, the speech-maker must cope with others. This may seem less important in public speaking than in conversation, but the apparent lack of interaction is deceiving. Speakers who overlook the interactive elements may be out of touch with the values, attitudes, and behaviors of the audience. Such speakers often use their words to shield themselves from the audience. Instead of seeing speech as a bond, such people use it as a barrier.

Finally, the speech maker must strongly desire to *communicate*, not just speak. This desire changes words into messages; it charges them with meaning. You relate to your audience, not just talk to it. This desire marks a commitment not only to the speech, but to the speaking situation, which includes your audience and its needs, values, and goals.

Approaching the Speech-Making Situation

So you have been asked to make a speech, give a talk, prepare a presentation. Maybe your boss asked you to make an oral presentation of a proposal that you developed. You feel honored, and you should. The invitation means that people feel their time will be well spent listening to what you have to say. But you are also anxious, unsure, even fearful. You are not sure that you can rise above the dictum laid down by country people in Vermont who say: "Don't talk unless you improve the silence."

As you approach this situation, realize that anxiety or fear are normal. Most people have stage fright or butterflies in their stomachs. If they did not, those phrases would have never become clichés! A moderate amount of anxiety may be useful. It is a physiological state of arousal, and it can promote heightened emotional and intellectual capacities.

So why are you afraid? Maybe a grade, a promotion, a sale, or your good name is on the line. But fear in public speaking situations is usually fear of the unknown. The audience, the setting, your capacity to give a worthwhile talk, whether you will succeed, are all unknowns at first. But your approach to your preparation should go a long way toward making the unknowns known.

Experienced speech-makers usually start their preparation by asking a series of questions about the purpose of the speech, the audience, and the situation in which it will be given. These include:

- To whom am I speaking?
- What is the purpose (to inform, persuade, motivate, impress, control, inspire, instruct)?
- What are the goals of the audience?
- What does my audience know about me?
- What experience has the audience had with my topic?
- How is the audience likely to feel about me and my topic?
- What kind of circumstances will surround my talk?

Knowing the audience.   Effective speakers are audience-centered rather than self-centered. Effective speeches appeal to the interests of the audience rather than those of the speaker. Meanings are in people, not in words. So how our messages relate to the audience's experience and response system will determine our success. To become audience-centered, to appeal to audience interests, and to have some hope for transferring meaning, you must know the audience.

How can the speaker know? Often, speeches are made to groups known only slightly, if at all. There is rarely time to survey or interview even a sample of the audience. Still, there are five ways to learn about your audience.

1. Someone asked you to speak. Ask him or her about listeners and the circumstances in which you will be speaking.

2. If you are speaking to an established group that meets regularly, and if you have the chance, go to a meeting in advance.

3. If you are speaking to an established group, find out its nature and purposes and who belongs to it.

4. Find an opportunity to meet casually with members of your potential audience. Draw them out about their needs, attitudes, interests, and values.

5. Put yourself in an audience member's shoes. Let imagination and common sense tell you how your audience might feel or react.

What do you know about your audience? Who they are; how old the members of the audience are; what they do for a living; what their experiences are; what their politics are; their special interests; their values, attitudes, and beliefs. Are they likely to respond emotionally or rationally? Will they be friendly, hostile, skeptical, apathetic? What are their cultural, social, and economic backgrounds?

Once you have the answers to these questions, you will have an idea how to present your topic, how to establish credibility, what language and delivery style to use.

The insights may even affect the content of your speech. Let us say that your purpose is persuasion. You have learned that your audience leans in favor of your position. You had intended a balanced, rational presentation, but you decide instead to take a one-sided, emotional approach, ending with clearly stated conclusions calling for specific action. If, on the other hand, you learn that your audience is ambivalent or hostile, or if you learn that the group is highly educated, you would prefer a balanced, rational approach.

Exploring the situation. The occasion and location of the speech will affect your success. You must consider the physical and psychological circumstances likely to surround your presentation.

You must consider the size of your audience (you do not speak to five people the same way that you speak to five hundred); acoustics (whether you are speaking indoors or out, whether microphones or public address systems are available, the size of the hall, its acoustics); lighting (one excellent talk was ruined because the speaker was in front of glass doors in the bright sunshine and people saw only a dark form against the blue sky); and physical distractions (the noise of air-conditioners, plates being cleared, airplanes overhead, heat, uncomfortable chairs). If negative factors are present, adapt your presentation. You may speak louder, make the speech shorter, insert extra humor, or ask the audience to participate to hold attention.

Pychological factors refer to the mood, receptiveness, and expectations of your audience. If you are the fourth speaker on a five-hour program, your audience will respond differently than if you were first. Speaking after a heavy meal is different from speaking before it. Speeches at birthday celebrations are different from speeches at funerals.

Speech topic and purpose: In many cases, you will be invited to speak on a set topic. Sometimes you will be asked to pick your own subject.

When you choose your own, make sure it is suitable to the audience, the occasion, and to yourself. Nothing is more disastrous than attempting to talk about something of which you are ignorant.

Even when the topic is assigned, you must pitch the speech at an acceptable level. A discussion of nuclear energy is appropriate for either a Rotary Club or a group of nuclear physicists, but you would not give both groups the same speech. Moreover, topic is different from purpose. Speeches on similar topics differ greatly depending on whether you wish to inform, persuade, or entertain, or some combination of the three.

While we are discussing the various purposes of speeches, let us explore persuasion. Much research has been done on persuasion, a function of speaking that is still misunderstood.

Virtually all of speech has a persuasion component. Any time speech is used to induce changes in behavior, beliefs, knowledge, or attitudes, persuasion is at work. Many public-speaking courses very nearly promise that through oratorical wizardry, you will be able to manipulate others.

There are no magical means by which your words can automatically cause others to behave as you wish. To persuade some one or some group, you must first get their attention. You must then have them perceive your message, give them the necessary knowledge, inspire belief in or commitment to your cause, and finally, induce the desired action. Successful attempts at persuasion are rare, considering how often they are made. When they succeed, it is because the persuader satisfied not only personal goals, but also those of the audience.

Preparing the Speech

Having considered the audience, the circumstances in which your speech will be given, and its topic and purpose, you are ready to start preparation.

Research. We have already discussed gathering information in Chapter 8. Research for public speaking requires additional work, however. Your research should collect information that is new to your audience, current, authoritative, valid, reliable, and relevant. You should look not only for facts, but also for illustrations and examples that will humanize and personalize the data and help you hold interest. True-to-life anecdotes, drawn from your own experience or from that of people you know, are useful. Historical anecdotes can be excellent. Anticipate your audience's informational needs. Ask yourself the questions you think they might ask. Your research should immerse you in your subject. Collect more information than you can use. You can use the best of it. Do not force structure or conclusions onto the information until you have collected it all. Even then, give the information a chance to "ripen." Digest it.

Sources of your material range from the local library to conversations with people who know the subject. Review your own experiences for anecdotal material that you can use with integrity.

Organization.   Once you are swimming in information, begin to organize it. Mold it into a form appropriate to your audience, occasion, and topic. Even the best information means nothing if it is poorly organized.

Several patterns are used regularly. These include:

1. Topical pattern, in which you present your main idea, support it, and end by restating it.

2. Chronological pattern, in which information is presented in the order in which it happened historically.

3. Inductive pattern, in which you cite specific examples in support of a general conclusion. Be sure to offer enough examples to warrant the conclusion, and to account for any contradictions. (It is often effective to present an apparent contradiction that you can show actually fits the pattern you have derived.)

4. Deductive pattern, in which you give a valid general rule and draw detailed conclusions by applying the principle to specific circumstances.

5. Cause-Effect pattern, in which you explain reasons for particular actions and conclude that certain sets of events are linked in causal ways.

6. Alternatives pattern, in which a problem is presented, alternatives are listed, and then the alternatives are eliminated for cause until a single solution remains.

7. Analytical pattern, in which a problem or topic is broken down into its parts and the relationship of each part is shown to the whole.

Other organizational patterns also exist. They include descriptive, illustrative, definitional, hierarchical, and comparison/contrast. Combinations of patterns may be used.

Construction. You must pay especial attention to the beginning and the end of your speech. The organizational patterns discussed apply mainly to the body of your talk. Winning speeches also have good openings and conclusions.

Your opening should get the audience's attention and acceptance, arousing their interest and letting them know what they can expect. Some speakers begin with a relevant anecdote, joke, story, or instance. Do not feel obligated to start with a "cute" story. Nothing loses audiences faster than an old joke that falls flat. However, a story with character and relevance can be excellent. Other effective openers include plunging immediately into the most dramatic or significant part of your speech. Or you can begin with intense directness or earnestness, or ask a series of unanswered questions.

The ending of your speech may summarize what you have said, draw clear conclusions, or recommend specific actions that your audience can take, depending on your original purposes. End your speech cleanly. Do not wind down like a neglected clock.

Overstructure. Inexperienced speakers often overstructure. They prepare a word-for-word script and then attempt to memorize it. Such presentations come off exactly as you might expect—cold, unspontaneous, unresponsive.

To avoid this, the speaker should approach the podium completely versed in the subject, with notes or an outline, and the method of delivery decided upon.

Delivering the Speech

Just how important is the delivery? Many a well-researched talk filled with useful, well-organized information has failed because of poor delivery. On the other hand, you will not find people saying they enjoyed a shallow, incompetent, misleading, inaccurate speech. Content and delivery go hand in hand. In this section, we shall look at the methods and goals of good delivery.

Establishing a relationship with your audience. The most effective speaker is one who is known to be honest, sympathetic to the audience, committed to and excited by the subject, and willing to risk rejection. These attributes can make a speech a success even if the speaker slaughters grammar, stutters, or lisps. Consequently, your first job is to establish your relationship and identity with the audience. This process is often aided by anecdotes— funny or not—that show elements of your personality or your experience, or that demonstrate your point of view. The speaker must show that he or she and the audience are on common ground while building what Aristotle called *ethos*. Today we call it *credibility*.

An audience should perceive the similarity between itself and the speaker, and the speaker should have credibility. These two factors will partly determine whether the speaker's ideas will be accepted. In technical terms, perceived similarity is called *homophily*. Perceived dissimilarity is called *heterophily*. To encourage homophily, the speaker may open by speaking about values, experiences, and background held in common with members of the audience. Once they are convinced that the speaker is "one of us," audiences become empathetic. They believe that the speaker has their interests at heart.

Homophily is just one of the important aspects of credibility. An audience can perceive the speaker as one of its own, and still doubt that the speaker knows the subject. Five other dimensions of credibility are: *competence, character, composure, sociability,* and *dynamism.*

Competence has to do with knowledge or expertness. It is the audience's perception of the speaker's intelligence and authority. An introduction by someone known and trusted is one way to present credentials convincingly to the group.

Character is related to homophily. It consists of perceived trustworthiness, integrity, and consistency. It depends largely on the perceived congruence of the speaker's value system with the audience's.

Composure has to do with the appearance of the speaker. Nervousness, visible trembling, stammering, displays of emotion, or the like raise doubts about the speaker in the minds of the audience.

Sociability is the likability factor. If the speaker is seen as attractive, cheerful, kind, and friendly, credibility is increased. People are slow to accept or believe someone they see as unattractive, misanthropic, mean, or cruel.

The final element is *dynamism.* Speakers who appear to be extroverted, strong, mildly aggressive, and to show true interest in their listeners inspire confidence.

The presentation itself.   Having looked at the speech-making situation, preparation, and identification with the audience, it is time to talk about words and their delivery. Voice, diction, gestures, and even silence are important here.

As noted, public speaking can be like an enlarged conversation. As audience members, we like speakers who talk with us, not at us. The public voice should sound as if the speaker were talking to each listener alone. For choosing the words you will use, William Butler Yeats has given the best advice: "Think like a wise man but communicate in the language of the people."

Vocal and oral problems usually have to do not with the voice, but with diction, intonation, and pacing. Vocal shortcomings that are not problems in conversation may become distractions in public presentations. These difficulties include: running words together, dropping word endings, dropping the voice at the ends of sentences, speaking in a monotone, or using monotonous and repetitious pacing and rhythm. All of these can be corrected if you pay attention to *how* you are speaking, as well as to what you are talking about.

Nonverbal aspects can be important. First, avoid wild gestures or carefully planned and executed movements. These can distract from your presentation. Forced, unnatural gestures are inappropriate and look ridiculous. Just remember to "be yourself."

Nonverbal communication rule number two relates to eye contact. Look at your audience, not at your notes, the ceiling, or the back wall. In speeches, as in conversation, people distrust those who do not look into their eyes.

Other aspects of nonverbal communication include stance, posture, and dress. These indicate interest in and respect for your audience. They can suggest confidence and honesty. Dress appropriately. Do not pace like a caged animal. And do what your mother told you—stand up straight. Nonverbal communication will be discussed more thoroughly in Chapter 14.

It may seem contradictory, but let us share a few thoughts about silence. Too many public speakers fear that even momentary silence will be considered the absence of mental activity. In fact, silence has positive attributes. Used at the beginning of a talk, it lends gravity. It can emphasize a point by allowing time for it to "sink in." The speaker who pauses before choosing certain words may give the impression of thoughtfulness—the carefulness of a reflective mind searching for precise meanings. Silence, at times, can be as important to a speech as speaking.

Using visual aids. Visual aids may become an accepted, even expected, aspect of public presentations. Audio-visual communication is discussed extensively in Chapter 19, but we need to consider it specifically in relation to speech making.

According to psychologists, people who have to use more senses have higher rates of interest and retention. Visual aids cause audiences to use more senses. Thus, such aids improve attention, interest, understanding, and retention.

The most common aids include: handouts, chalk boards, flip charts, felt or magnetic boards, transparencies, slides, films, and video tapes. All require special equipment and preparation.

Visual aids should supplement and reinforce your spoken message, not simply outline or repeat what you have said. They should never compete or conflict with what you are saying.

Some general guidelines for using visual aids include:

1. Be sure everyone can see. Details should be large enough; reproduction of adequate quality; sightlines clear.

2. Keep the visual aid as simple as possible. Multimedia shows are slick, but they can be distracting.

3. Make visual aids neat, attractive, and professional. Sloppiness and mis-spelled words reflect negatively on the speaker.

4. Make sure your equipment is in good repair and that you, or someone you can count on, knows how to run it.

5. While using visual aids, continue to talk to your audience. Your chalk board is not interested in your face, and your audience is not interested in your back.

PRESENTING YOUR REPORT: SPECIAL CONSIDERATIONS

Everything written in this chapter about public speaking in general applies specifically to oral reporting in business situations. As you plan and write your report, as you gather information for it, you should have in mind your ultimate oral presentation. In this sense, the oral presentation is an integral part of your report's preparation.

The audience for your presentation will not be casual listeners. They will be concerned primarily about two things: how your information can help the company and how they might personally benefit from what you have to say. Time is valuable to these people and printed copies of your report are usually available to them. Consequently, you should primarily deal with highlights and conclusions and be prepared to answer questions.

Presentations in business are usually made to small groups. Keep in mind what we have said about the similarities between conversations and public speaking. Your goal is to talk *with* people, sharing ideas, helping them to reach conclusions. Remember, ultimately you are on the same team, after the same goals.

PULLING IT ALL TOGETHER: TWO EXAMPLES

One evening a college professor/consultant was invited to speak to a group of bankers on "Private Enterprise." The speaker knew that he had been invited because he had recently impressed a local Rotary Club with a similar talk. He knew that his audience came from small towns. He knew that he was addressing a group that met regularly for social and educational reasons, with more emphasis on the former than the latter.

He assumed that his audience was politically conservative, and predisposed to the topic. He also assumed that he would be addressing a group with traditional religious views. Finally, he assumed that his professional and academic credentials would assure reasonable credibility.

The speaker arrived early. He made an effort to meet and talk with the people in his audience-to-be. He noticed that despite the cash bar, little drinking was going on, which confirmed his assumption about religion. He asked about the local congressional race and found that he was correct about political conservatism.

He noticed that many people were surprised at his looks, specifically his beard, his longish hair, and his relative youth. He saw that these factors could undermine his credibility and turn his audience against him, especially when he was critical of ways in which private enterprise was being practiced.

During the dinner before the speech, the speaker jotted some notes to himself. Although he had given substantially the same speech many times, he knew that his success depended on how he presented his material now.

After an introduction by the organization's vice-president, which included a listing of professional and academic accomplishments, the speaker took the lectern and silently scanned the room. He began talking about his grandparents, who lived in a small town not far away, and his father, who had once owned a store in another. He named towns, people, and establishments indicating that he knew the territory. He was, in effect, one of them.

Then he told a story to show what happens when people do not understand private enterprise. The story was about a young man who went off to college and found himself espousing socialism because he did not understand private enterprise. The speech became rhythmic and took on a pattern familiar to the audience. The speaker revealed that he was that young man. And borrowing phrases from the churches that his audience attended, he admitted, in effect, that he had sinned but that he had seen the light.

By this time, he had the audience in the palm of his hand. And by maintaining his cadence, he showed that others had also sinned out of ignorance and had therefore abused the system. He named big businesses; he criticized farmers because they sought to avoid competition and the discipline of the marketplace. He showed that ignorance and abuse are the twin forces that threaten the system from within, and that his audience was part of the problem and could be part of the solution. At the end, he suggested actions that members of the audience could take to work toward solutions.

After the speech, members of the audience crowded around the speaker asking about further actions they could take. By all standards, it was a successful speech, covering subjects that might have aroused hostility as easily as praise.

Several weeks later, the same speaker made another talk, this time to inmates of a federal penitentiary. Again, he took the time to look over his audience before addressing them. Again, he spoke his message in their terms. After this speech, he was again surrounded by listeners, one of whom asked: "Man, you sure you ain't been in here? You talk like you been one of us."

The bankers and the prisoners had responded in similar ways and for the same reason. The speaker had established that he could relate to the world as they did. In neither case was the audience positively predisposed to all that he had said, but he was careful to surround his more controversial points with points with which the audience could relate and agree. He established his credentials, but he did not rest on them. He built audience identification at every opportunity—not by pretending to be a banker or a convicted criminal, but by honestly presenting himself as a human being with wants, needs, and beliefs not unlike theirs. He "leveled" with them on their own terms without compromising his own message or integrity.

Accomplished public speakers are successful because they gather information about their audiences and can predict how the audience respond to their messages. They are flexible and creative. They adapt their presentations. They are constantly aware of how their audience is reacting, and they maintain flexiblity as they speak. They have clear ideas as to the goals and purposes of their speeches, and present their ideas with honesty and sincerity. Moreover, they offer their audiences a chance to relate to them personally by revealing aspects of themselves, usually anecdotally. "We face similar problems and concerns," they say in essence. "Why not try the way that I've found to deal with them?"

With this attitude, you can understand why a speaker could be flattered when a convict assumes that the speaker has been a convict too.

The message of this chapter is that if a speaker or a speech is to succeed, the goals of the audience must come first. Remember, organization, construction, credibility, and delivery will fail if the speech is not audience-centered.

We conclude with an "Audience's Bill of Rights." Think about it when called upon to speak.

PRINCIPLES
FOR
PRACTICE:
AN AUDIENCE'S
BILL OF RIGHTS

1. Listeners have a right to a message worth the time and effort they invest in listening.

2. Listeners have a right to information addressing their own needs, interests, and desires.

3. Listeners have a right to honesty and sincerity. Speakers may seek to guide them but not to manipulate them.

4. Listeners have a right to language they can relate to and understand.

5. Listeners have a right to an orderly presentation of material.

6. Listeners have a right to offer constructive feedback and to expect it to have an impact upon the speech or speaker.

7. Listeners have a right to a speaker's interest and enthusiasm.

8. Listeners have a right to material that is specific and factual.

9. Listener have a right to speeches that are thoroughly researched and prepared.

10. Listeners are the final judge of the quality, value, and success of the speech and the skill, credibility, and acceptability of the speaker.

FOR FURTHER STUDY

1. Read a five-minute passage of a favorite book into a tape recorder. Play it back. Critique your vocal delivery.

2. Attend several public lectures. (Schools, libraries, churches, political events, and civic associations are good places to find public lectures.) Analyze how each affected you and why.

3. Interview the executives of local companies or organizations to discover how and when public speeches are used in their organizations internally and externally. Find out how the individual speakers develop the process of speech making (preparation, research, construction, delivery, evaluation).

CHAPTER 13

To: The Reader
From: The Authors
Subject: Listening

After reading this chapter you will know that:

1. Communication breakdowns often result from listening failures.

2. Listening is the most common communication behavior.

3. Effective listening requires making efforts, taking responsiblity and assuming risk.

4. Effective listeners make better decisions, save time, motivate others, and more readily develop positive relationships.

5. Listening is a four-phase process: attention, reception, perception, and retention.

6. Active listening begins with listening to yourself— knowing your own beliefs, biases, and motives.

7. Active listeners respect others' potential worth, consider their rights, and have confidence in their capacity for self-direction.

8. The purpose of active listening should be defined in terms of the speaker's needs, not the listener's.

9. A psychological climate conducive to active listening include suspending judgment, and a feeling of equality and freedom.

10. Active listening is contagious.

Listening

Jim worked on the assembly line at the local automobile plant. He liked the money, but he frequently was bored by his repetitious job. A creative fellow, he devised a plan of job rotation which he shared with co-workers, who were enthusiastic about his ideas. But when Jim took the idea to his boss, he got this curt reply: "Jim, we pay you to assemble bumpers, not to think."

A month later Jim's boss was called on the carpet by his boss about the increasing number of defects found in cars coming off his line. The worst defect of all was that Jim's boss did not know how to listen.

When Kathy had a problem with her co-workers, she talked the situation over with her supervisor, a man with twenty years' experience in the company. In presenting her problem, Kathy became quite emotional. Her boss's advice was to "live with the situation," and he gave her a paternal talk about controlling her emotions in the man's world of business.

Two weeks later, Kathy quit—the third female to leave that position in a year. The supervisor claimed that women could not take it. In fact, he could not listen.

The marriage counselor shook her head—another case, like so many she had dealt with over the years. Mrs. Cox complained that Mr. Cox never listened. Mr. Cox said that Mrs. Cox never said anything worth listening to. Mr. Cox said Mrs. Cox wasted money, never understanding the family's financial situation. Mrs. Cox said Mr. Cox did not understand the cost of running a household. Mr. Cox said their sex life was dull. Mrs. Cox said that he never told her what he desired sexually.

The marriage counselor watched Mr. and Mrs. Cox bickering, seeing how each attacked and rebutted the other without hearing what the other was saying. "A classic breakdown in communication," she observed, neither listens to the other."

George was a practical joker. Once after a wedding, he went down the reception line saying to each person in turn, "My mother died this morning. . . . My mother died this morning." And each person responded with "Thank you so much. We're glad you could come." No one listened.

A professor, lecturing to tops of heads and scribbling pens, wondered if anyone was actually listening to his explanation of anti-trust law. He used an absurd example to see whether he would get any response. He did. A student raised his hand: "Do we need to know that for the test?"

The professor shook his head, his suspicions confirmed.

When we speak of communication breakdowns, we are often talking about failures in listening. There are messages galore, but is anyone paying attention? Exhibit 13-1 shows listening as the most common communication activity; yet we take it for granted. We get formal training in the other activities, but seldom in listening. Thoreau observed, "It takes two to speak the truth—one to speak and another to hear."

EXHIBIT 13-1

Source: Paul Rankin, quoted in Ralph Nichols, "Listening Is Good Business," *Management of Personnel Quarterly*, Vol. 1, No. 2 (Winter 1962), p. 2.

Listening	45%
Speaking	30%
Reading	16%
Writing	9%

Executive Communication Time 100%

Most of us, quite simply, are lousy listeners. Research shows that the normal retention rate of orally communicated messages is less than 50 percent. This is true even when retention is tested immediately after communication of the message. After eight hours, we remember about a third of what has been said.

Many factors contribute to poor listening: inattention, distraction, distorted perception, previously developed attitudes and expectations, inability to empathize, or a deprived communications environment. Too many of us will not put forth the effort, take the responsibility, or assume the risks that active listening requires.

Our poor listening habits are important because of what they cost us. Good listeners make better decisions based on better information. They stimulate better speaking by others. They use their listening time more effectively and save time. They motivate subordinates by truly listening to them, and they more readily develop deep, positive relations.

THE LISTENING PROCESS

Listening is a vital aspect of the processes of communication and perception. It attempts to bridge what pioneering psychologist William James called "The most immutable barrier in nature"—the gap between one person's thoughts and another's. Listening is associated with hearing, but it actually involves several senses and the full range of cognitive processes. What we see, how we feel, what we want or expect, sensations of touch and smell, what we are thinking about—all affect whether we hear. They affect whether we actually listen and the meaning we attach to what we hear. With these factors in mind, we can understand that listening is a four-phase process involving attention, reception, perception, and retention.

Attention: There is a joke about a farmer who had two prize mules that needed training. He had heard about a man who was the best mule trainer in three counties. "Mr. Brown," said the mule owner to the mule trainer, "I've heard you're the best mule trainer in three counties. But I don't want you to hurt my animals. Just how is it you train miles?"

"Sir, you don't have to worry about a thing. All I do is talk to them," Mr. Brown explained.

"You just talk to them?"

"I just talk to them."

Satisfied, the farmer left his mules with Mr. Brown and went walking down the road. But before he had gone fifty feet, he heard a terrible crack and a mule squeal. Mr. Brown was hitting the mules on the head with a two-by-four pine board.

"Mr. Brown," the farmer screamed, stop that immediately. I thought you said you trained mules by just talking to them."

"That's right," said Mr. Brown.

"But you're hitting my mules with a board."

"Well," Mr. Brown said, "I just talk to the mules, but to make sure they're listening, I have to get their attention first."

Attention is a prerequisite to the listening process. All too often, it seems that we have to hit people with a board before we get their attention.

Attention is a willingness to expose yourself to certain stimuli. It is a selective process. We choose (usually subconsciously) to attend to certain stimuli and to ignore others. In general, people attend to stimuli that relate to their own goals or objectives; that satisfy their social needs; that they have learned or habitually select; or that are unexpected. They will not attend to stimuli that are inconsistent with their own frames of reference. Moreover, attention varies with the relationship between speaker, listener, and the environment and involves such things as credibility, liking, and role characteristics. Factors like complexity (messages that are too simple are boring, and those that are too complex are confusing), intensity (loudness or other attention-getting qualities), and redundancy (repeated messages are more likely to be heard) are also related.

We humans naturally want to hear only certain kinds of information. We prefer to give our attention only to what we want to hear, to that which agrees with us or that we like. To listen effectively, however, one must overcome these tendencies. Discipline can help you be aware of your own biases and expectations. Only then can you become sensitive to information that may not accord with your pre-existing beliefs.

We have all known bosses, teachers, parents, spouses, and mates who hear only what they want to hear. Nothing else gets their attention. Those trying to get something across that does not fit the "listener's" preconceived desires feel frustration and disillusionment. Important information goes uncommunicated, or if communicated, unheard. Mistakes may go uncorrected. More productive ways to accomplish tasks may go undiscovered. Decisions may be made without considering highly relevant but unheard information.

As William James put it, "What holds attention determines action." Conversely, if something cannot get our attention, we cannot act upon it.

Reception: Giving attention is like being tuned to a particular radio station. Reception does not occur until you turn on your set. Reception is the actual physical impingement of stimuli on sensory organs. Two variables influence reception: ability and noise.

As it concerns listening, ability is the physical capacity to hear. Hearing impairments obviously decrease ability to listen.

"Noise" means stimuli that compete with a message, not only in the auditory channel but in all sensory channels. When confronted with many sounds, you can scarcely distinguish any given sound (although research shows that some of us listen better with at least some background distraction—the presence of noise seems to make us concentrate harder). Likewise, a flash of light or pain or some other strong sensation in another sensory channel may cut off the auditory channel. Certain physical environments that minimize but do not eliminate distractions are helpful to listening.

Perception: Three baseball umpires discussing their work found that they had different beliefs about their business. Their argument went on for hours, but it can be summed up as follows:

"Some's balls and some's strikes," the first umpire said, "and I calls 'em as they is."

The second umpire made a distinction. "Some's balls and some's strikes," he agreed, "and I call 'em as I sees 'em."

The third umpire disagreed with both. "Some's balls and some's strikes," he said, "but they ain't nothing 'til I calls 'em."

.Conveniently, the umpires present three schools of thought about perception. Like the first umpire, some believe that objective reality is accurately reflected through passive perception. A second group holds that while there is an objective reality, perception is an active process that does not always lead to conclusions that correspond to reality. Still others would agree with umpire 3, maintaining that for all practical purposes, reality exists only in our minds as a function of perception. Research suggests that the truth lies somewhere between umpires 2 and 3.

Perception consists of making sense out of experience. It assigns meaning to stimuli received through sensory channels. Sensing and perceiving differ greatly, as is shown by the fact that although most people's sensory equipment is similar, their perception and interpretation of phenomena differ widely. Consequently, it is not words themselves, but how listeners construe words, that determines what listeners may hear, how they may feel, and how they will respond.

Perception is a process of constructing meaning based on apprehended symbolic stimuli. It is based upon the listener's frame of reference, standards, values, attitudes, beliefs, ideas, expectations, roles, needs, experience, and personal history. Interpretations are influenced by the situation surrounding communication events and metacommunicational factors like expressive movements, vocal qualities, facial expressions, posture, and spatial positionings. To understand human communication and to be successful at it, we must consider the way people interpret what they see and hear.

As you have gathered, perception is remarkably complex. It is so complex that perceivers themselves simplify it. They reduce an ever-changing and chaotic world of sensations to a fairly stable environment, reasonably free of ambiguity and relatively predictable. Perception works when people relate incoming stimuli to their frames of reference. Thus we oversimplify. We force unique events into convenient prearranged categories and jump to conclusions based on insufficient information.

Through these characteristics of perception, we save time and effort, avoid ego-threatening ambiguity, and build efficiency into day-to-day activities. However, we also lose the capacity to deal with novel stimuli, the important differences between people or events, and the richness of human experience. To become effective listeners, we must overcome the innate limits of our perceptions.

Retention: The final phase of the listening process is retention. This means the storage in memory of information gained through attention, reception, and perception. Our capacity to transfer information into storage is affected by all the factors that influence other aspects of listening.

Failing to work at listening will reduce retention. By yielding to distraction, by letting your attention drift, by letting concentration lapse, you reduce your chances of retention. Even note-taking, that time-honored practice, can distract from learning if it replaces active listening.

A problem related to retention of information gained through the auditory channel is this: our capacity to process such information exceeds by three or four times the rate at which most people talk. We have "spare time" while listening to others. Most of us use that time poorly. Our minds wander, or we prepare rebuttals. If we use the time well—evaluating what is being said, searching out meaning, repeating major points—we improve our retention capacities.

FIVE LOUSY LISTENERS

All of us recognize that some people listen better than others. Before looking at what makes a good listener, take a look at some bad ones: the selfish listener; the lazy listener; the emotional listener; the fact listener; and the defensive listener. You may see yourself in one, some, or all of these characters. If you do, you should identify some areas to work on in your efforts to become a better listener. If you do not, you are probably fooling yourself.

Selfish listeners: Have you ever talked with someone who could hear things only the way he or she wanted to hear them? If so, you were talking with a selfish listener.

Selfish listeners are restricted to their own points of view and frames of reference. Such people listen only to what they want to hear as it relates to their wants, needs, or views. They can be the victim of autistic thinking, a confusion of reality with what is wanted.

Sensitivity and empathy are absent in the selfish listener. In fact, the selfish listener rarely takes any responsibility for communication, preferring to leave it to the speaker. Not realizing that the more one believes that everyone has something worth listening to, the more one gets out of listening, the selfish listener assumes that few people can say anything valuable. As this attitude is reflected in selfish listeners' overt behavior—the failure to communicate interest or concern—they become victims of their own self-fulfilling prophecies. Since they do not stimulate speakers by showing interest, they are not offered interesting information.

Lazy listeners: Lazy listeners specialize in passive listening. They do not seek beyond what they expect to hear. They will not do the hard work of listening: maintaining concentration and attention; indicating interest through eye contact, posture, and facial expression.

Lazy listeners are often apathetic. They are indifferent to most messages. When they become bored, they too reject any responsibility for communication, and blame the speaker. Lazy listeners do not realize that there is no such thing as an uninteresting subject; there are only uninterested people.

Emotional listeners: Most of us have certain words or ideas that set us off. Some people hear the word "communist," then hear nothing else. Some hear "private enterprise" and go deaf. Emotional listeners are overwhelmed by emotional responses. When this happens, they suffer "emotional deafness," an inability to listen to anything that follows their emotional response. It does not matter if an idea is positive or negative; the listener's critical faculties and capacity for empathetic understanding are destroyed.

Emotional listeners respond not only to words or ideas, but also to a speaker's appearance or delivery. They may reject a speaker's message because he has long hair or because she does not wear a bra. You have no doubt been excited or stimulated by speakers and then, on reflection, realized that you had no idea what they said. You were "turned on" by their deliveries and their use of a few loaded words.

Because listeners in emotional states cannot evaluate and act upon information effectively, they are subject to manipulation by demagogues and charlatans.

Fact listeners: "Just the facts, ma'am. All we want are the facts," said a famous television detective. People who are good at ferreting out the facts are often considered to be good listeners.

Journalists are supposed to be in the business of discovering and reporting the truth. They do so by finding and assembling facts. But any good reporter will tell you that facts by themselves do not constitute truth. Facts must be in context if they are to be understood. Moreover, objective journalists report that facts can easily be a barrier keeping us from the truth.

Listeners who heed only the facts are likely to miss the truth. Fact listeners almost certainly fail to attend to speakers' feelings, nuances, and nonverbal cues. These cues contribute much to the communication of meaning. They hear words instead of listening for ideas.

The fact listener is like the student who is more concerned about what will be on the test than about learning. People who cannot see the forest for the trees are likely to get lost in the forest.

Defensive listeners: Like selfish listeners, defensive listeners restrict perception to their own frames of reference. They are unwilling to risk seeing the world as others see it. They find the experience threatening to their own beliefs and values. Consequently, defensive listeners seek only information that reinforces their needs and beliefs. They often mistake disagreement for a personal attack.

Defensive listeners cannot listen effectively because they have never really listened to themselves. They do not understand the influence of their own feelings, attitudes, values, and needs on their perception. As a result, defensive listeners cannot effectively listen or understand.

ACTIVE LISTENING

Carl Rogers and Richard Farson have written:

> Active listening carries a strong element of personal risk . . . we risk being changed ourselves . . . we risk coming to see the world as he sees it. It is threatening to give up, even momentarily, what we believe and start thinking in someone else's terms.

Researchers who have studied the listening process conclude that "active" or "empathetic" listening is the key not only to effective listening, but also to effective interpersonal relations. Active listening requires particular attitudes and special skills. It creates a good listening climate. In its most advanced form, active listening means getting inside the speaker. We understand from his or her point of view just what is being attempted.

Too few people ever achieve active listening. Few are willing to give up their own thoughts, values, and preconceptions in order to understand what others are trying to say. Too few people, especially in the workplace, will deal with and accept feelings and emotions.

Your first step in preparing for active listening is to listen to yourself. Get in touch with your own beliefs, biases, and motives as they relate to the speaker, the listening situation, and the information being received. If we understand ourselves, we can tell when we stop listening and start concentrating on ourselves. By monitoring our reactions, we can better keep our attention on the speaker.

Second, active listeners develop particular attitudes toward speakers and listening situations. To become an active listener, you must respect other people's potential worth, consider their rights, and have confidence in their capacity for self-direction. The interpersonal attitudes required for active listening include respect for creativity, capacity to accept responsibility, and desire for personal growth.

You must also develop certain attitudes toward the listening situation. The purpose of listening must be defined in terms of the speaker's needs, not the listener's. The active listener thinks *with* people, rather than for them or about them.

Third, the proper climate for interaction must be established. "Climate" here refers not to the physical environment of interaction but to the psychological environment. Active listening can take place in a plush office, in a company cafeteria, or even on a shop floor. The variables that affect climate include the speaker's perceptions that the listener is neither criticizing, evaluating, nor making moral judgments concerning what is being said. In a situation supportive of active listening, the speaker feels equal to the listener. The speaker feels free to express thoughts, opinions, or feelings, knowing that the words will be heard with understanding, acceptance, and warmth.

Once self-knowledge, attitude, and climate are established, one needs to know as much about the speaker as possible—his frame of reference, point of view, needs, and values. Now the scene is set for active listening. All you need are the skills.

These skills include suspending judgment until transmission is complete, relating the ideas and feelings of the speaker to the actual words spoken, and monitoring nonverbal communication cues. The active listener can reach past the speaker's words and concentrate on ideas and feelings. Moreover, the active listener offers feedback and asks questions to help the speaker make meaning clear and more complete.

Benefits of Active Listening in Business

Managers who actively listen have advantages over those who do not. Active listeners get more and better information about their subordinates and their problems. They also tap the ideas of subordinates in day-to-day informal contacts. They create opportunities for employees to say what is on their minds, and they can remember more of what they hear.

Active listeners make better decisions based on information, opinions, and experience of both superiors and subordinates. They actually stimulate better communication.

Equally important, active listeners change those who have been listened to in this manner. People who consistently experience active listening become more emotionally mature, more open to their experiences, less defensive, more democratic, and less authoritarian. Employees become more flexible and open to change, more cooperative and less likely to perceive an adversary relationship between management and labor, and more committed and motivated. On a personal level, the active listener is more likely to build deep, positive relationships.

Best of all, listening habits are contagious. Once active listening starts, others become active listeners too. They spread the benefits throughout the organization.

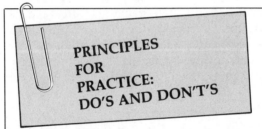

PRINCIPLES
FOR
PRACTICE:
DO'S AND DON'T'S

1. Do remember that communication is a two-way process. Listeners and speakers must share responsibility.

2. Do try to listen in terms of the speaker's frame of reference rather than your own.

3. Do realize that listening is an active process. It requires concentration and energy.

4. Do recognize that meaning is a personal construction based on a person's needs, values, and frames of reference.

5. Do review your own experience, knowledge, and attitudes in relation to what you are hearing.

6. Do sift fact from opinion.

7. Do listen to understand, not to refute.

8. Do judge content rather than delivery.

9. Do be objective.

10. Do attend to nonverbal cues such as eye contact, posture, and facial expressions. Listen for vocal cues such as tone, speech rate, inflection, and hesitations.

11. Do maintain a desire to listen.

12. Do learn as much about the speaker as possible.

13. Do create a psychological climate of equality, freedom, understanding, and acceptance.

14. Do try to think *with* people, rather than for them or about them.

15. Do try to establish good physical conditions for listening: minimize noise, find surroundings with good acoustics, pleasing surroundings, and comfortable furniture.

16. Do focus on ideas rather than facts.

17. Do attend to messages beyond those that apply to your own needs.

18. Do understand that people tend to simplify perception by categorization. Resist this tendency in yourself.

19. Do seek to bring forth differences; without differences there is no need for communication.

20. Do ask questions to show interest and to help the speaker clarify and develop points.

21. Do communicate interest to the speaker through eye contact, facial expression, and other nonverbal cues.

22. Do create opportunities for listening.

23. Do practice listening by exposing yourself to difficult messages such as recorded poetry, plays (particularly British versions of Shakespeare), and lectures on subjects to which you have not been exposed.

* * * * *

1. Do not take listening for granted.

2. Do not jump to conclusions before hearing all of a speaker's message.

3. Do not become defensive about your own thoughts and ideas.

4. Do not be afraid to deal with feelings or emotion.

5. Do not become preoccupied with words; listen for ideas and feelings.

6. Do not initially criticize, evaluate, or moralize.

7. Do not get too excited about a speaker's points until you are certain you understand them thoroughly.

8. Do not assume that meanings are absolute.

9. Do not confuse what you hear with what you want to hear.

10. Do not be overwhelmed by emotional reactions to words, ideas, appearance, or delivery.

11. Do not put beans in your ears.

A
CASE
STUDY*

A female employee who has received top pay for her job classification for some time goes to her supervisor to complain about her wages. During the interview she makes the following statements:

1. "The only pay increases that I have had in ten years are those where the top rate has been raised. Everyone gets those increases. I think that I should get an increase once in a while that isn't due to the top being raised."

2. "A woman with a good attendance record should be given an increase for that reason alone."

3. "New women come into the office and they get increases whether they are any good or not."

4. "Lots of women working for the company get more money than I do, and I'm just as good as they are."

5. "There is a woman who works for another company who gets $300 a week, and this company is making lots of money now. If others can pay those salaries, so can this company."

6. "I have had to fight for every raise I ever got, and that's what I'm doing now."

7. "You brought a new woman into our unit the other day. If you had given us women in the unit a raise, then we would work harder and you wouldn't need to hire the new one."

8. "If there's no more money for me here, why don't you transfer me? They have lots of good jobs in other departments and they don't work as hard as I do."

9. "If I were a pretty woman, you'd give me an increase."

10. "You don't want me here. You just want young women. I'm getting old; so I guess that I should get out."

*Adapted from Norman R. F. Maier, *Psychology in Industrial Organizations* (4th ed.; Boston: Houghton Mifflin, 1973), pp. 48, 49, 60, 61.

11. (Crying): "No one pays any attention to me any more."

12. "All my troubles seem to have started since my father died last year. Since then, things haven't gone good for me."

13. "If I could find another woman to live with me, maybe things would be better, but I can't find anyone I like."

14. "I won't be working very long anyway. I'm buying a 50-dollar savings bond every week, and that has mounted up, and with my pension I can get along all right."

Do these statements seem reasonable and related?

What do you think the woman is really saying?

What effect would rational responses and explanations have in this situation?

How could active listening be beneficial in this case?

FOR FURTHER STUDY

1. As you listen to a friend talk to you, try to get what he is saying so that you can tell it back to your friend to his or her own satisfaction.

2. Listen to a sermon. After you hear the title, write down the points you expect to hear. As you listen, check them off. After the speech, write down things you heard but did not expect. This exercise gains an added dimension if you do it with someone whose religious views differ markedly from yours and compare notes afterward.

3. Identify people you consider to be good listeners. What makes them good? What do they do that other people do not do? What do others do that they do not do?

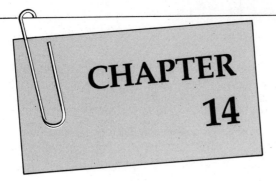

CHAPTER 14

To: The Reader
From: The Authors
Subject: Communication Without Words

After reading this chapter you will:

1. Be able to recognize the nonverbal communication messages that surround us in all organizational environments.

2. Understand the diferences and relationships between the four categories of nonverbal communication: body motion and posture, space, voice, and objects.

3. Be aware of the role of facial expressions in communicating emotional states.

4. Understand how we use space to define power and status in organizations.

5. Be familiar with the use of personal space zones and their effects on interpersonal communication.

6. Be aware of the effects of touch, smell, and time as nonverbal messages.

7. Understand the role and importance of clothing, furniture, wall hangings, and other objects in business communication situations.

8. Be aware of the nonverbal context of written messages.

Communication
Without Words:
Understanding
Nonverbal Messages
in Business Environments

A government agency called in a communication consultant to give its employees interview training. The employees were having trouble getting personal information from people applying for government assistance. The consultant asked to see the area where the people were being interviewed. He saw rows of identical desks, each with one chair on the side and just enough space for a person to walk between the chair and the next desk. Dozens of interviews were taking place as people milled about. Interviewers usually leaned across their desks, while interviewees sat looking at their hands.

The consultant turned to the supervisor and said, "You don't need interview training." The supervisor was confused. "Would you disclose private information in a place like this?" the consultant asked. "You need private, nonthreatening space. You need partitions, not training."

This advice points out the importance of the unspoken and unwritten environment in communication. No matter how expert the interviewers were, the public, impersonal setting in which people were being asked to reveal private information became itself a part of the message. All written and spoken messages are delivered in a nonverbal context. This context adds meaning to the communication process, for good or bad. In this chapter we shall discuss nonverbal messages common in business environments.

LISTEN TO WHAT YOU ARE NOT SAYING

The importance of nonverbal communication in daily life cannot be overestimated. It has been recognized for centuries. In 1640, Sir Francis Bacon called gestures "natural hieroglyphic writing in the air." Shakespeare's plays contained references: "Your face, my thane, is as a book where men may read strange matters" (*Macbeth*); and "There's language in her eye, her cheek, her lip, nay, her foot speaks, her wanton spirits look out at every joint and motive of her body" (*Troilus and Cressida*).

Scientific study of the subject goes back over a century to Charles Darwin's *The Expression of the Emotions in Man and Animals*, published in 1872. Sigmund Freud was also aware of the phenomenon. As he put it, ". . . no mortal can keep a secret. If his lips are silent, he chatters with his finger tips; betrayal oozes out of him at every pore." Still, relatively little formal study of nonverbal communication took place until the latter half of this century. Recently, the subject has had so much attention that it has become a victim of misconceptions. Books have offered to teach you how to "learn to read the body as you read a book," "tell whether the person you are talking to is lying," and "penetrate the personal secrets of others." The definite consensus of reputable scholars is that with few exceptions, gestures, expressions, and postures have no easily accessible specific meanings. The study of nonverbal communication will not provide a magical way to know people's thoughts without asking them.

Nevertheless, understanding and awareness of nonverbal communication can help you communicate more effectively in the organizational environment. In our chapter on interpersonal communication we will state that all communication interactions operate within certain stated or implied rules of behavior. These rules serve as boundaries of human interaction. The learning of rules and establishment of boundaries are largely a function of nonverbally communicated information concerning expectations, roles, and relationships; interpretation of attitudes and emotional states; and feedback.

WHAT IS NONVERBAL COMMUNICATION?

Any communication behavior that is *not* verbal (written or spoken words) can be considered nonverbal communication. In actuality, verbal and nonverbal dimensions are often so intimately woven together that the possibility of understanding either in isolation is small. In this chapter we will categorize the nonverbal message forms common to business environments.

Nonverbal communication can be divided into four categories: (1) Communicative body motion and posture, which include movements of the body, limbs, hand, head, and feet, facial expressions, and eye movement; (2) The space that communicators place between themselves; (3) Vocal rate, pitch, and inflection; (4) Material things ranging from clothing and cosmetics to furniture and architecture. Time, touch, and smell can also take on significance.

Our discussion of nonverbal communication divides into two message areas common in business: *person-to-person messages,* which involve any message form used in an interaction between two or more people, and *environmental messages.* The latter are not directly involved in interaction, but influence the interpretation of person-to-person messages.

Person-to-Person Messages

People talking face to face or even on the telephone send and receive many more messages than those borne by the words they use. Face-to-face meetings are considered the richest form of communication in terms of the amount of information they make available. This richness comes from the nonverbal signals available to enhance the verbal signals sent in such an exchange. These signals include all forms of body movement, clothing, personal appearance, and vocal qualities. Telephone messages supply less information, but still offer vocal signals in addition to words. Successful executives prefer face-to-face and telephone communication as ways of getting information. The nonverbal signals in person-to-person interactions give added dimensions of information.

Facial Expressions   The face is the primary communicator of emotional states. Ray L. Birdwhistell in his book *Kinesics and Context* says that a human face can make 250,000 expressions. Recently, researchers have shown that some aspects of facial expression are interpretable across cultural boundaries.

Next to speech, the face is probably the primary source of information in human interaction. It shows emotional states and interpersonal attitudes and gives feedback to others.

In relation to the expression of attitudes (i.e., "liking or disliking someone or something"), Mehrabian and Ferris suggest the following formula:

Perceived attitude = 7% verbal + 38% vocal + 55% facial

Verbal refers to the actual words used. *Vocal* refers to the way in which the words are spoken. Using this formula, we can conclude that 93 percent of the meaning in a face-to-face interaction comes from nonverbal cues. Among these, facial expressions are the most dominant.

As a source of feedback, Albert Scheflin points out, "facial displays . . . convey a running commentary on someone else's behavior." For these reasons we pay attention to other people's faces. We use the information gained there as the basis for judgments and actions.

Just as we attend to others' faces, we are aware of our own. To some extent, we manipulate and choose our facial expressions while we choose our words. However, facial expressions can communicate even when we do not intend to communicate. They may be "leaks" about our inner feelings; they may act as "covers" such as, for example, when we try to appear calm when we are anxious.

Eye Contact and Movement   Expressions about the power of eye communication are abundant: *icy stares, he looks right through you, shifty eyes, if looks could kill, the evil eye.* Face-to-face eye contact can express willingness to communicate. On the other hand, avoiding another's glance can be perceived as an evasive maneuver. You avert your gaze in a crowded bus to avoid interaction. Staring is a taboo in most places; a good way to call attention to yourself as a deviant is to stare at someone for several minutes. In many contexts, both pupil dilation and frequency of eye contact seem to indicate attraction.

Many eye behaviors are associated with emotions: downward glances may suggest modesty or shame; wide eyes have been associated with innocence, wonder, or terror; fixed eyes may indicate coldness or anger.

More importantly, eyes can control communication. They signal willingness or reluctance to communicate and offer positive or negative feedback.

Body Movements and Posture   Hand, arm, leg, and feet movements also have meaning. Certain hand symbols mean specific things. Examples of these are the sign systems of the deaf, the extended perpendicular palm meaning "stop," or the extended middle finger. These intentional motions are called *emblems*. The meanings of emblems may differ across cultural boundaries; for example, pointing a finger at another person may convey an insult in some cultures.

Most communicative movement of the limbs, however, is unintentional. It serves to illustrate, emphasize, or punctuate speech; to regulate interaction; to show emotion, particularly the degree of emotion; or to deal with bodily and emotional needs.

We are less aware of communicating with our hands/arms and legs/feet than we are with our words and facial expressions. Therefore, the limbs are good sources of "leakage"—cues to suppressed or hidden emotions or clues that suggest deception. Anxiety, confusion, stress, fear, aggressiveness, even sexual attraction may be revealed by arms, hands, and particularly by the legs and feet. This is true even when words and face give no hint of these emotions.

Posture, carriage, leaning, walking, and other movements can be communicative as well. For instance, the rate of working adopted by an employee high in informal status can act as a signal to other workers concerning acceptable norms and expectations for production. If an informal leader of a particular work group begins to show signs of disinterest and low motivation in the performance of her job, these symptoms may spread to the rest of the group without any actual discussion of the matter.

The study of how all of these elements of body movement and posture work together to produce meaning is called *kinesics*. While there is no "body language" in the sense that spoken and written languages exist, these elements do combine with other modes of communication to create messages.

Personal Space Space between people is extremely important. We approach people we like. We leave a lot of space between ourselves and those we dislike or fear.

When we are unable to arrange comfortable distances, we manage other variables, such as eye contact or body position. In an elevator, we are forced to stand close to strangers. It is common practice to pretend you do not notice them by avoiding eye contact, by turning your back and staring at the floor indicator, or by remaining silent even though you were talking with another passenger before getting on. Subway riders react similarly. The face is a mask. The eyes read a newspaper or stare away from people. Arms and legs are held close together in self-protective gestures. If a passenger is seated, the legs are crossed. All of these are substitutes for having more space.

We may also simulate closer proximity. At a party, displays of affection can be signaled by eye contact, animated facial expressions, brief touching, or the positions of legs, arms, and feet.

If you see your supervisor and another employee standing engrossed in conversation and you wonder whether to break in, you may get a clue from their feet. If they are facing each other, they form a closed system. They want no intrusion.

We lean toward people we like; we face them when sitting and promote eye contact. The opposite is true with those we dislike. It is, of course, likely that greater closeness can lead to liking. One study demonstrated that liking in a housing project was related to how close to each other the front doors of people's houses were. Stories about proximity breeding affection abound: being stranded on a desert island with another person, a relationship that develops with a person seated beside you in class. In organizations, close friendships frequently develop between people whose work stations or offices are close to each other. Other things being equal, the distance between you and another person can show the closeness of your relationship.

There seem to be *personal space zones* around each of us. In the United States these are about as follows:

1. *Intimate zone.* 0–1½ feet. This close, you must have an intimate relationship, be fighting, or be dominant. Touch and smell are important. Verbal communication may be whispered or murmured.

2. *Personal zone.* 1½–4 feet. At this range, you must be well acquainted. Words are likely to be hushed.

3. *Social zone.* 4–12 feet. You are acquainted with the other person and have some reason for speaking. Otherwise, the probability of saying much more than "hello" is slight. If a stranger enters this zone, you break off eye contact and perhaps turn away. If you speak, you use a full-throated, businesslike voice.

4. *Public zone.* More than 12 feet. More than 12 feet away, strangers do not exist for us. We may look at them so long as we do not maintain eye contact or stare too long. Interaction is avoided. Words must be shouted or projected very well, as in the theater.

How much space does a person need? The amount varies according to how much one is used to, and it varies in different cultures. Anthropologist Edward T. Hall tells about cross-cultural misunderstandings based upon the difference in distance zones favored by North Americans and foreigners (often Latin Americans). A New Englander and a Latin doing business may both wish to be in the social zone. The Yankee stands about five feet from the Latin, whose social zone might be three to four feet. When the Latin moves closer, the Yankee becomes uncomfortable and backs away. The Latin thinks the New Englander is cold and unfriendly.

One of the authors of this text experienced intense frustration in a recent hospital confinement. Off and on at all hours, without invitation, complete strangers (hospital personnel) invaded his intimate zone. No matter how necessary these "invasions" may have been, this author believes that the "invaders" could have at least grouped their "attacks" to minimize their frequency. For example, perhaps medicine could have been given at the time of blood pressure checks, etc. The ultimate violation was an intrusion to wake up the patient well past midnight to administer a tranquilizer.

Using Touch and Smell to Communicate   Touch and smell are senses that are important in person-to-person communication. The importance of touching in our society can be seen in what we prohibit. We usually avoid touching each other even in situations where it is almost impossible to avoid contact. In elevators, people turn their bodies in strange ways to avoid touching. Even friends in a cramped work area will apologize when one unavoidably brushes the other's arm. Because we spend so much energy avoiding touching, a great deal of meaning attaches to situations where deliberate touching takes place.

Who is touched, what part of the body is touched, and the circumstances under which touching occurs are crucial variables. The boss's pat on the back can be a sign of encouragement or a veiled threat. Which one depends on the conversation that preceded the pat. A man's arm around the shoulders of a woman in the office can be a sexual proposition, pure friendliness, or comfort. In our society one man patting another on the rear might be seen as homosexual if it was done anywhere except on a basketball court. However, in other cultures no one reads homosexuality into the sight of two adults of the same sex walking down the street holding hands.

To refuse another's outstretched hand is almost unthinkable. We go to much trouble to respond appropriately to the offer of a handshake. We shift books or papers from one hand to another. We apologize if the proper hand cannot be freed. People in business sometimes say they can judge by a handshake everything from the quality of a person's work to that person's honesty.

This ritual has presented problems since women have begun to fill management positions. Men and women may not be sure whether it is appropriate to shake the hand of a member of the opposite sex in a business situation.

Increased touching can affect other forms of communication and interpersonal attitudes. One study found that increased touching by nurses made patients talk more. It improved patient attitudes toward nurses. It has even been suggested that the Los Angeles Dodgers won the 1977 National League pennant because the coach often hugged the players.

In some cultures, people touch each other more often than they do in North America. North Americans touch mostly in courtship, greetings (handshakes), and to indicate dominance-submission relationships (a pat on the head or back). A pat on the head or a downward pat on the shoulder by a taller person may arouse anger in some individuals. North Americans are also particular about *where* you touch.

North Americans also do not use their sense of smell as much as people in other cultures do. Fear and anger, for instance, give off distinctive odors. Chemical changes occur in our bodies with particular emotional conditions. We do not notice these odors unless body or breath odor is strong.

Artificial odors applied to the body and mouth are used to mask natural odors. They are intended to evoke pleasant associations rather than to elicit direct responses. However, the presence or absence of these artificial odors is often the basis upon which opinions about a person are formed. This is epecially true if the odor is unusual. Therefore, it may be appropriate, even desirable, for a man or woman to wear some type of fragrance to work. If the odor calls undue attention to itself and the wearer, however, a negative message can result.

Vocal Emphasis   "It's not what you say, but how you say it that counts." This expression contains an element of truth. Robert J. McCloskey, a member of the State Department in a former administration, apparently meant to communicate different messages by varying his voice quality. He had three ways of saying, "I would not speculate." *Newsweek* magazine in an article about McCloskey reported that "spoken without accent, it means the Department doesn't know for sure; emphasis on the 'I' means I wouldn't but you may—and with some assurance; accent on 'speculate' indicates that the questioner's premise is probably wrong."

While McCloskey "said" the same thing on different occasions, perceptive reporters learned that depending on which word he stressed, he sent different messages. This difference in *how* something is said as opposed to *what* is said is called *paralanguage*.

Paralanguage includes stress, pitch, rate, loudness, timbre, inflection, rhythm, and enunciation—all of the vocal nuances that accompany speech. Moreover, sounds that are not words, such as laughing, crying, sighing, yawning, belching, marked breathing, coughing, clearing the throat, groaning, yelling, whispering, and the like, are also considered paralanguage. Even silences, pauses, and hesitations fall into this category.

Any message has two aspects: the statement itself and information concerning its interpretation. The latter is called *metacommunication*. It is often a function of nonverbal, particularly paralinguistic, behavior. In sarcasm, for instance, the message is that what is said is the opposite of what is meant. This is often the product of information carried by paralanguage, which also supplies information about a person's personality and emotional state. Paralanguage takes on real importance when other nonverbal messages are absent, as in telephone conversations, tape recordings, and public address systems.

Of course, we must keep in mind that actual interpretation occurs in the mind of the receiver, not in the message itself. For example, words have different connotations to different people. Likewise, nonverbal information may be subject to a variety of interpretations. Thus, a receiver may interpret another's comments as sarcasm, even though that was not the intended message, or may miss the sarcastic meaning intended in the message.

Environmental Messages and Unspoken Power

No matter how a message is delivered, whether it is spoken person to person, over the telephone, or written, the environment in which it is received contributes meaning. Sometimes the environmental signals become the primary message. They shadow any written or spoken messages that are received. Because of the importance of these messages, business organizations and those who manage them look closely at territorial boundaries, the things situated within territories, and the use of time by themselves and others. In fact, "human engineering" of office layouts has become—at least according to its practitioners—a science. Thus, we see room dividers, murals, modular work spaces, etc., replacing the old desks, swivel chairs, and standard filing cabinets. These elements are widely seen as statements about power and authority in American business firms.

Territorial Power Messages Proximity can suggest status, authority, or dominance. This is related to the idea of territory. Just as each of us carries a bubble of personal space around us, there are locations that we consider our "turf." These are places in which we feel comfortable, most in control of the environment: our home, a favorite chair, a desk, a study, or workshop. The boss takes an employee to his office for serious discussion. A teenager signals his right to his bedroom with a keep-out sign on the door. You can never completely understand a person until you have inspected his or her territory.

In his book *The Territorial Imperative,* Robert Ardrey notes that some dominant animals have larger territories than lesser animals. Dominant animals may visit the turf of lower-status animals, but the reverse is not true. Rich and powerful people often live on spacious estates or, at least, in roomy suburbs. They go downtown every day to work, crossing casually through the territory of lower-status persons on the way. Their spacious offices are on the highest floors of buildings. They have private restrooms, meeting rooms, executive dining rooms. Space itself communicates status.

Lower-status persons approach high-status territory rarely. When they do, they behave formally and are nervous. Watch workers approaching bosses' offices. There is discomfort, hesitation, formality—"Am I intruding?" or "Are you busy?" The lower-status person *asks permission* to enter the territory. The dominant person is a little threatening and is on his or her home turf. The subordinate acts timid, stands until invited to sit, and picks words carefully. The superior leans back in the chair, speaks loudly, and has the option of slapping the subordinate on the back. Note the relationship between a parent and six-year-old. The parent may barge into the child's room at any time. The child must ask permission to enter the parental bedroom. Those with status tend to control and demand more space; those with lesser status in turn respect the larger territory of these people. Perhaps to foster a climate of cooperation and trust within an organization it would be appropriate for everyone, even managers, to knock before entering a closed door. One of the authors recalls his negative reactions to a boss who had the habit of using his master key to enter subordinates' offices without knocking.

Time and Timing   If you ask someone to see you within five minutes, it is different from asking to see that person several days from now.

If the boss tells you to get into his office "immediately if not sooner," it is different from being asked to drop by "when you have a chance." Different cultures place different meanings on time. Edward T. Hall points out that in some cultures it is impolite to arrive on time when asked to dinner. A guest who came at the appropriate time in India might be inexcusably late in the United States. Cultures also differ in their uses of the times of the day. The Latin American custom of resting in the early afternoon is sometimes stereotyped as laziness by Western executives who do not understand the purpose of the *siesta*.

Hall reports a more dramatic case from the South Seas. It falls into the "ugly American" category. American supervisors of a factory had blundered by hiring too many workers from one native group and not enough from another. Since the Americans could not solve the problem, leaders of several native groups met to discuss it. After a long meeting, they found a solution. A large group of them hurried to tell the plant manager. Unfortunately, they called on him at about three o'clock in the morning. They did not realize that to wake an American in the middle of the night is a sign of great urgency. The plant manager, understanding few local customs, thought the natives were rioting and called out the Marines.

Time of day, amount of advance notice, timing, or time kept waiting for an appointment can be eloquent messages. Status is shown by control of time as much as by control of space. Lower-status workers have rigid time regulations in most organizations. Executives have more flexibility. Numbers of hours spent on the job is not crucial in this message of power. In fact, executive employees probably spend more hours at work than production workers. However, their schedules are more flexible. Their status enables them to go to lunch or take a break when they wish. They can take an afternoon off without asking permission. In most organizations, the higher people's status, the more control they have over their own time. Recently some organizations have begun to experiment with time as a means to enhance employee motivation. Various methods of "flex-time" scheduling have been demonstrated to be effective messages to employees about the amount of maturity and responsibility management would like them to exercise in their duties.

Object Language: The Symbols of Power and Authority

When you enter a person's office, you generally find a lot of artifacts that give clues to the individual's personality and tastes. Some communicators develop real abilities to translate such clues as these. Each of us sends messages through the clothes we wear, our haircuts, or the contents of our pockets, purses, and briefcases.

Communicators manipulate entire environments. Furniture in a room is often placed for a certain effect. The arrangement and decorations in an executive's office may point out important aspects of personality and attitudes. The executive desk can sit between the executive's chair and the chairs in which employees sit. This puts greater space between communicators. The desk might be turned to allow conversation at closer range. Often a more comfortable sitting area in another part of the office allows a more relaxed climate in which formal barriers such as desks and conference tables are not present.

Research has shown that such things affect perceptions and communication patterns. Rooms and buildings can be built to promote better communication. Nightclubs and expensive restaurants are dark and noisy so that customers can hold intimate conversations; stores arrange furniture and merchandise to let customers associate related items to each other and to feel relaxed.

Objects on an executive's desk, indeed the desk itself, are statements about that person. Proof of this is easily found. Most of us carefully select the things that adorn our offices. They project an image of ourselves. Sometimes we do not have complete freedom to select the things in our offices, being limited by rules, money, or the availability of the objects themselves. However, even the things we may have in our offices against our will tell much about our power to influence our surroundings. The effect of the title "Administrative Assistant" may vary, depending upon whether or not there is a typewriter on that person's desk.

Sometimes managers violate their subordinates' space expectations with foolish, trivial restrictions. For example, one office manager ordered a switchboard operator to remove a personal lamp. Other practices that might be reconsidered are prohibitions against any personal objects being hung on office walls or imposing artwork or paint schemes on employees without consulting them. Such policies, which ignore employee needs, perceptions, and values, may explain why managers find it so difficult to get employees to treat company property as though it were their own.

Written Messages Beyond Words   We should emphasize that the meaning received from written messages goes beyond the words used. Style of writing produces effects similar to those of a speaker's vocal expression. Written messages have a "feel" to them. That "feel" goes beyond verbalization.

The appearance of a written message contributes to the meaning received. Although correctness of format will vary from situation to situation, we can recognize a general range of formats that are acceptable for business messages. A number of letter formats are used in business (block, modified block, etc.).

However, we would be safe in saying that a business letter typed without any form or paragraph divisions would not, as a rule, be received favorably. The reader, of course, could understand the words in the letter. The additional message conveyed by the format, or lack of it, would be negative.

In addition, the forms of the letters used to make the words of a written message can affect the meaning received by a reader. The study of typefaces is termed typography (Exhibit 14-1). The importance of typography in constructing written messages has been recognized by the advertising industry perhaps more than any other group. After a message has been composed by a writer, the graphics specialists of an advertising agency will select a typeface to evoke the proper emotional response of the reader and to fit with the other graphic illustrations being employed. Typography is also important in everyday business messages. In most office situations it is not considered appropriate to type a letter with a script type element. This informal style of type is general reserved for special effects or personal messages.

Graphics of all kinds give important signals. Graphics include letterheads, drawings, logos, photographs, charts, and graphs. All of these communicate information. A letterhead or logo may create the desired image for a writer or company. Charts and graphs can give factual information nonverbally in a brief space.

Even the quality of the paper can be a signal about the importance of the message. Whether the message is typed individually, copied mechanically, produced by computer, signed personally, or stamped, "says something" to readers.

Understanding Nonverbal Communication in the Workplace   If you notice a hand gesture, facial movement, or item of dress, it might be a random event of no significance. But it could be a subconscious sign of the personal style of the sender or a conscious effort to communicate. The *same* gesture or movement might be any of the three. Which it is depends upon the situation, that is, on how communication systems interact with visual systems. Communication emerges from interactions of verbal, vocal, visual,

EXHIBIT 14-1

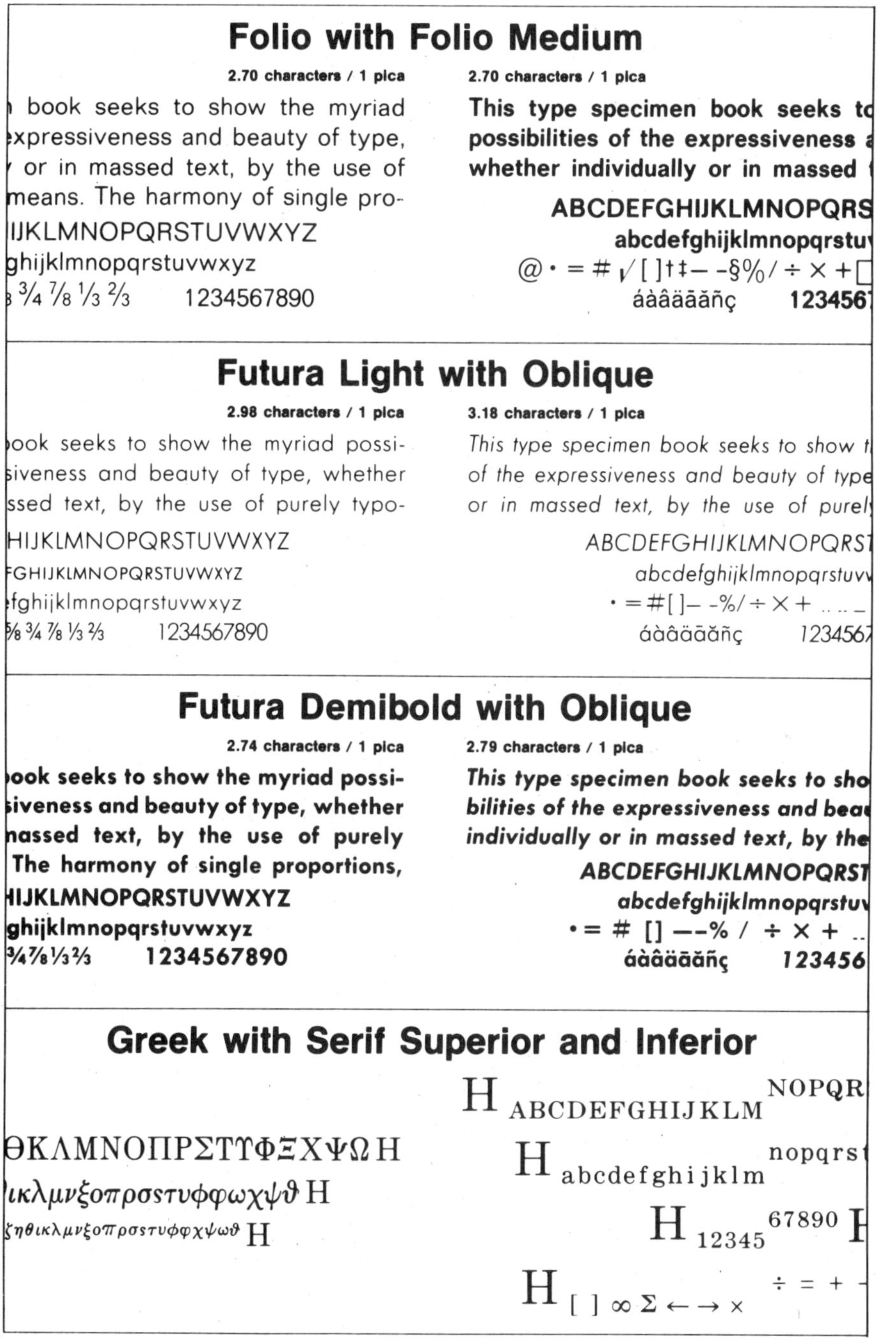

Folio with Folio Medium

2.70 characters / 1 pica

book seeks to show the myriad
xpressiveness and beauty of type,
or in massed text, by the use of
means. The harmony of single pro-
IJKLMNOPQRSTUVWXYZ
ghijklmnopqrstuvwxyz
¾ ⅞ ⅓ ⅔   1234567890

2.70 characters / 1 pica

This type specimen book seeks to
possibilities of the expressiveness a
whether individually or in massed

ABCDEFGHIJKLMNOPQRS
abcdefghijklmnopqrstuv
@ • = # √ [ ] † ‡ — -§%/ ÷ × + ☐
áàâäãñç   123456

Futura Light with Oblique

2.98 characters / 1 pica

ook seeks to show the myriad possi-
siveness and beauty of type, whether
ssed text, by the use of purely typo-
HIJKLMNOPQRSTUVWXYZ
FGHIJKLMNOPQRSTUVWXYZ
fghijklmnopqrstuvwxyz
⅝ ¾ ⅞ ⅓ ⅔   1234567890

3.18 characters / 1 pica

This type specimen book seeks to show t
of the expressiveness and beauty of type
or in massed text, by the use of purel

ABCDEFGHIJKLMNOPQRS
abcdefghijklmnopqrstuv
• = # [ ]– -%/ ÷ × + ... _
áàâäãñç   123456

Futura Demibold with Oblique

2.74 characters / 1 pica

ook seeks to show the myriad possi-
siveness and beauty of type, whether
nassed text, by the use of purely
The harmony of single proportions,
HIJKLMNOPQRSTUVWXYZ
ghijklmnopqrstuvwxyz
¾⅞⅓⅔   1234567890

2.79 characters / 1 pica

This type specimen book seeks to sho
bilities of the expressiveness and bea
individually or in massed text, by the

ABCDEFGHIJKLMNOPQRST
abcdefghijklmnopqrstuv
• = # [] ––% / ÷ × + ..
áàâäãñç   123456

Greek with Serif Superior and Inferior

ΘΚΛΜΝΟΠΡΣΤΥΦΞΧΨΩ H
ικλμνξοπρστυφφωχψϑ H
ζηθικλμνξοπρστυφφχψωϑ H

H ABCDEFGHIJKLM NOPQR

H abcdefghijklm nopqrst

H 12345 67890 H

H [ ] ∞ Σ ← → × ÷ = +

and other code systems, plus past events, personal styles, and preferences connected with the goals of the communicators.

With all these elements involved, it is not unusual for messages to contain conflicting information. A supervisor smiles at an employee, stares, and remarks with heavy irony in his voice, "Good morning, Smith, I appreciate your punctuality." It is 9 A.M. Work was scheduled to start at 8. The nonverbal cues will be believed more than the verbal ones. The employee is not likely to miss the supervisor's meaning. The ironic tone and hard-eyed smile carry the heaviest meaning. Sometimes our nonverbal messages betray our real feelings even when we attempt to hide them. For example, when a manager replies "Come in" to an employee's knock on his door but keeps on writing and does not bother to look up, the employee will, no doubt, correctly interpret the manager's lack of interest in her and her problem no matter what is said.

To understand the meanings of complex messages, you must analyze the content of a communication event. Why does the salesperson work so hard on the initial approach to a customer? Why do lonely people appear aloof and unfriendly when they wish to interact? One reason is that there is a low level of awareness among most of us about the importance of nonverbal communication. Education centers around the verbal. Can you imagine a class in the public schools about how to control gestures, facial expression, or space? Nonverbal messages have not received official recognition as messages. Typical of this lack of awareness is the case of the manager who is perplexed at the reaction of a new female employee in his department when he compliments her work while lightly touching the tip of her nose with his index finger. "All I did was tell her she did a good job," he complains. But, whether he realized it or not, that was *not* all he said. His nonverbal message added "for a girl" to his compliment.

Keep your eyes open. You'll be surprised.

**PRINCIPLES
FOR
PRACTICE**

1. Everyone who works in an organizational environment must be aware of the fact that his or her behavior, clothing, and use of space and time communicate messages to others.

2. To be effective in business situations, we have to be receptive to the nonverbal messages that others transmit and aware of our own nonverbal cues.

3. Understanding the role and effects of nonverbal communication can improve the effectiveness of verbal interactions.

4. Nonverbal communication is particularly important in relation to feedback, the communication of attitudes and emotions, and the establishment of organizational expectations, power, status, and authority.

5. Nonverbal communication takes four basic forms: body motion and posture, the communicative use of space, and vocal emphasis.

6. Time, touch, and object language are also very important in business relationships.

7. It would be a mistake to attempt to interpret nonverbal messages in isolation from the context in which they occur.

8. In organizational situations, nonverbal cues can often be important or even primary messages.

FOR FURTHER STUDY

1. After reading this chapter, how much of your own communication do you think is verbal? How much is vocal? How much is facial expression?

2. What forms of nonverbal communication, other than vocal emphasis and facial expression, do you use most?

3. Make a list of the nonverbal communications you notice from others. Evaluate their effects on you: are they positive or negative, confusing or clarifying?

4. List the forms of nonverbal communication you normally use. Divide the list into things you want to continue and things you wish hereafter to avoid. Discuss your list with someone who knows you.

5. Get a copy of the annual report of a large corporation. See if you can make an estimate of the percentage of verbal and nonverbal communication in the report.

6. Visit the offices of a business that hires a lot of people in clerical and management positions. List the nonverbal messages you received while there. Compare them to the verbal messages you received.

7. Handbook B discusses some rules of punctuation. Speakers do not punctuate, at least not by saying "comma," "semicolon," etc. Instead, speakers punctuate by nonverbal devices. What nonverbal cues have you noticed yourself and others using to punctuate their oral messages? See if you can find nonverbal equivalents for the following: question mark, comma, period, exclamation point, dash, and hyphen.

8. Suppose (a) you called a meeting to lecture to ten people about some new regulation requiring their understanding but not their discussion; and (b) you called a meeting of the same ten to get their ideas and discussion in developing the regulation. Assume you could have any furniture you wished arranged any way you wished. Which of these arrangements would you choose in each situation:

a. U shape, with several tables.
b. T shape, with several tables.
c. Circle of tables.
d. Box or square shape of tables.
e. Classroom style with two rows of five each.
f. Classroom style with five rows of two each.
g. V shape with the opening toward you.
h. V shape with the point toward you.
i. Large "coffin"-shaped table.
j. Other.

9. Suppose you could design a room for interviewing prospective employees. On a piece of graph paper sketch a room to scale. Show location, size, and type of furnishings. Show window and door locations. Assume you would test employees somewhere else. Also assume you might sometimes have one other staff member present.

10. Here are some methods of communication. Which nonverbal cues does each offer or lack: person-to-person; closed-circuit line TV; videotaped playback; conference call by video phone; telephone; typewritten letter.

11. Polygraph ("lie detector") tests are based on involuntary nonverbal messages that conflict with verbal messages. What other involuntary nonverbal messages can you list? (Hint: blushing.)

12. How does a mannerism differ from a gesture?

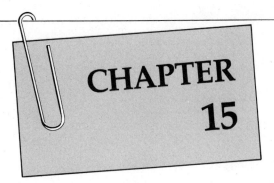

CHAPTER 15

To: The Reader
From: The Authors
Subject: Interpersonal Communication in Business

After reading this chapter, you will know that:

1. People coordinate short-term activities through
    interpersonal communication.

2. Interpersonal communication occurs within constraints
    that are determined by "rules" imposed by culture,
    organizational structure, work groups, and participants,
    or developed through interaction.

3. Rules make interactions more predictable, stable, and
    comfortable.

4. Formal and informal communication differ in the extent to
    which rules are imposed.

5. Coorientation is a system of mutual rules, meanings, and
    expectations.

6. Some communicators seek direction and control; others are
    more interested in understanding and facilitation.

7. Communicators are characterized by differing levels of
    need for inclusion, affection, and control.

8. Leadership is dependent on interpersonal communication.

Interpersonal Communication in Business

Interpersonal communication is a fact of organizational life. It is the way that people coordinate their efforts from minute to minute and day to day. The quality of interpersonal communication influences frustrations and satisfactions, personal relationships, happiness, motivation, and productivity. Individuals are the "building blocks" that structure an organization, and interpersonal communication links people together. Trying to understand this, we think back to the discussion of systems in Chapter 2. Interpersonal communication is a system operating within larger systems that constrain and direct interaction. Interpersonal exchanges in part are a function of explicit or implicit rules accepted by the participants. These rules may be imposed by outside sources, brought to the relationship by the participants, or developed during the interaction.

Certain rules are found in the culture. For example, conflicts in work organizations usually are not settled by physical violence. Such behavior breaks the rules of our culture. Other sources of rules are organizational structure and work groups. Of course, the rules differ greatly in differing situations.

These rules deal with two aspects of interaction: content, or the information being conveyed, and the relationships between the communicators. A major factor that helps to achieve good interpersonal communication is an acceptance of the unstated rules governing conduct.

You have probably been in situations where interpersonal communication rules have been broken. Imagine a relationship between a worker and his boss. Conversation between them has always been about business-related topics, or "safe" subjects like sports or the weather. One day, out of the blue, the boss starts talking about his marital and financial problems. The boss is breaking the rules. He is discussing subjects that have been beyond the scope of the relationship. Moreover, the boss's broaching of personal subjects presumes on the relationship itself. It implies closeness and intimacy, and the worker cannot help but be uncomfortable. He does not know how to respond. He wonders why his boss is telling him these things. His expectations about how interpersonal communication with the boss is supposed to happen have been violated.

Rules make interactions more predictable, stable, and comfortable. When they are broken, unknown, or when participants are using different sets of rules, interpersonal communication is difficult, exhausting, and problematic. You pay so much attention to the interaction that little else is accomplished.

FORMAL AND INFORMAL INTERPERSONAL COMMUNICATION

In business organizations, sources of communication rules can be the authority structure and peer groups. Some rules are set out in the organization's official documents and are easily identified as *policy:* "Always make copies in triplicate"; "Direct all inquiries regarding employment to the personnel office," etc. However, members of all organizations know that there are expectations that cannot be found in policy statements. Even though these rules must be learned by experience, they are as binding as codified regulations. "Go to your boss's office when you want to see him or her. Never ask the boss to come to you" is often an unwritten rule.

No matter how many rules an organization has, there is always at least some freedom of action. This freedom requires that communicators establish some of their own rules. The boundaries of one's freedom are the lines between formal and informal communication in organizations. This concept is best seen as a continuum. It ranges from entirely "imposed" to entirely "developed" rules (Exhibit 15-1). Of course, the end points of this continuum represent extreme conditions, and most relationships fall between them. *Formal* communication happens where most of the rules are set by an institutional source that is not a direct part of the interaction. *Informal* communication happens in situations where the people involved make most of the rules.

The most comprehensive attempt to create a system of imposed rules is found in the literature of Scientific Management. However, even organiza-

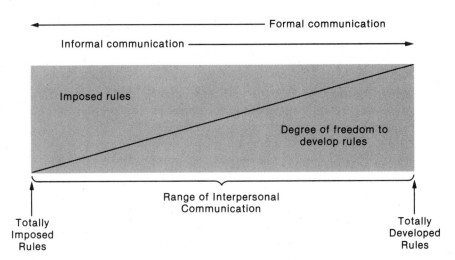

Formal communication

Informal communication

Imposed rules

Degree of freedom to
develop rules

Range of Interpersonal
Communication

Totally
Imposed
Rules

Totally
Developed
Rules

EXHIBIT 15-1

From: Interpersonal
Communication in
Organizations by Otis
Baskin and Craig Aronoff
(p. 151) © 1980 by
Goodyear Publishing
Company Reprinted with
permission.

tions as rigidly structured as those envisioned by Frederick Taylor would require managers to develop an interpersonal relationship (mutual rule system) with subordinates to encourage acceptance of the imposed rule system. The third of Taylor's four principles of Scientific Management makes this need clear:

> Heartily cooperate with the men so as to insure all of the work being done in accordance with the principles of the science which has been developed.

Thus, even in formal relationships, some rules must be developed interpersonally.

In contrast, consider the case of a design engineer at an aerospace firm. As a professional, he is free to do his work however and whenever he chooses. He frequently does not come to the office during the day but works at home. Sometimes he works at the office after most employees have gone home.

Obviously, few imposed rules exist here. Supervisors and subordinates work out their own rules systems. Communication between the engineer and his supervisor is informal because of their freedom to develop mutual rules concerning their relationship. This, however, does not imply that the interpersonal relationship will be free of imposed rules. Although the engineer and his supervisor enjoy much freedom within their relationship, contracts from clients impose deadlines and cost restraints within which they must function. Their interpersonal communication rules must conform to these imposed considerations.

COMMUNICATION BETWEEN SUPERVISORS AND SUBORDINATES

The most crucial interpersonal communication relationships are those between managers and subordinates. Famed organizational researcher Fritz Roethlisberger says: "It is in the relationship between a superior and a subordinate that more breakdowns of coordination and communication between various parts of the industrial structure finally show up."

Coorientation

People enter into communication relationships, formal or informal, with differing needs, values, and perceptions. They discover and create commonality of needs, values, and perceptions to produce a common rules system, mostly through reciprocal influence. Communicators learn each other's expectations and develop mutual expectations through what is called *coorientation*. Three factors must be present for coorientation to exist and for interpersonal communication to be successful. They are: agreement, accuracy, and understanding.

Agreement refers to the similarity between the expectations and meanings held by each person in the communication situation. *Accuracy* represents the degree to which each can predict the rules and meanings of the other. Accuracy differs from agreement. It suggests that communicators need to know each other's positions whether they agree or not. You can never improve agreement without accuracy.

Interpersonal communication can survive on little agreement if high accuracy is present. If Sam realizes that George's position is different from his, he can avoid that subject and avoid conflict. *Understanding* depends upon, but is not the same as, accuracy. It is more than knowing the other person's position. It is realizing that "they know that you know." Coorientation, therefore, depends on shared understanding of the degree of agreement and accuracy in the communication relationship.

Agreement Most research about interpersonal communication between managers and subordinates concerns itself with agreement rather than accuracy or understanding. One study asked first- and second-level managers in manufacturing firms whether the lower-level manager had authority to do certain things. Supervisors and subordinates agreed with each other on this subject about half the time. Another study found that subordinates are likely to describe their supervisor as someone who is as "open" as they see themselves to be. Moreover, the more agreement the subordinate sees between himself and his supervisor, the more satisfied the subordinate is with the company, the job, and management. The perception of agreement, even if erroneous, appears to create a sense of security and satisfaction. A third study measured the similarity between superiors' and subordinates' descriptions of five jobs (such as vice-president, clerk), and six persons (such as the personnel director, the supervisor). People who agreed in their descriptions also saw their own communication as more effective than those who did not agree as much.

Researchers who find discrepancies between the way that supervisors and subordinates perceive things attribute the difference to breakdowns in communication. However, participants enter into communication relationships with different needs, values, and perceptions. Because of their different backgrounds, discrepancies in perception are to be expected. Even within the same organization, individuals have differing experiences which result in dissimilar views of identical situations. The varied positions of superiors and subordinates explain a good bit. For example, a supervisor in a chemical plant sees the shutdown of a unit as necessary for maintenance, whereas the plant manager, who accounts for overall production, sees it as a mistake. It will cause other units and support functions to slow down or stop. Such lack of agreement may not indicate a problem of communication, but rather a natural, possibly desirable, difference in role perceptions. Individuals who perform different roles must often perceive the same objects, events, or persons differently.

Accuracy/Understanding The accuracy with which one person understands another's views is a better basis for evaluating communication effectiveness than simple agreement. When accuracy is added to agreement, coorientation becomes a function not of similar perceptions, but of accurately defining differences in perception and mutually understanding those differences.

Understanding, therefore, becomes more than a superior and subordinate accurately predicting each other's attitude or opinion on a subject. Understanding is a realization that each person correctly perceives the position of the other. This brings a particular quality to an interpersonal situation that transcends agreement. We can "agree to disagree" if we understand each other's perceptions. Where disagreement exists with understanding, you are less likely to have serious error or conflict. However, if a superior and subordinate assume they agree when they do not, or if they assume they disagree when they do not, serious consequences can result. Coorientation is a result of, and a basis for, successful interpersonal communication.

As communication researchers R. V. Farace, P. R. Monge, and H. M. Russell say in their book, *Communicating and Organizing:*

If two persons disagree and both recognize it, each can make allowances for the other's point of view. But if one person is inaccurate about the other person's viewpoint, and expects it to be the same as his or her own, then the stage is set for some potentially serious misunderstandings.

A scene from a widely used training film shows such a misunderstanding. An executive, deeply involved in a conference, is buzzed by his secretary. She explains that she must leave for the afternoon for a doctor's appointment. A typist from the steno pool will answer the phone and do routine clerical work in her absence. A few minutes after the secretary has gone, the executive emerges from the conference with the only existing signed copy of an important contract. He hands it to the stenographer sitting at his secretary's desk and says: "Here, burn this." He closes the conference room door, expecting his photocopied contract to be delivered momentarily. The steno holds the contract over an ash try and touches a lighted match to one corner. As the contract goes up in smoke, so do the executive's illusions that the typist from the steno pool can be expected to perceive his "verbal shorthand" the same way his secretary does. This example is extreme. But it shows the tendency to assume that others hold the same needs, values, and perceptions as we do.

Understanding/Facilitation and Communication Orientation

Understanding as we have defined it does not supply a cure for all management–subordinate problems. Coorientation concerning rules in an interpersonal relationship mostly involves give-and-take. We enter into communication situations with differing needs, values, and perceptions, but our agreement upon a mutually acceptable rule system does not automatically mean our relationship will promote productive behavior in the organizational context. As researchers Mark Steinberg and Gerald Miller write in their article "Interpersonal Communication: A Sharing Process":

> . . . individuals may agree to share rules systems that can only be labeled "sick" by most of the society's normative criteria. "Beat me!" pleads the masochist. "Go to hell!" replies the sadist, and their bizarre exchange not only illustrates the intricacies of some interpersonal relationships, but also highlights an interpersonal bond which most people would renounce as a social abomination.

How these rule systems evolve, be they "sane" or "insane," is set to a large extent by the personal orientations of the communicators themselves.

For our discussion of communicator orientation, we will describe two approaches: those that seek *direction and control* of the behavior of others; and those that seek *understanding and facilitation* of the behavior of others.

Director/controllers have a need to assume command. They implement communication strategies that will put them into power positions in interpersonal relationships. They tend to be involved frequently in conflict relationships because they fear that others threaten their control. Managers with direction/control orientations prefer to direct their subordinates rather than consult with them. They resist close relationships and insist on keeping a "safe distance" from others.

Understander/facilitators, on the other hand, need to analyze their own behavior and that of others. Because they wish to develop mutually beneficial relationships based upon shared trust and respect, they head off many potential conflicts.

Of course, the orientations of individuals are not often as clearly defined as we have just described them. All of us have needs, values, and perceptions with some of the characteristics of each communicator type. These characteristics also change with each relationship. However, all of us can see within ourselves assumptions that affect our approach to dealing with others. The fundamental orientations of individuals influence the development of rule systems for their relationships.

Relationship Orientation

Others have described these orientations differently, but their conclusions have been similar. William Schultz, writing in the *Harvard Business Review*, saw three interpersonal needs:

Inclusion: This is the tendency to include others in your interpersonal relationship or the desire for others to include you in theirs. It involves the need to belong. Director/controllers would characteristically resist attempts by subordinates to be included. Understander/facilitators would be comfortable either with inclusion or without it.

Affection: This is the need to give affection in interpersonal relationships and the desire to receive it. Director/controllers might use affection or friendship as part of their communication strategy. However, they would resist offers of close friendship from subordinates. They would not wish to be placed in a position of "compromise." Understander/facilitators could seek close relationships and receive affection from subordinates without fearing a loss of power.

Control: This is the desire to exert control over others or to have them exert control over you. Director/controllers obviously need to control others. They cannot permit anyone to usurp their power by controlling them. Understander/facilitators take a more moderate view. They can give up control in some situations and assume it in others without being threatened by either. They would be comfortable where control is shared by others.

As noted, each of us has expectations that are characteristic of both director/controllers and understander/facilitators. Although our basic orientation may be closer to one than the other, it can be altered by the situation in which a relationship exists.

LEADERSHIP AND INTERPERSONAL COMMUNICATION

Leadership can be defined in one sense as coorientation between manager and subordinate. Mutual rule systems are imperative between manager and subordinates if leadership is to be effective. Psychologist E. A. Fleishman defines leadership as ". . . an attempt at interpersonal influence, directed through the communication process, toward the attainment of some goal or goals." This parallels most definitions of interpersonal communication. Leadership, then, is goal-directed interpersonal communication. Work groups, bridge club members, families, as well as managers and subordinates, can share interpersonal communication rule systems that permit goal-directed communication.

Casual Relationships

Supervisors and subordinates interact on many levels in their organizational roles. One often-overlooked level involves nontask-related interactions. These include such everyday rituals as "Hello," "Nice day isn't it," "How are you?" These are called "phatic" communications, nonthreatening exchanges that help to pass time or define situations. They certainly are not, as we often hear, phrases without meaning. The meanings found in interpersonal relationships of this type have profound effects upon those involved, even though the words appear to have little to do with the situation at hand.

In her book *Communication: The Process of Organizing,* Bonnie Johnson quotes the former chief engineer of a cargo ship as an example: "They [the crew] knew what to do," he said. "I didn't have to tell them. I talked to them because I'd have gone crazy if I didn't talk to somebody. They were my friends." Of course, the situation presented by a three-month ocean voyage is different from the work experiences of most of us. Nevertheless, casual talk makes our situation more bearable in any relationship.

In addition to being a vehicle for strengthening interpersonal bonds, this type of "conventional-polite" communication can be used to keep others at arm's length. Thus, "Hello, how are you?" "Nice day, isn't it?" and other "small talk" can also be barriers to communication. The conventions of our society dictate "polite" responses. When a relationship is not allowed to develop beyond these "polite" exchanges, no normal mutual rule system can develop. Interactions are governed by rules that are imposed. Many managers who have a direction/control orientation perceive such aloof relationships as necessary for them. This need for distance is usually based upon some conventional and untested wisdom, such as "familiarity breeds contempt." Those who wish to keep tight control of interpersonal communication situations often talk to keep others at a proper distance. Director/controllers prefer communication rules that let them monopolize the situation. They create content rules to direct attention to themselves.

Being less concerned with direct control, understander/facilitators spend more time and effort on listening than on talking. Of course, by listening and talking we really refer to sending and receiving messages in the broad sense that allows for all forms of verbal and nonverbal communication. Understanding/facilitating managers do talk. But they also assume the role of active listeners, as discussed in Chapter 13. They give their attention to other people and help them with feedback. Understander/facilitators encourage others to talk by being involved and interested. They do not hesitate to ask for feedback themselves. To accomplish the goal of coorientation in casual relationships, understander/facilitators create relationship rules that assist shared communication and content rules that support other-directed interactions.

Leadership: A Two-Way Communication Process

Those who approach manager-subordinate relationships from a directive/controlling point of view assume that their purpose is the exertion of their influence over their subordinates' behavior. They wish to win the subordinate over to their way of thinking. On the other hand, understander/facilitators see leadership as a two-way interaction.

Contemporary leadership theory recognizes the importance of followers influencing leaders, as well as vice versa. This is the natural result of the process of coorientation. As G. C. Homans put it: "Influence over others is purchased at the price of allowing one's self to be influenced by others. . . ." Douglas McGregor, in his classic book *The Human Side of En-*

terprise, says that subordinates are not alone in their dependence upon others in organizations. Managers at every level must depend upon their subordinates if they are to achieve personal and organizational goals. He illustrated the relationship with a story:

> An agent of the Textile Workers Union of America likes to tell the story of the occasion when a new manager appeared in the mill where he was working. The manager came into the weave room the day he arrived. He walked directly over to the agent and said, "Are you Belloc?" The agent acknowledged that he was. The manager said, "I am the new manager here. When I manage a mill, I run it. Do you understand?" The agent nodded and then waved his hand. The workers, intently watching this encounter, shut down every loom in the room immediately. The agent turned to the manager and said, "All right, go ahead and run it."

It is folly to consider only the behavior of the leader in the study of leadership.

FACILITATING INTERPERSONAL COMMUNICATION

In this chapter (1) we have defined mutual acceptance of communication rules, and (2) we have shown the differences between an orientation toward understanding and facilitating and an orientation toward directing and controlling. These differences involve crucial aspects of effective interpersonal communication. These factors, coupled with the lessons on active listening in Chapter 13, provide a basis for positive interpersonal relationships in business and other organizations, and offer an underpinning for successful leadership, problem solving, and decision making.

FOR FURTHER STUDY

1. To help see whether your orientation toward communication is characterized by direction/control or understanding/facilitation, please take this test. Indicate whether each statement is true or false.

T F a. Communication problems can be solved by getting the right information to the right people at the right time.

T F b. Poor communication is a basic cause of low productivity.

T F c. Organizational communication is primarily a management responsibility.

T F d. It is important to regulate communication among workers and management.

PRINCIPLES FOR PRACTICE

1. Recognize the rules that constrain your interpersonal relationships.

2. There are always room and need for interpersonal communicators to seek coorientation. It is never sufficient to simply "play by the rules" or "go by the book."

3. Understanding, agreement, accuracy, and coorientation do not just happen. They must be consciously and conscientiously pursued.

4. Understanding is not agreement, and vice versa.

5. Understander/facilitators are generally more flexible and adaptive than director/controllers. The development of trust and respect in communication relationships helps to achieve coorientation and cooperation.

6. Realize that leadership is a two-way process of communication and influence.

T F e. The written word is the most effective means of communication within organizations.

T F f. A worker will follow company orders and policies if the reasons for them are understood.

T F g. Work is different from other kinds of human behavior and should be dealt with differently from other kinds of behavior.

T F h. Communication is a managerial tool, a process that facilitates more basic organization functions.

T F i. The major purpose of communication is to get other people to do what you want them to do.

Count up the number of true responses and false responses. The more times you answered true, the more prone you may be toward a direction/control orientation. The more times you answered false, the more likely you are to have an understanding/facilitation orientation.

2. Devise a strategy by which you can become more oriented toward understanding/facilitation.

3. Describe the interpersonal communication rules existing for your relationship with:

a. an employer,
b. a teacher,
c. an acquaintance,
d. a good friend,
e. your parents,
f. your boyfriend/girlfriend/spouse.

Discuss your rules with the other person in the relationship. How could your rules be changed to improve the relationship?

4. Discover how it feels to break communication rules. Try price bargaining at the checkout counter of a supermarket or walking around in the middle of a professor's lecture. How do you feel just before intentionally breaking implicit communication rules? How do people react? What efforts are made to get you to return to "normal" behavior?

5. Refuse to engage in "trivial" phatic communication. Go one day without "meaningless" greetings or "small talk." How do people respond? What motivations do they ascribe to your lack of responsiveness? How long do you think it will take to patch up the damage done to your relationships? (Considering the damage to your interpersonal relationships that might result from actually doing this exercise, we suggest you merely imagine the consequences of such behavior!)

6. Think of the last time you had a "meaningful" conversation. What is your definition of "meaningful"? What made that conversation "meaningful"? With whom, on what subject, and under what circumstances did it occur? Why are "meaningful" conversations rare?

CHAPTER
16

To: The Reader
From: The Authors
Subject: Communicating In Groups

After reading this chapter you will know that:

1. Groups provide a major part of the context for
    interpersonal communication.

2. We usually communicate as members of a group.

3. Group members develop shared expectations and use
    feedback to enforce them.

4. Shared expectations are the basis for cooperation,
    coordination, and integration in groups and
    organizations.

5. Group norms and roles relate expectations to individual
    behavior.

6. The definition of social reality and the attainment of
    group goals are the major functions of groups.

7. The amount of communication directed toward a given group
    member depends upon perceived differences, group
    cohesion, and the status of the individual within the
    group.

8. Groups are increasingly used in business organizations
    for information sharing, decision making, problem
    solving, morale building, coordination, motivation, and
    control.

9. Broad participation in group meetings requires the right
    climate and coorientation on meeting content, process,
    purpose, and outcome.

Communicating
In Groups

In our last chapter, we said that an organization can be seen as a network of interpersonal communication relationships. These relationships are governed by systems of rules developed in part by their participants, and, in part, imposed upon the participants. Perhaps the most significant sources of imposed rules are the groups to which we belong. Groups are an important part of all our lives. Understanding groups is basic to understanding the communication behavior of individuals in organizations. Organizations consist of overlapping groups. Groups are responsible for getting work done and providing social relationships among the people who are part of the organization.

Later this chapter will show you how you can improve work communication through groups. But first, let us look at some recent research on how people behave in groups.

INTERPERSONAL COMMUNICATION: A GROUP PERSPECTIVE

Much interpersonal communication can best be studied as group communication. Groups provide the closest reference point for interpersonal interactions. People speak to each other as members of groups. An interaction between a manager and subordinate might begin with talk about the local baseball team. Both participants are members of the same reference group—home team fans. They share a common system of expectations on that subject. As the conversation goes on and the mutual rule system becomes more apparent, the supervisor might decide to bring up the employee's recurring tardiness. The supervisor hopes to carry over some of the commonality already established into the "management group" versus "worker group" confrontation that follows. As the topic changes, the reference group changes from sports fans and friends to management and union member.

We all have reference groups for various parts of our lives. We shift from one to the other easily. When involved in a relationship, we draw many of our expectations for it from one or more of the groups to which we belong. If participants have a common reference group for the subject being discussed, they are likely to begin with at least some of the same expectations. The greater the differences in reference groups, the smaller the chance that coorientation will occur. Coorientation, as discussed in Chapter 15, is the process by which communicators learn each other's expectations and develop mutual ones. This process naturally speeds up between members of the same reference group. It slows down between communicators affiliated with groups that have opposing philosophies. For example, members of a labor union are likely to achieve coorientation quickly when discussing the rights of workers to bargain collectively, because they begin with common expectations derived from a mutual source. However, when the same people talk football, their respective reference groups (favorite teams) may be opposed to one another. Thus the chances that mutual expectations will result are reduced.

Group Communication and Expectations

Expectations are established and maintained through communication within the group. Expectations within groups, like those within person-to-person relationships, fall into two categories: process and content. Process expectations define the appropriate procedures of the group. Violation of expectations, either process or content, can cause a breakdown in relationships within the group. For example, a manager's unilateral decision to change work procedures in a department where group expectations include consultation is likely to meet resistance, even if the decision made is best for the problem at hand. The famous Hawthorne experiments showed how communication is used to establish and maintain expectations about job-related behavior of individuals in a work group. The Harvard researchers conducting those experiments identified certain messages that the group used to encourage conformity to group expectations. One of these group expectations was a production level that appeared to have no direct relationship either to the group's ability to produce or to company-set quotas. The group "enforced" its expectation of a fair day's work by labeling those who fell below production level as "chiselers" and those who produced above it as "ratebusters."

Work groups develop expectations that govern both casual and talk-related interactions. Many content expectations take the form of "communication themes" within the group. Themes are subjects of discussion that are relatively stable over the life of a group. Once a subject becomes sufficiently ingrained in the expectations of a group, it becomes a recurring theme. Acceptance of certain themes is part of the socialization process through which new members are inducted into the group. If the theme in a work group is, "no one in management ever appreciates your work around here," it will be hard to change this attitude. It is part of the rule system of the group. Likewise, new employees in the group are likely to incorporate the negative theme into their belief system as they become socialized into the group. Such rule systems reduce uncertainty within the group environment. Members know what to expect from other members. Themes are safe, predictable topics of discussion, and they assist interpersonal relationships between members.

Group expectations define the boundaries of individual behavior. Psychologist Leon Festinger contends that each person needs to compare his or her beliefs, perceptions, and values with those of others. He says that we tend to choose from all the people available for comparison those most similar to ourselves. A group in this sense is not merely a collection of persons lumped together. Members of this kind of group are aware of their mutual expectations, which psychologically define them as a unified body within an organization. Festinger's definition is only incidentally concerned with the number of people involved, the task performed, the spatial proximity of members to each other, and the relative status of members in the organization. These factors are important only as they contribute to the group's recognition of itself as a group. The mere fact of their existence, however, does not make any collection of people into a group. Groups must develop process and content rules to govern their behavior if the persons involved are to think of themselves as a group.

The operation of mutual expectations in both task- and nontask-related behavior is seen in a case by Donald F. Roy. Notice how communication is governed by a clear set of expectations to which each member responds.

"Banana Time"*

In an isolated area of a plant, four men perform the routine operation of placing strips of plastic under the head of a punch, then starting the ma-

*From Donald F. Roy, "Banana Time—Job Satisfaction and Informal Interaction". Reproduced with permission of the Society for Applied Anthropology. Adapted from: "Banana Time," Human Organization. Vol. 18, No. 4. (Winter 1960), 158–168.

chine. This requires them to stand in the same spot all day with little variety in their job and none in their surroundings. Instructions often are announced to the men over the public address system. The only man who has daily contact with the plant superintendent is George. He has the most seniority but is not formally designated as group leader. Other workers include Ike and Sammy, two European emigrants, and Roy, a new employee.

At first, Roy finds the monotony of the work unbearable. Then he begins to realize that "break times" and "chatter themes" have developed within the group. First there is "Peach Time," during which Sammy produces peaches from his lunch box. Each worker eats a peach and much conversation ensues over their quality, the character of the donor, and the lineage of the recipient who happens to criticize the gift.

"Banana Time" follows "Peach Time" by about one hour. Sammy again is the provider. However, Sammy brings only one banana. Ike steals the banana from Sammy's lunch box and then yells "Banana Time." Sammy protests and begins to castigate Ike. George soon joins in and chastises Sammy for making such a fuss. Sammy brings his banana every day, and every day Ike steals it; though Sammy never does eat his banana, he always brings one.

"Window Time" is next. In retaliation for the abuse Ike perceives he has taken from Sammy over the banana, he opens the window to let cool air blow in on Sammy. This always brings about a great deal of conversation between the two. George joins in, extolling the virtues of fresh air and encouraging Ike in his window teasing.

"Lunch Time" follows "Window Time." Ike tampers with George's clock to get a few extra minutes for lunch. These "break times" continue throughout the day until "quitting time."

In addition to the "times," there are "chatter themes." Roy, being the youngest, becomes the object of the "spoofing-about-his-love-life" theme. Other themes are the "Ike is a very bad man" theme, and the "George is a very good daddy" theme. The most solemn is the "professor" theme. George's daughter has married the son of a professor. George goes to extremes to tell how he dines with the professor and takes long Sunday walks with him on the Midway. When he discusses the professor, the others listen with deference.

The Roy comes upon an idea for a variation of the professor theme. He gets Ike to tease George by saying he has seen the professor giving instruction at a barber college in the wrong part of town. George turns very red but does not speak. He is obviously angry, so much so that he says nothing for the rest of the day. No breaks are taken and the "times" and "chatter themes" stop. George confides to Roy that there is too much play and not enough work and that things are going to change.

For twelve days the "times" and "themes" are eliminated. All communication is work-oriented. Soon everyone complains of work strain and leg fatigue. Even George grumbles about sore feet and weariness. On the thirteenth day communication between Ike, Sammy, and George is reestablished, and within a few days the old "times" and "themes" are again in use. However, there is one exception. George never again mentions his Sunday walks or dinners with the professor.

In this work group, "break times" and "chatter themes" are mutual expectations. They define the group. To be a member, one must participate in these communication interactions and understand the rules governing them. Some of the interactions involve the whole group, but others are relationships between individuals mediated by the group. "Banana Time" is basically a relationship between Sammy and Ike. However, interaction between these two follows the same expectations as "Peach Time," in which everybody takes part. Also, the "Banana Time" interaction is valuable diversion for the other members. The same system of rules govern "Window Time," "Lunch Time," and the themes of conversation.

One of the expectations held by the group is respect for the "professor" theme. Whenever George discusses the professor, everyone responds with respect. When Roy persuades Ike to shatter this rule, communication within the group immediately breaks down. It does not resume until a way is found to restructure the system of expectations. The teasing by Ike makes George uncertain about the possible behavior of other group members, and George's response to Ike had made the other members uncertain about George's behavior. Because the other expectations are relatively strong (fulfilling the needs, perceptions, and values of the members), the group is able to reestablish them and continues to function as a group by removing the "professor" theme from its system of expectations. Other options, such as withdrawal from George, were open, but removal of the theme provides the least amount of change in the system. The ability to maintain a mutual rule system within a group reduces uncertainty between members. It makes it possible for individuals to work together in an integrated effort.

Communication, Cooperation, Coordination, and Integration

Cooperation, coordination, and integration are prerequisite to the existence of any organization. Cooperation means the existence of mutual support among individuals. Coordination refers to actions synchronized to produce a common benefit. The actions of assembly line workers must be coordinated to some extent to produce results. However, coordination does not require a cooperative relationship among the individuals involved. Integration describes a higher level of organization. It includes both cooperation and coordination and produces a molding of individuals and activities into a unified whole.

For an organization to exist, it must have a system of expectations that is accepted by the members. These expectations specify what actions should be taken, which members should be involved, the functions of those involved, the time that the action should occur, and its rationale. In other words, integration is the result of mutually accepted rules that define the *who, what, where, when, why,* and *how* of a group. When these conditions are met, we can say that a group has become organized. The coordination of functions is accomplished through the subsystems within that system. Individuals develop interpersonal communication relationships (coorientation) within the context of one or more groups to which they belong. These linking relationships produce integration between the members of the subunits of the organization.

Intergroup communication or coorientation develops integration between groups. Coorientation between groups is brought about through the boundary-spanning relationships of individual members. "Banana Time" shows us integration within and between groups. Integration in the work group was created through "themes" and "times." The men did not need cooperation from each other to do the jobs they had been given. Only minimum coordination was needed, because no supervisor was present. But the group was more than a collection of individuals on a job. It became a functioning unit by developing a system of mutual expectations. Although the tasks were routine and required little definition by the group, the interpersonal environment in which the tasks were done had a significant effect upon each individual's ability to be satisfied in his work. Each "theme" and "time" had agreed-upon participants, time frames, roles, locations, and purposes. The broad purpose, of course, was to relieve boredom and make the tasks bearable.

George helped integrate the group with the rest of the organization through daily contact with another group—management. However, simple coordination between George's group and the organization could have been brought about through instructions broadcast over the public address system. George's boundary-spanning role made coorientation between the group and management possible. When individuals and groups in organizations develop mutual expectations, integration is achieved.

COMMUNICATION AND GROUP DYNAMICS

The need for balance or coorientation pressures growth toward uniformity, agreement, and conformity. These pressures create mutual expectations among group members.

Uniformity is a felt need. It exists within all groups to reinforce similar needs, values, and perceptions about subjects central to the group's functioning. Integration depends upon the amount of pressure a group feels toward uniformity. Groups with high uniformity have well-developed systems of mutual expectations. They show a high degree of integration in their behavior. Communication lets groups express and maintain their uniformity. Communication from other members shows new group members, or someone who aspires to be a group member, the expectations to which one must conform. Likewise, the communication of individual members becomes an important measure of the would-be member's conformity to expectations. These mutual expectations define the stated or implied rules of behavior that are the boundaries for interaction within the group. The pressure toward uniformity, whether its purpose is social or task-related, affects and is affected by interpersonal communication.

Communication Rules and Group Identity

Pressures toward uniformity show that anyone who is a member of a group is affected by the group's expectations. The fact that a person's behavior is affected, however, is not enough to establish membership. Although someone who wants to become a member may conform to the expectations of the group, he or she will not become a member until other members are willing to share a system of mutual expectations.

Groups, as stated earlier, are more than an aggregate of persons. Groups develop an identity that sets them apart from any mere collection of persons. The interpersonal communication relationships between members are the source of group identity. Dorwin Cartwright and Alvin Zander in their book, *Group Dynamics*, describe the process of group formation as follows:

> If a collection of people engages in interaction frequently and over an extended period of time, it is likely that their interactions will become patterned, that they will develop expectations concerning one another's behavior, and that they will come to identify one another as members of the same social entity.

The conditions for group identity involve a pattern of interactions among members that is frequent and long lasting. A system of shared expectations concerning the behavior of group members results.

As we said in the last chapter, all interpersonal communication relationships operate within stated or implied rules of behavior. These rules are acknowledged by the participants and serve as boundaries of interaction. The system of shared expectations that identifies a group as a social entity is the set of rules that creates the boundaries of the group. These boundaries define who is "in" or "out." They prescribe the limits of acceptable behavior for members and establish the functions of each member in relation to other members.

Group Norms and Role Expectations   Group norms are expectations or rules within the group that define standards of behavior for members. Such standards are developed to reduce uncertainty about the behavior of others. Reducing uncertainty between individuals increases interaction. People who can predict each other's reactions are more likely to develop rewarding communication relationships. As discussed in Chapter 15, consensus in interpersonal relationships depends more on accuracy regarding another's opinion than agreement. By reducing uncertainty, norms help relationships between group members to last.

Roles are rules or expectations that define a set of activities or behaviors for each person within the group. A group norm might be a certain level of production. However, the part each individual plays in achieving it is that person's role. Role conflict may arise if an individual fails or refuses to fulfill what is expected. Even if this deviant behavior does not violate the group's norms, refusal to conform to one's role may set off pressures to conform. If an individual assumes a leadership position that the rest of the group does not perceive as a proper role, that person may come into conflict with the other members. This can happen even though the person is advocating a group norm, such as a high standard of production.

Social Reality   Two sources of pressure toward uniformity that create group boundaries are social reality and attainment of group goal. Social reality is the individual's need to anchor opinions, beliefs, and attitudes in a group holding similar beliefs, values, and perceptions. Each of us needs to have others reinforce our expectations. That need brings together people with similar viewpoints. The need for *social* reality becomes stronger when our ability to rely on *physical* reality is low. People who felt that American involvement in the Viet Nam War would have ended sooner if President Kennedy had not been killed had to depend for support on social rather than physical reality. So it is with most expectations upon which we predicate our behavior. We cannot experience the physical reality of every situation; therefore, we look to social reinforcement for support. As our knowledge about the environment becomes more abstract, we rely more on social reality, and we feel more pressure toward uniformity within our reference groups.

A study by Edgar Schein, which appeared in *Psychiatry,* deals with the importance of social reality to human existence, and the role of reference groups in establishing and maintaining social reality. Many Americans worried about the behavior of U.S. prisoners of war during the Korean War. Studies showed that American P.O.W.'s in Korea were less likely to escape, suffered more disease, died at a higher rate, and collaborated with their captors more than their counterparts did in Germany during World War II. Physical differences in German and Chinese P.O.W. camps were not enough to explain the striking differences in prisoner behavior and survival. However, the differences in the social conditions in prison camps in the two wars do appear to have affected the social reality of the prisoners.

German P.O.W. camps were run in military fashion. American officers were expected to control their enlisted men. Therefore, groups formed and were even recognized by the German guards. Prisoners were housed together, making frequent interaction possible. Internal organizational structures were formed and rules of behavior were established. If a prisoner were interrogated, he knew he would be going back to his unit later and would have to answer for any breach of conduct.

In the Chinese camps, formation of strong groups that could establish a social reality for prisoners was discouraged. Officers were usually separated from enlisted men, which broke down social order. Sometimes enlisted men were deliberately put in charge of noncommissioned officers. In these and other ways, the Chinese broke up existing groups and kept new ones from forming. Prisoners were regularly moved between barracks to prevent organization.

Schein concluded that the low morale and poor survival rate of American prisoners in Chinese camps resulted from inadequate military or social structure. Prisoners collaborated with their captors because they lacked a reference group to set norms or to define roles for them. Individual prisoners felt isolated. Facing their captors alone, they could easily be intimidated. Prisoners seldom escaped because escape is usually a group activity. The Chinese did not allow prisoners enough interaction to develop mutual expectations. Instead, American prisoners in Korea distrusted each other because their opportunity to interact was so limited.

Informal groups in organizations can structure reality for their members in ways that are counter-productive to organizational goals. A negative social reality developed within a subsystem of an organization can result in sabotage on the production line. Without proper integration with other subsystems, groups may develop faulty social relations. Irving Janis, in his book *Victims of Group Think*, describes how groups can insulate themselves from communication relationships with others who have different views of a situation. When other views are cut off, the group has no mechanism for "reality testing." It may adopt a faulty social reality. This can be serious, because the social realities constructed by groups in an organization are the basis for decision making. Thus, for integration to take place within an organization, each subsystem must develop a social reality compatible with every other subsystem.

Achievement of Goals   If a group perceives uniformity as desirable or necessary to the attainment of its goals, the tendency toward uniformity will increase. The strength of the pressures toward uniformity is mediated by variables such as the desirability of the goals themselves and whether or not uniformity is seen as useful in moving toward the goals. Where members depend upon the group to achieve their own goals, the tendency toward uniformity within the group is greater. Pressure toward uniformity affects communication among group members in four areas:

1. Amount of communication.
2. Direction of communication.
3. Individual reactions.
4. Group membership.

Perceived Differences   As the amount of perceived difference in opinion about a subject increases among members, the tendency to communicate in a group increases. We need to anchor our beliefs, values, and perceptions in social reality. Therefore, pressures to communicate increase as members learn of discrepancies in the group over relevant issues. The pressure becomes intense if there is little "physical reality" to validate the opinion. However, differences in beliefs, values, or perceptions result in pressure to communicate only if the group is perceived as a reference group for the subject in question. Although there might be striking differences in opinion over religion in a work group, the topic would seldom be discussed. The members do not perceive the subject as relevant for this group. But if the discrepancy was over how much work should be done in a day, relevance would be high, and pressure to communicate would also be high.

Group Cohesion   Cohesiveness of the group also affects communication. When the forces that make members want to stay in the group (cohesion) increase, the tendency to communicate about accepted expectations also increases. The tendency to withhold unacceptable communication also increases. M. E. Shaw's review of research on group behavior says:

> . . . high cohesive groups engage in more social interaction, engage in more positive interactions (friendly, cooperative, democratic, etc.), exert greater influence over their members, are more effective in achieving goals they set for themselves, and have higher member satisfaction.

In another study, three types of cohesion (linking the members, prestige attached to belonging, and possibility of getting a reward for performance) were used to measure the effects of cohesion on communication. The results compare low and high cohesive groups. In the high cohesive groups, there was more pressure to communicate, more rapid discussion, and a greater attempt to exert influence. The amount of communication seems to increase with the presence of cohesion, relevant issues, and disagreement among members.

Deviate Members In groups where members express conflicting opinions, the pressure to communicate is strongest on members whose opinions differ most from the rest of the group. The tendency to communicate among members holding the same opinion is less. One study found about five times as much communication directed toward members with opinions differing from the rest of their group. Another study looked at groups with a wide range of opinions among members. It concluded that 70 to 90 percent of the communication was directed toward members who held extreme points of view. As opinions began to cluster together, fewer messages were transmitted between members with similar viewpoints. Thus, more communication is directed toward those holding opinions perceived as substantially different from the rest of the group.

Acknowledged or Desired Members The extent to which a person is perceived to be a group member and the extent to which others want that person to be a member influences the amount of communication directed toward that person. "Membership" clearly means more than nominal or appointed membership. It is the rule system of the group itself. That system defines the psychological or perceptual boundaries of the group. Therefore, membership is largely a function of the group's perceptions about who its members are and who they should be.

Members avoid communicating with those they do not perceive to be a part of their group, or whom they do not wish to remain members. Psychologist Stanley Schachter's research shows that members who do not want individuals holding divergent opinions to remain in the group withhold communication. Another study concludes that communication decreases in the direction of people with different opinions if they are not considered group members.

Communication and Change The extent to which members believe that communication may change divergent opinions affects communication flow within the group. Such communication seeks to bring the opinions of a divergent member into line with those of the rest of the group. Therefore, it follows that more communication will be directed toward members who seem open to change. If a member is judged highly resistant, the group is less likely to direct communication toward that person. There will also be a tendency not to communicate if it seems that doing so will increase differences in opinion between the rest of the group and that person. In the "Banana Time" case, further communication toward George concerning the "professor" theme would have made matters worse.

When a disagreement occurs between two members, with the rest of the group remaining fairly neutral, members with more moderate opinions will tend to communicate less with the entire group. When conflicts happen, members who hold more moderate opinions seem to realize that communication designed to bring an extreme member into line may set off an even more extreme reaction in the other disagreeing member. Because of this, moderate members tend to direct their messages to individuals rather than to the whole group. Conflict between two members results in communication flow becoming more directional and less general within the whole group.

Effects of Group Communication on Individual Behavior

Two forces for change related to communication result from pressures toward uniformity. First, attempts to change the opinions of disagreeing members will increase in groups where there is increased pressure toward uniformity. Because of this, we expect greater change in groups with pressures toward uniformity. Also, the desirability or need for uniformity makes all members more ready to change. Thus, pressures toward uniformity can produce change in the opinions of all members, not just the divergent ones to whom the communication is directed. Such groups produce more messages intended to change opinions, and their members are more susceptible to these messages. Therefore, we assume that change is more likely in groups where the pressure toward conformity is great. Research on these matters shows that high pressure groups had more change, medium pressure groups were second, and low pressure groups were last in the movement toward uniformity. In "Banana Time," all members changed their expectations. They excluded the "professor" theme when group activities were threatened.

Cohesion and Coercion in Group Communication   How much influence a group can have on one of its members is related directly to how strong the forces are that attract that member to the group. Where cohesive forces are strong, the group has real power to change the beliefs, values, and perceptions of the member through communication. The change is not coerced. If a member is kept from leaving a group (coercion) rather than attracted to stay (cohesion), the group may influence outward behavior, but it will have little effect on real opinions and attitudes.

For example, if a work group member disagrees with other members about an important matter, such as how much work should be done, communication directed from the other members toward the deviate will seek to change his or her opinion. The results will depend upon many factors, including cohesion in the group. If membership in the group is attractive for the disagreeing member, then that person is more likely to be influenced in the intended direction. This change is likely to be a real change in opinions and attitudes. It is based on the attractiveness of group membership for the conflicting member. But, if the disagreeing person cannot find another job and stays in the group because of financial coercion, the change will be superficial, affecting outward behavior only. Such changes to avoid punishment (unemployment) are unlikely to produce a good climate within the work group. The force that a group can apply to a disagreeing member to change opinions and attitudes cannot be greater than the force of the attraction that the member feels toward the group.

Other Affiliations Another factor affecting opinion change can be a divergent member's affiliations with other groups. Actual change in opinion and attitudes in response to communication from group members decreases where divergent opinions and attitudes are anchored in other group memberships. Change also decreases where the opinion and attitudes satisfy important needs for one individual. If a work group member is asked to take part in activities which that person believes are morally or ethically wrong under the norms of religious or professional groups to which he or she belongs, communication from other members of the work group saying that the activity is not objectionable will be less effective. In "Banana Time," George was not likely to change his opinion about the professor, because it was strongly rooted in his family group.

Communication and Group Membership As forces that create pressure to communicate increase (pressure toward uniformity, divergent opinions, cohesion), so does the tendency to reject deviate individuals. As group members communicate more and more to try to bring an individual member's opinions into line, the group is more and more likely to perceive the individual as someone outside its psychological boundaries.

Groups respond to the need for uniformity or mutual expectations in two ways, as already noted. They communicate with divergent members to try to influence their opinions. At the same time, they are more susceptible to influence themselves. The need for mutual expectations or a common rule system increases the tendency to expel disagreeing members as their differences increase. Therefore, some groups achieve uniform or mutual expectations by redefining their memberships.

Where group cohesiveness is high and the issue in question is relevant, a group will tend to reject nonconforming individuals. The same forces (cohesiveness and relevance) combine to increase the pressure to communicate within a group. As that pressure grows, the group becomes more apt to reject those who do not share their system of expectations. This system of relevant expectations creates the psychological boundaries of the group and defines its scope of interaction.

Groups as the Means of Participation in Organizations

Now that you know some of the aspects of communication in groups, let us see how the unique characteristics of group communication work in business organizations.

In recent years, an increasing number of organizations have recognized that worker participation is a key to increasing both productivity and the quality of working life. Informal and formal groups are the means by which participation is best promoted. Groups are used for sharing information, making decisions, solving problems, building morale, achieving coordination, accomplishing integration, assisting motivation, and maintaining control. In a survey of corporate chief executives, group meetings were most often named as the "most effective single communication technique" in organizations.

Part of the reason for the rise of participation in organizations is changing sociological reality. J. Lee Hess, general manager of Dana Corporation's Victor Products Division, says: "People used to be satisfied with merely having a job. But that's not true today. Now they want to get involved." People throughout society demand more involvement. In organizations and businesses, employees demand greater participation in decisions affecting their lives.

In a sense, the extensive use of groups in modern organizations reflects the fact that we live the majority of our lives in groups. We need them to accomplish tasks and achieve goals that cannot be reached individually. As Michael Doyle and David Straus have written:

> We are a meeting society—a world made up of small groups that come together to share information, plan, solve problems, criticize or praise, make new decisions or find out what went wrong with old ones. Governments, businesses, schools, clubs, families—all are built up from groups of men, women and children. Regardless of their values or goals, individual members of these groups must get together in order to function.

Organizations that Use Groups and Their Results

All organizations use groups. In traditional organizations, the more successful you become, the more time you spend in meetings. Middle managers spend about 35 percent of their working week in meetings, and top managers may spend more than 50 percent. In more modern organizations, first-line managers and employees also spend much time in work groups. Let us look at two examples of modern group management:

Questor Corporation's Spalding Division, makers of golf clubs, uses work teams. They are made up of production workers and their supervisors, and they coordinate work flow, division of labor, and quality control. The work teams manage these matters successfully and also improve performance in other ways. They help with employee motivation and satisfaction, absenteeism, turnover, and productivity.

PPG Industries Incorporated's Crestline, Ohio, Glass Division introduced a work-team approach to problem solving. In it, "people whose job responsibilities are interrelated meet regularly and discuss problems as a team," according to plant manager Ken Gibson. Results include a 24 percent reduction in man-hours per square foot of glass shipped, and a low absenteeism rate of 3 percent.

Several hundred major companies now have worker involvement policies, which have increased the use of group meetings. Worker involvement has produced excellent results: increased production, better quality products, more agreeable bargaining atmospheres, better safety records, more efficient work practices, more satisfied and stable work forces, fewer grievances, and higher profits and wages.

All of this means that supervisors are finding themselves in situations where they must run meetings and lead groups. The time and effort is well spent, however, because the process, when well done, can turn workers into problem solvers.

No special magic takes over when people gather in groups. The benefit lies in the psychology of individuals and social dynamics of groups.

All people need to "belong." We need to associate and communicate with other people. Not surprisingly, a recent study showed that isolating employees from other personnel negatively affects their morale. The need to feel like part of a group or a member of a team; the need to feel unity, togetherness, belonging, and trust; the need to ease the loneliness and burdens of responsibility; and the development of a sense of commitment are all sound psychological reasons for meetings.

Meetings intensively involve others in solving problems and making decisions. When someone helps solve a problem, he or he is likely to accept and support the solution.

Interaction in groups causes alternatives and ideas to emerge, something that is less likely to happen where people are working alone. Because groups are systems, the synergistic principle discussed in Chapter 2 comes into play. Group interaction and interdependency make the whole more than the sum of its parts. A group develops solutions that its members could not have come up with alone. This is even more true when a problem requires the knowledge and experience of several people. The problem can usually be solved best by bringing all the people together.

Moreover, group meetings have an impact even on people who are not present. There often is a "ripple effect," so that a meeting involving half a dozen people may ultimately affect the work of 50 or 100 or even thousands of others.

The rest of this chapter describes ways of getting better communication in groups—whether you are a group leader or a member.

GROUP MEETINGS AND HOW TO MAKE THEM BETTER

Despite all the good things we have been saying about groups in organizations, group meetings still have bad reputations. You have heard the mock definition: "A committee is a collection of the unfit chosen from the unwilling by the incompetent to do the unnecessary." Criticisms of group meetings include: "meetings are so boring"; "we keep getting off the track"; "the same people do all the talking"; "there's too much griping"; "the meeting was unnecessary"; "some people won't participate."

Any meeting can be a triumph or a bomb. Meetings called for the wrong reasons (or no reason) can be disasters. When expected outcomes of meetings are not made clear, when they are poorly prepared, structured, or run, they can cause more problems than they solve. They can create frustration, disillusionment, and bitterness when mismanaged.

But if meetings are properly prepared and led, they can be an organization's greatest asset. They can enhance coordination, planning, participation, and employee commitment. Let us now find out how to take advantage of the benefits of meetings and how to avoid their pitfalls.

Criteria for Successful Meetings

There is no formula that will assure successful meetings, but a number of factors can tilt the scales toward success. They include:

1. Determining if the meeting is really needed.

2. Having a clear idea of its puprose.

3. Involving the right people.

4. Establishing a good meeting environment physically.

5. Maintaining enough structure to keep things moving, but staying loose enough to allow interaction.

6. Encouraging input and interaction from all participants.

7. Achieving consensus on what outcome is expected.

Is that Meeting Really Necessary? How many times have you been at a meeting and wondered why you were there? Were you just going through the motions, meeting to be meeting?

Sometimes meetings are called too easily, too quickly. Sometimes they are a habit. A meeting that should not have been held is unlikely to have positive results.

Sometimes, even often, however, meetings are the only practical means for achieving communication objectives. Meetings *should* be called:

1. When issues require that several people be involved.

2. When interaction is needed to spur creativity or critical analysis.

3. When there is time to prepare for and to complete meetings.

4. When participants must act on the decision.

5. When a mutual exchange (feedback) is needed to assure that participants understand.

Meetings *should not* be held:

1. When time pressures prevent adequate preparation.

2. When communication is to be one-way and no participant response is wanted.

3. When the problem is simple and can be handled by one person.

4. When commitment and input from participants are not required.

5. When participants cannot handle the conflict that is usually found in the problem-solving process.

In sum, meetings should be called when participation is desired, necessary, and feasible. A meeting should not be called when it is not needed or not feasible. Meetings should never be used merely to give an *impression* of participation.

Clarifying the Meeting's Purpose Every Friday at four the salespeople at Gurley Cars are assembled for a sales meeting. Every Friday the same "pep talk" is given by Mr. Gurley. The session has long since become a joke among the sales force, some of whom resent it as an intrusion on their efforts to sell automobiles.

A real problem in this case is the lack of a clear purpose for the meeting. The rationale, if there ever was one, is long since forgotten. Was the meeting supposed to help sales? Was motivation the objective? Was it sharing information? Training? Decision making? No one can say.

The purpose of a meeting is the "goal to be achieved." *Purpose* should not be confused with *outcome*, which is the tangible, measurable product of the meeting.

A perfect example of confused purpose is a meeting that has been called to ask for input into a decision already made. People attending such meetings are disaffected. They feel deceived, and grave damage can be done to morale, commitment, and personal relationships by such meetings. Getting *feedback* on a decision already made is a different thing altogether. It is just as legitimate as asking for input, provided the rationale is so stated.

We have spoken of the necessity for coorientation. If participants are cooriented to the purpose of their meeting—that is, if their expectations about its purpose are largely similar and these expectations are not violated—then the meeting is more likely to be effective and successful.

Involving the Right People Clarifying the meeting's purpose is part of the process of identifying those people who can and will work to achieve that purpose. Effectiveness and success depend upon involving the right people; after all, a meeting's participants are its major resource.

Individuals bring expectations, values, needs, attitudes, information, ideas, status, and roles to meetings, all of them potential assets or liabilities. All participants should be selected on the basis of their potential contributions.

The outcomes of meetings go beyond announcing decisions or taking actions. Meetings affect individual satisfaction, commitment, motivation, and expectations, as well as group norms and values. Participant selection, therefore, must seek to increase positive outcomes of these kinds.

Once the purpose of a meeting has been established, six factors should guide your selection of participants:

1. Group size.

2. Maturity level of potential participants.

3. The knowledge, information, skills, and abilities of potential participants.

4. The compatibility of potential participants.

5. The status of potential participants within the organization.

6. The extent to which potential participants will be affected by meeting outcomes.

Group size: Your decision on who should participate is naturally limited by the number of people who can be effectively involved. Some variables will affect group size in problem-solving meetings. They include the complexity of the problem, the methods to be used in running the meeting, and the amount of participation wanted.

Research on group size shows that a meeting with five to seven participants is optimal. It works best in terms of participant input and efficiency and quality of task completion. Less than five can be good for simple tasks or when time is pressing. Groups larger than seven are usually inappropriate for problem solving.

Maturity level: Mature people can deal better with the ambiguity and the conflict usually found in problem-solving groups. They can take a variety of roles in the meeting.

Knowledge, information, skills, and abilities: Many problems require specific knowledge, information, skills, or abilities. People who have all of these must be invited. Knowledge need not be strictly cognitive, however. It is sometimes important to include people who represent the feelings of a constituency.

Compatibility of potential participants: The "mix" within the group is important. You should select members on the basis of their ability to work together. This is not to say that only people who think alike should be included, nor that groups should be structured to avoid conflict. Conflict is often a spur to creativity and helps to avoid "group think." Consequently, while compatibility is desirable, diverse viewpoints are equally essential.

Status: In some cases, high-level participants should be included in group meetings, especially when outcomes must be "sold" to top management, or when the importance of the group must be impressed upon people in or outside the group.

Effects on participants: Particularly in problem-solving groups, those who will be affected by projected outcomes should be represented. Objections can be foreseen, and individuals involved in the meeting tend to develop commitment and understanding of the group's decision.

Establishing a Good Physical Environment   Successful meetings have been held under bad conditions, but meetings tend to be more effective when the physical environment works for rather than against you. Sufficient lead time can usually assure a helpful environment in terms of location, size of the room, lighting, seating arrangement, and removal of physical distractions.

When possible, meetings should be held away from the participants' usual workplace. Those taking part can then avoid the interruptions and distractions of their everyday surroundings. A new location also lends an aura of importance to the proceedings.

The meeting room should be large enough to serve the participants but not big enough to dwarf them. Lighting should be soft, designed to reduce glare, shadows, and fatigue. Carpets, drapes, acoustical tile, and other sound-absorbing devices ideally should be present to deaden sound.

The seating arrangements can influence effectiveness. Months of negotiations decided the shape of the table at the Viet Nam peace talks. Seating arrangement indicates status. Also, research shows that people communicate most often with those they can see. To promote equality and to increase interaction, emulate King Arthur and his round table.

Maintaining Appropriate Group Structure   One of the hardest things in running effective meetings is keeping a proper degree of structure. Too tight a rein kills creativity, initiative, and commitment. If you loosen controls too much, the meeting can go off in all directions. Hence, group leaders walk tightropes that can be too taut or too slack. Both are dangerous.

Proper structuring begins long before the meeting starts. Often, the preparation and circulation of an agenda announces the meeting's time and place, identifies those invited, states the purposes, describes major topics, and estimates the meeting time. The agenda creates clear expectations, permits those invited to prepare worthwhile contributions, and serves as a structural framework.

To stick rigidly to this or any structure, however, would be an error. Meetings must adjust to individual needs and inputs and must facilitate group conflict and consensus. Robert's Rules of Order, full of complex rules for conduct of meetings, may be needed to keep very large groups in some semblance of order. But to use such a standard in a problem-solving group of five to seven people would be a mistake.

Facilitating Input and Interaction   If group meetings are to do what they are supposed to, their leaders must get all participants to take part. Two things are needed for broad participation: establishing the right climate and achieving coorientation concerning the meeting's content, process, purpose, and outcome. We have already discussed coorientation, so let us look at meeting climate.

The way the participants feel while they are in the meeting establishes the climate of the meeting.

You have certainly felt differently in different meetings you have attended. At various times, you may have felt threatened, intimidated, stifled, manipulated, or resented. At other times, you may have felt accepted, valued, encouraged, or stimulated, feelings that obviously lend themselves to effective meetings. But how is this kind of climate fostered?

Many things contribute to climate: the purposes and expected outcome of the meeting, the circumstances under which it is held, and the relationships between those taking part. Perhaps the most important factor, however, and the one most directly controlled, is the "facilitator role." Someone must be responsible for assuring an open and balanced conversational flow. Someone must protect individuals from personal attack. Someone must be neutral and nonevaluative, concerned with keeping the group on track and maximizing its effectiveness. Whether formally designated or not, that someone is the facilitator.

When someone is withholding participation, the facilitator invites input. If conversational traffic is heavy and a voice is having trouble entering the flow, the facilitator plays traffic cop or runs interference, as the situation demands. If interaction becomes rough or nasty, the facilitator protects the party under attack or defuses explosive situations.

Effective facilitators help to create and maintain good meeting climates. They relieve tension and conserve energy for listening (see Chapter 13) and for worthwhile contributions.

Facilitators often ask questions. A well-timed and phrased question can defuse an attack, point a way into the discussion for a reticent participant, or get a wandering conversation back on target.

Good questions are pointed, brief, and specific. Those with *yes* or *no* answers are not the best ones. "What do you think?" or "Don't you agree?" usually do not stimulate the best answers. To draw someone into the discussion, try, "Joan, you've had some experience with that kind of problem. What would you suggest?" To get back on track, use: "But isn't our main purpose here to develop a marketing strategy? The decision to produce has been made."

A supportive meeting climate and a good facilitator can bring about input and interaction. All that is needed then to assure success is the conclusion: achieving consensus on meeting outcomes.

Achieving Consensus   What comes out of a successful decision-making meeting? Some would say: "Making the best decision." Others believe that the "feelings" that emerge are most important.

Even if the "best" decision is made, however, it will not matter unless group members accept it and carry it out. On the other hand, if good feelings are all that is accomplished, the group has failed in the operational sense.

Success in group meetings can be defined as making the best decisions consistent with the needs of the organization, the group, and the people taking part in the group. This means reaching consensus.

Before groups make decisions, they decide how to decide. The result of this process is called a decision rule.

Consensus is a decision rule, an agreement that a decision will not be reached until an alternative is found that all participants can support. Other decision rules exist, of course. They include unilateral mandate (a powerful leader announcing a decision); win/lose bargaining; averaging; majority votes; or coin flips. All of these others may reduce conflict and save time, but they may leave a significant portion of the group unhappy. Moreover, important inputs and feedback may have been suppressed, reducing the chances of finding a good solution.

Japanese corporate executives say that the phenomenal performance of Japanese industry is due in part to the fact that decisions in Japanese corporations are made in groups. Consensus is the decisional rule. *Nemawashi*, the first phase of decision making, is a process of informal discussion and consultation. It takes place before proposals are presented. Objections are heard, compromises are reached, the proposal is changed on the basis of the input and information of all who may be affected. *Nemawashi* is followed by the *ringi* system. This allows everyone likely to be involved in carrying out the decision to approve it in its final form.

American executives sometimes criticize the Japanese system as frustrating and time-consuming. Indeed, more time is spent reaching a decision in Japan. Much less time is spent implementing the decision, however. People who helped make the decision help implement it. Thus Japanese corporations are more rapidly committed to and prepared for effective action than are their American counterparts.

Consensus does not always result in the best solution from any particular viewpoint. Research shows, however, that group decisions are generally superior to those made by individuals. Group members are more committed to decisions made by consensus than to those settled by majority vote or handed down by one individual.

Here are some tips that can help both group leaders and group members achieve consensus:

1. Avoid arguing for your own views. Make your point lucidly and logically; then sit back and listen to reactions before pressing further.

2. Do not assume that some must win and some must lose. . . . Find a solution that seems most acceptable to everyone.

3. When agreement seems to come too quickly and easily, be suspicious. Conflict avoidance may be taking place. Differences of opinion are natural and expected. They help the group reach better solutions.

4. Put concern for the whole group above your desire to have your solution accepted.

So What's Wrong with a Camel? Group decision making has been maligned. We hope that in this chapter, you have learned that under the right

1. Be aware of the groups you and others represent in interpersonal communication.

2. Violate group expectations at your own risk.

3. The capacity of a group to influence individual behavior depends more on cohesion (the desire to remain a group member) than on coercion.

4. We all belong to many groups. This factor modifies the influence of any given group.

5. People want to get involved. Groups are a means of getting them involved.

6. To assure successful meetings: determine whether the meeting is needed; clarify its purpose; involve the right people; set up a good environment; maintain appropriate structure; encourage participation; and achieve consensus.

7. Whenever possible in group decisions, seek consensus rather than settling for majority rule.

8. To be a good group member or leader: avoid arguing for your own views; do not take win/lose positions; distrust easy agreement; be concerned for the group as a whole.

circumstances, using proper methods, group meetings can be effective, even essential, in organizations.

You may have heard it said that "a camel is a horse designed by a committee." Yet if the problem was to design an animal for transportation in the desert, the group that decided on a camel was right. It made a more effective decision than the person who recommended a horse.

FOR FURTHER STUDY

1. Why are groups usually more effective decision makers than individuals?

2. How much of what we usually consider individual behavior is really a function of groups of which individuals are a part?

3. How do groups improve an organization's capacity for cooperation, coordination, and integration?

4. Analyze the communication of a group in which you have recently taken part. How could communication have been improved to help achieve group objectives?

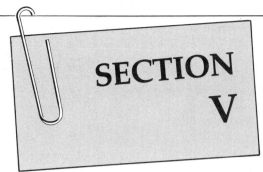

SECTION
V

Getting Your Message Across Through Other Media

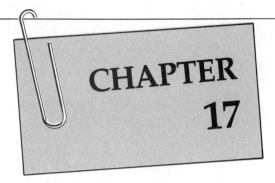

CHAPTER 17

To: The Reader
From: The Authors
Subject: Writing, Planning, and Managing In-House
           Publications

When you finish reading this chapter you should:

1. Realize that some of the most important and frequently
   used communication tools in any organization are the
   newspapers, magazines, and newsletters published "in-
   house."

2. Have a better understanding of the role in-house
   publications play in an organization's total
   communication system.

3. Be aware of the major considerations that must be faced
   by anyone who attempts to put out an in-house
   publication.

4. Understand the difference between content that is
   newsworthy and stories that may be dull or trivial to
   your reader.

5. Have a knowledge of the basic techniques of writing,
   laying out, editing, and managing this kind of
   publication.

6. Be aware of some useful strategies for getting news and
   enlisting the cooperation of individuals from various
   parts of the organization.

Getting Your Message Across Through In-House Publications

Not long ago the personnel manager for a small chemical plant that was part of a large multinational corporation found himself facing a management situation that his college professor never warned him about. One afternoon a package came to his office by parcel post. As he signed for it, he noticed that the return address was the company's corporate headquarters. Eager to see what corporate headquarters was sending, he ripped open the box to find a 35-mm. camera and numerous accessories. No explanation was included, only an instruction manual. The personnel manager was puzzled, to say the least. He did not recall entering any contest that would produce such a prize. He had not ordered this equipment. His greatest photographic achievement to date was the partial decapitation of his wife on the rim of the Grand Canyon. He decided to lock the camera in a file drawer and wait for the sender to ask for its return.

A few days later a letter about the camera arrived from the public affairs office at corporate headquarters. The letter did not ask for the return of the camera, but directed the personnel manager to begin immediate publication of an in-house newspaper for his plant. The personnel manager's staff consisted of himself and a secretary. Naturally, his first thought was to hire someone with experience in these matters. Unfortunately, corporate headquarters had issued the directive without providing an increase in budget. Thus, editing, writing, photography, layout, printing, and all the other duties associated with an in-house publication fell on the shoulders of the personnel manager and his secretary. Neither his university nor his pro-

303

fessional training had provided the kind of knowledge he needed. This is not surprising. Most managers are not prepared to manage one of business's most widely used communication media: in-house publications. At that distressing point, one of the authors of this book was called in to help. He and the personnel manager developed a comprehensive plan, communication strategy, and production process for putting out the newspaper.

The chances are good that you also will be involved with such publications as a manager or an employee. Even in small businesses, in-house publications are recognized as important tools of communication. The chemical plant in our example had only 70 employees. The value of an in-house publication, like that of any other tool, depends on the ability of those in charge of it. This chapter will discuss the purposes, function, and techniques of using such publications in business organizations.

WHAT ARE IN-HOUSE PUBLICATIONS?

In-house publications take about as many forms as the organizations and individuals who publish them. Effective, professionally written publications can be mimeographed newsletters, newspapers with editorial staffs, glossy full-color magazines, or any variation thereof. The one thing all internal publications have in common is that they give an organization the chance to tell its story the way it wishes it told. This is the reason why in-house publications have become popular. It is also the reason why so many fail to meet their objectives. When management tells its story from its own point of view without considering the intended readers, in-house publications are only "propaganda sheets." However, like the other media discussed in this book, in-house publications can be effective tools if produced with the needs of their intended audience in mind.

There are more than 50,000 in-house publications in the United States with a combined circulation of more than 300 million. Many large organizations find it useful to have more than one publication. One automobile producer, because of its size and the variety of its audiences, has 38. Most in-house journals are internal publications not intended for the general public. However, occasionally they are distributed to influential people outside the organizations or even used as a marketing tool.

THE PURPOSE AND POTENTIAL OF IN-HOUSE PUBLICATIONS

The need to distribute information about the company and its goals is keenly felt. The trouble most organizations have in "getting through" to their

EXHIBIT 17-1
In-House Publications

employees is illustrated by the troublesome discovery made by one firm. It was honoring an employee for 25 years of service. While talking with this person, management was shocked to realize how little he knew about the organization he had been a part of for a quarter of a century. The employee did not know the name of the company president, the location of head-quarters, the number of plants the company had, the year the firm was founded, or the source of the raw material used in the manufacturing process. After 25 years of experience, he could name only two of his firm's 200 products.

Such examples often come up. Everyone then says that "what we have here is a problem of communication." However, as pointed out earlier, while every management problem does have a communication aspect, simply labeling it as such, or even deciding to increase communication, does not guarantee a solution. Too often, a stressful situation results in a sudden increase in print communication that just makes the problem worse. Communication problems cannot be solved by simply increasing the flow of printed messages. While printed media have their advantages, they cannot be regarded as the response to just any problem. Printed communication must take its place as a part of an overall program. Such a program includes all the modes discussed in this book: face-to-face, public speaking, meetings, verbal, nonverbal, written, and spoken. In-house publications can do a lot of good work within an organization. But they can never take the place of person-to-person manager–subordinate relationships. Company publications are effective *supplementary* communication tools, but they are not primary ones.

Communication Functions of In-House Publications

Downward communication is the most common use of in-house publications. The need of management to "inform" its employees is the justification behind most company publications. Internal publications, because they publish regularly, can report new developments in a timely and relatively inexpensive way.

Internal publications are sometimes used as propaganda tools. There is a fine line between telling intended readers what management wants them to know and providing the information they want and need. The former is the leading cause of failure for in-house publications. The latter insures success. If a company publication gets a reputation as a "management line," it loses readers. Those who do read it do not take it seriously, and then the publication becomes a part of the problem.

Upward communication is another function of the in-house publication. It can help avoid the propaganda problem just mentioned. Those responsible

Brennan: selling the philosophy of the basics

EXHIBIT 17-2
Downward
Communication

From *Sears South News*,
Sears, Roebuck and Co.,
used by permission.

Nine months ago Edward A. Brennan brought to his new job as territorial executive vice president, 22 years of experience in 15 assignments and the unshakeable conviction that *Sears is still Sears.*

Despite the fact that retailing has become an increasingly competitive and segmented industry, causing Sears to respond with adjustments in promotional strategy and changes in organizational structure, Brennan believes that the basic fabric of the company is intact and that its source of strength—as well as its hopes for the future—rest with the people who work there. And those people, he maintains, have always responded to the challenge of a solid program.

"People can make a difference," he never tires of reminding management. "I sense we have exceptionally strong, fine people here who want to do their jobs,

of profits Sears will need in the future to remain the world's leading retailer. He pointed to the company's overall performance in 1977 to emphasize that a double-digit sales increase alone cannot substantially increase year-end earnings.

For the South's part he advocates a rededication to the fundamentals of sound retail practices. "We have to move our expense levels into line with the rest of the company and move our margins up. When you do that you don't need a huge sales increase to improve your profits," he noted.

The vice president added that the situation in the territory need only be adjusted to show improvement; drastic change, Brennan warned, is never the answer. Instead, he espouses a business philosophy that emphasizes the basics of smart retailing, the same principles upon which the company's

ed Brennan. "The outside salesperson can plan his calls better; the division manager can prepare more thoroughly for a promotion by planning effective displays and seeing that his or her salespeople receive the proper merchandise training. If we all did a better job of planning at every level, the company would perform better."

Brennan concedes that all game plans are subject to adjustment. Each season sees the introduction of new products, the discontinuation of others, shifts in strength and aggressiveness among the various headquarters merchandise departments, and of course, changes in the general economic climate. But always the territorial goal of providing maximum service to customers and ending up with a reasonable return on sales, remains the same.

"We'll have the same program next year, the year after next and

provement in gross profit. At summer's end, it was apparent that the South had made substantial gains in this area. "I'm delighted with our progress in sales and profits and I believe we'll continue to improve," predicted Brennan. "It's no accident. The improvement is a direct result of what is being done in both merchandising and operating today."

Brennan assigns much of the credit for the South's performance to its division managers. "The professional division managers hold the key to the company's success," he often remarks. "I can't conceive of how Sears could operate without them. They're the real link in merchandising between the buying of the goods and the actual sale to the customers.

"In the end," he added, "they have responsibility for implementing any corporate plan."

The vice president, however, shrugs off his own role as harbinger of the mood of optimism now sweeping the South by observing, "I never talk about the past or changing things—only about what I feel is important."

What *is* important to Brennan—and in the final analysis to Sears—is that everyone, no matter what their job, perform to the best of their abilities. "The future of this company depends on how well each of us does his or her job. It demands that we all perform at a very high level," he said.

Putting it into perspective Brennan went on, "If you think of the company in terms of a single store, it's easier to see how people who do a good job in a unit contribute to that unit's success. The total is the sum of its parts. If all the employees in a store do well, then the store does well. If the store does well, the group or zone will do well. And if all 13 administrative units including the catalog organization do well, so will the territory.

"All this,"—he made an intense sweeping gesture with his hand that seemed to include his ninth floor office, the Atlanta headquarters and Sears Tower—"exists to serve one store." —*Donna Peterman*

"...We have exceptionally strong, fine people here who want to do their jobs, to derive satisfaction from those jobs and to take care of customers by treating them the way they themselves like to be treated..."

to derive satisfaction from those jobs and to take care of customers by treating them the way they themselves like to be treated. It's up to us as managers to challenge them."

With the Southern Territory encompassing some of the fastest growing markets in the nation, Brennan feels that the South has the greatest opportunity of any of the five territories to boost sales and profits. "We are fortunate because the population shift is in our direction," he said. "Unlike some other sections of the country—which at best can only gain 2-3 per cent real growth a year—we have the chance to make great progress as the markets in our area continue to expand."

But Brennan cautioned against the folly of relying solely on shifting demographics to trigger huge sales increases to generate the level

historic successes were fixed: correct merchandise assortments, including a proper mix of regular and promotional goods; good operating expense control; effective merchandise presentation, meaning well-marked, full bins in sparkling clean stores; competitive pricing, and Sears traditional customer service.

Underpinning Brennan's approach is his firm belief in good planning—and faithful execution of those plans. "You've got to live day in and day out with a plan," he said. "Decide what is possible and then run your business that way."

But corporate planning alone does not hold all the answers, said Brennan. He believes that individual employees too have the responsibility to set objectives for their jobs and then carry them out. "All of us can plan better," stress-

the year after that," grinned Brennan. "With good planning we can adjust for the other conditions and be able to stay on a steady course. Then if we execute well, we'll out-perform everyone else."

Thinking out loud he continued, "We're always looking for magic ways to be successful. But there are no magic ways."

With understandable pride, Brennan points to the South's successful in-stock effort as a shining example of what can be accomplished in a relatively short time through planning and teamwork. "It brings tears of joy to my eyes to be No. 1 with the lowest out-of-stocks in the nation three months in a row," he admitted. "I'm thrilled with the way our people responded to get us in-stock."

Another source of satisfaction to him has been the territory's im-

3

EXHIBIT 17-3
Upward
Communication
From The Georgia Power
Citizen, used with
permission.

Bob Scherer's Straight Talk

How can we know our insurance claims were figured correctly?

How can we determine if an insurance claim has been figured correctly? Why can't insurance claims be itemized (hospital, doctor, prescription, etc.) when insurance is paid? Why keep switching from one insurance company to another?
Name withheld by request

The group insurance area of employe benefits has among its primary goals the timely and accurate processing of medical claims. We have not been able to eliminate every error, however, and occasionally we are faced with a claim that has been processed incorrectly. Several safeguards assure that the error will be found and corrected.

When a claim has been processed, the checks are totaled to ensure they correspond to the benefits calculated for the covered expenses. This would reveal any error in addition or in typing of drafts.

Then the original work sheet and the bills are forwarded to the Provident Life and Accident Insurance Company. Provident audits the claims to verify that the benefit calculations are correct and that payments are made in accordance with the provisions of the policy. This should indicate any underpayments or overpayments.

Another safeguard is you, the employe. When a claim is processed, a check stub is sent to you. This stub lists the charges you submitted and the amount of money deducted to cover co-insurance and deductible. For further checking, you get a list of doctor and hospital fees that should correspond to dollar amounts on the stub.

The check stub includes only brief information on processing the claim. Certainly, a copy of the complete work sheet would be more helpful in reviewing the claim. A revised work sheet is being printed. Soon, the group insurance area will begin sending the completed work sheet to the employe.

With such procedures and with the emphasis employe benefits places on accuracy, we hope you never receive benefits that are incorrect. If you do, the error will be revealed and corrected before the file is closed.

Group insurance costs are high. Our management is prudent in having reputable carriers bid occasionally on the insurance programs. This ensures that Georgia Power and its employes are getting maximum benefits for their premium dollars. In 1975, we again offered our group insurance in competition, and the Provident Life and Accident Insurance Company won the contract. The only reason for changing from one insurance company to another is to get the best value at the lowest rate.

May spouses work at the same location?

Does the company have a policy concerning a husband and wife working for the Company at the same location?
Angie Lipscomb
Plant Bowen

The policy of our Company is that when a husband and wife work in the same department or office, or if one of them works under the supervision of the other, such steps shall be taken as are deemed necessary for the good of the organization, even to the extent of the transfer, resignation, or discharge of one or the other of the employes.

Why the long delays in processing raises?

We would like to inquire as to why the payroll department functions so unpredictably. It seems to us that this department is grossly inefficient when it comes to processing pay raises, retroactive

pay and in getting W-2 forms out to the employes. However, when an employe is docked, a mistake is made in an employe's insurance, or there is any error in favor of the Company, corrections are made almost immediately.

Can't anything be done to better organize the payroll department so they can handle all matters concerning employes with the same promptness and efficiency with which they handle the correction of errors in the Company's favor?
Minola Road line section employes

Every two weeks, our payroll section processes pay data and paychecks for more than 10,000 employes. This process entails a complete system update with new and changed data relevant to rates of pay and all of the various payroll deductions as well as time report information. In the processing of this volume of data, occasional errors do occur. Were it not for the dedicated effort of a fine group of payroll section employes in verifying data accuracy to the fullest possible extent, paycheck errors would be far more numerous.

Some errors, such as the incorrect reporting of hours worked, cannot be detected by payroll personnel. Nor can payroll employes control the delays that occur in the preparation and approval of pay change documents. The accurate and timely submission of these documents is the responsibility of the numerous reporting locations throughout the Company.

Payroll personnel are sometimes criticized for the time that is required to establish revised rates of pay and to pay retroactive wages to union employes. Delays that are experienced in performing these functions originate from the intricacies that are incorporated in Company/union wage settlements. Under these agreements, rate of pay increases are applied in varying amounts to different job classifications and steps.

4 Citizen

for in-house publications must never forget that management itself is a prospective audience. Letters to the editor, question-and-answer columns, articles written by employees, and other devices such as readership surveys give information about issues important to employees. This is valuable— perhaps vital—to management decision making.

Lateral communication is a growing need in modern organizations. Hierarchical organizations are usually designed only to pass information up and down. Yet management needs some plan for communication between employees at the same level. They may never meet face-to-face. Horizontal communication flow increases employee knowledge about the overall operations of the company. It helps to create a sense of community among the divisions of an organization. Moreover, lateral information can help foster new ideas and prevent duplication of effort. Lateral communication should be a primary goal of in-house publications.

The Objectives of an Internal Publication

In the broad sense, the goal of an in-house publication is improving the relationships between its readers and management. But setting policy and defining objectives for such a publication are complicated undertakings. Without specific guidelines, however, it is hard for an in-house publication to be successful. It is harder still to measure its success.

As stated, in-house publications must fulfill the needs of both the organization and its employees. The information in the publication must be useful and meaningful to the readers, not small talk and management "propaganda." Most important to the success of such a publication is the selection of content combining the common interests of management and employees. Following is a list of some objectives that might apply to good in-house publications.

Recognition of employee achievements both on the job and in the community can encourage internal cooperation by helping management and employees become better acquainted with other members of the organization. This type of recognition also serves as official commendation for outstanding service and sets an example for others in the organization. Social activities can also be recognized, but they should not take precedence over job-related and community service accomplishments. Proper recognition of this type can produce objectives such as:

- strengthening positive community relationships
- building a sense of accomplishment
- stimulating new ideas for company and community service

EXHIBIT 17-4
Horizontal
Communication

From Transco Companies
Hot Tap, used with
permission.

The controllers

The Gas Control Department is "Mission Control" for Transco

Linden sales dispatcher Jerry LaChere talks with a customer company about their gas needs.

Remember the days when Mission Control at NASA in Houston controlled spaceships on their way to the moon?

Transco has its own version of "Mission Control" embodied in the Gas Control Department.

From their control rooms in Houston and Linden, N.J., they are responsible for moving Transco's gas from the production area to the market area.

"We like to consider ourselves the nerve center of Transco," says Department Manager Bob Withers. "Our objective is to move natural gas as safely and efficiently as possible. Consequently, we represent Transco daily with gas producers and customers, and we interface with nearly every other department in Transco."

Controlling the gas is a 24-hour-a-day business, so there are always at least two people on duty at each of the Gas Control centers located in Houston and Linden, N.J.

Customers begin calling Gas Control early in the morning, giving reports to the sales dispatchers on how much gas was delivered on the previous day and an estimate of the current day's requirements. The Houston office receives about 40 calls, while the Linden office gets between 25 and 30.

About three-fourths of Transco's 80 customers call in daily. The remaining one-fourth are smaller customers whose gas requirements are estimated by Transco.

Ronald Sampay, a Houston-based sales dispatcher, estimates that he spends between four and six hours a day on the telephone. That's enough to give anyone a sore ear!

"The hardest part of our job," says Weldon Laird, superintendent, "is trying to guess, or *out* guess, our customers. We have to anticipate their needs every day."

During the day, Gary Warren, the production dispatcher, monitors calls from between 150 and 200 gas producers.

"That's not an absolutely accurate figure," says Warren, "because you don't have time to count the calls!"

By combining the calculations of the sales and production dispatchers, the department can estimate the amount of gas that will be flowing into the pipeline each day and adjust amounts to be injected into or withdrawn from storage.

Next the dispatcher on duty totals all the gas needs and subtracts the amounts that customers request be placed in storage, resulting in the "burn figure" — the gas the customers will actually use.

This information goes to one of the four senior gas controllers, Bill Roempke, Bill Landes, Mike Blackwood, or Bubba Jaenecke, all based in Houston. The controller balances the production (inflows) and sales (outflows) of gas with adjustments to storage figures. At this point he determines how much horsepower will be necessary at each compressor station to propel the given volume of gas, and then gives the orders to the stations.

Every two hours, on the odd hour, the controller calls every compressor station along the pipeline and records each station's pressures. He communicates via Transco's microwave system, which has one channel on the Gas Control telephone designated strictly for dispatch purposes.

According to Controller Jaenecke, the whole process takes only about 15 minutes. He calls the station's numbers in ascending order, and they reply with their pressure readings. Since the stations give their reports from Refugio, Texas, northward, the pressure run makes for an interesting blend of Southern drawls and Yankee brogues.

The senior gas controller in Houston determines any changes which must be made in a daily operating plan due to weather changes and other conditions, and the Linden dispatchers monitor certain operating pressures and flow information in the Pennsylvania, New Jersey, and New York areas. By constant communications with larger customer companies in that area, he

EXHIBIT 17-5
Employee
Recognition

From Southern Bell *Views,*
Issue 4/August 1978.
Published by Southern
Bell, Atlanta, Ga., used
with permission.

Surfing Champ

Surfing champions have to be picky about where they live. Jon Motes, installation/repair technician, requested a company transfer from South Florida to Jacksonville because "the waves in Miami were too small."

"Now I keep my surf board at a friend's shop on the beach," he said. "If the waves are good at lunchtime I change into my baggies and hit the surf for an hour. I go out after work too. With daylight savings time, the best thing that ever happened to surfing, you can stay 'till about 8:30.''

It's that type of dedication since age 13 that won Motes first place at the Florida State Surfing Championships last October. "You can show people how to do it, but they can't learn without a lot of practice," he said.

Motes' six-year-old son, Jason, proved himself among the younger surfing set by winning the "minihune" division in Eastern Surfing Association competition last year.

"Jason's been surfing for two and a half years now — almost as long as he's been walking," said Motes proudly. "He's scared to go out to the big swells, but he tears up the shore breakers. He's just learning now, but he'll be something else one of these days."

Motes involvement in surfing includings his directorship of the 175-member North Florida Division of the Eastern Surfing Association.

That organization is buying litter barrels for the beaches and trying to open more areas to surfers.

Big brother

Ray Jones, a Florence, S.C., installation/repair technician, has a philosophy about child raising. "Kids who turn out bad are usually not to blame," he said. "The badness comes out of the family life — the atmosphere they live in."

As a result of his efforts to improve the atmosphere for some of the boys around Effingham, his hometown, Jones was named "Big Brother" of the year for 1977 in the five-county Pee Dee Area.

"Big Brothers is a program for boys without a father," explained Jones. "It's older boys like me spending time with younger boys — kind of directing them, showing them which way to go."

He has a personal understanding of growing up in a fatherless household. "I didn't have a daddy around either, but a friend's daddy acted sort of like my big brother. It's easy to see the value of it when you've been there yourself."

His two current little brothers, 11 and 16 years old, are often found at the Jones' home. "I try to make them feel like part of the family by doing things with them such as helping around the house or going fishing. My wife and two little girls are as much an influence as I am," Jones said.

Children come into the world as innocents, says Jones, who believes the duty of grownups is to shape that purity into productive maturity.

"You never lose anything by taking up time with kids. I can tell they appreciate it because they usually ask me 'When are you coming back?' when I take them home."

21

Employee well-being and safety can be promoted through information on safety practices, rules, and procedures. There is an endless need to explain benefits, vacations, holidays, taxes, workmen's compensation, affirmative action, and equal employment opportunity policies. Employees can be told of community issues and educational and training opportunities. Objectives of this type can include:

- promoting employee activities
- promoting health and safety
- interpreting local, state, and national news as it applies to the company

Employees' understanding of their role in the organization can be improved. The publication can stress the importance of each worker's job in meeting the goals of the company. Information about the final use of products illustrates the importance of everyone's part in the process. Internal publications must promote the idea that each employee is a salesperson for the company. They should pay attention to:

- building loyalty to the organization
- improving cooperation and coordination
- giving a sense of belonging
- improving production and efficiency
- reducing costs and waste
- getting everybody on the public relations team

Clarification of management policies must consider the point of view of management *and* employees. Employees must be accurately informed about business activities if management wants support for its programs. Understanding can be helped through:

- explaining policies and rules
- building confidence in management
- combating rumors and misunderstandings

An in-house publication can be effective in accomplishing these objectives: *if* it meets the needs of employees; *if* it says something that employees want to think about and talk about; and *if* it is attractive and easily read.

YOU MADE IT ALL HAPPEN IN '78

Environmental Clean-up
We worked hard to clean up our environment. Shown here is the new 38-acre, 250-million-gallon secondary treatment system (aeration lagoon) constructed at G-P's Bellingham, Wash., Division during the year. Mill process water flows into the lagoon and is cleaned and oxygenated for release into Bellingham Bay seven days later.

Millions of New Trees
More than 26 million seedlings were raised in our company nurseries during '78, promising beautiful, managed, green forests on a continuing basis for future generations of Americans.

Community Involvement
We had a good year which allowed us to share with our friends and neighbors. All around the country in '78, we lent a helping hand—to people like Steven Powell (pictured with H.S. Mersereau, Southern Division senior vice president), of Augusta, Ga., who was one of 97 G-P scholarship winners. More than 1,000 high school graduates have received nearly $3 million from G-P in recent years.

Energy Conservation
Our energy-conscious company made news around the country during '78 as it continued to conserve and devise ways to turn wastes into energy sources. This dust cell, installed at Toledo, Ore., last year, uses a waste product —wood dust—as a fuel. By suspending flammable dust in air in the right concentration, the dust supplies a sustained source of heat. Two other dust cells are at our Eugene/Springfield Division. Creation of the dust cells earned G-P national acclaim, for the second year in a row, the latest an award from Keep America Beautiful, the public service organization that promotes involvement in environmental improvement around the country.

20

EXHIBIT 17-6
Improved Understanding of Employee's Role
From Georgia-Pacific *Growth*, Georgia-Pacific Corp., used with permission.

EXHIBIT 17-7
Clarification of
Management Policies

From *Sears South News*,
Sears, Roebuck and Co.,
used with permission.

Voluntary employment goals work, says Graham

"Sears is the nation's second largest private employer of women and one of the largest employers of minorities, with almost 80,000 on payroll," Ray Graham, the company's director of equal opportunity, said in a sworn affidavit filed in support of recent company motions for dismissal of EEOC charges.

"Sears has had a formal, voluntary affirmative action plan since 1968," Graham told the court. "In 1973, Sears formulated, and in 1974, implemented its Mandatory Achievement of Goals (MAG) Plan, which among other steps, requires each Sears unit to hire one underrepresented member for every white male hired until the presence of the underrepresented group in a particular job grouping equals or exceeds its presence in the local trade/hiring area.

"For non-traditional jobs (e.g. women in craft jobs such as automotive mechanics and men in clerical and secretarial positions), the MAG Plan requires that one underrepresented group member be hired for every five males (or females if the position is clerical) until a goal of 20 per cent is reached.

"In addition, terminated minorities and women (and, where applicable, men) in underrepresented job classfications must be replaced in kind on a one-for-one basis before any other assignments within that job classification are made.

"Before they can deviate from the MAG Plan requirements, Sears unit managers must request advance authorization and state the reasons for not hiring an underrepresented group member," said Graham.

"Based on my experience in administering Sears affirmative action plan and my knowledge of other companies' plans, it is my opinion and belief that Sears equal employment and affirmative action programs are unsurpassed in scope and effectiveness in American business and industry," said Graham.

Percentage of Female and Minority Employees in Each EEOC Job Category
(Categories as defined by Equal Employment Opportunity Commission)   "Sears Where America Works"

Job Categories	Female %		Black %		Asian/ Pacific Islander %		American Indian/Alaskan Native %		Hispanic %		Employees in each job category (in thousands)	
Date	Feb. '66	Jan. '79	Feb. '66	Jan. '79	Feb. '66	Jan. '79	Feb. '66	Jan. '79	Feb. '66	Jan. '79	Feb. '66	Jan. '79
Officials and Managers	20.0	37.0	.4	7.3	.2	.5	.1	.3	.7	2.8	33.4	51.3
Professionals	19.2	57.9	.8	6.1	.5	1.5	.0	.0	.4	2.7	1.3	1.8
Technicians	48.1	51.5	1.1	11.9	1.5	1.9	.0	.2	.7	4.4	1.5	2.0
Sales Workers	56.9	64.6	3.2	11.3	.6	.8	.1	.2	1.5	4.5	98.7	124.9
Office & Clerical	86.0	86.9	3.1	13.4	.6	1.1	.1	.2	2.0	5.3	78.6	111.5
Crafts Workers	3.8	8.4	2.8	9.2	.7	1.1	.1	.4	2.8	5.7	20.8	30.3
Operatives	12.0	22.4	13.8	19.9	.8	1.1	.1	.3	3.5	6.9	23.4	11.8
Laborers	34.3	32.6	18.4	23.0	.3	.8	.1	.3	6.5	7.8	15.2	48.9
Service Workers	32.3	44.1	44.9	32.3	.5	1.1	.1	.2	2.0	7.1	9.9	12.7
All Categories	50.7	57.0	5.9	13.6	.6	.9	.1	.3	2.1	5.2	282.8	395.2

"On Aug. 1, 1979, *Employment Relations Report*, a weekly newsletter, published an article based upon confidential memoranda obtained from the EEOC. According to the article, the memoranda were written in June 1979 by Issie Jenkins, the EEOC's acting general counsel and by other attorneys in the General Counsel's office.

'Errors And Flaws'

"The memoranda advised the EEOC that the case against Sears was riddled with 'errors and flaws' and that the evidence was too weak to pursue litigation on the broad scale recommended in the Commission Decision. However, it was reported that lawsuits would be prepared as a bargaining ploy."

In the memoranda, said Graham, "The EEOC's then top lawyer admits that 'Sears has been in the vanguard of voluntary affirmative action since 1974, and with respect to minorities, possibly as early as 1969.'"

The memoranda also stated, "Although we (the EEOC attorneys) are unable to fully evaluate the progress achieved by the MAG program, its existence may render it impossible to prove any discrimination occurring after 1973, except for certain equal pay claims...The absence of discrimination after 1973 may affect both a court's receptiveness to our arguments regarding pre-1974 discrimination and the issue of what relief may be appropriate for any proven violation."

Graham said, "the EEOC implicitly confirmed the accuracy of the quotations from the memoranda in a press statement issued Aug. 1, 1979, which said that the quoted memoranda were based on a 'preliminary review of the data and analysis in the case,' and that 'additional information and further analyses have since been obtained.'"

However, concluded Graham, EEOC Chairman Eleanor Holmes Norton commented on the EEOC's decision to bring national charges against Sears and several other large companies in a statement made to the Associated Press Aug. 22, 1979: "In retrospect it was perhaps overly ambitious," said Norton"...and the cases were brought, as it turns out, in the most troubled time of the Commission."

Sears moves for dismissal of EEOC suits

Last month Sears filed motions for dismissal of five lawsuits brought by the Equal Employment Opportunity Commission (EEOC) against units in Atlanta, Chicago, Memphis, Montgomery and New York.

The EEOC suit filed in Chicago alleges job discrimination against women at Sears facilities nationally.

The other four suits allege local discrimination in the hiring of minorities in those cities.

In moving for dismissal of the suits, the company maintained that the case is "a culmination of more than six years of governmental abuse and unfair treatment."

Reasons cited by Sears as grounds for dismissal include:
• conflicts of interest, or the appearance of such, within the charging, investigative, conciliation, and decision-making structure of the EEOC undermine the fairness of the proceedings and destroy the credibility of the Commission decision;
• the Commission's refusal to conciliate individual issues, as required by law — issues which are included in the present lawsuits;
• attempts by the EEOC to deprive Sears of property by the use or threat of adverse publicity after the EEOC had insisted that Sears forfeit its right to confidentiality;
• the refusal of the EEOC to grant Sears a hearing after facts disclosing a violation of due process were presented to the Commission;
• disclosures on record which indicate the prosecution of Sears was without foundation, unreasonable, brought in bad faith, and continued even after it clearly became so.

Sears also maintains that the Equal Pay Act allegations should be dismissed, because they are barred by an earlier equal pay suit, brought by the government against Sears and denied by the courts. (Excerpts from Sears brief appear on page 6.)

Earnings off 9.9% in 3rd quarter from '78

The company has reported net income for the third quarter ended Oct. 31 fell 9.9 per cent to $212,117,000 or 67 cents per share from last year's record of $235,487,000 or 73 cents.

Net sales for the third quarter were $4,528,406,000, an increase of 1.6 per cent above last year's $4,458,379,000.

The company's net income for the nine months ended Oct. 31 was $555,753,000 or $1.74 per share. This was 6.1 per cent below last year's net income of $591,645,000 or $1.84 per share. Operating income from sales and services for the nine months ended Oct. 31 increased 3.7 per cent.

Net sales for the nine months were $12,409,965,000, a decrease of 4.7 per cent from last year's record of $13,015, 688,000 for the same period.

Net income of the Allstate Group of Companies was equal to 39 cents per Sears share for the third quarter compared with 38 cents for the same period of 1978, and $1.07 per share for the nine months compared with $1.09 last year.

"The EEOC appears to have used its power and authority as a law enforcement agency...to advance the partisan interests of private political groups," stated briefs prepared by Sears chief counsel Charles Morgan.

2

Planning for Successful Communication

Who will read the publication? Deciding on the audience will shape all other decisions. Do not try to be "all things to all people." Do not try to rival *The New York Times.* An internal publication serves the needs of the organization that sponsors it. Successful house publications are those that identify, acknowledge, and stick to a purpose: serving the employees.

Identification of a publication's audience may not be as simple as it seems. Its nature usually limits its primary audience to people inside the organization. Yet these individuals are often divided into several groups. A large petrochemical company has blue-collar workers who belong to one or more unions. It also hires engineers and research scientists with professional affiliations, as well as white-collar midmanagement and clerical personnel. Each of these groups has differing information needs.

When only one publication is possible, you should identify a primary audience and treat the other groups as secondary. The secondary groups can be served through special columns or stories that will interest them. Secondary audiences might include suppliers, distributors, other company plants or divisions, competitors, and the surrounding community. Many of these secondary audiences will read your publication even if you do not want them to. Therefore, the contents must reflect good judgment. Issues of substance must be discussed if the publication is to have credibility. However, the in-house publication is not the place to air dirty laundry, a process that would embarrass the company and its employees. Some companies have begun publications that serve outside groups important to the firm.

What type of publication does your organization need? Once the primary and secondary audiences have been identified, you should decide what kind of publication will meet their needs best: a newsletter, a tabloid newspaper, a magazine, or some other format. Frequency of publication and method of distribution should also be decided in advance in terms of the primary audience's needs. Most house publications are published monthly. Some appear quarterly and some weekly. The easiest, cheapest, and simplest method of distribution is to make them available around the work areas. However, to get wider distribution, some organizations hand them to employees, use the in-house mail, or send them to employees' homes. All of these matters are interdependent. The format (size and shape) may limit the possibilities for distribution. All considerations discussed here depend on two factors: budget and audience needs.

After budget constraints are understood, information about the needs of the audience must be gathered. Interviews and questionnaires can tell a great deal about content, frequency, and distribution needs. To help select a format, many companies use employee panels to review sample publications from other organizations. The panel can also evaluate data obtained in interviews and questionnaires.

The results of your planning effort should be written down and kept. They can help you plan future issues and evaluate past ones.

Starting the Publication Producing an internal publication takes organization and coordination. Of course, you will want to publish at regular intervals. If your newsletter, newspaper, or magazine is distributed at regular intervals, readers will develop expectations concerning it. Such consistency requires budget and staff. Putting out a publication on a shoestring may be worse than never putting one out at all. A publication that cannot be maintained properly creates negative attitudes by building expectations it cannot fulfill. Therefore, organizing the details of production is important to success.

What makes news? What goes into a house publication will vary from one organization to another. Still, there are some topics about which employees will not read and even more they do not have time to read about. Such topics, even when educational, do not belong in a house publication. There are some subjects, however, that will attract the interest of even the busiest executive or blue-collar worker. You should identify these topics and develop them into stories.

Anything that concerns what people do, feel, or think is interesting. You should select topics that grow out of the activities in the sponsoring organization. News is everywhere. Every job, group, program, and employee has news value. To identify potential stories, an editor or writer should consider the topic from the intended reader's point of view. Include items that will interest many groups within the organization. Although you should always keep the needs of your primary audience in mind, you can expand readership with items of interest to others as well. Look for stories that inform and entertain. No one will read everything, but almost everyone will read something. A rule of thumb for an appropriate "mix" is:

- 50 percent company information
- 20 percent employee information
- 20 percent relevant noncompany information
- 10 percent small talk

And remember, company information must satisfy the audience's needs, not those of management. If the publication is to serve the goals of the sponsor organization, readership is essential. Topics with generally high interest are:

- new equipment or changes in existing equipment
- remodeling or expansion
- quality control procedures and requirements
- safety requirements
- achievement of quotas
- wage rates and increases
- new jobs created
- new assignments
- meetings
- changes in union officers or policies
- important business-related visitors
- sales and earnings
- management policies
- president's or general manager's message

Employee information is an excellent source of columns or even feature articles. It has high readership because its subject is the audience. Never be condescending or patronizing in reporting employee news. Some possible topics are:

- promotions
- new employees
- retirees
- in memoriam
- community involvement
- memberships—clubs, community organizations, and associations
- volunteer service
- educational achievements
- awards

Relevant noncompany information consists of matters that affect the company or its employees. Events reported in the popular media can be followed up with stories predicting their effect on employees, the company, and the industry. Relevant noncompany information usually comes from the following:

- national news
- industry news

EXHIBIT 17-8
Employee
Information Column
Reprinted with permission
from *Hot Tap*, Transco
Companies, Inc., Houston,
Texas.

In Memoriam

Julia Branagan, mother of transmission foreman *James T. Branagan* of Linden, N.J., died December 16. Mrs. Branagan resided in Bayonne, N.J.

Lindsay E. Cary, Sr., father of *William E. Cary*, Engineering, died November 28. A native Houstonian, Cary was 87 years old.

Muriel Moore, mother of *Marjorie Maurer*, Property Accounting, died October 15.

On the Move

Promotions

Marjorie A. Barron
from senior administrative clerk to land R/W specialist, Land.

Richard D. Bland, Jr.
from accountant trainee to plant accountant, Property Accounting.

John C. Boutwell, Jr.
from assistant supervisor to supervisor, General Accounting.

Woodrow W. Brown, Jr.
from operator-A to chief operator, Ellicott City, Md.

Kenneth Carter
from maintenance man-B to maintenance man-A, Lake Charles, La.

Joseph L. Chambers
from maintenance man-A to repairman-A, Unionville, Va.

Kathleen S. Conley
from accountant trainee to general accountant, General Accounting.

Sylvester Cooley, Jr.
from maintenance man-B to maintenance man-A, Seminary, Miss.

Terrance E. Crosby
from controls specialist to area foreman, Austin, Pa.

Gavin J. Cuccia
from maintenance man-C to maintenance man-B, Schriever, La.

Kathy L. Eriksen
from senior word processing specialist to lead word processing specialist, Information Services.

Alex Fuselier, Jr.
from maintenance man-C to maintenance man-B, Eunice, La.

Joe L. Gilmore
from maintenance man-A to operator-A, Sandersville, Miss.

Richard T. Gomez
from garage attendant, Purchasing, to administrative clerk, Production Accounting.

Gregg H. Hammond
from maintenance man-B to maintenance man-A, Moore, S.C.

Jimmie L. Harrington
from maintenance man-B to chief operator, Cameron, La.

Walter W. Horner
from measurement technician-A, Masonville, N.J., to measurement engineer, West Chester, Pa.

David S. Husband
from maintenance man-C to maintenance man-B, Lake Charles, La.

Clarence F. Johnston
from maintenance man-C to maintenance man-B, Eunice, La.

Gary W. Kana
from maintenance man-B to maintenance man-A, El Campo, Texas.

Sue V. Kendrick
from senior land and R/W specialist to records supervisor, Land.

Olen K. Kolb
from general accounting supervisor to assistant general accounting manager, General Accounting.

Mark B. Landry
from maintenance man-C to maintenance man-B, Kaplan, La.

Michael J. LeMaire
from maintenance man-C to maintenance man-B, Kaplan, La.

Donald W. Little
from transmission engineer to senior transmission engineer, Lithonia, Ga.

Charlene Marek
from gas accountant to corporate accountant, Gas Accounting.

Tom A. Martin
from laborer, Seminary, Miss., to maintenance man-C, Sandersville, Miss.

Felix L. Martinez
from maintenance man-C to maintenance man-B, El Campo, Texas.

Gordon E. Marttila
from measurement engineer, West Chester, Pa., to measurement division superintendent, Linden, N.J.

Frank J. Michelli
from maintenance man-A to operations clerk-A, Eunice, La.

Anyer L. Miller
from dispatcher-B to material expeditor-B, Cameron, La.

Jimmie T. Miller
from maintenance man-C to maintenance man-B, Davidson, N.C.

Jack Porter
from operator-A to chief operator, Tilden, Texas.

Stephen M. Price
from maintenance man-B to maintenance man-A, Cameron, La.

Willie L. Richardson, Jr.
from laborer, Seminary, Miss., to maintenance man-C, Laurel, Miss.

James R. Seymour
from accountant trainee to production accountant, Production Accounting.

William R. Shannon
from maintenance man-A to operator-A, Tilden, Texas.

George W. St. Julien
from laborer to maintenance man-C, Kaplan, La.

Jeffery A. Stallings
from maintenance man-C to maintenance man-B, Refugio, Texas.

Jesse D. Trahan
from maintenance man-B, to chief operator, Cameron, La.

Raphael Weizman
from accountant trainee to gas accountant, Gas Accounting.

Anton J. Wetter
from area foreman to area superintendent, Austin, Pa.

Marie Whalin
from administrative trainee to buyer, Purchasing.

George W. Zepp
from maintenance man-A to operator-A, Ellicott City, Md.

Transfers

David W. Freestone
from General Accounting to Corporate Accounting.

Tony A. Gant
from planning analyst, Financial Planning, to contract administrator, Gas Purchases.

James M. Hamilton, Jr.
from Linden, N.J., to Corpus Christi, Texas, Measurement.

Fletcher W. Hartley
from supervising engineer, Engineering Technical Services, to staff engineer, Engineering.

John M. Kryvanick
from Linden, N.J., to Jackson, La., Communications.

Harley N. McDonald
from Engineering Technical Services to Gas Control.

Terry D. Sparks
from material control accountant, Property Accounting to contract administrator, Gas Purchases.

Carol E. Tucker
from senior credit union specialist, Personnel to accountant trainee specialist, Production Accounting.

"R" Wegner
from Corporate Communications to Records Management.

Catherine E. Hicks
from Communications to Office Services.

New Employees

Diane L. Adams
Production Accounting

Kenneth L. Adamson
Unionville, Va.

Peggy M. Duck
Communications

Johnnie Fleming, Jr.
Cameron, La.

Edward J. Gaspard
Cameron, La.

Lynette M. Hayes
Lake Charles, La.

Ronald L. Honefenger
Environmental Affairs

Harold R. Johnson
Davidson, N.C.

EXHIBIT 17-9
How External Events
Affect the
Organization
Reprinted courtesy of
J D Journal, the employee
magazine of Deere &
Company, Moline, Illinois.

Space-age agriculture: What we can expect

If you think John Deere farm equipment is sophisticated now, wait until the year 2000.

Trying to predict the future of American agriculture is just as difficult as predicting the future of American society. After all, the kind of life a farmer will be living in the year 2000 depends upon who will be buying his crops, at what prices, and for what purposes. It depends upon the energy sources available to power his tractors, dry his grain and fertilize his crops. And it depends fundamentally on the purpose and even the very definition of agriculture.

Although many people can afford to debate the question at leisure, John Deere and other farm machinery makers have no time to spare. Many tractors that will be working fields in the year 2000 will be bought in, say, 1985; these machines are in the design stage today. Agricultural engineers must have a pretty firm idea already of what is in store for us 21 years from now.

One engineer who has done a good deal of thinking—and debating—about the future of farming is Gordon Millar, vice-president of engineering for Deere & Company. Millar speaks at food conferences where he encounters critics of today's high-productivity agriculture. He defends this kind of farming so strongly that he says he has become known as the "ogre" of agribusiness.

"There is a whole set of historical facts, a whole set of reasonably quantifiable projections, which all have to fit together," says Millar. "In order to survive, people need a certain amount of food. It looks like we'll have between 6.5 and 8 billion people at the end of the century. That's about twice as many people as we have now.

"Should the food for these people come from farmers who live on six to 10 acres of land and practice low-productivity, subsistence agriculture? Or should we have high-productivity farmers who can feed 20, 30, 50 people? Is farming a way of life, a recreational activity, or is the primary purpose of farming the production of food, so that the billions of people who are not

- state news
- local news
- union news

In-house publications are most often criticized as "gossip sheets." Some people believe that the way to get employees to read a publication is to get as many names and faces into print as possible. This over-reliance on small talk will cause credibility, and eventually readership, to decline. Serious content will foster a climate of belief, and successful communication can then occur. Small talk is important if used properly, but it must not dominate the publication. Appropriate topics in this category are:

- hobbies
- births
- marriages
- employee sports (bowling league, softball, golf, etc.)
- social achievements

Other topics for articles overlap the previous categories. Some are: safety training, security procedures, benefits, vacation schedules, accident and injury record, housekeeping, educational assistance programs, emergency procedures, and charity fund drives. Information about future events, especially those close at hand, makes good reading if the events concern the audience. Again, moderation is important. Some in-house publications have become little more than calendars because of requests from groups who want their activities publicized. Set and maintain strict policies about what will be published and how much space will be given. The following can help you to evaluate a topic's newsworthiness:

1. *Timeliness.* Is the topic timely enough to interest most of the readers?

2. *Scope.* Does it affect enough people directly or indirectly?

3. *Noteworthiness.* Is someone or something important or well known involved?

4. *Human interest.* Does it deal with things vital to the interests of the readers or those involved?

A "tickler" file is used by newspaper editors to "tickle their memory" about future news stories. The editor of a house organ can use such a file. A futures book or file can be started with headings such as "use next issue," "if space available," and "short fillers." Updating the file keeps material ready for each issue.

Writing for House Publications Most house publications use two types of articles: news stories and feature or human interest articles. Both are important, although they serve different purposes. News stories concentrate on information about current events as they affect company policy, market conditions, safety, company-sponsored events, and other happenings. Articles that focus on people and their lives are called feature or human interest pieces. A balance between these two types should be decided upon on the basis of reader feedback. Both, however, must meet the criterion of general interest.

Company publications are not daily metropolitan newspapers. People who write for them should not try to be investigative reporters. Objectivity is an important goal, but in-house publications should have a more personal tone than public newspapers or magazines. They should reflect a sense of closeness and common interest that says to the reader, "We're all in this together." One writer says that a house publication "should look and read like . . . a letter from home . . . a pat on the back . . . a friendly handshake."

Journalists use the inverted pyramid style of writing, which covers the most important points first. The inverted pyramid is equally useful for house publications. Exhibit 17-10 shows it. Also see Chapter 9. We begin with five questions: *who, what, when, where,* and *why?* These are sometimes followed by *how*. The story's lead (the first one or two paragraphs) should answer these questions, starting with the one most important for that story. Each successive paragraph should contain less important details. Studies of reading habits show that most readers skim or skip around. A strong lead gets readers' attention. It directs them into the rest of the article.

Tips for those who write or edit house publications are:

- Use short, simple words.
- Use short, simple sentences and paragraphs.
- Write in the active, not the passive, voice.
- Avoid slang and jargon.
- Use adjectives and adverbs sparingly.
- Be brief. One or two double-spaced typewritten pages is enough for most stories.
- Give the actual date of an event. Do not say "next Friday" or "day after tomorrow."
- Be consistent when using numbers: spell out numbers one to nine and use numerals for 10 and above.

EXHIBIT 17-10   INVERTED PYRAMID FORM*

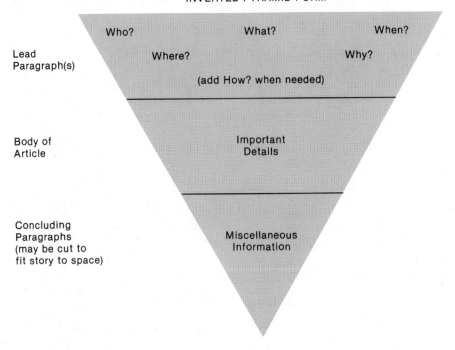

Lead
Paragraph(s)

Who?   What?   When?
Where?   Why?
(add How? when needed)

Body of
Article

Important
Details

Concluding
Paragraphs
(may be cut to
fit story to space)

Miscellaneous
Information

*Levels presented in order of declining importance.

All copy must be carefully edited. Cross out unnecessary words. Use a good stylebook, such as the one published by the Associated Press. *Be consistent.*

Layout and Format   Bad layout and format have cost many well-written publications the readership, credibility, and recognition they deserve. In-house publications need a clean simple format. An attempt to be unique or artistic often calls attention to itself and interferes with the message.

Careful planning for each page is needed no matter what format is used. Each page should have a purpose that fits the goal of the publication. Generally speaking, the first page should contain news of high interest to your target audience. The second can be set aside for editorials and related opinion material. The remaining pages are for features, columns, and news stories of lesser importance.

Page makeup refers to the way stories, headlines, and photographs are arranged on a page. To encourage readers to read the entire page, many editors use the primary optical area dramatically. This area is the upper left-hand corner of a page, where readership studies show most readers look first. From this point, most readers skim down the page in the pattern of a reversed "S" (Exhibit 17-11). Page makeup can be planned to catch the reader' attention at the visual impact points illustrated in Exhibit 17-11. Photographs and headlines are useful at these locations.

Avoid "grey" pages that do not have enough white space or photographs to break up the solid print (see Exhibit 17-12). Paragraphs should be no longer than eight lines when set in type. Articles that measure eleven inches or more in a column should be broken up with subheadings. Be careful not to overdo boldface and italic type, which are too dark to be effective in large quantities. However, boldface is best for cutlines and captions with photographs. Dark type blends better with the photograph and helps the reader link the two.

Headlines attract attention to an article. They should be complete statements with a subject and a predicate. They should not be labels. One-column headlines should be no longer than three lines and multi-column headlines no longer than two. The main headline on each page should generally be about one column longer and one type size larger than the

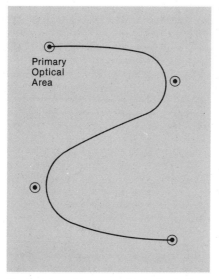

EXHIBIT 17-11

Primary
Optical
Area

Most readers skim a page beginning in the upper left corner. They move down the page in a reversed "S" pattern.
⊙ Visual impact points.

EXHIBIT 17-12
Good Use of White
Space
Reprinted with permission
from *New Jersey Bell
Magazine*. Copyright ©
New Jersey Bell 1979.

Bea Gleeson,

Directory Assistance, Rutherford

When Bea finishes her day's work, "I could walk out of here and if someone said, 'Let's go dancing,' I'd say, 'Fine.' That's how much easier computerized directory assistance is than the old way of flipping paper pages."

An operator in the Rutherford directory assistance office, which handles calls from New Yorkers seeking numbers in the 201 area code, Bea welcomed the conversion.

The technological process can be compared to a baby's efforts, according to Bea. First the baby crawls, then it walks and, finally, it runs. Human technological advancement is at the walking stage right now:

"We can't have progress without this process. I just hope that when we're at the point of running, we won't be relying more on machines than on the human element," she said.

The relief of human physical labors is a big blessing, particularly when human drudgery surrounding such tasks as housework is alleviated, according to Bea, who is the mother of five sons.

"Of course we still have to preserve human judgment. Let's not forget that any machine or computer operates because of human beings who design, plan, manufacture and run it.

"Even if I could use, say, an instant computerized traffic route detailing the most trouble-free highways, I might prefer to take the scenic drive instead of the quickest route. I'd have to weigh whether the pleasure I'd derive from the drive itself would be greater than the advantage of speed."

Will computers make us lazy?

"I see increased leisure time becoming more of a learning process for individuals. The time could be used for self-enrichment, community service and other activities — sports or hobbies, maybe. Yes, I think people will use the extra time well. The quality of family life will also improve." ■

25

next largest headline on the page. Avoid placing headlines of the same length and type side by side on a page. If this is unavoidable, one of them should have more lines than the other to provide visual separation. Because people read headlines one line at a time, it is never a good idea to break phrases onto two lines.

Photographs can be tied into the copy of a publication, and they are excellent nonverbal communication. When a photograph is used on top of a related story, the headline should be underneath the photograph rather than above it. However, if the photograph and its story are placed horizontally on the page, you may extend the headline over both. Each picture should have its own caption. The importance of a photograph and its story should determine size. When several related pictures are used together, one should be at least 50 percent larger than the others. Place the smaller photographs so that they face into the page. This will direct reader attention to the other parts of the page. Do not be too extravagant with photographs. Too many can be gaudy. Cutting them into shapes for artistic effects or tinting them is neither beneficial nor professional.

"Jumping" an article from one page to another is acceptable. It may be necessary if the article is long and would crowd out other pieces that need to be on that page. However, continued articles seldom carry as much readership over to the second page a they had on the first. When an article must be continued, the "jump" headline should be smaller than the original. Stories should always "jump" from front to back in a publication.

White space can creatively focus attention (see Exhibit 17-12). Every inch of space need not be filled with type or photographs. Empty space at the edge of a page can draw the other graphic elements together. White space should be used between stories and columns to prevent a grey look. But be careful not to leave the impression that you simply ran out of copy. And do not leave "holes" in the middle of the paper.

Staff   All editors know that a high-quality publication requires more of them than just sitting in an office and waiting for stories to come in. You must have a system for gathering information and preparing it for publication on time. You must do more than write and rewrite stories. Editors of house publications are managers in the best sense. Managing, as noted in Chapter 1, is generally defined as "getting things done through other people." The editor's task includes getting others to provide information and to write stories for the publication. Even when an editor has a paid staff, it is never large enough to cover all the sources of information in the organization.

Ways to get news.   The only reward offered to those who write articles (except for paid staff) is the *byline.* This is a powerful recognition for many

EXHIBIT 17-13
Good Use of
Photography
From TVA's Division of
Construction *ONSITE*,
used with permission.

In the early 1940's, TVA building programs sometimes took a back seat to the Nation's military needs. At Fort Loudoun, workmen stayed busy despite funding cutbacks, which killed an extension dam and delayed installation of two generating units. Above right, two workers find a rare empty spot at the base of the dam's massive spillways. Far right, a gantry crane lowers a turbo-generator into place near the end of construction. Tellico, too, has had its share of cutbacks and delays. But now some TVA officials say that by February Tellico Lake will be filled and joined with the Fort Loudoun reservoir by canal. Standing atop an earth plug in the canal, Winfred Miller drains rain water from the Tellico construction site into Fort Loudoun Lake at left.

26

people. Reader interest goes up if the writer comes from the target audience. Others will provide information and news tips just to help out. There are several ways to organize a news-gathering process:

1. *The "beat" system.* The organization can be divided into territories and a reporter assigned to cover each. Each territory is called a "beat." This is an excellent system if there are enough people willing to be reporters. One way of recruiting correspondents is to identify the people in each area who have been there longest. Ask them whether they will help you. Then ask their supervisor if they can be a reporter for the house publication. This support is valuable motivation. When all the reporters have been selected, invite them to a "news clinic" on company time.

2. *The telephone network.* If an editor cannot recruit enough reporters, people who are willing to phone in information can be used. The editor should stay in touch with every link in this network even if there is no news. Constant contact with the editor keeps lines open. Regular conversations may turn up information that the contact did not realize was newsworthy.

3. *News request forms.* Memos or notices asking for information are seldom effective. Most people don't understand what news means. They seldom think what is happening to them is important. A news request form that asks for information about specific things such as promotions, awards, and achievements can produce excellent story topics.

Editorial staff. A house publication needs columnists, feature writers, photographers, and artists. Budget will determine how many of these skills can be bought. However, recognition can often be effective in place of pay. A list of the names of all those who contribute to an issue is one way to recognize those who do not have bylines.

Controlling In-House Publications

Every publication should evaluate its progress toward its objectives. Purpose, content, and frequency of publication should all be evaluated in terms of the needs of the target audience. The panel that was used originally to identify the target audience can be used again to evaluate progress. Surveys and questionnaires also give useful information about how well a publication is fulfilling expectations. National magazines have found that even simple surveys can provide excellent insight into the interests of readers. To pre-test the potential readership of planned articles, for example, a questionnaire can be prepared with a list of headlines. A sample of the intended audience can be asked to indicate which articles they would read. An editor can thus get feedback about the probable success of stories.

**PRINCIPLES
FOR
PRACTICE**

1. In-house publications are secondary tools. Despite their usefulness, you must remember that they cannot take the place of interpersonal communication between managers and subordinates.

2. Persons who are responsible for in-house publications must perform a dual role as members of the managerial hierarchy and as representatives of the needs and interests of their audiences.

3. The reason that most organizations have an in-house publication (to tell their story their own way) is also the reason why so many publications fail. The needs and interests of the target audience must be represented if credibility and a wide readership are to be gained.

4. Secondary audiences must also be planned for. Many people other than the target audience (suppliers, distributors, competitors, the community) will read the publication.

5. In large organizations, in-house publications can be an effective way to share information between divisions and other work groups, as well as to increase the flow of upward communication to top management.

6. Even without large budgets and staffs, an in-house publication can be an effective supplementary tool of communication if it meets the needs and interests of its audience.

FOR FURTHER STUDY

1. Where would the editor of a typical in-house publication fit into the organization chart of most companies—staff or line?

2. What types of power and authority would the typical in-house publication editor have in his or her organization—formal or informal?

3. Why should in-house publications always be considered secondary rather than primary media in an organization's overall communications mix?

4. Visit an organization that has an in-house publication and investigate the following:

a. What part does the publication play in the organization's overall communication plan?
b. Interview the publication's editors to find out the major problems they face and how they go about their job.
c. Read a recent issue and compute the percentage of lines devoted to each of the following: company information, employee information, relevant noncompany information, and small talk.
d. Critique two of the major stories using the inverted pyramid form.
e. Analyze the page makeup, headlines, photographs, and use of white space.

CHAPTER
18

To: The Reader
From: The Authors
Subject: Preparing and Distributing Supplementary
           Publications

When you finish reading this chapter you should:

1. Be familiar with many of the ways supplemental
   publications can be used to augment an organization's
   communication system.

2. Be aware of legal requirements that affect some
   supplemental publications.

3. Understand the differences between various forms of
   supplemental publications and how they can be used in
   various situations.

4. Understand the unique roles of bulletin boards, posters,
   billboards, information racks, exhibits, and displays.

Supplementary Publications and Other Printed Messages

Understanding grows out of good communication. Understanding involves more than knowing the facts. It includes an appreciation of the other person's point of view and a realization that yours is also understood.

One area of misunderstanding in most organizations is the employee benefit program. Managers claim that employees "just don't appreciate what they have." Perhaps this lack of "appreciation" results from poor communication. This was certainly the case in one organization.

Management could not understand why employees had been attracted to a benefits package offered by a union that had just been successful in organizing them. "Those benefits offer no substantial improvement over the package we already had," complained one executive. Upon closer examination, however, it was discovered that the company had never prepared publications to explain its package. Employee meetings to discuss benefits were irregular, almost nonexistent. No employee handbook or guide had ever been published. There was no orientation program for new employees.

There is little doubt that when the employees cast their ballots for the union, they were not voting for better benefits, but for a plan that had been explained to them.

Another company was alarmed by inaccurate grapevine information about an outstanding benefit package. Consultants called in to investigate found that the company's communication program consisted solely of a confusing booklet on group insurance and a dull monthly newsletter. The newsletter never addressed the issues circulated on the grapevine. The communication void in that company was a breeding ground for misunderstanding, mistrust, and dissatisfaction.

U.S. Chamber of Commerce figures show that from 1957 to 1977 the cost of benefits in American companies rose 78 percent. More than one-third of employee costs paid by businesses in the United States goes for benefits. With such an investment, good communication about those benefits should command a high priority, but workers are often left unaware of the scope of the benefits they have.

When an organization does not tell its employees about their benefits, the value of the benefits as incentives is lost. If workers do not understand what their benefits are, they may be more likely to change jobs. The money spent on benefits has no motivational value if information about the benefits is not effectively communicated. We shall now look at some of the publications used for this purpose. We shall also look at media used to communicate a variety of other messages in organizations.

OCCASIONAL AND SPECIAL PUBLICATIONS

Most companies use a number of publications that are published only when needed. These publications range from mimeographed one-sheet leaflets to books produced by professional writers and publishers. Responsibility for these publications often rests in the personnel department, but other areas may become involved because of legal requirements, government regulations, or company policy. These publications generally can be divided into three categories: (1) orientation literature, (2) reference material, and (3) position or special topics publications.

Types of Special or Occasional Publications

Orientation literature indoctrinates new members in an organization. This literature can help a new employee "get off to a good start" by setting forth the "ground rules." Goals and objectives of the organization are often included. They give a sense of where the company is going and the employee's role in helping it get there. In large organizations, it is often hard for a new employee to grasp the scope and range of the company's products and activities. Publications that give new members a readable and accurate view of the scope of the organization help the team-building efforts essential to development of good employees. In addition, orientation publications should give new employees a guide to the small details that are so much a part of everyone's routine. These include: pay periods, lunch and break areas, security procedures, where to pick up your check. This publication may be read once and discarded. It should be brief, attention-getting, easy to read, and inexpensive.

Reference material is designed to be kept for future use. Because of the nature of reference material, it is unlikely that anyone will ever read it from cover to cover. Therefore, reference publications must give fast and easy answers on any subject covered. This information changes sometimes, and such publications should be designed for supplements or for material to be added later. Reference material would deal with such matters as benefit programs, insurance plans, recreation programs, etc.

Position or special topics publications are put out only once. They deal with a specific subject or occasion. The subject can be any topic that an organization feels it should discuss. The private enterprise system, charitable and social commitments, history, awards, and scientific or technological developments are among the most frequently treated subjects. Occasional publications give an organization the chance to tell its story. The same requirements of credibility and interest that apply to newsletters must apply to position publications if they are to be read and believed.

Whatever the purpose of a publication, it must be remembered that these media, like house organs, are supplementary. They supplement face-to-face communication. They do not replace it. Occasional and special publications are employed as *part* of an overall communication system. Their formats dictate their uses and limitations.

Leaflets, Inserts, and Enclosures Inexpensive publications that can be read and thrown away are often printed on one sheet. Folding techniques can produce several formats from a single sheet. They increase the applications of this kind of publication. Leaflets or handbills are inexpensive and fast to prepare. They can be typed on a good typewriter and duplicated on a copying machine. With more attention to detail, these single-sheet publications can be folded into brochures for information racks, in-house distribution, or direct mail. Many organizations use them as inserts in pay envelopes to deal with immediate problems. Credit card companies and other organizations have shown this to be an effective way to communicate inexpensively.

A popular insert is a regular (sometimes monthly but at least quarterly) update on the dollar value of fringe benefits for each employee. These fact-sheets can be generated for each employee by computer. They are effective reminders of the value of an organization's benefit program.

Single-sheet publications can be used for many messages in an organization (Exhibit 18-1):

1. To give information on a topic of interest.
2. To make an announcement.
3. To ask for support or encourage action.
4. To correct an error.
5. To explain certain actions.
6. To greet visitors.
7. To report on the progress of long-term projects.
8. To give information about forthcoming changes.
9. To supplement other publications.

EXHIBIT 18-1
Brochures and other
publications

EXXON COMPANY, U.S.A.'s
Energy Outlook
1979-1990

December 1978

EXXON BENEFIT PLANS SUMMARY

BAYTOWN RESEARCH CENTER
EXXON RESEARCH AND ENGINEERING COMPANY

The following summarizes the more important provisions of several of the Company's benefit plans and policies which apply to regular employees. Additional details of the Benefit Plan are provided in the loose-leaf binder entitled "How your benefits work for you." The complete official text of the Benefit Plan, which is available in Employee Relations, will govern.

SAVINGS AND INVESTMENT PROGRAM

The Thrift Plan of the Savings and Investment Program is designed to encourage regular savings for both long and short range goals. It offers flexibility to meet some of the needs of employees and their families as well as options for investments during employment and at retirement time.

If you have completed one year of credited service, you may make regular contributions of 6% of your pay by payroll deduction. The Company will match your regular contributions to your Thrift Fund Account. In addition, the Trustee will annually credit your account with fund earnings based on your monthly cash balances. Your total account including Company contributions will be provided to you upon termination of employment if you have completed five years of credited service. However, in the event of your death, your total account will be paid out regardless of length of service.

In addition, you may make special contributions of up to 10% of your compensation while continuously a participant in the Plan. Special contributions may be made by payroll deductions or by lump sum amounts. No corresponding Company contributions are made for special contributions.

You may use cash in your account to buy Exxon Corporation stock provided your loan collateral (if any) is not impaired. If the stock is registered in your name, you will receive dividends directly; if it is registered in the name of the Trustee, the dividends will be credited to your account. Also available is investment in an equity portfolio of certain moneys credited to your Thrift Fund account or in the Fixed Income Account which provides an annual rate of return on your investment of not less than 8.85%.

At retirement, you may receive distribution of your entire Thrift Fund account in a lump sum, or you may direct the trustee to pay all or part of the cash equivalent of your account to an insurance company selected by the trustee for the purchase of a life annuity or a contract providing payments for a specified period. Annuity purchases under this option will be in addition to payments received under the Company's Annuity Plan.

In general, your contributions, both regular and special, less any withdrawals constitute your tax paid credit balance. You may withdraw from your account any amount up to your current tax-paid credit balance provided the withdrawal does not impair collateral for any loan you may have outstanding and you have not made a withdrawal during the preceding six months. Exceptions to the six months time limitation are (a) withdrawals of any gains that result from the sale of stock or equity units in your account, (b) any regular withdrawals you authorize for the payment of your medical insurance contributions, and (c) no withdrawals can be made without penalty unless the **remaining** amount in your account after a withdrawal is at least equal to the amount of the Company's and your regular contributions made during the preceding 2 years. The "penalty" for making a withdrawal which will reduce your account to less than 2 years of the Company's and your contributions is a mandatory 6 months suspension from the Plan.

Booklets and Manuals   Because of their expense, booklets and manuals are made to be read and saved for reference. Their greatest shortcoming is that they can be hard to read and use if they are not designed properly. Employee orientation manuals or insurance plan booklets need an index and might also use tabs or color-coded pages to improve accessibility of information. Regardless of the information inside, employees will remain uninformed unless they can locate what they need when they need it.

Booklets and manuals must be written with the needs of employees in mind. If management allows them to be written in technical language or the jargon of insurance, law, accounting, or finance, readability will be lost. When copy is being prepared for a booklet or manual, the needs and interests of the intended audience must come first. Too often, publications meet the regulations of insurance companies or government agencies rather than the needs of employees.

One of the largest organizations in the United States was recently made aware of the difference between employee understanding and publishing information to meet legal requirements. They learned it in a court ruling. When an employee charged violation of Equal Employment Opportunity statues, the federal court ruled against the organization. The court's ruling said the company must not only publish and distribute EEOC information to its employees, but also see that the employees understand it. To enforce this, the court directed federal officials to "spot test" the knowledge of employees of the organization across the country. In this company, the readability, clarity, and point of view of their publications suddenly became a major concern.

Federal law is also concerned with employee understanding of benefit plans. The 1974 Employee Retirement Income Security Act (ERISA) requires that descriptions of benefits be written "in a manner calculated to be understood by the average plan participant." As a result, great emphasis must now be put on the focus and readability of employee booklets and manuals.

Some of the areas in which booklets and manuals can be used successfully are:

1. To orient new employees.

2. To explain the safety regulations as they comply with OSHA standards.

3. To explain the benefit plan and its value to the employee.

4. To explain company policies and their compliance with government regulations.

5. To explain the costs and benefits of the organization's insurance package.

6. To explain the company retirement plan and its requirements.

EXHIBIT 18-2
Some uses of
booklets and
manuals.

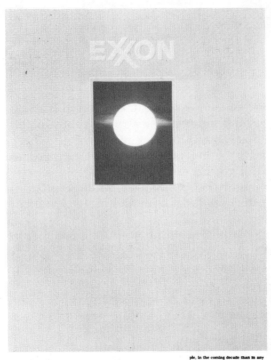

expects to employ about one-third more people in 1985 than it does today. The company's growth will come as the nation shifts from near total dependence on oil and gas to reliance on many energy sources, including coal, our greatest fossil fuel resource, plus nuclear, solar, and other less traditional alternatives. As this shift occurs, Exxon expects to broaden its scope of operations to include energy in all its forms. Further growth is also expected in nonenergy operations. Exxon Minerals Company, for example, hopes to develop major base metals discoveries and will be constructing mines and carrying out mining activities. In all these areas, career opportunities will abound.

Opportunities? Perhaps challenges would be a better word. For those who choose Exxon will be challenged to explore the unknown in a dazzling variety of fields. Consider:

Research

Here's where it all begins — in the minds of 12,000 men and women staffing Exxon's 19 research labs and 5 engineering centers worldwide. Here, scientists and engineers probe the hidden world of energy, seeking to develop new energy sources and improve existing processes. Recent innovations now being studied include a method to change coal into gas by the use of a catalyst, and an energy-saving way to scrub flue gases to prevent air pollution. In the interest of helping Exxon to protect the environment while carrying out its far-flung operations, scientists have invented a seismic energy source

ple, in the coming decade than in any similar time period in the company's history. The energy industry, for example, will be growing, not shrinking. Just think. Between now and 1990, Exxon estimates the U.S. will need 520,000 new oil and gas wells; 17 additional refineries; 206 more large coal mines; 29 new uranium mining and milling complexes; and 15 synthetic fuel plants to meet its anticipated energy demands. If all this is done, and sound conservation of energy practiced as well, the nation may be able to meet the energy demands of the future. To achieve the economic growth necessary to the country's welfare, energy must be made available in satisfactory quantities.

That's why Exxon Company, U.S.A.

should you consider a career with Exxon?

Yes, if you are looking for challenge and opportunity in a lifetime career.

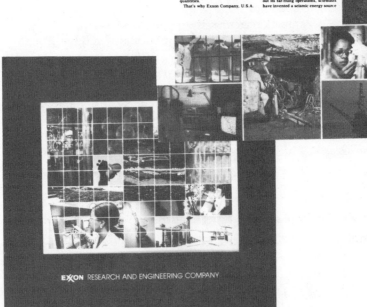

EXON RESEARCH AND ENGINEERING COMPANY

7. To give information helpful to the employee in his or her job.

8. To give information about social or community issues.

9. To explain organizational compliance with environmental standards.

Exhibit 18-2 illustrates some of the uses of booklets and manuals.

Printed Speeches and Position Papers   Printed speeches and position papers comprise another type of occasional publication. Organization officials frequently make important talks to professional, community, or other groups. These speeches often concern topics of interest to employees. It may be useful to print them for distribution within the organization. The extra expense usually amounts only to the cost of the paper needed, since copies of the speeches have usually been made available to news media anyway (Exhibit 18-3).

Reprints of magazine articles of concern to the organization and its employees can be bought rather inexpensively. Magazine reprints have the advantage of "outside" credibility. If general-interest magazines are used, the readability of the articles will probably make them suitable for wide distribution. However, if a more technical or professional publication is used, the style of writing may suggest limited use.

EXHIBIT 18-3

THE COURAGE TO WORK TOGETHER

Remarks By:
C.R. Sitter
Senior Vice President
Exxon Company, U.S.A.
Presented Before
American Council on Consumer Interests
San Antonio, Texas
April 27, 1979

Annual Reports   Annual reports to shareholders have recently evolved far beyond the financial statements required by law. They have become statements of philosophy as well as financial stability. Profit and nonprofit organizations have begun to use them as tools to communicate news of their progress and plans. In addition to financial statements, most reports now include information relating to one or more of the following:

- internal scope of the organization
- economic impact on the areas where the company has facilities
- international operations and agreements
- products or services related to social and environmental problems
- management's position on public issues

Content and scope of annual reports have changed. So have its readerships. Annual reports enable a company to reach a range of individuals in addition to investors including competitors, suppliers, dealers, community and government leaders, and employees. Employees who are not shareholders will read and keep an annual report. Because annual reports are attractive and expensive, employees and their families keep them as conversation pieces, if for no other reason.

A well-designed and written annual report can be a source of pride for an employee (Exhibit 18-4). To be effective it should contain some of the following:

1. A cover design that will get attention and reflect the unique attributes of the organization.

2. A table of contents for longer reports.

3. A summary of the highlights usually displayed graphically.

4. Names, titles, functions, and, preferably, photographs of top officials.

5. An overview statement from the organization's chief executive officer. It should give a summary of the past year's progress and goals and objectives for the future.

6. Financial data required by law. Some financial highlights are given in graphic form.

Message Displays

All organizations must now *display* messages in different locations. A growing number of laws and regulations require the posting of notices. Display messages are a quick, inexpensive medium for reaching large numbers of

EXHIBIT 18-4

people. Message displays are usually printed or artistically designed. They include posters, billboards, bulletin boards, information racks, and exhibits.

Bulletin Boards   Bulletin boards display messages in regular locations with minimum effort and expense. They are a much-used and effective means of communication in organizations. They often do a supplementary or follow-up job. Notices that have been mailed or given out to employees can be posted as reminders. Details of announcements made in meetings or in the house publication can be posted for those who wish more information. Bulletin boards can post notices required by law. They can post information that is of value but does not warrant publication.

Bulletin boards are a fast, effective means of communication when used and kept up properly. To insure credibility and readability, bulletin boards must be carefully planned.

Location is a primary consideration. No matter how professionally written and designed a board may be, if it is hidden in a corner it will not be read. Management must pick locations that meet the needs of most of those who should read a bulletin board. The convenience of the manager charged with keeping it current is secondary. Too many bulletin boards are outside supervisors' offices.

Bulletin boards should be placed in or near areas of heavy traffic. As many employees as possible should pass the message. The boards should be at eye level where the reading light is good, and where employees can stop and read without blocking traffic. Bulletin boards should never be put where they present safety hazards.

Neatness will improve readability. Order and arrangement invite reading. If a board becomes cluttered, even with important notices, it will no longer communicate its messages.

Someone should regularly service each board to be sure that it does not become overloaded and disorganized. Boards that have information on more than one topic should be arranged so that all the messages on one subject are kept together. Whenever possible, have a separate board for each topic to avoid confusion.

Timeliness is a key to credibility in bulletin boards. Out-of-date notices have little interest. When an organization's bulletin boards always have up-to-date information, employees will check their contents regularly. Constant attention is required to post current material and to take down outdated messages.

The "wear-out" potential of a message must also be considered. Even if the content is still current, the notice itelf should be changed periodically. Once employees have read a notice, they are likely to skip over it when checking the board. If the information is "repackaged," it will once again attract notice. This method can keep employees alert to long-term issues.

Interest of the intended readers can be assured by picking messages that meet their needs. Like any other publication, posted items should reflect the interests of the intended audience. Messages posted must be significant to the employees. Personal items, advertisements, and entertaining odds and ends should be kept to a minimum. The presence of nonofficial information can create a relaxed atmosphere, but too many nonessential items destroy credibility.

Responsibility for the upkeep of each bulletin board should be fixed. One person must be charged with maintaining the condition and integrity of each board. Bulletin boards are important media. They should not be assigned to a secretary or clerk. Decisions about what should be posted and how it will be presented are the job of management.

Posters and Billboards   Like bulletin boards, posters and billboards offer fast, effective communication. Most appropriately, they emphasize an idea. They are not for careful reading. Posters and billboards provide messages that can be grasped quickly. Details can be published in other media. Posters and billboards should be in high-traffic areas where they can be easily seen by most employees. "Wear-out" potential is also a consideration here. Messages should be changed or revised periodically.

Because posters and billboards rely on artistic design, they need to be prepared professionally. Unless the topic is important and lasting, posters and billboards may not be cost-effective media. Commercially produced posters are available on topics such as safety, productivity, workmanship, waste reduction, quality control, and free enterprise.

Information Racks   You can combine the effects of posters, bulletin boards, brochures, and booklets with an information rack. Racks can be designed with posters to get attention. They can invite the reader to take a copy of the material in the rack. This is a way to get attention for topics that cannot be handled with short messages. Because the booklets are selected by readers without pressure from management, interest in them is likely to be higher. There are economic advantages to information racks. Only interested employees are likely to take material from them.

Information racks work best in areas where employees can look at the material at their leisure. Lunchrooms, break areas, waiting rooms, and dressing areas are good locations. Empty information racks suggest that management is uninterested in them, so regular maintenance is needed.

Exhibits and Displays   Exhibits and displays rely primarily on visual messages. Their effectiveness comes from seeing a sample or model of what is being discussed. Many organizations recognize the value of exhibits and displays at industrial meetings or in sales-related contexts.

Exhibits and displays can be used to show how production facilities work, to display products, to honor those who receive awards, and to depict organizational or industrial history.

PRINCIPLES FOR PRACTICE

1. Management can utilize a wide variety of publications and other printed messages to supplement its communication efforts.

2. Most supplementary publications can be classified as indoctrination, reference, or institutional messages. Examples include: leaflets, brochures, booklets, manuals, inserts, enclosures, position papers, printed speeches, and annual reports.

3. As the proportion of an organization's payroll that goes to pay for fringe benefits increases, so does the need for better communication about those benefits.

4. Governmental regulations are forcing organizations to do an effective job of communicating information about their benefit plans to employees.

5. Bulletin boards, posters, billboards, information racks, exhibits, and displays are other supplemental media that can perform unique services in an organization's communication system.

FOR FURTHER STUDY

1. Why is it important for an organization to do a good job of communicating information about its benefit programs to its employees?

2. Why are employees not likely to read a booklet or manual about the company's retirement plan? Discuss the use of such publications as reference material. What can be done to make them more useful?

3. Design a communication plan for an organization with which you are familiar. Include in your media mix as many of the publications discussed

in this chapter as possible. (Assume that you would have adequate resources to support any program you design.) Explain the role of each publication in the overall communication plan.

4. Visit an organization that is large enough to have several of the publications discussed in this chapter. Collect samples of all the supplementary
publications. Prepare a critique of these publications based on the information in this chapter and the purpose of each publication.

CHAPTER 19

```
To:         The Reader
From:       The Authors
Subject:    Audio-Visual Communication in Business

After reading this chapter, you will:

1.  Understand the importance of including audio-visual media
    in the organization's total communication plan.

2.  Be aware of some of the factors to be considered when
    selecting audio-visual media.

3.  Know the advantages and disadvantages of overhead
    projectors, slides, filmstrips, motion pictures,
    television, and video tape recorders.

4.  Understand the problems many managers have in adapting
    their communication skills to audio-visual media.

5.  Be aware of some techniques for using audio-visual media
    more effectively in organizational settings.
```

Audio-Visual
Communication
in Business

Face-to-face meetings via satellite between business parties in various corners of the earth may be a part of the future, but it also happens today. When the management of Hills Bros. Coffee in San Francisco needed to meet face-to-face with the account group of their advertising agency in New York (BBDO), they did so without either group leaving its city.*

The group in New York and the people in San Francisco traveled only a short distance to a closed-circuit television studio. Designed like a conference room, it enabled the participants in each coast to talk face to face. It was much like a normal meeting. The cameras in each studio automatically focused on the person speaking and pulled back to a wide-angle shot when no one was talking.

While a BBDO manager was speaking, another person in the same room in New York added a comment. Immediately the voice-activated camera switched to the new speaker. The Hills Bros. management in San Francisco could not only hear the comment but also see the facial expression.

On both ends of the conversation, the studios were equipped to allow the use of slides, motion pictures, video tapes, and photocopy transmission. It was almost like being in a room together.

This service is now available only at Bell System offices in major U.S. cities. However, technology will make the service available in organization

*Rewritten from "You Stay There, We'll Stay Here: But We Can Still Have a Meeting," *BBDO Newsletter*, April 1977.

offices anywhere in the world when and if demand for it grows. The savings in time and money make this form of communication very attractive.

THE AUDIO-VISUAL BOOM

Audio-visual technology is widely used in American organizations. Audio-visual communication in its broadest sense means communication media that engage both sight and hearing. In the strict sense, audio-visual communication has been around since the first cave artist explained his or her work to other prehistoric humans. Flip charts and chalkboards would count, since they are used to illustrate a vocal explanation. However, these devices now seem almost primitive. Audio-visual communication today usually means electronic media. When organizations realized that face-to-face communication with everyone was no longer possible, public address and telephone/intercom systems were installed. Soon motion pictures and slide/filmstrips were used to add visual effect to messages within organizations. More recently, closed-circuit television and video tape have combined the advantages of almost all audio-visual media into what is becoming a flexible and cost-effective method of communication within organizations.

Electronic audio-visual communication in America has been growing in recent years. It is estimated that the use of such media in business and industry is expanding 40 percent each year. Moreover, the state of the art in the last five years has reduced initial investment cost. Many organizations can now afford to join the audio-visual age.

This does not mean that audio-visual communication is superior to all other forms, or that it is just an expensive fad. Electronic audio-visual communication will continue to grow, creating new communication channels and expanding old ones. But electronic media still must depend upon the communicator and his or her message to be effective. No medium alone creates good communication. It only facilitates it. The skills of preparing and delivering oral and written messages discussed elsewhere in this book will never be replaced by hardware. Electronic media are supplementary to interpersonal communication, not a replacement for direct person-to-person contact. Such media must be fitted into an organization's total communication plan.

Planning Message Content and Objectives

Before a medium is selected, the message itself should be completed. A communicator should decide what needs to be said before deciding how it will be delivered. Audio-visual media must be selected to fit both message and audience. This stage of planning is much like the preparation of a speech discussed in Chapter 12. The seven questions recommended for speech preparation can be modified to apply to audio-visual messages:

- For whom is the message intended?
- What do I want those who hear and see the message to do?
- What are the goals and interests of the audience?
- What does the audience know about me or those I represent?
- What experience has the audience had with the topic?
- How is the audience likely to feel about me or those I represent?
- What kind of circumstances will surround the presentation?

Once these questions have been answered, the next step is to organize the content of the message. There should be a workable order of presentation to accomplish the desired ends. A complete script is not as useful at this point as an outline of ideas. These basic ideas, or major points, then become the body around which an introduction and conclusion can be planned. Attention should be given to planning a request for action to meet the purpose and objectives of the presentation. Action requests can range from the mere acceptance of information to physical activity.

Audience Characteristics and Setting   The message must meet the needs and interests of the audiences who will be exposed to it. The language used should reflect the audience's education and level of knowledge about the subject. A message for aerospace engineers may be too technical for the workers who assemble a spacecraft. The message should match the vocabulary and experiences of the workers. Naturally, a different message need not always be prepared. Many groups have enough common experiences to understand one audio-visual presentation that touches on these areas of common need and interest. Careful planning will help to identify these cluster groups, as well as audiences that are different enough to need separate messages.

Media Selection and Mix   Once the purpose, objectives, audience, and content have been decided, you are ready to choose a medium or combination of media. The newest, most expensive, or most technically impressive medium is not always the best. A medium can overpower a message. It can emphasize the wrong aspect. For example, audio-visual media alone cannot inform employees about their benefit plan. Other media must be used as well—face-to-face interviews, booklets, group meetings, articles in the company publication. In the overall communication effort, audio-visual media are only one part of the mix. They must complement the other media.

Some factors to consider when selecting audio-visual media are:

- Size of audience. Some media are more appropriate for small groups and rooms. Others are better in large areas.
- Composition of audience. Executives? Clerical? Blue collar? Union? Non-union? Educational level? Technical knowledge?
- Interest of audience. Were they forced to attend, or did they come of their own free will? The presentation may need to be extra impressive and shorter if the audience has been forced to attend.
- Location of audience. If audiences will be in diverse locations, the presentation will have to use a medium that is portable and easily adapted to different settings.
- Equipment. Are the production as well as presentation facilities adequate? Is the cost reasonable in relation to what can be accomplished?
- Wear-out potential. If a message is expensive to produce, this cost can be offset if the message can be reused.

Exhibit 19-1 provides some useful information concerning the relative costs and benefits of various audio-visual media. Such information should be carefully considered before a decision is made regarding audio-visual media.

Overhead Projectors   Overhead projectors are a good support for an oral presentation. There are two types. Transparency projectors are the most popular. They can be used in a fully lighted room. The transparency can be easily made from typed material or photographs. An office copy machine will do the job. Opaque projectors are not so common. But they have the advantage of not needing a transparency. They project an image from any copy of a photograph directly onto a screen. However, the room must be darkened.

Overheads can give an impression of order and careful preparation to any oral presentation. The production and presentation equipment are inexpensive, versatile, and portable. Unlike flip charts and blackboards, overhead projectors let the speaker face the audience. Presentations are easy and quick to prepare and are effective with small- to medium-size audiences.

Slides and Filmstrips   Although more expensive than overhead transparencies, 35-mm slides are still relatively inexpensive. Projectors are common. Slides can be made with relatively inexpensive equipment. Projection equipment is compact and portable. It produces an image suitable for a room of any size. A darkened room is necessary, except for rear-projection. Slides present information with impact.

Filmstrips have the attributes of slides. They are connected on a continuous piece of film, so they cannot get out of order. This advantage is also a disadvantage; filmstrips cannot be edited as easily as a slide presentation.

Filmstrips and slides can be supplemented by audio tape recordings. This makes a complete audio-visual package. Projectors can automatically change the slide or film frame to fit an audio tape. When professional narration, music, and photography are combined with an effectively written script, the results can be excellent. Filmstrip and slide presentations are often used to communicate information about employee benefits and company policies. They are excellent for new employee orientation. They can be easily updated (especially slides) without great expense. Filmstrips and slides can be shown in large or small rooms to audiences ranging from one to hundreds. Where there is a supplemental tape, no speaker is required.

Motion Pictures   Movement is the key to the dramatic effects of motion pictures. They can be combined with sound-on-film, color, animation capabilities, and shown on large screens. They can be shipped anywhere and shown by a person with only a basic knowledge of projectors. Each time the message is presented, it has the same content. Little is left to speakers or operators.

The projection equipment for 16-mm sound film is inexpensive and portable, but the production equipment is not. In addition, sound film productions require several highly trained professionals. They take a great deal of time. It is generally inexpensive for organizations to rent motion pictures for training or information purposes. High production costs mean that they are usually not cost-effective, unless rented or produced in response to a very special need.

The Super-8 film cartridge is a relatively recent innovation in motion pictures. Super-8 equipment is less expensive than the standard 16 mm for both production and projection hardware. However, Super-8 production equipment has a number of technical drawbacks that prevent most professionals from using it. Generally speaking, the quality of the image is noticeably inferior to that of 16-mm film. The Super-8 film cartridge projection system has found wide acceptance as a distribution-only medium. That is, a film can be produced in 16-mm and then transferred to Super-8 cartridges for distribution because of their low cost and portability. This technique is used frequently as point-of-purchase sales support and displays. There have been some problems because of the production of four incompatible cartridge formats by the leading manufacturers.

Both 16-mm and Super-8 film production usage has slowed in recent years because of the increased reliability, quality, and portability of video-

EXHIBIT 19-1

A Guide to Making Audiovisual Equipment Decisions

Figures are based on current information and experience of users

Equipment	Reasons for using equipment	Equipment costs (and weight)	Presentation materials costs	Audience size	Image area size	Lead Times Needed — Preparing scripts	Lead Times Needed — Producing materials	Equipment rehearsal & first set-up time
Flip Chart	Short lead time; little investment warranted	$63 (15 lbs.)	Per word cost: $25–$40 for 1–5 words per page: $75–$90 for charts, cartoons, etc.	10 or under	27" to 34" maximum	From hours to days	Up to 18 pages per day per worker	Minimal, but needed
Chalk Board	Informal in-house communications in board rooms & offices	$15–$150	None	Approx. 20	18" × 24" to 48" × 96"	None	None	None
Veloro Boards, Felt Boards, etc.	Informal but professional presentation to valued audience	$70–$100 (21 to 33 lbs. for portables)	$1.50 per letter	Up to 24	48" × 36" to 72" × 48"	From several days to weeks	Usually several days	3 to 4 hours or more
Overhead Projector (3M)	Complex materials requiring extensive discussion	$300–$500 (15 to 21 lbs. for portables)	$4–$7 made in-house; $25–$85 professional	48 maximum	60" × 60"	Hours to days	Up to several days	Allow a few hours
Slides (1 Projector Presentation) (Kodak)	Important audience & message; professional tone wanted	$110–$875 for random access (10 to 15 lbs.)	Type only: $5–$50 Art: $15–$75 +	Usually ltd. only to room size	6' or more	Plan on 2 or more weeks	Ideally, several weeks from story-board to finished art	Several hours or longer for script presented live, less with programmed tape

R. C. Reinhart, "How to Select Your A/V Equipment," Public Relations Journal, May 1979, p. 28.
Reprinted with permission from the May 1979 issue of *Public Relations Journal*. Copyright 1979.

System	Characteristics							
Filmstrip with Sound, Pulse Advance (Singer)	Mechanically somewhat easier than slide & sound	$360 + (20 lbs. +)	Same as slides	Same as slides	Same as slides	Same as slides	Same as slides; (Note: frame ratio is different from slides)	Same as slides
16mm Sound Movies (Kodak)	Highly important audience; greatest impact; long life; simple, universal display	$735–$1775 (35 to 40 lbs.)	$1500–$6000 per minute of finished film	Usually ltd. only to room size	6' or more	Several weeks	1 to 5 min. of useable footage per day's shooting	One hour or so
Videotape 1. Seen on monitor from pre-recorded videocassette (Sony)	1 & 2: Important audience; credibility; cheaper, quicker production than film; quality not as critical as film	1. $1350 (50 lbs.)	1 & 2: Very roughly, half the cost of film and less	1. 1 person per 1" of monitor size; e.g. 25 for 25" mon.	1. up to 25'	1 & 2: days to weeks	1 & 2: 3 to 5 days to duplicate videocassettes	1 & 2: several hours
2. Seen projected on screen (Sony)		2. $3000 (up to 200 lbs.)		2. 36 or so	2. 40" × 30"			

Other speciality systems which may be of interest are: 3M's sound-on slide; multimedia using multiple slide projectors or slides with movies: Super 8 sound movies; sound tape presentations or sound with auxiliary materials; opaque projectors which are best for small conference situations.

Note: Overtime for professional assistance, studio or lab time can add 50% to 100% to production costs.

351

tape recording equipment. Before the improvement of mini-camera video systems it was common practice to produce a motion picture on film and then transfer it to video cassettes for distribution. The increased production of motion pictures directly onto video tape has had a profound effect on both 16-mm and Super-8 production and projection equipment.

Room and Seating Requirements for Projectors   When a projected image is used for communication purposes, it is necessary to keep certain limitations of audience and room size in mind. If a projector is used in a setting that hampers the ability of the audience to see clearly, more information may be lost than gained.

When arranging a meeting room for projection presentations, it is important to understand that only a portion of the room will yield a good viewing area. If a room is filled (wall to wall), it will not be possible for everyone to see the screen clearly. Exhibit 19-2 illustrates the relative proportion of the good viewing area to the size of the room.

EXHIBIT 19-2

Reprinted from: Kodak Projection Calculator and Seating Guide, Kodak Production No. S-3. (Reproduced with the permission of Eastman Kodak Company.)

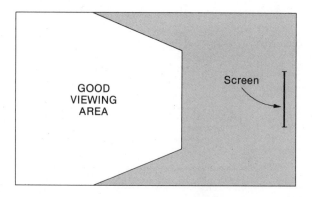

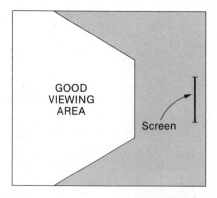

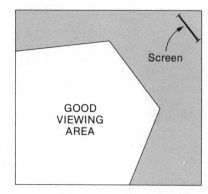

Screen size is an important factor to consider along with room size. For best viewing, the screen should be large enough to allow the back row of viewers to be a distance that is eight times the image height (8H) from the screen. Sometimes, especially in the case of an overhead or opaque projector, it is necessary to move the projector closer to the screen to increase the brightness of the image. Moving the projector in to an image distance of 11H will double the image brightness and only slightly reduce the image size. Exhibit 19-3 illustrates the image distance ratio that should be applied for most projection situations. For best results, viewers should be seated within the 50°–60° angles and should not be closer to the screen than 2 times or farther than 8 times the height of the projected image.

Exhibit 19-4 provides typical room ratio, viewing angle, and seating capacity information for a variety of room sizes. It should be noted that these calculations apply to theater-style seating. For conference situations where tables are used, the seating capacity is only about one-half that of a theater arrangement. To use Exhibit 19-4, locate the size of the room available and look under the 50°–60° angle column to determine how many people can be accommodated. Some exceptionally bright screens can increase the acceptable viewing angle to 90°. In most cases increasing the viewing angle will increase the audience capacity for a room.

Television and Video Tape Recordings   The use of closed-circuit television and video tape recordings began principally in plant security and employee training. Today it is the fastest-growing audio-visual medium for intra-organizational communication. More than 1,000 private-sector organizations use some form of television to communicate with their employees.

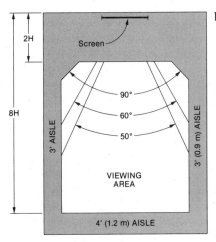

EXHIBIT 19-3

EXHIBIT 19-4
Seating Guide

Theater-style seating for different room sizes
(For conference-style seating, use one-half the seating capacity shown)

Room Ratio 1:1

Room Size L × W (ft)	Viewing Angle* 50°	60°	90°
16 × 16	10	11	13
20 × 20	18	21	25
24 × 24	28	33	41
28 × 28	41	48	60
32 × 32	56	66	83
36 × 36	73	87	109
40 × 40	93	111	139
44 × 44	115	137	173
48 × 48	139	167	210
52 × 52	166	199	252
56 × 56	195	234	296
60 × 60	226	272	345
64 × 64	259	313	397
68 × 68	295	356	453
72 × 72	334	402	512
76 × 76	374	452	576
80 × 80	417	504	642
84 × 84	462	558	713

Room Ratio 4:3

Room Size L × W (ft)	Viewing Angle* 50°	60°	90°
16 × 12	8	8	8
20 × 15	15	16	17
24 × 18	24	26	28
28 × 21	36	39	43
32 × 24	50	55	60
36 × 27	66	73	80
40 × 30	85	93	104
44 × 33	106	116	130
48 × 36	129	141	159
52 × 39	154	169	191
56 × 42	181	200	226
60 × 45	211	233	264
64 × 48	243	269	305
68 × 51	277	307	348
72 × 54	313	347	395
76 × 57	352	390	445
80 × 60	393	436	497
84 × 63	436	484	552

Room Ratio 3:2

Room Size L × W (ft)	Viewing Angle* 50°	60°	90°
16 × 11	6	6	6
20 × 13	13	13	13
24 × 16	22	23	23
28 × 19	33	34	36
32 × 21	46	48	51
36 × 24	61	65	69
40 × 27	78	84	90
44 × 29	98	105	113
48 × 32	119	128	139
52 × 35	143	154	167
56 × 37	169	182	198
60 × 40	197	212	232
64 × 43	227	245	268
68 × 45	259	280	307
72 × 48	293	318	349
76 × 51	330	357	393
80 × 53	368	399	440
84 × 56	409	444	489

Room Ratio 2:1

Room Size L × W (ft)	Viewing Angle* 50°	60°	90°
16 × 8	—	—	—
20 × 10	7	7	7
24 × 12	14	14	14
28 × 14	22	23	23
32 × 16	33	33	33
36 × 18	45	46	46
40 × 20	59	60	61
44 × 22	74	77	77
48 × 24	92	95	96
52 × 26	111	115	117
56 × 28	132	137	139
60 × 30	155	161	164
64 × 32	180	187	191
68 × 34	206	214	219
72 × 36	234	244	250
76 × 38	264	275	283
80 × 40	296	309	317
84 × 42	330	344	354

Room Ratio 3:1

Room Size L × W (ft)	Viewing Angle* 50°	60°	90°
16 × 5	—	—	—
20 × 7	—	—	—
24 × 8	5	5	5
28 × 9	9	9	9
32 × 11	16	16	16
36 × 12	23	23	23
40 × 13	32	32	32
44 × 15	42	42	42
48 × 16	53	53	53
52 × 17	66	66	66
56 × 19	80	80	80
60 × 20	96	96	96
64 × 21	112	112	112
68 × 23	131	131	131
72 × 24	150	150	150
76 × 25	171	171	171
80 × 27	193	193	193
84 × 28	216	216	216

*The 90-degree figures should be used only with screens capable of producing good brightness characteristics in that range, and then only when maximum seating capacity is necessary.

© 1969, Eastman Kodak Company.
Reprinted from: *Kodak Projection Calculator and Seating Guide*, Kodak Production No. 16. (Reproduced with the permission of Eastman Kodak Company.)

At least 80 percent of these produce some or all of their own programming. The programs produced in-house are growing about 20 percent per year. A conservative estimate puts corporate spending on in-house closed-circuit television in the United States at more than $1.6 billion. Most *Fortune* 100 organizations have more than $1 million already invested in video tape and closed-circuit systems.

Because of increased use and recent technological advancements that have cut costs, organizations will have to learn to deal with this powerful medium. As television "graduates" from specialized applications, such as training and security, it will require managers to know its potential and its limitations. Television, like any medium, is just a carrier of a message. We know that an expensive printing press cannot help a publication that is poorly written. A fancy typewriter cannot make a vague letter easier to read. Management must give direction if an in-house TV system is to be effective. Managers must learn which messages are appropriate for this medium, just as they understand when to send a memo or to use the telephone.

From the viewers' standpoint, corporate television systems seem natural. Employees readily adapt to watching television on breaks or lunch hours. A generation of employees has grown up with television as its main source of news and entertainment. To them, television is usually not an interruption or irritant, although printed material sometimes is. Television requires minimum effort by the viewer, and it is unlikely to be resisted or ignored. It shares the advantages of motion pictures. Sight, sound, and motion can deliver a dynamic message and can entertain and inform.

Video tape can be reused, easily edited, and quickly recorded. It is fast becoming a relatively inexpensive technique for producing in-house messages, which were once bought from film distributors. Now, an organization can produce a safety program to meet its own needs rather than buying a film about safety in general. If a video-taped message is produced to tell employees about an organization's benefit plan, it can be updated when changes in the plan occur. This cannot be done on film. Because of video tape, organizations can now prepare messages on subjects that change often. Even the criticism of television's small screen has been overcome. There are now video projection systems that can be viewed by tens of thousands of people simultaneously.

The uses for television and video tape messages seem endless. As organizations and managers recognize their potential, they discover new ways to use them. For example, CNA produces programs on video tape for all employees. They are called "Services News and Commentary." The tapes are sent to all CNA offices and inform field office personnel about developments and policies.

Shell Oil has a video-taped presentation describing its benefit package.

Even though it lasts one-and-a-half hours, Shell has found that employee response to it is better than to similar messages using other media.

Barnes Hospital in St. Louis, Missouri, has a series of patient education programs that it shows on the hospital's closed-circuit TV network. The network reaches waiting rooms as well as patient rooms. Monday through Friday, at regular times, patients see programs on anatomy and physiology, pregnancy, nutrition, contraceptives, and the "Patient's Bill of Rights."

Many organizations are starting to explore the opportunities for live two-way televised conferences and meetings. We described one at the start of this chapter. A sophisticated and effective system is in use at General Telephone Company of Florida. A description of it follows, and shows its potential for effective, fast, and accurate communication in organizations.

GT/F: A Success Story in Corporate Television

In 1973 amid negotiations between General Telephone Company of Florida and the International Brotherhood of Electrical Workers, President Richard Nixon announced a wage and price freeze. Confusion and rumors were abundant. Employees and management needed to know at once what effect the freeze would have.

Before rumors could get worse, a video tape was made with labor and management officials giving their ideas on the situation. Within hours, the company was broadcasting the tape to all employees over its microwave television network. This one message filled the need for an immediate response in a volatile situation. Each side candidly discussed its perceptions. Contract negotiations were routinely completed within a few weeks.

Three years later, GT/F was reorganized, and President George Gage announced the move in a live two-way television meeting. All employees saw and heard the explanation simultaneously and could ask questions. Because no group of employees got the message before another, rumors were held to a minimum.

General Telephone Company of Florida has continuous programming on its system. One of the most popular is a 10-minute news program, produced weekly. Much like a company newspaper, it aims at both hourly and salaried employees. The program presents a balance of spot news and feature stories. Features focusing on the jobs of various people in the company have been popular. The television programs present highlights, while company publications give complete details.

Longer programs monthly explore issues in more depth. These semi-documentaries, which run 20 minutes, typically deal with subjects such as corporate policy, legislation, or new products and reviews. Other programs are produced as needed.

All major lounges and break areas at General Telephone are equipped with one or more television sets fed by cable or microwave. Video tape cassettes serve remote locations. Each remote location has one or more video-cassette playback units. Between major programs, the TV screens are filled with useful announcements and other information for employees. This video bulletin board keeps employee attention high. Major programs thus have ready audiences when aired.

The GT/F example is become common practice today. Corporate television is growing rapidly and steadily. More and more companies are finding closed-circuit television to be fast, flexible, and cost-effective. Meanwhile, today's managers find it necessary to adapt their communication skills and habits to include this new message carrier.

Multimedia Presentations   This hybrid form combines two or more of the media mentioned to achieve even greater impact. Such a presentation will usually use two or more visual media with recorded sound. Slides, motion pictures, and recorded sound can be combined in a single message that steps up the amount of information sent and calls into play the sensory capacities of the audience. Elaborate productions that use several screens and electronic mixers and phasing units give the audience an impression of one continuous message.

A few years ago an executive of a leading tire manufacturer was scheduled to deliver an address to an industry convention. He was to appear late on the last day. His talk concerned a breakthrough in tire manufacturing, and his organization felt it should be forcefully presented. Faced with last-day weariness and inattention, the staff decided to do something different. A multimedia presentation was prepared. It used stereo sound, slides, motion picture film, and three large screens. This colorful action-packed presentation gave the complete history of the industry from the invention of the wheel to the moment of the new discovery. That segment lasted less than five minutes. The audience's attention was quickly directed to the speaker and his subject in such a way that the speech was a startling success, despite its inappropriate place on the program.

Multimedia presentations are not always so elaborate. But they are often more effective than single-medium messages in showing comparative information. Combined images can create a wide-screen effect. Or several images can be presented simultaneously to offer "bits" of information that are easier to absorb.

Telephone Messages   Telephone centers that give pre-recorded information are gaining in usefulness. Such centers have long been used for time and weather service. In recent years their effectiveness in combating rumors and misinformation in a company has become clear. The effectiveness of telephone message centers is due to the speed and ease with which a message can be put into service. Within minutes, management can have a recorded message ready for anyone who dials a selected telephone number. Employees can confirm rumors or check for new information by dialing and listening. An employee who might be unwilling to ask a manager about a rumor can get information without embarrassment. Proof of the success of these telephone message systems can be found in their heavy use during periods of crisis and uncertainty. Recorded messages offer a live human voice with authoritative information. This means high credibility and frequent usage when most needed.

PRINCIPLES FOR PRACTICE

1. Audio-visual media are an accepted part of the communication system of most organizations.

2. Audio-visual media include any presentation that electronically combines sight and sound into one message unit.

3. Slides, films, and closed-circuit television are frequently used to communicate messages of all types in business settings.

4. Audio-visual media depend upon well-prepared content to be effective.

5. The communicator must select a proper type of presentation based on the interests and needs of the audience, the message, and the requirements of the setting.

FOR FURTHER STUDY

1. Develop a media mix for the following organizational messages: (1) Explanation of a new product to be used at trade shows; (2) Explanation of company benefit program for new employee orientation sessions, which are conducted each time someone is hired; (3) Speech by your boss to a meeting of top management explaining your department's progress on an important project. For each of these messages recommend media, production time, and production and presentation costs relative to the message, situation, and audience.

2. Visit a local business firm and interview the manager of audio-visual services. Write a report describing that organization's audio-visual communication systems.

3. What do you think is the reason for the audio-visual boom in American business? Will it continue?

4. Why is it important for a manager to understand the use and nature of various audio-visual techniques?

5. Which audio-visual media would you recommend to a small firm with a limited budget and no real expertise in production techniques?

The Getting Your Message Across Handbook

Communication Strategies for Getting the Right Job

For most of us, getting a job (some kind of job) is not a problem. However, getting the right job, one that is suited to our skill, education, aptitude, and experience is much more difficult. Some experts estimate that as much as 80 percent of our working population is underemployed. Most of us have jobs, but they are not the right job. Even if you are just beginning your career, it is important to get a job that is right for you, a job that will allow you to develop the knowledge and skills you already have.

SELECTING THE RIGHT EMPLOYER

Job hunting should be organized and carefully executed to achieve the desired results. If you start in a panic to apply for any job available, you may get some kind of job, but to get the right job, you should begin your efforts with some careful research.

Know Yourself   Getting a job is essentially a process of selling yourself, so get to know the product. Begin by making a list of your unique qualifications. Remember that all prospective employers will be asking themselves the same question: What does this person have that my organization needs? You have to be prepared to answer that question.

Begin by gathering together all documents, transcripts, awards, current and former job descriptions, old resumés, and anything else that may apply. With this information in hand, you are ready to start your self-analysis.

Begin to write down brief descriptions of *all* your strengths and weaknesses. Organize these personal assets and liabilities into two lists. No item is too old, small, or insignificant to be included. Try to recall everything that may be of some help in your own analysis of the situation; even small items may trigger other more important facts. Write everything down and then begin to eliminate trivial items.

Begin by reflecting on your past experiences at school, work, or other organizations. Take each experience one by one, answering such questions as: What were my accomplishments, achievements, or contributions? What specific responsibilities did I have? What did I learn that can be applied in other situations? It is also important to ask yourself what you disliked about your experiences. This list of negative factors can help you identify the types of jobs that you would not enjoy regardless of the salary.

Organize Your Selling Points After you have made your two lists, examine the strengths in more detail. Look for common themes or threads that seem to appear over and over. Frequently skills and knowledge can be organized into one of four categories: people, ideas, data, things. Sort out all of the experiences that you have had that relate to these four and any other categories you feel are important. Once you have them distributed under these various headings, go through each list and weight each strength according to its importance. Some skills are more highly developed than others; some knowledge is more complete. This will give you two methods of comparison between your categories: quantity (number of items per list) and quality (significance of items).

A final step in deciding which strengths may be attractive to a potential employer is to review your list of weaknesses. Compare the experiences that you feel were unrewarding or negative to your categories of strengths. Don't be surprised if you find some similarities. We often develop skills and knowledge in areas that we do not particularly enjoy. Circumstances may have forced us to pursue a field in which we had little interest. Frequently we don't realize that we will not enjoy an experience until we have had it. Sometimes students spend months, even years, studying a subject only to discover that they do not want to continue in that field. It is important to identify these areas as soon as possible. You do not want to spend your energy and effort getting a job that will make you unhappy.

Selecting the Proper Target Once you have identified your skills and knowledge, those that you would like to develop in a career, the next step is to locate a job field in which they are needed. This may or may not be a difficult step. If your strengths are in a specialized field such as engineering or accounting, it will be relatively easy to match your education and experience to specific jobs and organizations. However, if your strengths are in more general areas such as people and ideas, you will need to concentrate your efforts in this phase of the job-hunting process. Everyone, even those with specialized skills, can benefit from some effort at this point. Remember, the *best* jobs are never easy to find, and they never fit a standard mold.

The key is *research*—research about the area of the country in which you would like to work; research about the kinds of organizations that need your skills and knowledge; and research about the prospective organizations themselves. This is one of the most important and most frequently skipped phases of the job search process. It is important because research is the best way to screen and choose your new career, geographical area, and employer.

The things you need to research are:

1. Your skills and knowledge.
2. Your selected geographical area.
3. The organizations for which you may wish to work.

First, find out what types of jobs use most of your strengths. A good place to begin is in *The Dictionary of Occupational Titles,* which describes more than 35,000 job titles. This three-volume source book describes what people who perform these jobs do. It is a valuable resource because the occupations can be classified by physical demands of the work, working conditions, necessary aptitude, educational requirements, and many other skill and knowledge areas.

Occupational Outlook Handbook and *Occupational Outlook Handbook for College Students* are two other valuable resources. These books provide an outline of numerous occupations and their future prospects. The nature of the work itself, usual training requirements, employment outlook, potential earnings, and working conditions are covered for each occupation. All of these government publications can be found in almost any library. There are several other sources of similar information which your librarian can help you find. You can dig deeper into the career fields that interest you most by reading the journals and trade publications in that field. This will also help you begin step 2: identification of geographical areas where your selected career fields are available and where you would like to work.

Researching areas of the country where you do not live now may present an extra challenge. There are several helpful sources of information including the Chamber of Commerce in the area you are considering. Ask for a list of local organizations that may employ people in the job categories you have identified, as well as other information about climate and economic conditions. Several sources will be available at your local library including a yearbook of newspaper advertising compiled by *Editor and Publisher* magazine. In addition to great quantities of other information, this yearbook will provide profiles of major U.S. communities. Also, if the town you are considering has a library, you can write directly to the librarian for information you cannot obtain locally.

Next, try to find out about specific organizations in the communities you are interested in. You should answer the following questions: Which organizations are most likely to need my skills and knowledge? What problems do they face that my particular abilities could help solve? Who has the power to hire in my job classification at each of these organizations (usually not in the personnel department)? Again, your local library is a good place to start. Some helpful sources are:

1. *Dun and Bradstreet Million Dollar Directory.*
2. *Dun and Bradstreet Middle Market Directory.*
3. *Standard and Poor's Register of Corporations, Directors, and Executives.*
4. *Thomas' Register of American Manufacturers.*
5. *Fortune* Magazine's "Directory of Largest Corporations."
6. *Fortune* Magazine's "Annual Directory Issue."
7. *Black Enterprise* Magazine's "The Top 100."
8. *College Placement Annual.*
9. Membership directories of professional and trade organizations.
10. Annual reports and other publications of the organizations.

Naturally, you can write or call the organization and ask for information. Thorough research on your part will assure that you will have the right questions when the time comes.

The results of this process should provide you with a specific plan of action for getting the job that is right for you. You should now be able to compile a list of jobs that use your skills and knowledge, geographical areas in which those jobs can be found and in which you would like to live, prospective employers who meet your criteria, and individuals within those organizations who have the authority to hire you.

STRATEGIC JOB HUNTING

Now you must develop an organized plan of attack. Organization is important. You will probably want to establish a file for each prospective employer. This will help you keep track of the jobs you are applying for and the progress you are making toward each. Every piece of correspondence should be filed along with basic information about the company and individuals who make employment decisions. Also, it is a good idea to keep a record of the following steps of Strategic Job Hunting:

Resumé and Letter of Application   Once the target organizations and persons have been identified, you should prepare a resumé and letter of application for each. This step is an initial screening to identify organizations that may have an interest in you. Early elimination of organizations that are not interested will save you time, money, and frustration. We will discuss letters and resumés later. At present it is sufficient to say that they must be personalized and directed toward a specific job. Keep a record of when you sent your first letter of application and resumé, as well as copies of them. You may wish to send a follow-up later.

Initial Interview   In response to your letter and resumé you may receive an invitation to be interviewed by someone in the target organization. Reply immediately by telephone to the person who issued the invitation. When setting the date for this initial interview, try to leave yourself enough time to prepare and yet not appear too eager. Follow your telephone conversation with a letter of confirmation. This two-step approach allows you to (1) make a personal contact with the interviewer before the interview and (2) remind the interviewer of your interest just before the interview. After the interview, jot down your impressions and other information you obtained for future reference. Always follow this initial interview with a letter to the interviewer thanking him or her for their time and consideration. This is a good opportunity to reinforce your expression of interest in the job.

Of course, you may receive a rejection letter instead of an invitation for an interview. If you do, it is usually best to take this organization out of your file and forget it. It is not likely that they will contact you again, even though they did promise to keep your resumé. If you do not hear anything, a follow-up letter and another resumé will be in order after sufficient time has passed. Use this opportunity to restate your interest in the organization. A follow-up phone call can be substituted if you have a specific person to contact.

Handling Job Offers   Handling job offers is not a problem when you know you have already been offered the best position of all those for which you applied. However, it is frequently impossible to know if a better offer may result from one of your other inquiries until everyone has had an opportunity to review your qualifications. Therefore, if you receive an early job offer that you feel may not be the best possible opportunity, it is appropriate to request a reasonable delay before you accept. You may do this either by letter, telephone, or both. If you do ask for more time to take care of unfinished business and consider the offer thoroughly, be certain your request is reasonable. An employer may be able to wait a few days or even a week, but a longer delay would disregard his or her need to fill the position. On the other hand, you must be careful not to accept a job you really do not want, just because it was the first one offered to you.

When you determine which job offer you wish to accept, make your acceptance in writing, even if you were notified and have already accepted by telephone. If you receive other offers after you have accepted a position, promptly respond with a letter of refusal thanking the person who made the offer for his or her consideration. If you have asked for time to consider other offers, respond to them with similar letters as soon as you have accepted a job and received confirmation of your employment in writing.

Now that we have outlined the basic job-seeking strategies, we will discuss several key elements in the process. In the remainder of this section we shall consider letters of application, resumés, and interviews.

Application Letters

A letter of application for a job is often the first step in the job-getting process. A good letter will not usually *get* you the job. It will get you an interview; at the interview, you must present yourself as qualified, energetic, reliable, and enthusiastic. Few companies hire without an interview.

Even so, the application letter is crucial to you. Sometimes you make a telephone call to a company you are interested in, and the personnel manager or some other official suggests that you send a resumé or data sheet. (These are sometimes called the vita, qualification sheets, or personal profiles.) You will, of course, send it in response to this invitation.

Many letters of application are *solicited*. Most solicited letters, however, are sent in response to advertisements. The United States Congress has passed laws regulating equal employment opportunity. As part of their efforts to comply, companies use advertisements much more than they used to. Although many of these ads run in newspapers and in magazines of general circulation, most run in specialized newspapers, magazines, and publications. If a person were checking advertisements for engineers or for a teaching position, a good place to look would be specialized engineering publications or professional journals for teachers.

It is also proper for you to send letters of application that are *unsolicited*. Analyze your qualifications carefully, pick out companies or institutions that you wish to work for, and send the strongest letter you can. It is not uncommon for persons graduating from college to send twenty or twenty-five such unsolicited letters. Usually, some of these will be answered, and a chance for an interview can develop. Mass mailing of unsolicited letters, however, is expensive and takes a lot of time. It is often better to narrow your sights and write only to companies or institutions in which you have a real interest. Follow the suggestions for selecting the right employer we discussed earlier.

In preparing a letter of application, what general rules should you follow?

1. Present the strongest case favorable to yourself. Emphasize your strong points. In one sense, you are writing a sales letter. Do not exaggerate.

2. Consider the "You" approach. Remember that each time a company hires somebody, it takes a risk. Think about what the company wants and take it into account in preparing your letter. If you have done your research properly, this will be easy to do.

3. Never say critical things about other places you have worked, or other people you have worked for. Most potential employers believe that if you were unhappy elsewhere, you will be unhappy with them.

4. Do not talk about what you want in salary and benefits. Normally these subjects will come up in the interview.

5. See that your letter is perfectly prepared. A smudgy letter could ruin you. A typographical error or an incorrect spelling will be spotted at once. Use good quality bond paper. Never send a carbon or photocopy of a letter.

6. Where possible, address your letter to a person, not to "Personnel Manager" or "Vice-President" or "President."

7. Remember that there is no one format for your letter. People are different, and so are letters of application. Two samples will be presented shortly, but they are "guides" rather than "forms." Use these "guides" intelligently and adapt them to your own uses and personality.

A few years ago, there would have been an eighth rule: send a photograph. This no longer applies. A photograph will usually identify you by race and sex (if your name has not already done so), and some employers are not comfortable receiving this information. Many do not wish to know the race of the applicants or the sex. The general rule about photographs now is to send one *if you wish*. It will do no harm. But do not be surprised if some potential employers send it back.

Most job applications are in two parts—the letter itself and an attachment or enclosure. The attachment or enclosure is the resumé/vita/data sheet/ qualification sheet/personal profile. Although all five titles are correct, we shall hereafter refer to the resumé. Both letter and resumé are important; neither should be slighted.

The letter usually should be typed. You often see letters of application that are printed, but they suggest a mass mailing, which means that they will be taken less seriously than individually typed ones. Seven rules for writing a letter of application have already been given.

Here is a perfectly acceptable letter of application for a teaching position at a university. The position had been advertised in the *Chronicle of Higher Education*. The *Chronicle* is a specialized publication that is widely read among college and university personnel.

EXHIBIT A-1

January 26, 19—

Dr. Harvey E. Davenport
Chairman, Department of Journalism
Georgia State University
Atlanta, GA 30303

Dear Dr. Davenport,

I have read your advertisement for an assistant
professor of journalism in the Chronicle of Higher
Education and I am enclosing my resumé with this
application.

I lived in Atlanta for seven years as a child and I am
quite congenial to the area and to Georgia State
University, which I know well. My brother, Edward
Langhorn, is a graduate of the College of Business
Administration of your University.

Both teaching and research interest me, and your
advertisement specified an interest in someone who can
do both. I am presently on leave from Metcalfe College
in Montana where I have taught three courses per quarter
for the past five years with good results. I shall be
happy to supply you with all my student evaluations for
that period so that you can see for yourself that I have
had a success in this field.

My experience also has been varied, as is shown in the
resumé. I have had nine years experience as a newspaper
reporter and as a news executive on three daily papers.
I am a candidate for the Ph.D. in mass communication
research at Temple, and expect to receive the degree in
August. My dissertation topic is communication law,
especially the right of privacy.

I am in excellent health, am 37 years old, and I hope
that I may pursue my career goals of being an excellent
teacher and researcher with you and your colleages.

A list of persons you may wish to contact is on the
resumé. However, I invite your investigation beyond this
list.

I shall look forward to hearing from you.

Sincerely,

Patricia Langhorn

This letter follows the general rules.

Suppose you are graduating at the end of the present quarter with a degree in Business Education. You have selected twenty firms in the town in which you live, and you plan to send them unsolicited applications. You wish to begin your business career as a secretary, and most firms have occasional secretarial openings. You telephone Harston Manufacturing Company and get the name of the personnel director, double-checking the address and the spelling of the director's name.

EXHIBIT A-2

January 16, 19—

Ms. Edwina Evans
Director of Personnel
Harston Manufacturing Company
1 Harston Road
Wichita, Kansas 67202

Dear Ms. Evans,

I shall be graduating from Kansas State University on March 16 with a degree in Business Education, and I should like very much for my first full-time job to be with Harston Manufacturing Company as a secretary. I am a native of Wichita and have known of the excellent reputation of your company all my life.

At Kansas State, I have been regularly on the Dean's List, and am a member of The Honor Society of Phi Kappa Phi along with several other organizations, all of which are specified on the attached resumé. I believe that these honors and associations show that I have taken my collegiate work seriously and that I have achieved near the top of my class.

While at Kansas State, I have worked as receptionist and part-time secretary for Dr. E. P. Howell, a distinguished dentist. I have done this through all four of my years in school. During the summers, I have also done related work with the Wichita Chamber of Commerce, and for the past two summers with the United Appeal of Greater Wichita. I would now like to work in Wichita in the private sector of the economy.

```
I have had a success in all of my prior employment and I
hope that I may have the opportunity to be interviewed
and employed by you. A list of references is on my
resumé. I shall be glad to have you drop me a note
setting an interview time.

Sincerely,


Elena Vastakis
```

Resumé

Several general statements may be made about resumés. They are a kind of tabulation of a candidate's qualifications. There are no wasted words and few personal words, because the resumé is an impersonal document. The contents are balanced on the page so that they look good. When it is necessary to carry the resumé over to a second page, a carry-over tag goes on the top of the second page: "Resumé of Elena Vastakis," or some such.

Most resumés have several parts, although the order in which they come is not fixed (except for the Heading), and the exact form in which the information is placed on the page is flexible. Resumés do not all look alike. The Heading, however, always comes first. It gives the name of the person applying, the address, and the telephone number, where appropriate. It may give the name of the company to which application is being made, but it may omit it if the resumé is being sent to many companies after being mass-produced. (Resumés may be mass-produced in any attractive way, but should never be mimeographed, which would make them look sloppy.)

After the Heading, the applicant should put the strongest part of the resumé: Education, Experience, Personal Details, Activities and Achievements, References (sometimes). In the case of Ms. Vastakis, both Education and Experience are strong, but she probably will consider Education to be slightly stronger and will lead with it. Here is a resumé that she can properly attach to her letter of application. The parts of the resumé are indicated.

This resumé could have been placed on the page differently; almost any arrangement would have been acceptable, provided it was balanced and neat. The contents also could have been varied. The Education section could have been expanded to include academic courses taken that were appropriate to the job applied for. The Experience section could have included part-time employment while in high school or other minor jobs. The Personal Details section might have been shorter. As a general rule, personal

EXHIBIT A-3

```
                  RESUMÉ OF ELENA FLORA VASTAKIS
           GIVING HER QUALIFICATIONS FOR SECRETARIAL WORK
                   AT HARSTON MANUFACTURING COMPANY


    Name: Elena Flora Vastakis

    Address: Box 1643
             Kansas State University
             Manhattan, Kansas 66506

    Telephone: No telephone at present

    Education

    Graduate, North Wichita High School
    19—       Wichita, Kansas
              Fourth-ranking graduate in a class of
              163.
              Business education sequence.

    Attended Kansas State College, Pittsburg, Kansas, for
    six months, 19—

    Graduate, Kansas State University, degree expected March
              16, 19—. Bachelor of Science degree in
              Business Education.

    Experience

    Four years as receptionist and part-time secretary to
    Dr. E. P. Howell, dentist, of Manhattan, Kansas.

    Two summers (19— and 19—), secretarial intern for the
    Wichita Chamber of Commerce.

    Two summers (19— and 19—), apprentice secretary for
    the Greater Wichita United Appeal office.

    Excellent typist; can operate word-processing and
    standard business equipment.
```

data sections of resumés used to be considerably longer and were always placed first. However, much of this information is not important to the hiring decision for most jobs. Indeed, it is unlawful to consider several of these factors in hiring. Some personal data probably should be included, although not first, because employers will expect to read something about you as a person that will help them visualize you. What data you include depends on what you feel is most helpful to your chances of being selected.

Personal Details

Height: 5 feet 4 inches

Weight: 104 pounds

Hair: Black

Health: Excellent

Marital status: Single

Hobbies: Tennis, cooking, sewing, stamp collecting.

Activities and Achievements

Dean's List, nine consecutive quarters at Kansas State
University
The Honor Society of Phi Kappa Phi
Sweetheart of Alpha Tau Omega fraternity

References

Professor N. P. Braswell
Department of Business Education
Kansas State University
Manhattan, Kansas 66506

Professor Norma Lamont
Department of Business Education
Kansas State University
Manhattan, Kansas 66506

Mr. R. P. Brascombe
Manager
Wichita Chamber of Commerce
Wichita, Kansas 67201

Dr. E. P. Howell
Suite 1101, Tower Building
Manhattan, Kansas 66504

Activities and Achievements could have included youth organizations, religious organizations, and others. The reference list could have been expanded. However, applicants seldom give fewer than three references, unless they give none at all and simply include the statement that references
will be furnished upon request.

Remember that a resumé needs constant updating, even when you are
not in the job market, so that it will be ready whenever needed. Resumés

are frequently used for more than just job hunting. If you are asked to speak at a meeting, the chairperson may ask for a resumé to use in the preparation of introductory remarks. Frequently organizations ask that personal data in one form or another be submitted when a person is being considered for promotion. Perhaps most importantly, keeping an up-to-date resumé helps you maintain a healthy view of the way your career is progressing.

Communicating in the Job Interview

As we indicated earlier, job interviews are an important part of the hiring process in American industry. Even organizations that do a poor job of interviewing seem to place a great deal of emphasis upon the process. When you are invited for an interview, remember that you are an active participant in this interaction, just as you would be in any other person-to-person encounter. Therefore, you must be prepared and willing to do your part to make the interview a success.

Planning for the Interview   Now that you have been invited to an interview, refer back to your files for helpful information. From the organization's file you can develop a data sheet that will help you prepare for the interview. Your research should have yielded certain information about the organization, such as: major products or services, names and facts about top executives, other locations, gross sales, assets, number of employees, market share, financial position, history, closest competitors, problems—especially those that need your skills and knowledge.

This data sheet should also help you identify the gaps in your knowledge about the organization. Recognition of such gaps can help you to prepare questions that you want to ask during the interview. In addition, be sure that you have the name of the interviewer and can pronounce it. If you have any doubts, check with the secretary or receptionist before you go into the interviewer's office. (Also get the secretary's name; you may find it useful later.)

While you are preparing for the interview, refer back to your original self-analysis inventory and identify the particular strengths that you think would be appropriate for this job. You will want to think back over your educational and job experiences and single out examples of the skills and knowledge you have to offer. Organize these examples in your mind so that you can describe each and make your point—a valuable skill, etc.—quickly and effectively. These personal success stories are ammunition you can use during the interview to sell yourself.

It is also useful to attempt to predict what questions an interviewer may ask you. David Gootnick, in his book *Getting a Better Job*, lists twenty questions that are likely to come up in most interviews:

From Getting A Better Job by David Gootnick. Copyright © 1979 McGraw-Hill Book Company. Used with permission of McGraw-Hill Book Company.

1. Tell me about yourself!
2. Why are you interested in working for this company?
3. Why do you want to leave your job?
4. Why have you chosen this particular field?
5. Why should we hire you?
6. What are your long-range goals?
7. What is your greatest strength?
8. What is your greatest weakness?
9. What is your current salary?
10. What salary do you require?
11. What do you expect to earn five years from now, ten years from now?
12. Tell me about your boss, your company.
13. In your opinion, what are the characteristics of the person filling this job?
14. What is important to you in a job?
15. What do you do in your spare time?
16. Which feature of the job interests you most?
17. Which feature of the job interests you least?
18. How do others describe you?
19. What are your plans for continued study?
20. Tell me about your schooling!

Your answers to questions like these can appear more direct and sincere if you think through them before you go to the interview.

Strategy for the Interview Remember, you are not a passive object in this selection process. You must take an active role in directing and shaping the interview. Although the interviewer expects to control the interaction—you should not violate this expectation—you do have considerable latitude in your responses to his or her questions. Make the most of these opportunities to showcase your experience, education, skills, and knowledge. Most skilled interviewers will ask you broad open-ended questions that require more than a brief reply. This is done to find out what you think is important.

Then the interviewer will follow up with more specific questions about areas that interest him. Use these open-ended questions to mention as many of your unique selling points as you can.

Good interviewers want you to talk more than they do; be sure you have something to say. However, you must be aware that not all interviewers are good at their job. If an interviewer does not encourage you to talk and seems to prefer to do the talking, do not get in the way. You must be prepared to take the role of active listener. Sometimes people are hired as interviewers because they enjoy talking to others and have outgoing personalities. However, if they do not understand the function of the employment interview, they may end up giving far more information than they receive.

The best way to handle such interviewers is to let them talk, even encourage them. It is not your place to teach the talkative interviewer his or her job. Even though you have prepared all of your selling points in advance, do not try to force them in when they are not wanted. Instead, be attentive, respond with positive feedback such as: "isn't that interesting," "I see your point," "please tell me more," etc. Remember that this person enjoys the sound of his or her own voice and will like you if you seem to enjoy it as well.

Have some questions ready to ask that are based on what you have heard. Questions indicate your interest and perceptiveness. You will want to make notes about some details. Take brief notes during the interview unless it bothers your interviewer. As soon as possible after the interview, write out all of the facts and impressions you have gained for future reference.

Nonverbal Communication in the Interview   Nonverbal cues take on great importance in an interview situation. Interviewers are usually very sensitive to these signals; so give some thought to them. Eye contact is very important to establishing a climate of trust between you and the interviewer. Be sure to look him or her in the eye when you talk. Do not stare, but indicate that you feel comfortable looking directly at the interviewer. Do not let your facial expressions give away thoughts you may not want known. If you are disappointed or even thrilled by something you hear, it may not be to your advantage to show your feelings.

Hands and legs can betray nervousness and anxiety. Control your motions at all times to give a confident impression. Avoid habitual or nervous gestures, swinging your foot, toe tapping, and other possibly irritating movements.

Dress is important in job interviews. No matter how strongly you feel that you should be hired for your talents rather than your clothes, you must consider the interviewer's initial impression. Frequently, you would not wear to the interview the type of clothing that you would wear on the job.

If you are in doubt, visit the interviewer's office unannounced ahead of time and observe the way people there dress, wear their hair, etc. These personal features should not get in the way of the interviewer's perception of your ability.

Getting the right job is a matter of careful planning and preparation. There are no magical tricks or easy formulas, but if you are willing to follow the suggestions presented here, you will be well on your way to finding the job that is right for you.

HANDBOOK B

The Mechanics of Writing: Punctuation, Grammar, Spelling

The mechanics of writing may seem to be minor matters, not because they are trivial but because you can correct them easily. You probably learned in school how to correct them. If not, or if you are not certain about some of the principles of mechanics, this handbook can help you.

COMMON USES OF PUNCTUATION

Punctuation is really no mystery; it is simply a code. You and your reader share a translation of punctuation marks. Your punctuation tells your reader: "Read this material a certain way, the way the punctuation shows." You punctuate (1) to make your meanings clear and (2) sometimes, just to follow common usage, as in placing a colon after the salutation in a letter.

This section does not treat punctuation completely, but it does explain some common uses of punctuation, especially those arising in letters, memos, and reports. If you feel unsure of some details, you can find rules for punctuation in any good grammar book. An even better source would be the *United States Government Printing Office Style Manual*. The grammar books do not stress one rule enough:

Use punctuation to prevent misreading or to make reading faster.

Most punctuation marks prevent misreading or simplify reading:

- Comma means "slight pause."
- Semicolon means "pause longer than you pause for a comma."
- Dash (double hyphen on a typewriter) means "strong pause, with a shift in thought."

- Parentheses and brackets means "pause to state information to make preceding statement clearer."
- Period means either (1) "pause at the end of a statement," or (2) "this is an abbreviation."

The comma, telling your reader to pause briefly, can often prevent a misreading. Note how a pause, shown by a comma at the spot marked by parentheses, keeps the reader from being misled:

> No matter what we might expect (,) the supervisor will not approve these time-cards.
> When the office closes down (,) the line will still continue.
> While increasing (,) production is still below the schedule.

Without the commas, a reader would read without pausing, rushing through the sentence as though running up a blind alley.

You normally use a comma

- *to separate items in a series:*

The main parts are scope, suspension, and bearing and azimuth circles.

- *to separate main clauses (which could be complete sentences if written by themselves) when they are joined by coordinating conjunctions, such as* and, but, or, for, nor, so, yet, *or* while:

New instructions will soon be ready, and all departments must comply.

- *to set off nonrestrictive modifiers, such as appositives and relative clauses:*

James Jensen, incoming chairman, will choose the schedule.
James Jensen, who is incoming chairman, will choose the schedule.

Note that any modifier coming after a proper name will almost surely be nonrestrictive—that is, not severely limiting in meaning—and therefore will be set off by pauses.

- *to separate dates from years* (although custom is changing this usage):

On January 1, 1990, these units must be ready.

- *to set off introductory phrases or subordinate clauses calling for a pause:*

Measured each hour, the readings should match.
Being unwilling to accept a transfer, she may resign.
When the cope is ready, you can then prepare the drag.

- *to set off parenthetical words or phrases:*

Lubricants, however, must be carefully specified.

Note two special rules for using commas:

- *Commas setting off appositives, nonrestrictive clauses, or parenthetical elements within a sentence come in pairs, one before and one after the element being set off:*
Some, however, cannot meet that schedule.
- *Commas come* inside *quotation marks, unless the quotation marks stand for inches or minutes of arc:*
The section on "workmanship," written by the subcontractor, will specify that detail.

The semicolon helps to set apart larger sentence elements when these elements contain smaller elements set off by commas. The difference in pause lengths helps to separate the items:

Line orders this month included No. 39, 173; No. 40, 265; and No. 41, 7.

The semicolon also shows a long pause between two complete sentences joined without a coordinating conjunction:

No orders were placed; no shipments were made.

When you join the two sentences with a coordinating conjunction (*and, but, or, nor, for, so, yet,* or *while*), you usually do not need to show a long pause. Therefore, you do not normally need a semicolon; the comma plus the conjunction will make one sentence flow to another:

No orders were placed, and no shipments were made.

When you join two sentences with a conjunctive adverb, such as *however, therefore, nevertheless, consequently, also, hence,* or *thus,* you change thoughts somewhat abruptly. You need a stronger pause than a comma would show. Thus you use a semicolon before the conjunctive adverb. Depending on how you want the reader to read, you will sometimes put a comma after the conjunctive adverb:

No orders were placed; therefore (,) no shipments were made.

The dash can help break up a long, confusing sentence. Use the dash to let the reader's train of thought change track. Without the dashes, the sentence would be confusing:

During the recent ice storm, the company tried to remove fallen wires—before any bystanders were killed—by use of special crews.

Use of too many dashes can make writing look choppy; sometimes revising the sentence structure removes the need for a dash. However, the dash is often a useful mark.

Parentheses can make reading clearer by telling the reader to pause in a special way. Putting part of a sentence in parentheses will give your reader a logical stopping point. It will let your reader feel the end of a sense package and change thought slightly.

Use parentheses

- *to enclose explanatory phrases, such as identification of abbreviations:*
"Metropolitan Atlanta Rapid Transit Authority (MARTA). . . ."
- *to enclose numbers or letters setting off items in a series:*
For three reasons this plan will not work: (1). . . .
For three reasons this plan will not work: (a). . . .
- *to cite references:*
. . . graphs. (See the appended charts.)
- *to give the double forms of numbers, when required by custom or policy:*
. . . there will be six (6) units. . . .

Brackets resemble, but are stronger marks of punctuation than, parentheses. You use brackets

- *to enclose material that has internal parentheses:*
. . . is being considered. [For three reasons this plan will not work: (1)
. . . (2) . . . (3). . . .]
- *to show explanatory ideas inside a quotation:*
"The specification [from ASTM] read in part. . . ."

Brackets and parentheses have special uses in mathematics and science, but this section does not cover such uses.

The period has two main meanings: (1) used at the end of a statement, a period indicates a longer pause than a semicolon, and (2) it identifies a nontechnical abbreviation. Technical abbreviations in science, etc., usually do not use periods. You have probably seen many examples, such as "cm" and "sec" for "centimeter" and "second."

You can also use a period raised half a line as a "bullet" to call attention to items in a list. Pulling items out of a paragraph and setting them off with bullets makes them easier to read and remember. You have already seen bullets used in this chapter.

A series of three periods, one space apart, means "material has been left out of the original being quoted."

The regulation ". . . shall be examined every twenty-four months. . . ." (The fourth period stands for the end of the sentence.)

Like brackets and parentheses, periods have special meanings in mathematics that are beyond the scope of this book. However, certain uses of the period are general:

- in monetary units ($2.50)
- after paragraph or section numbers (1., 1.1)

Other Marks of Punctuation

You may sometimes need other marks of punctuation:

The hyphen: This mark signals the reader to "speed up your reading":

- C-clamp
- a well-zeroed meter
- decision-maker
- one-half watt or one half-watt load

You also hyphenate two-word spelled-out numbers as a guide to reading:

twenty-nine

and to set off certain prefixes, such as *ex-* and *self-*:

self-sealing

The hyphen has the same meaning ("speed up") when you break a word at the end of a line. However, do not break a single-syllable word at the end of a line. Do not break any word at the end of a line if a single letter will have to stand by itself. Try not to break a word to leave two-letter syllables on the next line. Try not to divide a word at the end of a page to continue that word on the next page. Also, try never to break a numeral by hyphenating its parts.
The hyphen also has special uses in chemistry.

The colon: Coming at the end of a sentence, this mark usually means "Heads up! Here comes a list or an example":

The micrometer has five parts: (1) barrel. . . .

The colon also means a proportion; a double colon means a ratio:

1:2:4:: cement:sand:stone

Sometimes you can use a colon instead of a semicolon to join two sentences when the second sentence derives from or explains the first:

The manager found many reasons to suspect theft: he had watched the cash box carefully.

You also use a colon for these situations:

- after the salutation of a business letter (Dear Mr. Doe:)
- for clock times and engine operating hours (10:00 A.M., 151:8 hours)

The apostrophe: This mark shows (1) possession or (2) a letter left out in a contraction:

- the company's (singular)
- the companies'; (plural)
- you can't

You use the apostrophe in other ways:

- compound-pronoun possessives (everybody's concern)
- usages set by custom (hour's work, day's pay)
- possessive with the gerund (the clerk's being busy)
- for joint possession (manager's and supervisor's scales)

Over-Punctuation You should also know when not to punctuate. The general rule is, "Punctuate only when you need punctuation"; but some specific rules will help:

- *Do not insert commas when you join only two modifying adjectives by "and."* The machine-finish was bright (no comma needed) and smooth.
- *Do not insert a comma between two adjectives that you could not join by "and."* *The recently promoted (no comma—because you would not insert and)* general manager. . . .
- *You normally do not need a colon after an incomplete sentence:* The five parts are (no colon here) the scope, the journal, ...

Correcting Grammar

"Grammar" frightens many people, because it conjures up visions of schoolteachers flunking students for saying "ain't." But grammar should not frighten you if you understand what it really is: a set of habits that help your reader understand you. This sentence

Ditches openly have driver into ran truck a the into careless

is nonsense to you as written. You understand each word, but the words have no clear relationship. Correct grammar and *syntax*, or word arrangement, could make a clear sentence:

The careless truck driver has run into a ditch.

Thus, you should think of grammar as a coding/decoding machine. When you write, put your thoughts into codes called sentences. Equipped with the same code, your reader translates your sentences into thoughts. Obviously, this system works best when you and your reader use the same code, that is, follow the same rules of grammar.

This book does not have enough space to cover all the rules; if you are weak in grammar, you should either take a refresher course or study a book on grammar. (Two good books are the Prentice-Hall *Handbook for Writers* and the Harcourt, Brace, Jovanovich *Harbrace College Handbook*.) Instead, this section will review the problems most common in writing letters, memos, and reports. The section will also solve some problems often left uncovered in standard handbooks:

- *Make each verb agree with its subject:*
A number of problems *have* arisen. (not *has*)
The number of problems *has* increased. (not *have*)
Some of the *parts were* chrome-plated. (not *was*)
Some of the *part was* chrome-plated. (not *were*)
Payment of the invoices *was* delayed. (not *were*)

- *Treat the name of an organization as a singular word:*
Smith Company *has* a stock-option plan for *its* employees.

- *Make every pronoun agree with the word to which it refers:*
Each of the new-hires will draw *his* or *her* badge.
All of the new-hires will draw *their* badges.
Smith is the only one of the salespersons who *is* being reassigned.

- *Always make the reference of a pronoun clear:*
"We sent for the rest of the component which was completed," is not a clear

sentence; "which" may refer to "rest" or "component."
Instead, write
   . . . completed rest . . . or completed component . . .

● *Avoid weak or confusing constructions:*

There are included in this unit. . . .
should read
This unit includes. . . .

By taking every precaution will enable the supervisor
should read
By taking every precaution, the supervisor. . . .

The weak sentence
If the supervisor takes every precaution, she. . . .
could better read
By taking every precaution, the supervisor. . . .

Place modifiers as close as possible to the word or words to which the modifiers relate:

● *Place such modifiers as "only" very carefully:*
(Only) Ten units (only) were produced (only) last Tuesday (only).

● *Treat compound pronouns as singular:*

some	*P*		
			one
any	*L*		
			body
every	*U*		
			thing
no		*S*	
			body

are considered singular:
Has anyone filed a claim?
However, the word *none* can be singular or plural.

● *Make a linking verb agree with its real subject:*
The purpose of the meeting *is* to discuss sheet-courses and to prevent lay-offs.

Parallel structure: Skill in using parallel structure will almost always mark you as an experienced writer. Parallel structure means use of the same grammatical form or the same format for items or ideas with the same rank or emphasis. Parallel structure is thus both a grammatical device and a symbol of logical thought. You can best understand parallel structure by studying an example of faulty parallel. See if you can find the flaws in parallelism in the list below:

> Steps in Evaluating a Data Base Management:
> 1. Setting up criteria for a desirable system.
> 2. Make a list of vendors who could meet the criteria.
> 3. Each vendor should be invited to make a presentation of the proposed system.
> 4. Evaluating the vendors to cut out any who fail vital criteria.

You no doubt sensed quickly that the list was awkward. The four ideas are parallel, that is, equal in stress or rank; so they should appear in the same form. However, the first item begins with the gerund "setting up." The second item is a complete sentence starting with the imperative (command) verb "make." The third item is also a complete sentence, but the main verb, "should be," is not a command. Like the first item, the fourth is a partial sentence starting with a gerund ("Evaluating").

Parallel structure is more than a matter of grammatical nicety. Far more important, it can aid your reader and make your writing more useful. Your use of parallel structure for parallel items or ideas subtly tells your reader: "These items or ideas have equal rank and should get equal stress or attention."

You can use parallel structure in:

- format (layout and arrangement on a page)
- grammatical structure
  point of view
  sentence structure
  tone

Let us set up a parallel structure in each of these ways:

Format includes all variables in the way your writing appears on a page: margins, indentions, typography, and spacing. The key word in parallelism of format is "consistency." You should place all page numbers at the same spot on each page. You usually count but do not number the first page. You should indent the same number of spaces for each item in a parallel list. Thus, in describing four steps, if you indent seven spaces to start the first item, you should indent seven spaces to start each of the others. Moreover, you should space vertically in equal amounts. For example, if you single-space *within* paragraphs for the four instructional steps and double-space

388THE MECHANICS OF WRITING:
PUNCTUATION, GRAMMAR,
SPELLING

between paragraphs, do so consistently. If you group material under headings, all parallel items should have the same heading rank and the same treatment. Thus, you might center, capitalize, and number with Arabic numbers *all* major headings. You might then pull *all* second-rank headings to the left margin, and capitalize first letters only.

Grammatical structure includes point of view, complete versus partial sentences, sentence structure, and tone. Let us look at each of these:

Point of view includes person and number of subjects and voice, mood, and tense of verbs. You should keep the person viewpoint consistent (first, second, or third person). You should also keep the same verb voice (active or passive) and verb mood (declarative, imperative, interrogative, or subjective); and verb tense (past, present, future).

Sentence structure involves the use of partial or complete sentences for parallel effect. Sometimes you will want to use complete sentences to express items; at other times you will want only partial sentences or a list of objects. To keep structure parallel, try to use complete sentences consistently, or partial sentences consistently. Do not mix complete and partial sentences in a list.

The sentence structure itself should reflect proper parallelism. For example, if your partial sentences consist of a verb plus modifier and object, all parallel items should follow the same pattern.

"Tone" refers to the connotations, the meanings you imply, and the attitudes your reader infers. Throughout your memo or report you should keep the same tone. Thus, when you state steps as requests, you should state all of them in request form, not some as requests and some as commands. However, a break in parallel tone can sometimes help your writing. Just as parallelism suggests the same rank or emphasis for all items in a list, so a break in parallelism can give special emphasis to an item. Thus, you might write instructions in an operator's manual as requests or mild commands. You could ask, or perhaps tell, your reader to take these steps. But to call special attention to a safety precaution, you might break the parallel structure by stating a command strongly. You might break the parallelism of format by having the command typed in italics, set off, indented, or printed in red ink.

Parallel tone usually concerns you only slightly when you outline your report. Unless someone expects to see the outline, the headings and subheadings need not be parallel. You need only arrange ideas by ranks. Thus, a working outline might look like this:

1.1 Clean the disc
    1.1.1 All pieces torn off by hand
    1.1.2 Use solvent on rest
    1.1.3 Can finally remove some mechanically

1.2 Apply the new cement
    1.2.1 Use cement No. XXX
    1.2.2 Putty knife or spatula
    1.2.3 Have clean rags for wipe
    1.2.4 Solvent
1.3 Put new piece one . . . etc.

Despite its many faulty parallelisms, the list would still give you an adequate writer's outline (unless someone had to approve the outline itself).

You should correct the faulty parallelism when you revise the draft. These outline headings could become headings in your actual writing. You would then want them to read:

1. *ATTACHING SAND PAPER*
    1.1 *Cleaning the disk:*
        1.1.1 *Removing large pieces first by tearing*
        1.1.2 *Rewashing small pieces with solvent*
        1.1.3 *Removing other pieces mechanically*

Note that all ranks on this list are in parallel form: gerund plus object. But for proper parallelism you need not use the same form for items of different rank. For instance, this list is also in proper parallel:

    1.1 *Removing the old paper*
        1.1.1 *Hand removal*
        1.1.2 *Solvent removal*
        1.1.3 *Machine dressing*

Item 1.1.3 might at first seem out of parallel. Actually, it is not. It is basically the same form as 1.1.1 and 1.1.2.

You can also think of parallel structure as items on an organization chart. In fact, you might consider parallel items like people with parallel jobs. The people at the same level of an organization expect and—rightly or wrongly—want someone the same treatment. They do not expect different rank-levels to get the same treatment.

Correcting Abbreviations, Symbols, Acronyms, and Trade Jargon

An abbreviation is a short form of a longer word or phrase. It has been clipped to save time or space. A symbol is a letter or graphic device standing for a word, a phrase, or even a relationship. Sometimes a letter may be both an abbreviation and a symbol, as in "T" representing "Temperature" in an equation. An acronym is a word coined from the first letters of a phrase. Perhaps the best-known acronym is "radar" (radio detecting and ranging). A trade-jargon term is a word or phrase with special meaning for a certain industry or type of work. For example, some machinists call a micrometer a "mike."

Here are some guidelines for using abbreviations, symbols, acronyms, and jargon:

• Abbreviate only when (1) you need the space saved, (2) the abbreviation is convenient, or (3) the abbreviation is more familiar than the full term.

• Use only standard abbreviations, symbols, and acronyms.

• Make sure your reader will understand the abbreviation, symbol, acronym, or jargon term. If in doubt, identify the term the first time you use it.

• Never allow a single abbreviation or symbol to stand for two different quantities or ideas in the same context.

• Generally you do not place periods after technical abbreviations, except when the abbreviation could be mistaken for an English word, as *in.* (for *inch*), *sin.* (for *sine*), and *tan.* (for *tangent*). You usually put periods after nontechnical abbreviations.

• In abbreviating the name of an organization, follow the organization's practice.

• For readers who do not know trade jargon, put the jargon in quotation marks and identify or define it at first usage.

Two publications can help you in finding standard abbreviations: Publications of the American National Standards Institute and the *U.S. Government Printing Office Style Manual*.

Correcting Capitalization

Capitalization gives you a way to identify certain nouns. Also, some capitalization depends partly on habits of language. Capitalization usually causes few problems, but you should consider these principles:

• Capitalize, spell, and punctuate a trademark exactly as the owner prefers.

• Capitalize names of people the way they prefer (*Von* or *von*, *De* or *de*).

• Capitalize the name of an organization the way the organization prefers.

• Capitalize a letter that shows the shape of an object (*C-clamp*, *I-beam*).

• Capitalize the first letter of a complete sentence, including a complete sentence following a colon.

● Capitalize abbreviations to match the capitalization of the full form.

● Generally do not capitalize acronyms or derivatives of proper names (*radar, loran, volt, ampere*).

● Capitalize the first letter of regions and place names: "Southeast"; but do not capitalize compass directions ("south of the building').

● Capitalize terms in science according to current practice.

● Capitalize a title coming before another proper name or clearly used instead of, or as part of, a proper name ("President J. J. Jones").

● Capitalize names of specific sections, divisions, etc., of larger organizations ("Production Engineering will. . . .").

● In the title of a report, a book, or an article, capitalize the first word and all other words except *a, an, the,* conjunctions, and prepositions shorter than five letters ("The report entitled *Predicted Applications of the Modification.* . . .").

● Capitalize common names that are part of a proper name ("The annex on Broad Street is now. . . .").

● You may capitalize for stress ("WARNING: Do not touch the. . . ."). However, this device loses its effect if you overuse it.

● Do not capitalize unless you have a good reasons for using capitals.

Editing Numbers and Figures

How to write numbers—whether to spell them out or to use figures—must surely be one of the most vexing, even if minor, problems in writing memos or reports. No one rule covers every situation, and for every rule you can probably find exceptions. If you want a good review of the many "rules," again consult the *U.S. Government Printing Office Style Manual.* Meanwhile, these guidelines can help you:

1. *Spell out numbers*

● at the beginning of a sentence (or revise the sentence)

● when you can write isolated numbers as one word ("one" through "twenty," "thirty," etc.)

● as general abbreviations, such as "hundreds," "dozens," "half," "one-third"

2. *Use figures for*

● all numbers greater than 100

● exact amounts of money, distances, and clock times including minutes, dates, and street numbers

- heading numbers, section numbers, illustration numbers, table numbers, paragraph numbers, and page numbers in reports
- serial numbers for reports
- numbers in tables
- any number that contains a decimal point
- technical data, such as times, angles, temperatures, latitudes and longitudes, pressures, volumes, velocities, dimensions, electrical units, weights, drill sizes, wire gauges, and tolerances
- percentages, ratios, and proportions
- exact fractions
- telephone and cable numbers, street addresses, post office box numbers, zone numbers, room numbers, and building numbers
- correlations, conversion factors, and coefficients
- all units in equations, formulas, and displays of calculations

Specific Applications

- Try to treat all related numbers in a single sentence the same way—put them all in figures or spell all of them out.
- When a typographical error could cause a serious mistake, or when you want to emphasize the need for extra care, you can use both the figure and the spelled-out number. (This practice is seldom necessary.)
- When deciding between the British and SI (metric) units, follow current practice in your line of work. (Note that some proposals require numbers in the SI system.) If in doubt, give measurements in both systems, as, for example, 1.0 in. (2.54 cm.).
- For a decimal number less than 1.0, put a zero (0) to the left of the decimal (0.314).
- In hand-lettered numbers, be careful to avoid any confusion between Z, 2, and 7. One way of avoiding confusion is to use $\mathrm{\not{Z}}$ and $\mathrm{\not{7}}$.
- Round off large numbers as much as the precision needed in the example will allow. But do not add extra zeros to rounded-off numbers. For example, 1.0 is not equal to 1.000; 3.1 million is not equal to 3,100,000.
- If you have no measurement at a particular point in a table, put in "not available" or "not measured." Do not put a zero at that point; zero is a measurement.
- Use a combination of spelled-out numbers and figures to prevent confusion (eight ½-inch strips).
- In checking numbers, avoid reversing digits.

- Do not mix approximations and exact numbers; for example, do not write, "approximately 5.76 employees."
- Hyphenate fractions standing alone (one-third).

Correcting Spelling

As you edit, you should check the spelling of all words. In proofreading you should check spelling again before you send the memo or report. While editing, you should correct any misspelling; if you do not, a misspelled word may slip past you or someone else who proofreads.

The dictionary is your most ready aid. For checking spelling only, you can use one of the books of commonly misspelled words. If you write a technical report, you may not find the technical words in your dictionary, even if it is a large one. You should have access to a good scientific or other specialized dictionary such as Van Nostrand's *Scientific Encyclopedia*.

Correct spelling is important for several reasons:

- Sometimes a slight misspelling can change the meaning. For example, the words "except" and "accept" sound and look alike but differ greatly in meaning.
- A misspelled word can distract your reader.
- If you do not correct misspellings, your reader may conclude that you did not check what you wrote. This suspicion could cast doubt on your whole memo or report. At the least, leaving misspelled words suggests sloppiness.
- You can easily check the spelling of most words in a dictionary.
- Readers who may not know the finer points or obscure rules of grammar may still notice misspelled words.

Check especially your spelling of two types of words: proper names and trademarks. Misspelling a person's name may offend that person. Misspelling a trademark, especially your own company's trademark, is very serious. Continued misspelling of a trademark may result in that trademark becoming a common noun, what is called a "generic term." You would not want your carelessless to cause your company the loss of a valuable trademark.

A dictionary is your first guide to any question of spelling. You should be especially careful in checking any of these often misspelled words:

all right	accidentally	accompanying
accessories	accommodate	achievement

advisable	finally	precede
arrangement	financi(al)(er)	principal
believ(e)(ing)	fore	principle
beneficial	forecast	procedure
benefited	formally	proceedings
changeable	formerly	quantity
collectible	government	questionnaire
column	grievance	recei(pt)(ve)
commitment	incidentally	recommend
comparison	interest	reference
conceive	judgment	referral
convenien(ce)(t)	liquefy	relevant
deficit	maintenance	representative
definitely	management	safety
desirable	manufacturer	separate
develop(ment)	ninety	similar
efficiency	noticeable	simulate
eliminate	occasionally	stationary
environment	occur(red)(rence)	stationery
equip(ment)(ped)	omission	success(ful)
evidently	pamphlet	temperature
existence	personal	transferred
feasible	personnel	usage

You will find these words often misspelled, sometimes because writers are careless, and sometimes because they do not pay attention to all syllables.

Other problems of spelling arise because pairs of words may (1) sound alike but differ in meaning, or (2) look alike but differ in meaning. Here are some troublesome twins and triplets:

a, an	disinterested, uninterested
accept, except	everyone, every one
all ready, already	farther, further
all together, altogether	fewer, less
affect, effect	imply, infer
among, between	its, it's
amount, number	later, latter
anyone, any one	lie, lay, lain, laid
beside, besides	loose, lose
can, may	maybe, may be
continually, continuously	percent, percentage

principal, principle   sometimes, some time, some times
raise, rise, raised, risen   their, there

If you are not certain how to use the words, look them up. Also, add to the list any words that give you problems in spelling.

PRACTICE IN CORRECTING
THE MECHANICS OF WRITING

(Note: you should review Chapter 10 before working this exercise.)

1. Revise the sentences below to make them more forceful and concise. (The numbers in parentheses suggest lengths for the revised sentences.)

• We will provide you with a list showing all specifications related to these jobs at a time when they are ready. (16 words)

• Offset reproduction will be the preferable choice for the simple reason that it is of a higher quality than the draft which is already in existence. (13 words)

• The reason why we are unable to fill your order is that the instructions for shipping were printed in such a way as to be torn into two pieces. (19 words)

• If all complaints are handled by a sound policy it would save time. (19 words)

• There are four advantages to using the metric system. (7 words)

• It is unlikely that the group will be confronted with such a problem as this. (8 words)

• Cases of absenteeism which are flagrant have a tendency to become habit-forming. (7 words)

• The general manager is in favor of any method which is helpful to the line. (10 words)

• Make certain that the valve is in proper working order. (7 words)

• Anyone who is employed by our company has the option of purchasing stock for an amount not to be in excess of one week's regular salary. (16 words)

2. Delete from each sentence any useless information; revise each sentence to emphasize the important ideas.

• The brochure which is enclosed will help you choose a method which is preferable and suitable to you.

• In the month of January we saw an increase in our gross shipments.

• Attached you will find a very complete list of the canisters which were fuller.

THE MECHANICS OF WRITING:
PUNCTUATION, GRAMMAR,
SPELLING

- All price lists are shown in the appendix.
- The volatile liquids are enclosed in cans which are red in color and round in shape.

   3. Change any unneeded passive verbs to active by revising each sentence.

- This schedule must be revised by the chart clerk.
- Revise your plans so that a decision can be made.
- Negotiations will be concluded next Thursday.
- New rope-slings will be put to use by loading handlers.
- As is shown in Table 1, the returns have been tabulated.

   4. Revise each sentence to cut out any double or unclear meanings.

- Employers have been trying to find ways to get their workers to work for centuries.
- We are trying to please any customer with unsatisfactory service.
- The patrolman cited a speeding motorist although he did not stop.
- All employees are not eligible for a contract vote.
- No matter what else occurs this week has been difficult.

   5. Change these sentences to proper tone for a first memo.

- As should have been obvious to you, the crate was damaged.
- You must clearly understand that we cannot vary this policy.

   6. Change capitalization as these sentences require.

- john boltex, President of ozone refrigeration in wylie, ohio, will deliver the Proposal in person.
- this proposal will offer president boltex as a Consultant to the Client.
- furthermore, the proposal clearly states, "no substitutions will be made in the administrative time proposed before february Renegotiation session at fort belvoir."

   7. Punctuate (and capitalize if needed) these sentences correctly.

- the specifications read in part as follows each mix shall consist of these ingredients cement sand and crushed stone in the ratio of 1 2 4 by volume the moisture entrained in the sand and crushed stone shall be calculated approximately care shall be taken in adding water at the job site also the resultant mix shall not be allowed to free fall more than allowed by specifications vibration shall accord with section 2 of the standards so as to produce a well compacted concrete in place

   8. Correct any mistakes in grammar.

- We look forward to him appearing in person, however a substitute will have been acceptable. (possessive case needed; punctuation weak between main clauses; verb form wrong)

• The weakness of this program are: inefficiency, poor format, and the syntax has some mistakes. (wrong use of colon; faulty parallel)

• Arriving at the security office, no guards were seen on duty. (dangling modifier)

• The follower has seriously worn its channel thus the retrieval motion is uneven. (two sentences fused with no punctuation)

• Between you and I your promotion will be late. (wrong form of pronoun)

• To quickly count the packages, a random check should be made by you. (split infinitive; awkward change in point of view)

• No matter where this sample is taken, and whatever the sampling techniques used. (partial sentence written as though a complete sentence)

• The other bidder is preparing a full proposal, and they expect to have it ready on time. (pronoun disagreeing with its reference)

• Included in this list are part number, unit price, and price extension. (subject disagreeing with verb)

9. Correct any misspelled words in these sentences.

• The customers have all ready replied, even through reponses to the questionnaire at their conveiance. When the maintenance documents are finely received, they will be already to dispatch for farther committment.

10. Revise the following memo by using all principles in Chapter 10 and in this Handbook section.

```
                                          27 February 19__
     To:        All Dept. Heads
     From:      Controller
     Subject    Bring Travel Expenses to a Minimum
     :

        1. In recent weeks many expense reports with a common
     problem has been reviewed. The problem of over extention
     of incumbred funds. Partly due to employes not keeping
     an eye on rising costs of travel. This memo is for the
     purpose of asking that undue high costs greater than
     usual be limited in your travel. If you would try and
     keep costs of travel down, it would be of help in
     reducing our overhead burden to a minimum, some of the
     ways to reduce travel are

     I. Inso far as you are capable, do not preform any non-nec-
        essary trips
    II. Always make use of the cheapest routeing. Some times you
        should fly, other times you should drive
   III. Travel costs can reduced lower by lmited nights out of
        town to as few in number as possible, consequently saving
        on motel bills and charges
```

IV. concentrate most on taking advantage of discount rates, some ticketing discounts can save a minimum of twenty (20) percent, of course at some time it becomes a question of travel at a time for which a discount applies in opposition to saving a night out of town

V. The three major factors in travel cost are: duration of travel, method of travel, and your attempts to eleminate any expense is also important. It is not expected of you by the company that you will all ways travel at lowest cost, however, your efforts in following these principles will be appreciated by the company.

HANDBOOK C

Visual Aids for Reports

Here are some tips for preparing various visual aids used in reports. You can use these tips to instruct your typists or illustrators. You can also use the tips to check the quality of work these people give you.

Planning Tables and Data Sheets

● Tables that "break"—run over to second pages—should repeat the column headings on the next page. Multi-page tables or data sheets should be attached at the ends of reports.

● Titles should be in all-capital letters, centered, and underlined (unless you use preprinted data sheets). Column headings should have initial capitals and underlining.

● Column headings should show any units needed (or individual measurements can show units). Use of powers of ten is very risky (subject to misinterpretation).

● Independent variables should be in the columns farthest to the left.

● Typed tables should be double-spaced if possible.

● Decimal points (if needed) should be vertically aligned.

Planning Engineering Drawings and Technical Illustrations

● Preparing such visual aids requires special skill. Unless they are already available, they can be costly.

● You should inspect such visual aids and ask yourself, "How will readers view these illustrations?"

● The best approaches may be combinations of various views or sketches.

● Such visual aids included in reports should be copies, not the originals.

● Any such visual aids not drawn to scale should carry warnings "NOT TO SCALE" or "SCALE ONLY APPROXIMATE." Drawings included for training should be so marked.

- Reducing or enlarging destroys scales (except bar scales).

- Larger drawings must be carefully planned for fold-out, fold-down, or inclusion in a back pouch. Such methods of inclusion increase cost of production.

- Some reproduction methods produce drawings that fade. Some methods produce copies that are hard to read.

Planning Graphs and Charts   Charts and graphs are of two general types:

1. Computational devices (close-grid lines, semilog, and log-log graphs; alignment charts or "nomographs")

2. True visual aids (line graphs, bar graphs, pie charts, histograms, pictograms, segmented bar graphs, area charts, cartograms, scattergrams, organization charts, and flow charts). These notes will emphasize true visual aids.

- Widths of lines and heights of letters suggest importance. For example, titles should have the boldest letters.

- Originals should be done in black ink, on a white background, and 100 percent oversize (for later reduction).

- Lettering should be done by letter pen, template, typeset, rub-on, or typing with a plastic ribbon.

- Ample margins (generally at least one inch) should surround the frame-line box.

- Graphs should show descriptive labels and, where proper, units.

- Particular specifications and suggestions are as follows:

    line graphs: Plotted lines, frame lines, and grid lines should be in the proportions 4 : 2 : 1. Dependent variables usually go on the vertical axes (as readers will hold the graphs). If axes start at other than zero or some index (such as 100), starting numbers should be oversized. Plotted lines go from point to point, unless some mathematical relationship permits plotting an averaged line. Vividness is more important than exact interpolation.

    bar graphs: Bars show discrete (unconnected) variables. Bar widths should be constant; only lengths should vary. Bar widths should be either slightly wider or slightly narrower than spacings, but not exactly the same width as spacings between bars.

    pie charts: Pie chart should not contain more than about eight slices. If values are important, numbers should appear in the slices. Adjoining slices should not have similar cross-hatching. The largest slices should not be solid black. Slices must total 100% = 360°.

The Line Graph

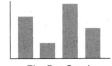

The Bar Graph

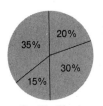

The Pie Chart

Pictogram: Reduction
in Cigarette
Consumption

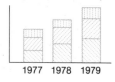

| 1 Billion Cigarettes

Segmented Bar Graph

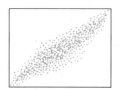

Scattergram

histograms: Bar lengths show percentage of totals, with bars touching one another.

pictograms: Pictograms are vivid because they symbolize variables. Although the variables may be keyed, for precise values the variables must still show numbers. Symbols should vary in number, never in size.

segmented bar graphs: Segments must be keyed or labeled for exact values. Darker segments should be at the bottom, lighter segments higher. Cross-hatching is better than single-angle diagonal hatching.

area charts: Areas should run from left vertical frame to right vertical frame. Darker hatchings or designs should be below lighter hatchings or designs, with lines marking boundaries. Areas should be keyed or labeled.

cartograms: Unless carefully done, cartograms (map graphs) may look cluttered. To show precise values rather than ranges, areas must contain actual numbers. For multi-color printing or patterns, registration of each color (placement of the printed image on the page) is critical.

scattergrams: Scattergrams show only very general relationships; that is, correlations. Scattergrams do not show the exact mathematical correlations.

organization charts and flow charts: Lines of authority or flow should be twice the width of block lines or operation steps. Organization charts should show dates of effectiveness. Blocks, nodes, or circles of the same rank or type should be the same size. The general flow is left to right and top to bottom. Broken lines show consultation or coordination. Flow chart should use standard symbols.

• Writers should avoid using graphs or charts that (1) try to show more precision than the data permit, (2) change scales without clear warnings, (3) are too detailed for the readers' understanding, (4) contain lines or lettering drawn with ball-point or show-card lettering, (5) lack clear titles, (6) are not as neat as the time and budget allow, or (7) do not really help readers to understand.

Planning Photographs or Copies of Photographs

• Generally, quality of reproduction is not as important as clear focus and good composition are; however, poor reproduction can ruin the effect of good photography.

• Pictures should be "cropped" or "air-brushed" to leave only important details showing.

• Reproduction of color photographs is very costly.

- Enlargement emphasizes the flaws in an original.
- Photographers should plan their pictures before "shooting."
- For most pictures, available light is better than the light from flashbulbs or floodlamps. Photographers should not use flashes or lamps where smoking is restricted for safety reasons.
- Photographers should not take candid pictures with flashes.
- You should not use in your reports any pictures that show people's faces unless the subjects grant permission.
- Photographers of equipment can include something—such as a meter stick or a person—to show relative size.
- Enlarging or reducing affects an entire picture, including any lettering, signs, or measuring devices in the picture.
- Making only a few copies of a picture can be costly, but printing many half-tone copies will result in a low per-copy cost.
- Film is the cheapest part of photography; hence, photographers should shoot more than the minimum number of shots.

Using Samples or Models in Reports

- Samples can often show such ideas as examples of good memos, work orders properly prepared, invoices filled in, etc.
- Pictures of models may show ideas better than drawings can.

HANDBOOK
D

Sources for Further Study

A tremendous amount of information is contained in this book. We hope that this book will serve as the first step in your study of business communication. Here are some good sources for further study that you may find useful.

Communication Theory

Dance, Frank E. X., ed. *Human Communication Theory*. New York: Holt, Rinehart and Winston, 1967. Traces contributions to communication theory from a variety of disciplines.

Mortensen, C. David, ed. *Basic Readings in Communication Theory*. 2nd ed. New York: Harper and Row, 1979. A comprehensive collection of classics in the field.

Writing

Flesch, Rudolf F. *The Art of Readable Writing*. New York: Harper and Row, 1974. This is the standard book against which others are measured. It gives you the means of measuring yourself.

Gunning, Robert. *The Technique of Clear Writing*. New York: McGraw-Hill, 1968. Plows much the same ground as Flesch. Between the two (and our chapters) you will have everything you need.

Strunk, W. J., and White, E. B. *The Elements of Style*. 3rd ed. New York: Macmillan, 1978.

Letter Writing

Buckley, Earle A. *How to Write Better Letters*. New York: McGraw-Hill, 1971. Buckley applies good writing principles to writing letters of all types.

————. *How to Increase Sales with Letters*. New York: McGraw-Hill, 1961. Much the same as the work above with specific reference to sales.

Report Writing

Brown, Leland. *Effective Business Report Writing*. 3rd ed. Englewood Cliffs, NJ: Prentice-Hall, 1973.

Lesikar, Raymond V. *Report Writing for Business.* 5th ed. Homewood, IL: Richard D. Irwin, 1977.

Sigband, Norman B. *Effective Report Writing for Business, Industry, and Government.* New York: Harper & Brothers, 1960.

These three books on report writing cover much the same ground. Any of them would be useful as an additional guide to report writing.

Information Gathering

To help you with research for your reports, letters, and other efforts, the following books are excellent guides.

Johnson, H. W., ed. *How to Use the Business Library.* 4th ed. Cincinnati: South-Western Publishing Company, 1973.

Murphy, Robert W. *How and Where to Look It Up—A Guide to Standard Sources of Information.* New York: McGraw-Hill, 1958.

Paradis, Adrian A. *The Research Handbook.* New York: Funk and Wagnall's, 1966.

Public Speaking

Here are four recent efforts in the area. *Thinking and Speaking* is a more general treatment, while the others "zero in" on speaking in business settings.

Hays, Robert. *Practically Speaking in Business, Industry, and Government.* Reading, MA: Addison-Wesley, 1969.

Holm, James N. *Productive Speaking for Business and the Professions.* Boston: Allyn and Bacon, 1967.

Walter, Otis, M., and Scott, Robert L. *Thinking and Speaking.* New York: Macmillan, 1973.

Wilcox, Roger P. *Oral Reporting in Business and Industry.* Englewood Cliffs, NJ: Prentice-Hall, 1967.

Listening

Too few books have been written on this subject. Of the few, these two are the best.

Barker, Larry L. *Listening Behavior.* Englewood Cliffs, NJ: Prentice-Hall, 1971.

Nichols, Ralph G., and Stevens, Leonard A. *Are You Listening?* New York: McGraw-Hill, 1957.

Nonverbal Communication

Birdwhistell, Ray L. *Kinesics and Context.* Philadelphia: University of Pennsylvania Press, 1970. The most comprehensive work by the father of the study of nonverbal communication. A bit complicated for novices, but essential for true students of the field.

Hall, Edward T. *The Silent Language.* Garden City, NY: Doubleday, 1973.

————. *The Hidden Dimension*. Garden City, NY. Doubleday, 1966. Both of these books have become classics. Highly readable and very informative.

Knapp, Mark. *Nonverbal Communication in Human Interaction*. 2nd ed. New York: Holt, Rinehart & Winston, 1978. A comprehensive overview of all types of non-verbal communication.

Interpersonal Communication

Baskin, Otis; and Aronoff, Craig E. *Interpersonal Communication in Organizations*. Santa Monica, CA: Goodyear Publishing Co., 1980. A treatment of interpersonal communication in the organizational context.

Lee, Irving J. *How to Talk with People*. New York: Harper and Brothers, 1953. Another classic in practical, usable terms.

Group Communication

Keltner, John W. *Group Discussion Processes*. Rev. ed. New York: Longmans, Green, 1974. A guide to understanding group discussion with a practical bent.

Maier, Norman R. F. *Problem-Solving Discussions and Conferences*. New York: McGraw-Hill, 1963. The late, eminent social psychologist offers great insights and usable techniques.

Shaw, Marvin. *Group Dynamics: The Psychology of Small Group Behavior*. New York: McGraw-Hill, 1975. A compendium of research in the field.

Zelko, Harold. *The Business Conference: Leadership and Participation*. New York: McGraw-Hill, 1969. A guide to better performance as a group leader or participant.

In-House Publications

The Ragan Report. Lawrence Ragan and Associates, 407 W. Dearborn St., Chicago, IL 60605. A weekly survey of ideas and methods used by industrial editors.

Editor's Newsletter. P. O. Box 243, Lenox Hill Station, New York, NY 10021. A monthly review of trends and technique in business communications, particularly company periodicals.

In Black and White. Associated Editorial Consultants, P. O. Box 2107, La Jolla, CA 92038. This bi-weekly publication for those who write, report, and edit is a valuable guide to clear writing.

Supplementary Publications

Alberding, Russell J. "Communicating Employee Benefits Under ERISA," *Financial Executive* (July 1975). Provides some guidelines to legal and governmental regulations that affect the way in which organizations communicate with their employees regarding company benefits.

Employee Benefits, 1975. Washington, D.C.: Chamber of Commerce of the United States, 1976. A study of the costs of benefits to American corporations.

Freeman, Thomas W. "Matching Concept to Content—Employee Benefit Communications Programs," *Personnel Journal* (November 1972). A critical survey of various employee benefit communications programs that provide examples of effective and ineffective efforts.

Hayett, W. *Display and Exhibit Handbook*. New York: Van Nostrand Reinhold, 1967. A useful guide to the do's and do not's of displays and exhibits.

Peterfreud, Stanley. "Employee Publications: Deadly But Not Dead Yet," *Public Relations Journal*, Vol. 30, No. 1 (January 1974). Explores the role and function of employee publications.

Audio-Visual Communications

Audiovisual Projection. Kodak Publication No. S-3. A technical guide to the use and selection of projection equipment for various room sizes and configurations.

Kodak Projection Calculator and Seating guide. Kodak Publication No. S-16. A handy guide for calculating best viewing angles based on room size and seating capacity.

Martino, Joseph P. "Telecommunications in the Year 2000," *The Futurist* (April 1979), pp. 95–103. A look ahead to the changes technological innovations will bring to audio-visual communication.

Reinhart, R. C. "How to Select your A/V Equipment," *Public Relations Journal* (May 1979), pp. 27–29. A useful guide to considerations that should precede any decision concerning audio-visual media.

Job Skills

Angel, J. L. *Job Finding Resumés*. New York: Pocket Books, 1980. Step-by-step guide to developing effective resumés.

Bolles, Richard N. *What Color Is Your Parachute?* Berkeley, CA: Ten Speed Press, 1978. A practical manual for job-hunters and career changers.

Gordon, Raymond L. *Interviewing: Strategy, Techniques, and Tactics*. Rev. ed. Homewood, IL: Dorsey Press, 1975. A helpful book for preparing for the crucial job interview.

Index

A

abbreviation, 388–389
active listening, 238–240
active voice, 62–63
Alberding, Russell J., 404
American Press Institute, 28
analyzing communication systems, 19–20
annual reports, 340
Angel, J. L., 405
apostrophe, 383
Ardrey, Robert, 253
attention, 233–234
"Audience's Bill of Rights," 228
audio-visual communication, 347–361, 405
    planning, 348–350
    deciding on equipment, 352–353

B

Bacon, Francis, 246
Banana Time, 279–281
Barker, Larry L., 403
Barnard, Chester, 4
Bateson, Gregory, 21
Barnes Hospital, 358
benefits communication, 333–334, 404–405
Birdwhistell, Ray L., 247, 403
Birmingham News, 28
Bolles, Richard N., 405
Brown, Charles, 215
Brown, Leland, 402
Buckley, Earle A., 402
bulletin boards, 342–343
Butler, Samuel, 213

C

Calhoun, John C., 214
capitalization, 389–390
Carroll, Lewis, 21
Cartwright, Dorwin, 283
change, 6, 11
Chrysler Corporation, 306
CNA Insurance, 357
colon, 382–383

Columbia University, 28
comma, 378–380
common-sense theories of communication, 14–16, 22
communication
    breakdowns, 15–16
    downward, 308
    normal, 264–265
    importance in business, 4
    informal, 264–265
    lateral, 311
    networks, 6
    problems, 3, 10
    theory, 13–23, 402
    training, 7, 9
    upward, 308, 311
conflict resolution, 8
consensus, 297–299
control, 7, 11
cooperation, 281–282
coordination, 6, 281–282
coorientation, 266–267
Couey, James H., 28–33
Couey Principle, 28–33
Curtis, J. Montgomery, 28
cybernetics, 19

D

Dana Corporation, 290
Dance, Frank E. X., 402
Darwin, Charles, 246
dash, 378, 380–381
decision making, 5–6, 8, 11
Deere & Company, 321
developing relationships, 5, 6, 8
dictation, 56–58
Dirksen, Everett McKinley, 34, 37
Doyle, Michael, 290
Drucker, Peter, 4

E

economic man, 6
editing, 41, 179–192
EEOC, 337

†